The
STARTUP
Equation

VISION
Minimum Viable Business Product

CORE IDEA

Id

CURIOSITY

Cu

Values

The STARTUP Equation

Xf

Te

Designer

A Visual Guidebook to Building, Launching and Scaling Your Startup

Ce

In

By Steven Fisher and Ja-Nae' Duane

Illustrations by: Caleb Sexton and Kate Rutter

Introduction by: Andrew Hyde

SCALE

Br

Key Performance Indicators

Crowd Funding

Angels

Sc

Ma

Dashboards

Sa

Fn

McGraw Hill Education

NEW YORK   CHICAGO   SAN FRANCISCO   ATHENS

LONDON   MADRID   MEXICO CITY   MILAN

NEW DELHI   SINGAPORE   SYDNEY   TORONTO

3 4 5 6 7 8 9 10   DSS   20 19 18 17

ISBN 978-0-07-183236-6
MHID   0-07-183236-X

e-ISBN 978-0-07-183237-3
e-MHID   0-07-183237-8

All art in this book was created for *The Startup Equation* unless explicitly noted.

McGraw-Hill Education books are available at special quantity discounts to use as premiums and sales
promotions or for use in corporate training programs. To contact a representative, please e-mail us at
bulksales@mheducation.com.

This book is dedicated to Ja-Naé.
She is on the cover with me but is really the reason this book is written
and in your hands. She is my wife, my life, my best friend. And from my
two page wedding vows, I reaffirm to always be your partner in fun
and adventure, your lover, your sounding board, your co-pilot, your sous
chef, your copyeditor, and your best friend. And to always flush the
toilet and remember to put the seat down when I am done.
Love you, babe.
Steve

Love you too.
Ja-Naé

In Memory of Karl Baehr
A Teacher, A Mentor, A Friend. And yes. Profit is good.

Contents

Acknowledgments

We want to thank our parents (Steve—Terry, Carol, and Joanne, Ja-Naé—Mike, Leslie, and Cindy) who really don't read business books so they won't know they are in here unless someone tells them.

We want to thank Caleb Sexton who was the creative glue who put up with Steve and interpreted his haiku and sketches to turn them into graphics that made sense.

We want to thank Kate Rutter who really got the essence of the Startup Equation and so clearly and quickly created sketchnotes that anchored each of the element chapters.

We want to thank Britt Raybould who patiently proof-read, edited, and re-edited our book to prevent this from becoming *Ulysees 2*, but without the stream-of-consciousness style that made that book great. She is awesome.

We want to thank our agent Carole Jelen at Waterside who understood the vision of this book and helped us find the perfect home for it.

We want to thank the team at McGraw-Hill, including Casie Vogel, Peter McCurdy, and most importantly, Donya Dickerson, who has been patient, creative, and just plain awesome.

We also want to thank caffeine and sugar, two elements that are not in the Startup Equation, but both helped us write this book.

Finally, we want to thank all of the entrepreneurs out there for whom this book is written. You are the pioneers, the explorers, and the rebels who create things for the world we never could imagine. You make this world a better place. This book is for you.

Foreword

"Why don't you just fix that?"

It was a late summer night at the office. Many of my friends were on romantic dinners or exploring Colorado on their bikes. I, however, was tucked away in an office drinking warm beer with some other stressed out software developers. It struck me that all these startup friends had never worked together. These three developers are now lifelong friends, but before that night had not really had a chance to work on something together. One of them had a problem with their newly launched application, and I happened to know just the right person to fix the problem who joined us at the office that night. "There should be a way we can work together on projects."

"Why don't you just fix that?"

I could have left it there. I could have just passed on it. It could have joined thousands of ideas in the trash can. For some reason that night, I jumped to action and within an hour, I had a website, ticketing system, and blog post with just a single line written, "Let's do this."

Looking back, the launch was both structurally embarrassing and completely perfect. No logo. Under 200 words describing it. No venue. No partners. No sponsors. No money. I wasn't known nor very connected. I chose the name "Startup Weekend," which was so generic that people claimed to have heard of it before we had even done anything. Even with all these obvious flaws, something big started happening: people were actually signing up. We had five people. Then ten people. Then thirty. Then, just three weeks later we had eighty-eight people show up to a small office above a bike shop in Boulder, Colorado.

Startup Weekend was born.

We all gathered at 6 p.m. to discuss what we all wanted to build. Ideas went around about event organizing, finding friends, parking, trail mapping, and voting were presented. This group was having a hard time building consensus, until we began discussing a product idea. That's when we struck gold. That's when we had consensus.

We made a voting application for groups just like us. Or we tried to. Throughout the weekend we picked a name (VoSnap), selected a programming language (Ruby on Rails), created a marketing plan, and created a group cheer (voooooooo-snap). We had all the functional things of a startup, in just one weekend, which was against everything we were told was possible. But it worked, because we had the basic elements of our own Startup Equation.

It was community building at its finest: A talented group who are individually challenged to remain as flexible as possible to solve a problem. That is the essence of what Ja-Naé and Steve talk about when they want you to assemble your "A-team." To get a group together who challenge themselves and encourage the others as well. Because we had that core team element, what really launched that weekend was a centralized movement of these Startup Weekend events.

But it wasn't easy. A bunch of blogs wrote about what we were trying to do and pointed out how we were going to fail! That was actually fantastic for getting attention and ironically they became our biggest word of mouth evangelists without even knowing it. And that got lots of people talking about whether we were on to something. Could a startup be built in a weekend? How about a prototype? We knew, just as Ja-Naé and Steve know, that you just need the right elements in place and a startup can be conceived in a day . . . or a weekend.

In the startup ecosystem of 2007, it was assumed that you needed to invest or raise a ton of money in the hopes of launching something within a few months to a year (or more). We were trying to challenge that assumption. What happened when a group of people were challenged outside of their usual work? Would we work smarter and faster? Could the new tools and methodologies carry us to an early launch? There were just too many questions that we were testing, and in the end, the bloggers were right: we alone couldn't launch a startup in a weekend. However, we could, and did, build a small community! Community was my calling and the discussion around launching in a weekend was the marketing plan.

A side effect of the weekend was that everyone in the room later described it as the primary spark of the an evolved startup community in Boulder. The narrative of "our community is too siloed" and "there isn't much going on here" went away. The startup community grew tighter, and I was amazed by the way members of it always lent a hand. We had a strengthening community with great ethics and leadership.

During our first weekend, we stayed up until 4 a.m. looking to launch this project. We kept on thinking that we were an hour away. We just needed to patch a bug. We just needed to write some copy. We just needed to finish the code. Well, we just needed to do about three weeks of work to launch, and we really never did. The weekend was a success, but it also failed many ways. But as this book explains, that it the chance for every startup. The true test is how you can learn from it and pivot as quickly as possible. That is what we did, and it made all the difference.

No matter where you are on planet Earth, building, launching, and scaling a company leverages many of the same elements in order to be successful. One thing that did come from that weekend were emails to me from people all around the world wanting to do a Startup Weekend in their community. I responded to these inquiries with a simple, "Sure, pick a date and I'll fly out!" Many people took me up on this and pretty soon we had programs in 20 states and four countries. I was working a fulltime job and flying places on Friday and facilitating for weekend. It was amazing. It was exhausting. It was a classic "I must work harder" mistake on my part. I didn't have the tools (like this book) and made a ton of mistakes on how to run a program. My X-Factor (which Steve and Ja-Naé cover in Chapter 17) was that I had that drive to start something and caught the energy needed to really run with it.

It is stated in this book and by other sources that by 2020, about 1 in 6 people on the planet will be an entrepreneur of some shape or form. How they come to being an entrepreneur could be one of 10,000 ways, but it excites me that so many will take that risk. Books like *The Startup Equation* will drastically increase the number of people that realize they can start something (and that is just damn exciting). This book is a key part of showing you who you are as an entrepreneur, helping you decide on the right approach, and then giving you the elements to build something you're proud of.

Looking back, I can identify a few things that were the reasons why Startup Weekend worked:

1. We put our full trust in the community and valued everyone that attended.

2. We gave a challenge to talented people and the flexibility for them to solve it.

3. We were clear with what we were, what we were not, and what to expect.

The customer of Startup Weekend was part what Ja-Naé and Steve identify as the creative economy. These are the makers, the doers, the tinkerers, and the creators. By reading this book, I'm going to assume that you are the type of person that is looking to fix a problem or identify an opportunity for something new in the world. If I were to list out my heroes, they would all fit into this group. The inventor, the singer, the artist, the builder, and the founder. I think the world needs more people who take charge and put their stamp on it. There are startup economies of all shapes and sizes around the world and Startup Weekend is helping power that. This book, *The Startup Equation*, is a perfect complement to every Startup Weekend team.

I don't think we need more dreamers. I think we need more founders. Think the world is a certain way? Test it. Think there is a market for something new? Talk to customers. Think you can make a change for the better in your community? Launch it, and take pride in the fact that you are the one to give it a chance to be great.

This is a living book that I think is a breakthrough in entrepreneurship and for entrepreneurs of all shapes and sizes, regardless of geography.

Leveraging many of elements discussed in this book, the team has grown UP Global, the non-profit that runs Startup Weekend, Startup Week, Startup Digest, and Education Entrepreneurs. I am excited to say that we are active in over 140 countries. Every weekend, hundreds of founders make their first step toward applying the elements of *The Startup Equation*. The energy grassroots organizers bring is something that still gets me excited about what entrepreneurship can do for the world.

So . . . here is some wise advice given to me that I'll pass along to you:

1. Be humble. Failure is a known and very common outcome. Failure itself is not failure, but an unhumble project is just that.

2. Be bold. Don't be afraid to lead or to set up an experiment and test some assumptions out. Take your views and style and put them into action.

Think about what you want to create. Ask yourself, "What problem am I looking to solve?" So I ask you, as someone asked me: *why don't you just fix that?* What is stopping you? Now that you have this book and the passion, my wish to you is that you go for it. Build something great and take the time to enjoy the process. This is what *The Startup Equation* is all about, and I'm excited for you read and leverage this book as you begin your journey.

Andrew Hyde, Founder Startup Week
@andrewhyde

Our Story and The Surprising Truth About Why You Need This Book

Steve slowly turned to Ja-Naé as she opened up her eyes. "Good morning, wife." It's true. We can say that now. While rubbing her eyes, Ja-Naé recalled the amazing party they had with 75 of their closest friends and family yesterday. What a great ceremony. What a great party. What a great day. But now, it's time. Well, after coffee.

"You know what we have to start today," Ja-Naé said while sipping her piping-hot first cup. Steve just looked at her because though they just got married yesterday, he knew that they had to begin and begin now. "Oh, yes I do." Months of research and years of personal experience needed to go onto paper. We needed to start this book.

We've both had two companies. We've made a lot of mistakes. We both have had a lot of successes as well. Now, we both teach, invest, and advise businesses on how to build and scale their startups. What drove

Hope is wishing something would happen.
Faith is believing something will happen.
Courage is making something happen.
—*Anonymous*

us to write this book really came from three major observations:

1. **We all need to be entrepreneurial:** The way people work has begun to shift. Now more than ever, people are finding ways to build up their skills so that they can design how they work and what they work on. This book helps you figure what it is that you need to focus on.

2. **There is NO book that unites them all:** From books like *The Lean Startup* and *Business Model Generation* to Steve Blank's *Startup Owner's Manual* all are great works. There are many great resources out there, but there is nothing that helps you combine them all in a way that is easy to understand. This book not only leverages some of these great methodologies and frameworks, but it does it in a visual way that is easy to understand and implement.

3. **Every entrepreneur and startup is different:** You are your own unique snowflake. Seriously though, every person is different and so is the type of business they are looking to start. This book takes into account not only your personality type, but your entrepreneurial approach. This way you can grow and scale the business YOU want. You are in charge.

> We can either be the ones who pave the way, or we can travel down someone else's road. Ironically, the choice and the journey is ours entirely.
>
> —*Ja-Naé Duane*

These observations made it abundantly clear that it was time for a book that not only taught people what we know, but helped entrepreneurs choose their own adventure. And that is what we have set out to do.

It is one thing to share your own experiences and lessons with readers, but at the end of the day, we are just two entrepreneurs. So it was vital to us to highlight and interview as many entrepreneurs and startups as we possible. So, not only will you be hearing from us but you will also get some awesome advice from *over 30+* other entrepreneurs.

Many will give you advice and tell you what worked for them. The truth is, there is no magic bullet that will work for everyone. The elements are always slightly different for everyone, and thus the formula is, too. We have constructed this book to help you understand who you are as an entrepreneur and what type of business you are currently looking to grow. You'll also figure out which elements are the right mix for that business at this time. We want you to understand that you are building something organically awesome and give you the ability to grow with it in a way that makes sense for you.

But know this: At the end of the day, this journey is yours. You can choose to figure it out on your own, or you can take some of the advice in this book and learn from the lessons of others. You can start experimenting with how to make this business work or you can allow us to help you find the right Startup Equation for you. You can choose to put this book down right now or you can give us the opportunity to show you a new world, a new way of growing a business, and a new adventure that may take you to places you could only dream of. But YOU have to make that choice.

Let's Get Started . . .

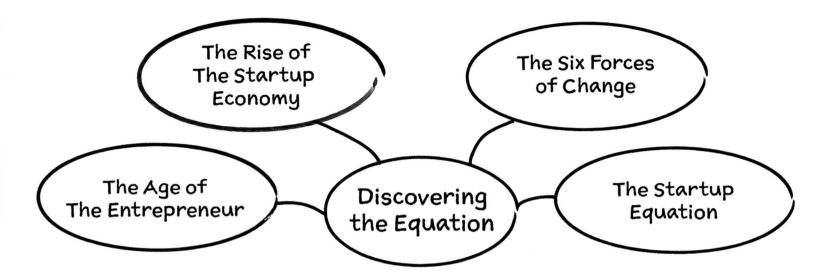

The human race is at its core, explorers. We are curious and adventurous. We are in pursuit of the new, the innovative and forging into the unknown. This drive to discover is what has driven us to accomplish great things and in this modern age we have made more advances in the last 50 years than in the previous 500. This exponential growth is powered by a global and connected human race that can communicate ideas at the speed of light and push the limits of our creative expression. Our global community is more empowered than at any time in history to take control of their future to create new business, be entrepreneurs and change the world.

But with this power there is a growing complexity that must be streamlined and demystified in order to keep it easy to access and easy to implement. It is this very reason that we felt it so important to write this book. As you read this book you will explore key concepts, equation functions and startup elements that help frame and open up how you build, launch and scale your startup. We begin this book and this first section with "The Age of the Entrepreneur" and discuss the impact of One Billion Entrepreneurs on the planet by 2020. We present, along with a short history lesson, that we are at the beginning of a new industrial revolution that will impact the rest of this century and how entrepreneurs are a critical part it. In chapter 2, we take a macroeconomic view of the global startup economy and what powers specific startup ecosystems in the various cities all over the world. Expanding on the idea that we are at the beginning of a new industrial revolution, we identify "Six Forces of Change" powering this revolution and the entrepreneurial opportunities that are just now beginning to emerge.

But with all of this global opportunity and complexity we knew it needed to be explained in a clear way that could be applied to any startup. We discovered over years of research profiling hundreds of startups and entrepreneurs to find common factors, best practices and really what just works. This has allowed us to present a functional framework or "equation" to chart the path for you to explore this book and forge into the unknown.

As you reach the end of this book you will be present with a way to take action and implement The Startup Equation for your business. We are excited to share this book with you and get started. Welcome to being an entrepreneur and enjoy the journey we are about to take together.

SECTION

1

DISCOVERING
THE EQUATION

THE AGE OF THE ENTREPRENEUR

In this Age of the Entrepreneur there are many ways to be an entrepreneur that are direct and indirect, here are six ways that you could be one in this age of the entrepreneur:

Independent Contractors
Contractors, freelancers, and consultants cost 30% less than maintaining salaried employees.

↑ No Supervising
↓ No Benefits
↑ Pay as You Go

Sidepreneurs
Flexibility allows creative entrepreneurs to build businesses or new projects on the side for extra cashflow.

Jack-of-All-Trades
For small businesses, generalists come out ahead with more work over highly trained specialists.

Master vs Generalist

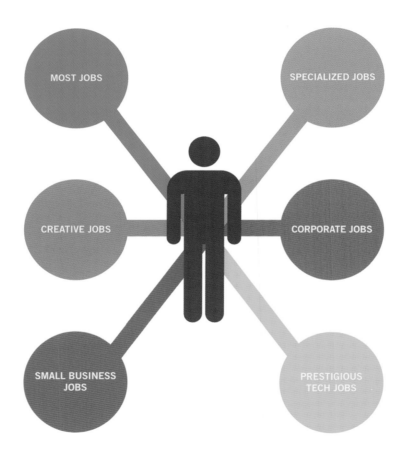

MOST JOBS

SPECIALIZED JOBS

CREATIVE JOBS

CORPORATE JOBS

SMALL BUSINESS JOBS

PRESTIGIOUS TECH JOBS

Outsourcing
With a growth in global specialization, many jobs that require specialization can be outsourced for less money.

Intrepreneurs
Those who innovate internally have a huge opportunity to help their corporation remain on the cutting edge.

Entrepreneurs In Residence

Aqui-Hires
Large companies acquire smaller firms to gain their talent pool.
"We buy companies to get excellent people." —Mark Zuckerburg, 2010

Twenty years from now you will be more disappointed by the things that you didn't do than by the ones you did do. So throw off the bowlines. Sail away from the safe harbor. Catch the trade winds in your sails. Explore. Dream. Discover.

—Mark Twain

The Age of YOU: The Entrepreneur

Entrepreneur. That word conjures up so many images. What comes to mind for you? Two people in a garage creating the next Apple or Google? Inventors like Tesla or Edison? Explorers like Columbus and Magellan looking for new trade routes? Your neighborhood shop or food truck owner? Friends selling their products online? All of them are entrepreneurs, and so are you.

The concept of being an entrepreneur is nothing new. We would dare say it's the world's second oldest profession. The personal qualities of drive and passion to create something new, something better, along with the ability to take calculated risks when the timing is right where others won't tread, are what separate the entrepreneur from the worker. Over the past 200 years, a rapid acceleration of industry worldwide created a new class of entrepreneurs. In this decade alone, the opportunity to start a business has increased exponentially. It's the age of the entrepreneur and it's an exciting time to have an idea with the entire planet as your potential customer.

According to outplacement consultancy Challenger Gray & Christmas, Inc., the number of job seekers starting their own businesses increased by thirty-three percent in the first half of 2013.[1] Even employees at large corporations are switching to a freelance role, giving corporations the ability to downsize full-time staff, cut costs, and hire based on the needed skill set for a specific project. As a result, employees have been replaced with entrepreneurs.

Over the last few decades, we've seen employment change. We went from spending a lifetime with one company to several jobs with many. In the wake of this change, both unemployment and entrepreneurship have increased. The *Kauffman Index of Entrepreneurial Activity* makes this new reality crystal clear. Every month more than 543,000 new businesses are created in the United States. In 2011 that meant more than 6.5 million new businesses were started in the U.S.[2] The number continues to grow.

PLANET EARTH: LAND OF THE ENTREPRENEUR Figure 1.2

GLOBAL AGE DEMOGRAPHICS

25–34 year-olds are the largest demographic for entrepreneurship globally with 35–44 the second largest group. Combined the two total at or near 50% of all global entrepreneurs.

ATTITUDES ARE IMPORTANT

Individual Self-Perceptions
- Awareness of a good opportunity
- Belief in one's skills and experience
- Attitude towards failure

Societal Impressions
- If starting a business is a good move
- The association of entrepreneurship with high status
- Awareness of positive media attention of entrepreneurship

INNOVATION-DRIVEN ECONOMIES

Many of the world's leading countries survive off innovation for growth, including: the USA, Italy, France, Japan, Israel, Switzerland, Taiwan, and the UK.

HIGHEST RATES

The highest rates of entrepreneurship come from Sub-Saharan Africa and Latin America. Zambia comes in at the top with 41% of all businesses in 2012.

↓ **Bad Economy and GDP**   ↑ **Entrepreneurship out of Necessity**

  =

NORTH AMERICA
U.S.A.

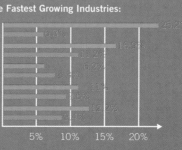

543,000 JOBS WERE CREATED EVERY MONTH IN 2011 FOR A TOTAL OF 6.516,000 IN 2011

Some of the Fastest Growing Industries:

Internet Publishing — 25.2%
Wind Energy — 16.9%, 11.2%
Video Games — 6.2%
Biotechnology — 11%
E-Commerce — 12.2%

- Revenue Growth 2000-2011
- Forecast Growth 2011-2016

5%   10%   15%   20%

DISCONTINUANCE

The three biggest factors across the world:

 Business isn't Profitable

 Inability to Finance

 Personal Reasons

Data Source: Docstock and the Global Entrepreneurship Monitor

THE NEXT BILLION ENTREPRENEURS

Globally, there are about 380 million entrepreneurs. That means if you had a network of 100 people, you'd probably know at least five entrepreneurs. With people living longer than ever before, we'll see the largest surplus of workers in history during the next 10 years. But with job choices diminished, people will find themselves adapting to entrepreneurship out of necessity. As a result, we expect to see an average of one billion more entrepreneurs in the next ten years.

Of that one billion, many will be women. The Global Entrepreneurship Monitor (GEM) found that over a three-and-a-half year period, 126 million women started or ran businesses and 98 million operated established businesses. That's 224 million women impacting the global economy—and this survey counts only 67 of the 188 countries recognized by the World Bank.

Most of these soon-to-be entrepreneurs live outside the global economic system. An overwhelming majority (94%) of these women live in developing countries and have little education. Others are housewives, stay-at-home moms, or women who are discouraged from working. But no matter what others may want, these women are a force to be reckoned with.

> We've been on this 200-year arc, moving from the Industrial Revolution to the industrial age to the information age. We are now about to start a new arc with a new Industrial Revolution.
>
> —*Steven Fisher*

CREATE OR DIE

Many entrepreneurs had absolutely no intention of becoming one. So why then did they become an entrepreneur? Here are three of the most common reasons:

- **Necessity:** They couldn't find a job or need more income than their current job provides.
- **Circumstances:** They lost their job or circumstances have changed so drastically that they need to start working for themselves.
- **Passion:** They had a hobby or a passion and wanted to spend more time working on it.

According to the Goldwater Institute, increasing entrepreneurship is key to lowering poverty rates.[3] The study shows that in areas with a higher than average rate of entrepreneurship, we see a corresponding decline in poverty. Every one percentage point increase in entrepreneurship corresponds to a two percent decrease in the poverty rate. Which is great for those who start a business out of necessity or based on their circumstances.

THE NEW INDUSTRIAL REVOLUTION

Even as we look to the future, we need to look to the past for inspiration and lessons so we don't repeat mistakes. Of course, we tend to repeat cycles, some good, some bad. Knowing where we came from will help guide where we go.

We live in revolutionary times. It's even referred to as a new Industrial Revolution. As we look back on the history of business and industrial innovation, both in culture and business, we can see how transformations appear to happen in waves. The three big innovations are the original Industrial Revolution, the post-Industrial Revolution, and today's new Industrial Revolution.

Phase 1— The Original Industrial Revolution (1750–1870)

In late-eighteenth century Britain, most people resided in small, rural communities. Life revolved around farming. It was difficult, even brutal, with incomes low and disease rampant. People made much of what they used and consumed, including food, clothing, and tools. Manufacturing happened on a small scale in homes and rural shops using rudimentary tools. It's also why we have the phrase cottage industry.

Rich in coal and iron ore, Britain's role as a colonial power also provided access to raw materials and a marketplace for manufactured goods. When consumer demand for British goods increased, merchants sought more cost-effective production methods, a contributing factor to the rise of the factory system.

Textiles and Industrialization

The textile industry experienced a significant transformation when production shifted to factories. Before mechanization, textiles were made primarily at home. Merchants often provided the raw materials and basic equipment and then picked up the finished product. The biggest challenge for merchants involved time. Workers set their own schedules based on their desire for a work/life balance centuries before the term became popular. However, as inventions like the cotton gin reduced the human energy and time required to create goods, work opportunities shifted to factories, forcing people into a system that gave them less control. This has only accelerated in today's world where we trade convenience for less control or privacy in our lives. It is a cautionary tale to be aware of if we are to balance innovation with progress.

> Did You Know . . . The biggest challenge for merchants involved time. Workers set their own schedules based on their desire for a work/life balance centuries before the term became popular.

Coming to America

The Industrial Revolution eventually moved across the Atlantic to America, leading to its own version of a "startup nation." American entrepreneurs or capitalists, (the buzzword of the day) overcame serious technical challenges by relying on inventiveness and a bit of industrial espionage.

America's economic pioneers, like the Boston Associates, tried to create utopian environments where communities could thrive and so a middle class of consumers emerged. Modern productivity spread and supported the start of a mass-consumption society. Like today's modern entrepreneurs, these intrepid creators realized that if you don't have a market, you sometimes have to create it. In the words of Steve Jobs, "A lot of times people don't know what they want until you show it to them."

Revolutions in Finance, Transportation and Communication

By the early 1800s, the transportation and communication industries had also transformed. American Robert Fulton (1765-1815) built the first commercially successful steamboat, and by the mid-1800s, steamships carried freight across the Atlantic, increasing demand and the dependence on a mass-production system. This transformed commerce and spawned entire industries related to this innovation. Before the advent of the steam engine, raw materials and finished goods were hauled and distributed via horse-drawn wagons and by barges along canals and rivers.

Today we'd use terms like "game changer" and "disruptive innovation" to describe the steamboat. It was a prime example of transformative entrepreneurship. Then came the railroads. As their reach expanded across the country, railroads became key to moving goods across a vast territory and building new markets, both necessary to sustain growth in these new industries. This was critical in the building of industry across large territories like America, Europe, and eventually Russia, India, and China.

As the size of the United States increased, a national communications network became critical. In 1844, Samuel F. B. Morse (the Morse code guy) created the telegraph, and by the 1860s, the telegraph network ranged along the East Coast and reached the Mississippi River. Financial markets also evolved from crude bartering systems to abstract and complex systems of ownership (e.g. stocks, bonds, savings accounts, etc.) that could be traded and moved around with pieces of paper.

Through the expansion of mass-produced goods, companies across America saw huge profits. This established America as a thriving, competitive power on the world stage and at the heart of it all were the entrepreneurs. We can parallel this time to today's startup entrepreneur working in coworking spaces and creating whole new industries with just a few people and some low-cost technology. Except it's not just in America; it's the whole world. Anyone can compete if they have the passion, some skills, and some affordable, even free, resources. *The World is Yours to Create!*

Phase 2—The Industrial Age (1870–1945)

By 1895, thirty years after the American Civil War, the United States blew by Great Britain and its colonies (whose wealth Britain relied on at that point) to become the greatest economic power in world history. At the time, railroad, steel, and oil monopolies dominated. In this well-known period of American history, industrial titans like Andrew Carnegie, John D. Rockefeller, and J.P. Morgan controlled multiple industries.

The economic shift between Britain and America has parallels with events happening today. A great example is the current standoff between China and America. Historian Charles R. Morris highlighted the parallels and differences in his book *The Dawn of Innovation: The First American Industrial Revolution*. His research shows that by sustaining an unprecedented 3.9 percent average annual rate of economic growth for more than a century, the U.S. was propelled into global economic leadership, beating Britain for the top spot. Now America finds itself in the uncomfortable position of being challenged by China for the top spot.

During the Industrial Revolution, one its phases was call the Age of Synergy.[4] From 1867 to 1914, most of the great innovations were primarily science based. New innovations included electricity, the radio, human flight, the telephone, and the automobile. These inventions brought people and nations around the world closer together. However, the specter of two world wars divided the planet and turned factories into war machines, delaying progress, but also providing a catalyst for innovations that eventually ended up in our daily lives. It was also a time of global expansion and a horrible depression that exposed us to the very worst and the very best that we humans can be and do.

Phase 3—The Information Age (1945–1999)

The conclusion of the Industrial Age coincided with the end of World War II. In the process, it ushered in a new era of an emerging middle class in the United States, Europe, and other Western societies. Entrepreneurship took on a new meaning as those who grew up in the era of a worldwide

---

Robert Fulton, Inventor of the Steamboat

THE INDUSTRIAL REVOLUTION

- The invention of steam power decreased need for muscle power from people and animals
- Vast advancements in transportation and communication technology created new markets
- Manufacturing brought people into collected groups to produce products and the workplace moved from the home to the factory
- Coal became a leading energy source for factory and transportation work and also supported mass production of raw materials into finished goods
- People didn't work from start to finish, but on smaller, discrete tasks as part of the whole
- Wage labor became common

The Industrial Revolution produced advancements in:

Technology   Energy   Transportation   Communications   Production

financial depression and a World War began to see abundance and had the means to become consumers in this new, post-industrial society. People moved to the suburbs and bought homes along with new conveniences and entertainment. Economist Daniel Bell popularized this concept in his 1976 book *The Coming of Post-Industrial Society*. According to Bell, "The post-industrialized society is marked by an increased valuation of knowledge."

Common themes around this change emerged:[5]

1. The economy undergoes a transition from the production of goods to the provision of services.

2. Knowledge becomes a valued form of capital (e.g., human capital).

3. Producing ideas is the main way to grow the economy.

4. Through processes of globalization and automation, the value and importance to the economy of blue-collar, unionized work, including manual labor (e.g., assembly-line work) declines. Professional workers (e.g., scientists, digital creatives, and IT specialists) grow in value and prevalence.

5. Behavioral and information sciences and technologies are developed and implemented (e.g., behavioral economics, information architecture, cybernetics, and game theory).

Bell's prediction pointed to a post-industrial economy dominated by the service and information industries that also raised the standard of living, leading to greater demand for goods and services.

The post-industrial society also benefited the creative culture. As education oriented towards individuals discovering their potential through creativity and self-expression, newer generations built on this philosophy. This transformed industry and the way we view creativity in the workplace and its impact on productivity. According to renowned architect Ellen Dunham-Jones, "This doctrine of 'speed, mobility, and malleability' is well suited to a dynamic creative industry and as industries of good production decrease in precedence, the way is paved for artists,

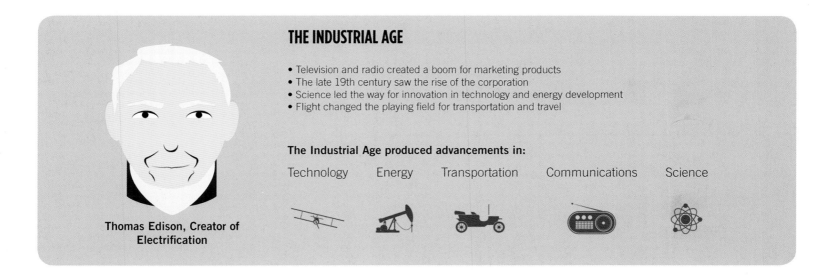

THE INDUSTRIAL AGE

- Television and radio created a boom for marketing products
- The late 19th century saw the rise of the corporation
- Science led the way for innovation in technology and energy development
- Flight changed the playing field for transportation and travel

Thomas Edison, Creator of Electrification

The Industrial Age produced advancements in:

Technology   Energy   Transportation   Communications   Science

musicians and other creatives, whose skills are better utilized by the tertiary and quaternary sector."[6]

The emergence of the post-industrial society during the second half of the twentieth century accelerated the move to an interconnected economic landscape, including globalization and increased automation. The development of the microprocessor, for instance, ushered in the era of innovations for the personal computer, the Internet, and the smartphone. Today we carry more processing power in the palm of our hand than what powered the first space shuttle. Economists have repeatedly stated that in a post-industrial society "knowledge is power and technology is the instrument,"[7] a perfect description of the information age.

With the shift from raw materials and a manufacturing economy to a service-based one, and later an intellectual focus, people exchanged more information (and still do). This chain of events led to today's information society. Over the last twenty years, we've used the Internet to develop a network society that leverages digital information and communication technologies to generate, process, and distribute information.

It's changed the way we communicate, the way we market products, and the way we collaborate today.

Phase 4—The New Industrial Revolution (2000–Present)

This arc of economic history began with the Industrial Revolution, moved through the industrial age, and then on to the information era. Today we are at the nexus of a new story arc that will propel the planet into a new era, and it begins with how we chart the next decade of our growth as a society and as a people. While the information age shifted our focus from the industrial to the digital, this new revolution shifts the power from larger, global corporations to small business owners with the global connections now possible in our digital world. Carbon-based fuels and technologies powered the previous Industrial Revolution, but new power sources and technology are coming online.

Since the global recession in 2008, we've seen the global economy search for a new economic narrative. As we've discussed throughout this

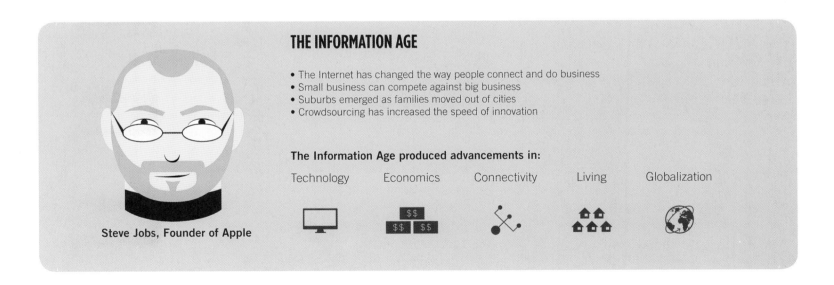

THE INFORMATION AGE

- The Internet has changed the way people connect and do business
- Small business can compete against big business
- Suburbs emerged as families moved out of cities
- Crowdsourcing has increased the speed of innovation

The Information Age produced advancements in:

Technology   Economics   Connectivity   Living   Globalization

Steve Jobs, Founder of Apple

chapter, economic revolutions in history occur when new energy systems are combined with new communication technologies. In the nineteenth century it was steam power and print technology. In the twentieth century it was electricity, the telephone, radio, and TV. Today, it's the Internet, 3D printing, and renewable energy sources setting the stage for what we and many others consider a new industrial revolution based on collaboration.

Emergence of the Era of Distributed Capitalism

As this new revolution emerges, our ongoing collaboration will help speed the end of the 200-year story of mass workforces and centralized businesses. In its place we'll usher in an era of distributed business practices that rely on a professional and technical workforce. By democratizing communication and increasing the number of available channels, we've empowered more than a third of the world's population to access and enjoy information, social lives, and knowledge in new and previously unthinkable ways. But that's only half the story.

Fossil fuels (e.g., coal, oil, natural gas) have powered almost everything. These systems require top-down command and control in addition to massive capital investment. This is not a surprise because centralized production and distribution sits at the core of modern capitalism and guides the rest of the economy.

When you think about it, modern finance, telecommunications, automobiles, utilities, and commercial construction feed off of the fossil fuel business funnel. Author Jeremy Rifkin highlighted in his book *The Third Industrial Revolution* that "three of the four largest companies in the world today are oil companies—Royal Dutch Shell, Exxon Mobil and BP. Underneath these companies are some five hundred global companies representing every sector and industry—with a combined revenue of $22.5 trillion, which is the equivalent of the one-third of the world's $62 trillion GDP."[8]

In sharp contrast, "the New Industrial Revolution is...organized around distributed renewable energies found everywhere and for the most part, free—sun, wind, hydro, geothermal heat, biomass and ocean waves and tides."[9] Imagine the possibilities. All this dispersed energy collected at millions of local sites and then bundled and shared with others through a "green, electric Internet." Over the coming years the centralized model powered by fossil fuels will give way to what many call distributed

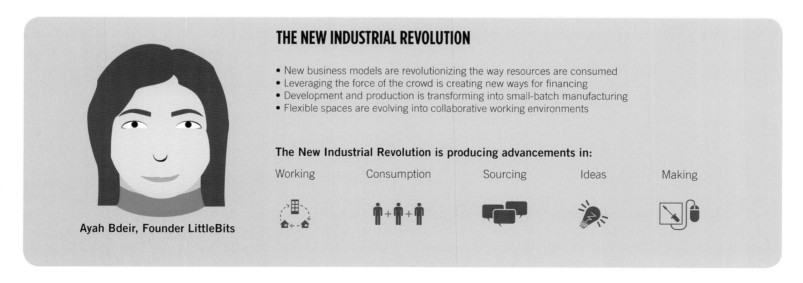

THE NEW INDUSTRIAL REVOLUTION

- New business models are revolutionizing the way resources are consumed
- Leveraging the force of the crowd is creating new ways for financing
- Development and production is transforming into small-batch manufacturing
- Flexible spaces are evolving into collaborative working environments

The New Industrial Revolution is producing advancements in:

Working   Consumption   Sourcing   Ideas   Making

Ayah Bdeir, Founder LittleBits

capitalism. In this model we'll leverage peer networks to allow everyone to become a potential entrepreneur, by creating information, knowledge, and power in the open, Creative Commons landscape.

This is a Global Movement, a Worldwide Revolution

The stories of our current revolution and ongoing innovation are global. China, Brazil, Russia, and India are growing rapidly and leading the way in manufacturing and outsourced service jobs. Within their countries, entrepreneurs like you and us are searching for a better way to serve a global market. This is only the beginning of a new era. Our era.

Throughout this book we will show how startups and entrepreneurs like yourself, can leverage technology and real-world social connections to solve your piece of the puzzle. By creating individualized ways to consume goods and services at a radically reduced cost, you'll prosper greatly as you realize wholly new sources of value that remain invisible to companies still bound by conventional business models.

It's an amazing world. We do live in revolutionary times. And you have joined the revolution.

CHOOSE YOUR OWN STARTUP ADVENTURE

Many people starting a business often have no clue where to begin. They often feel excited yet overwhelmed by the amount that needs to be done. Sound familiar? That's why we wrote this book. We'll walk you through, step-by-step, and help you understand the following:

1. The type of entrepreneur you truly are
2. The right startup formula for YOU
3. How to begin implementing it

Are you ready? Let's begin.

Savannah's startup economy is immersed in two key environments: on one hand, the community is a wonderful place to test a new business with many new opportunities, local resources, plenty of human capital, space, and hospitality; however, on the other hand, despite the efforts of many startups, several entrepreneurs have faced a variety of barriers to entry, including political issues and other problematic conditions.

CHAPTER 2

The best time to plant a tree was 20 years ago. The second best time is now.

—*Chinese Proverb*

The Rise of the Startup Economy

THE NEW STARTUP ECONOMY

Startups are at the heart of our world and are the driving force of our local economic development. The town you live in was a startup at some point. So was every company and organization you come into contact with in your daily life. You can easily find yourself within the startup economy as a customer, a partner, a service provider, and especially as an entrepreneur. As an entrepreneur you are not only growing your business but you are affecting your community.

A TALE OF TWO CITIES: SAVANNAH AND BOULDER

Savannah: A Story of Emergence

Savannah, Georgia, has a growing entrepreneurial community, but to truly understand the city, we need to examine it as an ecosystem that's connected across many divides, large and small. Like other cities, Savannah is built on the efforts of entrepreneurs, many of whom own small and medium enterprises (SMEs) that make up a combined total of 90.74% of Savannah's overall business economy.[1] Several of these individuals, businesses, and organizations collaborate to help support Savannah's current and future entrepreneurs, as well as aiding in the growth of a new, startup-driven economy.

Many outsiders describe Savannah as a tourist town (tourism does make up a large part of its economy), but that isn't all there is to Savannah. It's a university town that wears many hats. Savannah offers a rich educational experience with a variety of small tech schools, universities, art schools, and even a new law school. These schools act as feeders for the startup community by bringing in young, new, and fresh minds who want a different experience.

Over time, more graduates from the Savannah College of Art and Design (SCAD) and other local universities finish school, but didn't aspire to work for major firms or companies. They decided to start their own businesses. As these schools offered a wealth of opportunities for students to collaborate, they found ways to take their ideas and make them a reality.

Savannah shows that it's possible for a city to make a transition. Even though it still has a long way to go, the foundation now exists to support a new group of change makers. Local entrepreneurs, educators, researchers, mentors, and local businesses and nonprofits have come together to build an aligned vision for the city's startup community. Of course, making that vision a reality will take collaboration and a willingness to experiment, to fail, and to explore.

These collaborators now work together to provide new opportunities and services to the community. For example, you can now find a local co-working space in downtown Savannah. Thinc Savannah plays host to a new set of workshops and programs that help engage local business owners and schools.

Things are just getting warmed up in Savannah.

Someone who knows just how the momentum is building is Caleb Sexton, an entrepreneur down in Savannah. We asked Caleb to elaborate more on what is happening in Savannah.

SEQ: You mentioned startup economies in Savannah. What are the things you consider key to growing a startup economy in general?

Sexton: Obviously people are the biggest necessity. I am a firm believer in Brad Feld's Boulder thesis. I think it's a really great analogy for being able to understand the key actors and entities that are necessary for any good system to thrive. It has to be championed by the entrepreneurs, but it also has to have a strong support base. The community is starting to really cultivate that in Savannah.

SEQ: What to you is as an emerging startup economy? Can you talk about Savannah as an ecosystem and where you think it's going?

Sexton: Savannah is an ecosystem. It's a small city. We've got 130,000 people. It's diverse. Savannah has really great assets. Obviously it's got a really rich and vibrant cultural mesh. The entrepreneurial community is here, and it's starting to thrive. It's had some successes, but not as many as you would hope. I think there's a lot of work being laid in Savannah between organizations. You've got the pro-profit and non-profit institutions that are active. Even the entrepreneurs and some of the investor community getting involved. They're looking at, "How can we really help turn this into something new and something at the next degree of development?"

What's unique is that all the organizations in play are all very interconnected. Everyone knows each other, and everyone is tied to one another. That's another key point that I find interesting about Savannah. It's a great place to live.

Boulder: A Story of Sustainability

Boulder, Colorado, falls on the other side of the startup economy spectrum, and it comes with an interesting past. Originally territory of the Native American Arapaho tribe, Boulder saw its first wave of entrepreneurship in the 1850s as part of the gold rush in the American West. Another wave of entrepreneurs flooded the region after the discovery of tungsten, a rare metal, in the early twentieth century. Over the decades, Boulder became a quiet college town near great skiing and popular with people who loved being outdoors. However, as the technology industry grew in the 1980s, more companies opted to locate in Boulder, but the town maintained its charm and cool vibe.

In 1995, Brad Feld, a venture capitalist and mentor to many entrepreneurs, moved to Boulder. In his great book *Startup Communities*, Feld shared his story of coming to Boulder and his belief that it would become a new place for entrepreneurs to create, innovate, and grow their companies. It struck us that he called Boulder a "laboratory" of sorts and notes that it's a smart town.

Over the last decade, Boulder became a place where smart, independent people with a strong entrepreneurial drive went to build their dreams. Organizations like TechStars, events like Startup Week, and people like Brad Feld worked hard to build an inclusive community that's committed to making Boulder a place where you want to "do a startup."

It's clear that cities like Savannah are on their way to becoming the next Boulder. Cities around the world are in similar situations, maybe even the city or town you call home could be on its way to building a thriving, startup-oriented community. Now it's up to you, the entrepreneur, to take full advantage of your local startup economy and help take it to the next level.

WHAT MAKES A GREAT STARTUP ECONOMY?

Why do some cities flourish with innovation while others languish and struggle to progress? What components help a startup community

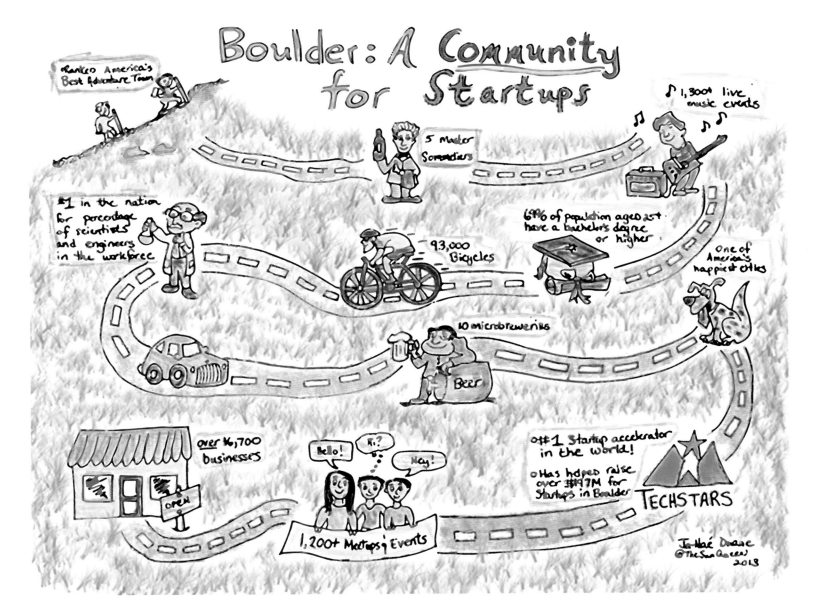

THE STARTUP ECOSYSTEM Figure 2.4

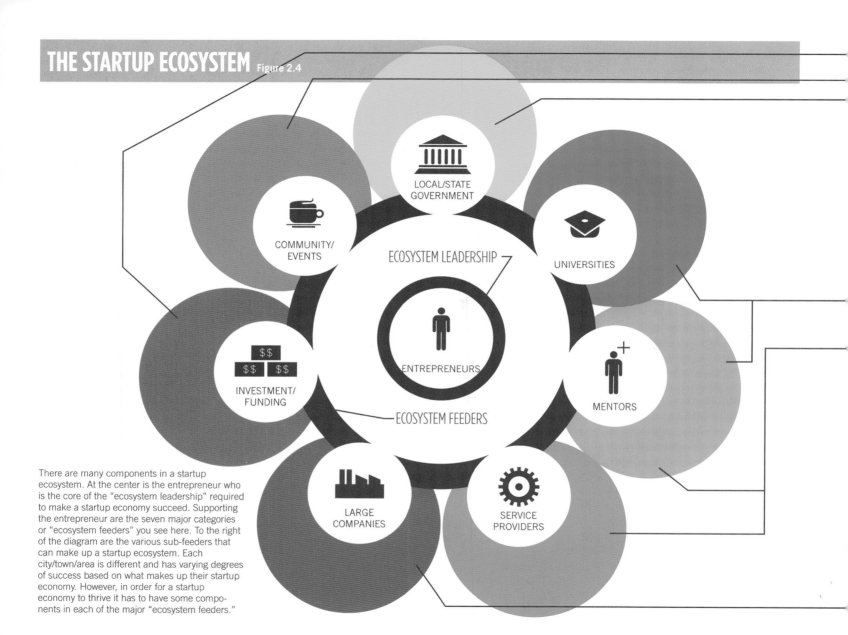

LOCAL/STATE GOVERNMENT

COMMUNITY/ EVENTS

UNIVERSITIES

ECOSYSTEM LEADERSHIP

ENTREPRENEURS

INVESTMENT/ FUNDING

MENTORS

ECOSYSTEM FEEDERS

LARGE COMPANIES

SERVICE PROVIDERS

There are many components in a startup ecosystem. At the center is the entrepreneur who is the core of the "ecosystem leadership" required to make a startup economy succeed. Supporting the entrepreneur are the seven major categories or "ecosystem feeders" you see here. To the right of the diagram are the various sub-feeders that can make up a startup ecosystem. Each city/town/area is different and has varying degrees of success based on what makes up their startup economy. However, in order for a startup economy to thrive it has to have some components in each of the major "ecosystem feeders."

POLICY

Government
- Research Institutes
- Financial Support
- Venture-Friendly Legislation
- Regulatory Framework Incentives

Leadership
- Social Legitimacy
- Open Door for Advocates
- Entrepreneurship Strategy
- Urgency, Crisis, and Challenge
- Unequivocal Support

INTERSECTIONS

Success Stories
- Visible Success
- Wealth Generation for Founders
- International Reputation
- Initiated by Creative Economy

Societal Norms
- Tolerance of Risk, Mistakes, Failures
- Innovation, Experimentation, Creativity
- Social Status of Entrepreneur
- Wealth Creation
- Ambition, Drive, Hunger

FINANCE

Financial Capital
- Micro-Loans
- Angel Investing, Friends, and Family
- Zero-Stage Venture Capital
- Venture Capital Funds
- Private Equity
- Public Capital Markets
- Debt

SUPPORT

Infrastructure
- Telecommunications
- Transportation and Logistics
- Accelerators
- Zones, Incubation Centers, Clusters

Support Professions
- Legal
- Accounting
- Investment Bankers
- Technical Experts, Advisors

Non-Governmental Institutions
- Entrepreneurship Promotion in Non-Profits
- Business Plan Contests
- Conferences
- Entrepreneur-Friendly Associations

MARKETS

Early Customers
- Early Adopters for Proof-of-Concept
- Expertise in Producing
- Reference Customers
- First Reviews
- Distribution Channels

Networks
- Entrepreneur's Networks
- Diaspora Networks
- Multinational Corporations

HUMAN CAPITAL

Labor
- Skilled and Unskilled
- Serial Entrepreneurs
- Later Generation Family

Educational Institutions
- General Degrees (Professional and Academic)
- Specific Entrepreneurship Training

STARTUP ECONOMIES Figure 2.5

UNITED STATES

BOSTON

- Mature Startup Ecosystem
- Strong Investor Community
- Big Data and Hardware Startups
- Enormous talent base (MIT, Harvard)

NEW ORLEANS

- Rated best emerging city for business
- Startups in culinary, tech and education
- Entrepreneurship 56% above US avg
- 70% of startups launched by students

AUSTIN

- Many success stories
- Strong tech base and talent pool
- Top city in the US for entrepreneurs
- Thriving creative class

NEW YORK

- Strong creative class and diversity
- Incredibly strong startup ecosystem
- Large amounts of investors
- Top place for women entrepreneurs

CANADA

TORONTO

- Strong startup economy
- Strong technology adoption
- Emerging investor sources
- Healthy mix of startups and events

VANCOUVER

- Competition for talent w/Seattle
- Thriving startup economy
- Many mobile-focused startups
- Tech company hub

MONTREAL

- Rapid cultural growth
- Cost of living is much lower
- Video game hub
- Strong talent base

WATERLOO (ONTARIO)

- Mobile and tech startup hub (e.g., RIM)
- Great talent pool and universities
- Great corporate HQ and partners
- Strong connections with Silicon Valley

LATIN AMERICA

SANTIAGO

- Startup Chile one of largest accelerators
- Highly educated workforce
- Low costs and strong infrastructure
- Strong government support for startups

SÃO PAULO

- Thriving startup economy
- Center of Tech Innovation
- Strong investor scene
- Bureaucracy and taxes

BUENOS AIRES

- Emerging startup economy
- Strong outsourcing hub
- Strong government support for startups
- Entrepreneurship is a career option

PANAMA CITY

- Hot real estate investments and tourism
- Destination for international business
- Easy and inexpensive to start business
- Large ex-pat entrepreneurial community

EUROPE

BARCELONA

- Government Zone 22 startup zone
- Top business and design schools
- Large app and tech startup scene
- Great work/life balance

DUBLIN
- Low corporate tax rate
- Best city for 'Human Capital'
- Accelerators and funding
- Attracts top engineering talent

LONDON
- Has a funding gap that is closing
- Tech City is a big success
- Google has a major outpost there
- Diversity influences everything

BERLIN
- Strong economy
- Entrepreneurship boom
- Funding sources are emerging
- Great location and talent pool

MIDDLE EAST

TEL AVIV

- Fairly established Startup Economy
- Highest density of startups in world
- Strong angel funding network
- Political tensions can be an issue

ABU DHABI

- Crowdfunding major source for startups
- Large focus on young entrepreneurs
- Former nationals are entrepreneurs
- Media and entertainment startups

DUBAI

- Hot bed of entrepreneurial activity
- Crowdfunding major source for startups
- VC's starting to increase their funds
- Interest is mainly around tech startups

CAIRO

- Vibrant Startup Scene
- Young entrepreneurs on the rise
- Seed funding is growing
- Bridging the entrepreneurial gap

AFRICA

CAPE TOWN

- The "Silicon Cape"
- Strong Investor Community
- Affordable, fast connectivity
- Outsourcing and Offshoring Hub

LAGOS, NIGERIA

- The "Silicon Lagoon"
- Emerging Startup Economy
- Crowdfunding major source for startups
- Many mobile startups

JOHANNESBURG

- Growing Investor Community
- Media and financial startups
- Coworking spaces
- Strong Education Base

NAIROBI, KENYA

- The Silicon Savanna
- 93% of citizens use mobile phones
- Konza Tech City
- 88mph Accelerator with Google Africa

ASIA

SINGAPORE

- One of the top places to live in the world
- Most developed startup ecosystem in Asia
- Access to Asia for many US companies
- Building a team is challenging

NEW DELHI

- High growth in female entrepreneurs
- Social and economic center for startups
- Over 2,000 investors in the area
- City has adopted a "fail fast" mantra

TOKYO

- 2nd largest economy in Asia
- Supportive educational system
- Vibrant scene of biz, VCs, and incubators
- Large focus on mobile, e-commerce

SHANGHAI

- Ecosystem for idea to follow-up funding
- Lack of government support
- Big problem with cloning startups
- Incubators and accelerators emerging

PACIFICS

SYDNEY

- Great quality of life
- Strong education and talent base
- Funding is focused on self-funding
- Tackle markets they know well

AUCKLAND

- Emerging startup economy like Boulder
- Needs better infrastructure and funding
- Startup equity is not part of startup culture

MELBOURNE

- One of the top startup ecosystems
- Good and growing funding base
- Great universities and talent pool
- Entrepreneurs reinvest in the startups

PERTH

- Emerging startup culture
- Needs more funding and talent pool
- Coworking spaces are the hubs
- Strong government support

achieve escape velocity? We pose these questions because it's important to discover what lays the foundation for a successful startup community.

As part of this discussion, we want to highlight a few frameworks in *Startup Communities* by Mr. Feld. The book reviews economic concepts like agglomeration economies, horizontal networks, and network effects that are really cool and explain much of how startup economies have formed over the years. Within the book, Feld covers another framework that he created called the *Boulder Thesis*. We see it as the best and most holistic approach of all the frameworks.

The Boulder Thesis is defined as follows:[2]

- Entrepreneurs must lead the startup community.
- The leaders must have a long-term commitment.
- The startup community must be inclusive of anyone who wants to participate in it.
- The startup community must have continual activities that engage the entire entrepreneurial stack.

We had a chance to chat with Brad Feld about his thesis and about Boulder's ecosystem.

SEQ: Back in 1995, you decided to move to Boulder for a number of reasons and helped pioneer a thriving startup ecosystem. What were the first few elements that became the catalyst to really get things going?

Feld: I've written extensively about this in my book *Startup Communities*. The essence of what drove things over the years in Boulder has been a vibrant and engaged set of entrepreneurs who are the leaders of the Boulder startup community. They aren't appointed, they just lead, just like they do as entrepreneurs. Over time, this group, and others, enabled a philosophy of "give before you get" where we all were willing to put energy into each other without having a pre-arranged relationship. We were willing to "give" without knowing what would come back to us. This wasn't philanthropy. We all expected to get a lot back, but the relationships weren't transactionally based.

SEQ: You created the Boulder Thesis, which has been a cornerstone for people creating startup communities. Has this changed?

Feld: When I came up with the four principles of the Boulder Thesis in 2010, I tried to make them broad enough to be long lasting, while specific enough to be actionable. They continue to be the basis for creating a startup community in any city. I've learned a lot about specific tactics that work and don't work in different geographies, but fundamentally the Boulder Thesis feels rock solid to me.

The Startup Ecosystem

Looking through the lens of an ecosystem gives us the best understanding of a new startup economy. Doing so allows us to view the community holistically, as interconnected parts working together (and sometimes against each other). After studying cities around the world, we propose that eight major components power a startup ecosystem:

1. Universities
2. Community/Events
3. Local/state governments
4. Mentors
5. Investment/Funding
6. Large Companies
7. Service Providers
8. And at the center, Entrepreneurs

While some of these components may be a little more robust than others from place to place, each city with a startup ecosystem has a dynamic mix of all eight components that you can see in Figure 2.4.

All cities that have a startup community or are thinking of growing a startup community have all of these components in some shape or form. There are many people in the community who are connectors and catalysts to help your startup be successful because it is in their interest and motivation to see that community thrive. As more startups come to a community there are more jobs for people in those startups and with the service providers that serve them. Startups also attract more venture funding and investment. The city/state tax coffers grow further supporting the need and politically positive entrepreneurial-friendly programs. It shows larger companies, who might have thought of leaving or relocating somewhere else, a new era of prosperity, potential acquisitions, partnerships and pools of talent to draw from that never would have existed without a startup ecosystem.

WHERE IS THE BEST STARTUP ECONOMY FOR YOUR BUSINESS?

Once a startup community has momentum, how does it sustain that energy and expand? At stake is the economic existence of your town, city, province, and region. From a global perspective, we need more than one Silicon Valley, because in a globalized business ecosystem, your market could be anyone located anywhere in the world. In fact, there are hundreds of startup economies around the world. You will see in Figure 2.5, The Global Startup Economy, that there are so many options that we could only take the top few in each region around the world.

Think about it. As a startup begins, the majority of its ecosystem stays local. The market becomes the community, and the customers are the people who live there. Every entrepreneur needs an ecosystem to grow and flourish. With many great places to start a business, it depends on you and what you need in a startup community. Entrepreneurship face similar struggles to build something from nothing and continue to find support worldwide.

Earlier in the chapter we spoke in detail about two startup economies in the United States, one (Boulder) more evolved because of hard work over the last 20 years and one (Savannah) with the potential to be that if the right connectors and catalysts are able to continue their work. But, as you saw in Figure 2.5, The Global Startup Economy, there are hundreds all over the world. In our research here are some things that really stood out to us:

- **Montreal, Canada** is a video game hub but has a rapid cultural growth that is challenging its past and really stirring things up
- **Panama City, Panama** is an easy and inexpensive location to start a business, with many ex-pats starting companies
- **Barcelona, Spain** is one of the most wired "smart cities" in the world and its great work-life balance culture it has attracted a large app and tech startup scene
- **Cairo, Egypt,** emerging from the Arab Spring, has a vibrant start up scene leveraging its youth-majority population to transform the country
- **Lagos, Nigeria** is known as the "Silicon Lagoon." It has a large mobile startup scene and leverages crowdfunding as a major source of funding for startups
- **Auckland, New Zealand** has an emerging startup economy like Boulder, Colorado. Equity is not part of the culture but that is changing

Let's highlight and dive a little deeper on two in particular—Santiago, Chile and Palestine.

Two Global Emerging Startup Economies— Santiago and Palestine

Santiago, Chile is an entrepreneurial hub flourishing and on the verge of becoming the entrepreneurship and innovation hub of Latin America. With a population of over 6 million, entrepreneurs are able to find opportunities there due to the lack of bureaucracy in this small country. To differentiate itself from other startup hubs in the world, it created "Start-Up Chile" with a final goal of creating a $1B company and globalizing the Chilean entrepreneurship culture. 1000 companies who are in or went through its 24 week program get $40,000 in equity-free funding and a 1 year temporary visa, along with the coaching, development and mentoring they would get in other programs.

Another budding ecosystem is in Palestine. Many people know of Israel's startup scene, but, in addition to that more mature startup scene, there are a number of connectors and catalysts working to create a new future for Palestine and its citizens. Most of the Palestinian startup activity is within the city of Ramallah including events like Startup Weekend and accelerators like FastForward and the BADER ICT incubator and ICT HUB led by connectors like Salah Amleh. There are startup spaces to host hackathons and educational events, and the community relies on one another to build their global go-tomarket strategies. Also, there are many who are part of the Palestinian Diaspora who have returned from being abroad to do their startup in the region. This is a testament to the power that startups and entrepreneurship can have to bridge divides and create communities of the future that could change the world for the better.

With all of the startup economies, when you really think about it, the world is one big startup ecosystem. It is about people helping people and about creating and being the change they wish to see in the world. So we encourage you to explore and investigate these amazing startup economies around the world so you can find the best place for you to take your first step as an entrepreneur.

The Six Forces of Change

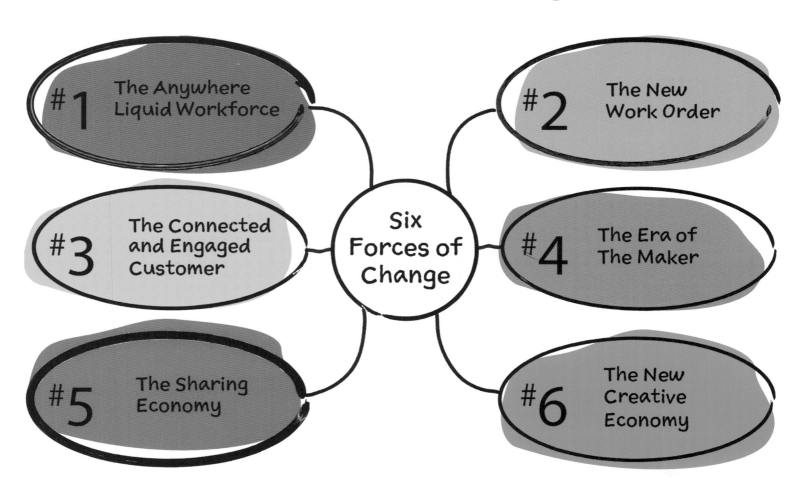

CHAPTER 3

The best way to predict the future is to create it.

—*Peter Drucker*

The Six Forces of Change

The world is changing more rapidly than many people can keep up. As you build your startup, shifting macroeconomic trends will be extremely important to you. We call these the *Six Forces of Change*.

FORCE #1: THE ANYWHERE, LIQUID WORKFORCE

Globalization, technology, and economic influences all contribute to ever more rapid change. These and other factors are changing the way we work. The jobs being automated are the stable; well-paying jobs that workers expected would last until retirement. If you can define a job, you can probably outline it enough to outsource the job, either to a lower-wage worker elsewhere or to a computer. Instead of fearing this change, see it as a motivator. If you want to control your career, don't sit on your butt and become complacent. It will also mean a new model for hiring a large portion of your future workforce.

The Move Toward Talent Clouds and Corporate Crowdsourcing

IBM pioneered the liquid workforce with their Liquid Challenge program. It set an ambitious goal: to transition 8,000 of 20,000 full-time jobs in Germany to freelance positions. The Liquid Challenge encouraged IBM project managers to outsource project design and programming to the IBM talent network (i.e., IBM Liquid Players). In this model, "teams are formed around individual client needs, and when those needs are satisfied, the team is dispersed."

Distilled to its pure essence, Liquid Challenge and other programs like it are about separating and assigning tasks. As the trend continues, companies will face the challenge of figuring out how to separate tasks and use platforms to create their own liquid workforce.

Startups have plenty of opportunities to leverage this liquid workforce. By having a startup team source specialist skills when they're needed, they can have that talent on demand for a limited time. When those in the talent cloud have more experience in different environments, they tend to have a broader understanding of the issues. Given the fast pace of the startup environment, this specialized talent can help trigger more innovation.

Force #1
The Anywhere Liquid Workforce

Someone who knows a lot about the Liquid Workforce is digital anthropologist and author, Brian Solis. We had an opportunity to chat with him about where he saw this trend going and what it means for entrepreneurs.

SEQ: You've previously mentioned the Liquid Workforce and Liquid Workplaces. How much time have you spent on this concept?

Solis: This is a powerful concept. This is what changes the nature of business. You have fluid workforces. You have fluid work locations. You have fluid hours. You still have traditional models that are governing all of these new trends and new behaviors that need to collapse in order to really capitalize on these trends. You have a revolution, you have a need, but nothing is really going to change unless things happen from the top down.

What we have to understand is that when people find out about the liquid workforce or entrepreneurialism, they often mean different things to different people simply because of the nature or the culture of the organization. That's okay.

It's really our job to figure out from a leadership perspective what are we really trying to do? What are we trying to solve? The challenge for the liquid workforce is that it's based on an old model. You create what's essentially a matrix organization. You borrow people for a period of time and then they move back.

It's all very dramatic but it's all very true and that comes back to the connected customer: people who live a digital lifestyle feel more empowered. As a result of being more empowered, they're more demanding, and as a result of being more demanding, they're impatient. They expect the world to absorb everything they do, say, share, and support and match these new values.

That means that whether it's an enterprise or whether it's a startup, you have to not only understand what's going on. You have to have the authority to design against it and execute against it and sell against it. That all comes down to a key word that I actually believe is the essence, the soul, of the future of all business and that's *empathy*. Empathy to me is one of the most powerful things that we can feel in order to feel something different, because many people live in a world where you've got the stakeholders, shareholders, investors, and employees, but you miss the human aspect of this, and why you did this in the first place, and why it's important.

Opportunities for Entrepreneurs

1. Work through organizational structures to prevent competitive silos.
2. Create a leadership lattice so those who work for your startup have the ability to learn a variety of skills and grow with your business.
3. Explore talent clouds for staffing instant experts in your startup.

FORCE #2: THE NEW WORK ORDER—CONNECTED, COLLABORATIVE, CREATIVE

During the first Industrial Revolution, workers shifted from farms to factories. In today's startup-rich environment, we find ourselves in the middle of a comparable transformation. Just as workers left the plow for the assembly line, they're now leaving the cubicle for the coffee shop. We're moving toward an economy where the majority of workers will be freelancers, creating a *new work order*. As an entrepreneur, you could be one of these people or you could be leveraging this force to power your startup.

The Rise of the Independent Workforce

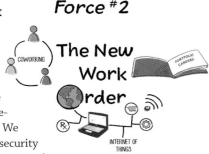

Everywhere you look, the global workforce is undergoing a massive change. We don't work at the same company for twenty-five years, hoping at the end for a retirement party and a gold watch. We also can't expect the benefits and security previously associated with full-time employment. Today, careers require juggling multiple clients and projects, while also learning marketing and accounting.

How we work is changing, and it requires crafting a lifelong, portfolio career. We're scaling a lattice, not climbing a ladder. Yes, freelancing isn't new, but today's talent also comes with cheap, readily available transformational tools and technologies. It's a world powered by ideas, enthusiasm, and collaboration. Coworking spaces, meet-ups, and hack days are the new catalysts of innovation. For the first time, we see the possibility of a real ecosystem of talent networks operating at a viable scale.[1]

The Age of Coworking: Redefining the Workplace

More than 110,000 people currently work in one of the nearly 2,500 coworking spaces available worldwide.[2] As coworking spreads worldwide, it attracts creative entrepreneurs and freelancers from a wide spectrum of vocations. Designers, developers, writers, photographers, lawyers, hackers, and even startup founders come together in shared spaces that offer the practical benefits of a traditional office without clinging to the standard cubicle and a nine-to-five mindset. Far from the utilitarian consideration of lower costs—everything from rent and printing to coffee and the Internet is cheaper when shared—these hubs offer a unique environment for what we like to call creative restlessness. Leveraging a coworking space can change things for an entrepreneur.

Alex Hillman, co-founder of IndyHall in Philadelphia, was a pioneer of the early coworking movement and likes to call coworking "community with a purpose." Back in 2007, he and his business partner raised money from the community to build a place in Philadelphia where people wanted to work. Their space, IndyHall, became an example of what a community can do when it comes together for a reason. Thirty people signed up for a space before it opened officially. We had a chance to chat with him about his experience growing this community.

SEQ: What is your philosophy on the power of coworking and its impact on a local community and its startup economy?

Hillman: When coworking is done with community in mind—and the experience focuses on how people connect with each other and build trust rather than just sharing desks—coworking can transform a local community. Because here's the thing: We're not creating a replacement for the cubicle that entrepreneurs have run so far away from. Battling against the cubicle is a reflection of our times and a valiant effort for sure.

SEQ: How does coworking impact/form a startup's culture, and what should a startup look for if they are considering coworking?

Hillman: Coworking can be great for startups, but startups are terrible for the other people in coworking spaces. Everyone comes for the opportunity to be around and interact with other people, otherwise they'd just work from home.

Opportunities for Entrepreneurs

1. Utilize coworking spaces to launch your business.
2. Connect with talent when you need it to support your new venture.
3. Turn creative restlessness into a collaborative environment.

FORCE #3: THE CONNECTED AND ENGAGED CUSTOMER

Customers develop an emotional bond or attachment through ongoing interactions that hopefully lead to satisfaction, loyalty, and engagement. When customers engage with an organization, they're more likely to feel passionate and connected to its products and services. An engaged customer will also feel aligned with the purpose and direction of the organization, creating a powerful connection, but one that must be maintained over time.

Force #3
The Connected & Engaged Customer
CROWDFUNDING
THE APP ECONOMY
GAMIFICATION

Atoms are the New Bits in the Long Tail and App Economy

Kevin Kelly talks about the engaged customer in terms of the 1,000 fans concept. He suggests that if you have 1,000 dedicated fans who bought everything you produced, that model beats trying for a one-time sale to 100,000 people. Writers and musicians with small but solid fan bases prove his point. In his bestselling book, *The Long Tail: Why the Future of Business is Selling Less of More*, Chris Anderson, CEO of 3D Robotics and formerly *WIRED's* editor-in-chief, writes about the transformation of industries using digital technologies designed to avoid wasting time on the big customer targets and instead aimed at leveraging small, dedicated customer groups. Not only can you make a living, but it's possible to do very well here.

Entrepreneurs need to recognize the ongoing role of digital to help disrupt business models that have existed for decades. We've already seen the democratization of business sectors like music, publishing, broadcasting, and communications. More disruption will come, and we're watching transformation happen through mobile devices and apps. Apple, Google, and Microsoft offer hundreds of thousands of apps for their mobile platforms to meet a need, help accomplish a goal, or just entertain you. Entrepreneurs may make money building apps and mobile web interfaces, but they're also creating businesses of all shapes and sizes that leverage these platforms to reach customers and support engagement.

Gamification: Beyond Quests and Badges

Years before the concept of gamification emerged, people used gaming principles to achieve all sorts of goals. For example, as a child you if you were a Boy Scout or a Girl Scout you could earn badges for demonstrating skills and completing projects. Little did we know that we were responding to an early form of gamification to gain our loyalty and dedication.

Another example are loyalty programs like frequent flyer programs that reward interaction with tangible benefits, such as coupons or other perks. In a way, school and work can be viewed as a sequence of challenges with a badge awarded at the end in the form of a diploma, a job promotion, or a year-end financial bonus.[3] The benefit to entrepreneurs is that gamification is a powerful tool for creating an engaging experience, leveraging the need to achieve, and driving meaningful engagement of their brand.

The Growing Power of the Crowd

Most of us are familiar with the concept of crowdsourcing. We see it in sites like Wikipedia, Quirky, and 99Designs where the talent of many is leveraged to bring the best and most innovative ideas to the forefront, with the crowd voting by mouse click. The concept originated in the seminal book *The Clue Train Manifesto*. Written in collaboration by four authors, it postulates that an organization's boundaries have become porous. It's led to an acceleration of emergent and smart markets that in many cases outpace the adaptive capacity of organizations. As a result, crowdsourcing evolved to meet that need.

Opportunities for Entrepreneurs

1. Leverage the concept of 1,000 fans to build your audience.
2. Utilize mobile apps as the gateway to your user's behavior.
3. Entrepreneurs should build on proven gamification principles to enhance customer loyalty and engagement.
4. Leverage crowdsourcing and crowdfunding as a way to validate your ideas and engage paying customers as your first beta testers.

FORCE #4: THE ERA OF THE MAKER

Chris Anderson[4] has also talked about "the massive increase in the range of both participation and participants in everything digital—the long tail of bits." In one sentence, he boldly summarizes the history of two decades. "If the last 10 years have been about discovering post-institutional social models on the Web, then the next 10 years will be about applying then to the real world." We see the same thing happening to manufacturing, the long tail of things, if you will.

The Era of the Maker and Digital Manufacturing

Ironically, the use of technologies like 3D printing blends the service and manufacturing sectors of an economy in a way that no one could foresee. While the star of this maker movement is the consumer 3D printer, the building momentum of digital manufacturing represents the real revolution. We're seeing an overall digitization of manufacturing (e.g., CNC milling and factory floor automation). This also involves leveraging software concepts such as automation, abstraction, and standards, giving home hobbyists or makers the ability to create solutions to real-world problems and create a whole new sector of entrepreneurial opportunities.

Right now, 3D is cool, but it's in the process of going digital as new models of distributed manufacturing begin to take hold. Many critics of this model believe it's responsible for bringing down the minimum viable economies of scale (i.e., the smallest amount that someone can efficiently produce something). However, we also see people developing prototypes at home or in hackerspaces like TechShop, Lowell Makes or Artisan's Asylum. This technology allows people to iterate faster and improve their results with each round. In the future, we see connected networks of MakerNets that accelerate local production on a global, connected scale to power the new industrial revolution.

We had an opportunity to chat with Kamal Jain of Lowell Makes about this shifting force. Here is what he had to say:

SEQ: What impact do you think Makerspaces will have?

Jain: I think the thing with Makerspaces is the keyword *make*. One of the big trends is this whole concept of entrepreneurship or micropreneurship. When you're doing entrepreneurship, you're creating a business or you're creating business activity and you're then creating economic activity, and that idea manifests itself in terms of dollars or jobs. That's the big thing. A lot of the reason for that is because we've seen repeated cycles of people going to work for large, capital-intensive operations. Lowell is a perfect example.

The Maker Movement is about taking down the barriers to creating your own business, your own products, your own services, and your own art and crafts, whether it's for play or for profit. It's about helping people make things from the tangible to the intangible.

SEQ: What do you feel is the impact of Makerspaces on the arts and on a startup economy in a local town?

Jain: I think it's a long-term impact. It's going to be phenomenal. I think the nearer term impact is one of social empowerment and change. What happens is you get folks, especially young folks, kids, maybe school-aged kids, grade school or slightly older, who may come from a highly disadvantaged socio-economic position and they are just constantly bombarded with things in life, directly and indirectly reminding them of how poor they are and how inferior their life is and how dim their chances are.

For many of them, they think, "Well, if I just go to college, that will solve the problem." Admittedly, college is great for a lot of people but it's not for everyone. When you bring these kids in, 8, 10, 12 years old into an environment, they realize that they can do something that very few people in the world can do.

It is so empowering for people to do something as simple as writing a little script that makes something happen or placing some wires together and making something happen or fixing something or modifying something and doing things with their hands and just blowing away the people around them. They'd go, "Wait a minute. You're this poor kid, this 12-years-old and you could get what?" That's really, really a big part of that and that feeds into the confidence building of economic development, which is the real question, and that kind of similar impact. These

GENERATIONS IN THE WORKPLACE Figure 3.5

CHARACTERISTICS	VETERAN (PRE - 1945)	BABY BOOMERS (1945 - 1960)	GENERATION X (1961 - 1980)	GENERATION Y (1981 - 1995)	GENERATION Z (BORN AFTER 1995)
Formative Experiences	Second World War Rationing Fixed-Gender Roles Rock n' Roll Nuclear Families Defined Gender Roles — particularly for women	Cold War Post-War Boom "Swinging Sixties" Apollo Moon Landings Youth Culture Woodstock Family-Orientated Rise of the Teenager	End of Cold War Fall of the Berlin Wall Reagan / Gorbachev Thatcherism Live Aid Introduction of First PC Early Mobile Technology Latch-key Kids: rising levels of divorce	9/11 Terrorist Attack PlayStation Social Media Invasion of Iraq Reality TV Google Earth Glastonbury	Economic Downturn Global Warming Global Focus Mobile Devices Arab Spring Produce Own Media Cloud Computing Wiki-leaks
Percentage of Workforce (Percentages are approximate)	3%	33%	35%	29%	Currently employed in part-time jobs or apprenticeships
Aspiration	Home Ownership	Job Security	Work-Life Balance	Freedom and Flexibility	Security and Stability
Attitude Toward Technology	Largely Disengaged	Early Information Technology Adapters	Digital Immigrants	Digital Natives	"Technoholics" - Limited grasp on alternatives
Attitude Toward Career	Jobs are for Life	Organizational Careers — Careers are defined by the employers	Early "Portfolio" Careers — Loyal to profession, not employer	Digital Entrepreneurs — Work "with" organizations not "for"	Career Multitaskers — will move seamlessly between organizations
Signature Product	Automobile	Television	Personal Computer	Tablet / Smart Phones	Google Glass, Graphene, Nano-computing, 3D Printing
Communication Media	Formal Letter	Telephone	Email and Text Message	Text and Social Media	Hand-held Devices
Communication Preference	Face-to-Face	Face-to-Face Ideally, but email or telephone if requires	Online — would prefer face-to-face if time permitting	Face-to-Face	Solutions will be digitally crowd-sourced

*Data Sources: Barclays "Talking About My Generation", William Strauss and Neil Howe "Generations"

CHARACTERISTICS	VETERAN (PRE – 1945)	BABY BOOMERS (1945 – 1960)	GENERATION X (1961 – 1980)	GENERATION Y (1981 – 1995)	GENERATION Z (BORN AFTER 1995)
Work Ethic	Respect Authority Hard Work Age = Seniority Company First	Workaholics Desire Quality Question Authority	Eliminate the Task Self-reliant Want Structure and Direction Skeptical	What's Next Multitasking Tenacity Entrepreneurial	What's Next Multitaskers Community Entrepreneurial
Work is...	An Obligation	An Exciting Adventure	A Difficult Challenge, A Contract	A Means to an End	Purpose Driven Portfolio Career
Leadership Style	Directive, Command and Control	Quality	Everyone is the same Challenge others, Ask why	Remains to be seen	Remains to be seen
Communication	Formal Memo	In Person	Direct, Immediate, Email, Voice Mail	Email, Texting, Video Chat	Texting, Video Chat
Rewards and Feedback	No news is good news. Satisfaction in a job well done	Money. Title Recognition. Give me something to put on the wall	Sorry to Interrupt, but How am I doing? Freedom = Best Reward	Whenever I want it, at the push of a button Meaningful Work	Instant and 360
Motivated By	Being Respected	Being Valued and Needed	Freedom and Removal of Rules	Working with other Bright People	Impact and Purpose
Work/Life Balance	Keep them Separate	No Balance: "Live to Work"	Balance "Work to Live"	Balance — It's 5pm — I've got another gig	Blurred Life and Work
Technology is...	Hoover Dam	The Microwave	What you can hold in your hand: Tablet, Cellphone	Ethereal - Intangible	Seamless - Expected

Data Source: Zemke, Ron; Raines, Claire; Filipczak, Bob. Generations at Work: Managing the Clash of Veterans, Boomers, Xers, and Nexters in Your Workplace. New York, N.Y.: American Management Association, 2000.

folks are going to be more inclined to start small businesses either as their full time thing or on the side to try to create their own job, to live their own dream job, and what winds up happening is you create a much more diverse, resilient ecosystem.

Small-Batch Businesses

Coinciding with the physical nature of MakerNets and digital manufacturing, people are more focused on the smaller volume, valuable production of things with higher quality. The phrase that seems to resonate in today's entrepreneur landscape is *small batch*.

When you hear that phrase, you might think bourbon or ice cream. It definitely applies to small quantities of high-quality products. You can also use terms like bespoke or craft or artisan, but they all refer to the same thing—this idea of a company or an individual producing limited amounts of high-quality products for a specific audience. People used to describe it as a boutique business or a mom-and-pop shop, but the ground has shifted.

Opportunities for Entrepreneurs

1. Utilize hackerspaces and 3D technology to develop physical prototypes quickly.

2. Leverage digital manufacturing supply chains to scale rapidly.

3. Explore how your startup might offer customers a small-batch experience.

FORCE #5: THE SHARING ECONOMY

The shift from an ownership economy to a sharing economy represents one of the most important movements of this decade. Rachel Botsman captured this concept eloquently in her book *What's Yours Is Mine*. In it, she describes the idea of "collaborative consumption." In this collaborative consumption world, people will share things with each other, and, in the process, create new economies. You may have heard of companies like AirBnB (short-term rentals), Uber (car service), or LiquidSpace (work-

spaces). Decentralizing resources enables us to have more by owning less, or as Kevin Kelly describes it, "Access trumps possession."[5]

Sharing remains a basic part of human life, and the sharing economy reminds us of learning as kids to share things with our siblings. Over time, this attitude of sharing became a key part of our lives. It's become apparent that while we may have "stuff," we don't use it one hundred percent of the time. In fact, many studies in cities all over the world confirm that cars sit for 95 percent of the time. That opens the door to some great opportunities for people who are looking to maximize their asset, while earning a little extra income on the side.

Someone who knows a lot about the sharing economy is Jeremiah Owyang. Jeremiah's career goal has been to help large corporations connect to their customers using their technologies. We had an opportunity to chat with him about where the sharing economy is headed.

SEQ: What is the mission of Crowd Companies?

Owyang: There's three things. There's the market, there's the mission and then there's the value. The market is the collaborative economy. This is just like social media: people create media, and then they share it with their peers.

SEQ: You're setting a whole new course, a new industrial revolution.

Owyang: That's absolutely right. It means that the crowd has become like a company. Fund, build, and share what they have and supply chain each other and avoid corporations if they want to.

They bypass inefficient corporations. That's the movement, the collaborative economy. The average funding this year of those startups, I just tallied it up this morning, the average funding is $100 million per start up.

THE MAKER MAP Figure 3.8

In this era of the maker we are witnessing the birth of a new industrial revolution. At the center of this are the makers and the manufacturing capabilities available today. We have identified six ways they are able to create new industries like artisan networks, citizen R&D and personal fabrication. To put the era of the maker front and center, below are six drivers that show how this is possible.

MANUFACTURING　　　**MAKERS**

LIGHTWEIGHT MANUFACTURING

Makerspaces offer a flexible location with tools and equipment for rapid prototyping and building.

CITIZEN R&D

Makers collaborate with their communities to develop, ideate, and gain insights on their work.

IF YOU CAN'T OPEN IT, YOU DON'T OWN IT

The nature of ownership is changing with the advent of beta development that allows others to help tweak and improve products.

NETWORKED ARTISANS

Makers and creating collaborative, local and regional networks where they can come together to share and showcase ideas.

GRASSROOTS ECONOMICS

Online marketspaces are offering new places for the retail of products and services over large retailers.

PERSONAL DESIGN AND FABRICATION

With the help of desktop design and production software, access to being able to create is rapidly becoming democratized.

6 LEADING DRIVERS

Platforms for Social Ability
Beyond the social networks for pictures of cats and your aunt's new sweaters, there are hubs of collaboration and problem solving that can leverage the wisdom of crowds that are powerful and wise.

Eco-Motivation
This is not about tree hugging or saving the world. It is about a new mantra of technology obsolescence - reduce, reuse, remake. It is green and it is cutting edge.

Rise of the Professional Amateur
Passionate hobbyists have blurred the lines between who is an amateur and who is a professional. These people are active creators whose dedication and results blow many "experts" and big companies out of the water.

Access to Tools
Think Moore's Law for Manufacturing - Cost of tools decreases and capabilities increase exponentially reducing the barriers of entry for new makers to jump into the mix.

Open Source Everything
Making software free and open to customization provides a gateway for innovation and businesses to be built on top of the very thing the original company gave away - see Linux and Wordpress as recent examples. And when we mean free, think free speech, not free beer.

Quest for Authenticity
Being virtual is limiting and people long for the ability to do physical, hands-on creating. These experiences are in reality and that is where the action is.

* Data Sources: The Future of Making

The people that you used to call customers are now competitors. It's like in social media. The people called the audience, they're now the media creators and producers and editors.

SEQ: There are so many startups that are members of this movement. Where do you see opportunities?

Owyang: There's three major business opportunities. The first one is responding to this trend. People don't need to own things now. They just need access to them. Now with Uber, you don't need to own a town car and a chauffeur, right?

Push a button, a car comes. It's access over ownership. As a result, we're seeing companies shift their business model. In San Francisco, BMW now rents their 1 series electric cars from their dealership lots. That's the first business model. Instead of buying, corporations are going to rent products on demand.

The second one is called the Marketplace Model. We see marketplaces emerging for just about everything. This also means people are going to sell their used goods to each other with mobile devices. It's easier sometime than buying new.

The third model is called Provide a Platform. Provide a Platform, just like a software company has a platform with APIs, that let's people launch new products without worrying about the infrastructure.

SEQ: There's no way to be perfect, like a crystal ball, but what is the trajectory of this?

Owyang: People need to own fewer things. It means you can summon them quickly using mobile devices. It also means we are more efficient with resources, and things are used more frequently. It also means that you can't tell the difference in a corporate perspective between employees and customers. They're going to be involved in delivering your goods. The freelancer economy, which you're looking at, is directly tied to this because people are empowered.

The Opportunities in the Sharing Economy

For communities that have established trust, sharing comes naturally. During her famous TED Talk, collaboration expert Rachel Botsman stated the obvious, but incredibly important, point that "the currency in this new sharing economy is trust." However, even as many companies focus on the sharing of physical objects, they may still overlook the sharing opportunities of physical and digital spaces.

Take a look at the New Opportunities for Sharing infographic in Figure 3.10. The greatest opportunities currently exist in transportation (e.g., car sharing), infrequent-use items (e.g., sporting goods), and physical spaces (e.g., coworking and short-term rental).

> The currency in this new sharing economy is trust.
> —*Rachel Botsman*

Opportunities for Entrepreneurs

1. Research services in the sharing economy to accelerate your startup while keeping costs low.
2. If you're looking to create a business that builds on the sharing economy, explore the opportunities on the New Opportunities for Sharing infographic (Figure 3.10).
3. Understand the dimensions of sharing and the market forces and drivers that power the sharing economy.

FORCE #6: THE NEW CREATIVE ECONOMY

Though you may not consider yourself creative, you may be one of the millions representing the creative economy. The creative economy spans a wide and cross-functional section of life. Some industries include performing and visual arts, cultural heritage, film, television, and radio, music, publishing, video games, new media, architecture, design, fashion, and advertising. The creative economy isn't new, but how governments view its economic potential has changed much over the past 15 years. It also helps that technological advancements have increased the number of potential jobs within this multi-sector economy.

The creative economy and its associated industries now represent a significant proportion of many countries' GDPs.[6] Both national and local economies globally recognize the importance of the creative economy.[7]

As the future of work changes from an industrial economy to a fluid, creative, and knowledge-based one, more economies are preparing workers for a digital future based on creativity and a collaborative brain trust.

Force #6

The New Creative Economy

ARTISANAL

MEDIA

PERFORMING ARTS

GUILDS

INDUSTRIAL
VS
CREATIVE

Ontario, Canada, provides a fantastic example of the creative economy at work. During the first decade of this millennium, the creative economy emerged as a growing source of GDP for Ontario. According to Ontario's Ministry of Tourism, Culture, and Sport, the creative industries in Ontario generate $12.2 billion in GDP for Ontario's economy annually and are number one in Canada by GDP. The creative industry GDP is now larger than Ontario's energy industry and approaches seventy percent of the auto manufacturing sector. It already surpasses the GDPs of agriculture, forestry, and mining combined.[8]

The creative economy contributes to Ontario's economic, social, and cultural well-being, and it's on track to grow at a significant pace over the next decade. The Canadian creative industries are forecast to grow at the same steady rate as the rest of the world.

Opportunities for Entrepreneurs

1. Find your niche in the creative economy.
2. Utilize any funding allocation to the growth of creative industries.
3. Focus on the customizable product or service, instead of mass production.

Someone Ja-Naé works closely with in the creative economy sector of Massachusetts is its Director of Creative Industries, Helena Fruscio. This is what she had to say about the sector and its opportunities for entrepreneurs:

SEQ: Where do you see the creative economy going in relation to entrepreneurship?

Fruscio: It's funny to me that when you talk to creative people in the creative industries and you say, "Well, you're an entrepreneur," because it's not the first way they would describe themselves. Once you start to dig into what they are actually doing and what entrepreneurship really means as an action not as the description, that's exactly what all of these creative industries, businesses, organizations and individuals are. They are problem solving. They're growing businesses.

SEQ: When you think about how the creative economy has influenced Massachusetts, where do you see that influence going over the next five to ten years?

Fruscio: I work in an economic development office, and one of the things we've been thinking about is how to get the creative industries involved in all industries. I always talk about manufacturing: imagine wearing a shoe that wasn't designed.

The creative industries are in a lot of ways making those pieces that are then manufactured, but they're really giving that spin to whatever is being made that gives it competitive advantage. I think the more we can involve the creative industries across industries in our economy, the more successful we'll be.

SEQ: If there are creative entrepreneurs out there that don't already have an ecosystem built, what can they do to start that?

Fruscio: You have to start thinking about how do you make those ties when you might not see everyone everyday, especially if they're an hour and a half, two hours away. How do you really do that? We try to really leverage technology and I know it is sounds silly, but just using Facebook taking pictures at events and tagging people and then having people be friends with people on social media, it helps.

We always use the joke that you just couldn't walk into a bar on a random Tuesday and think it would be full. You have to be very intentional about that. We created something called "The List" where you could send out, "I'm having a barbecue" or "We're going to this restaurant" so that people could come and see what was happening. It's a different way of approaching it and I think you have to be a little more intentional, but I guarantee you that there are like-minded people somewhere in your community. If you have to get in your car and drive a little bit, that just might be what you have to do.

Collaborative Economy
Honeycomb Version 1.0

The Collaborative Economy enables people to efficiently get what they need from each other. Similarly, in nature, honeycombs are resilient structures that efficiently enable many individuals to access, share, and grow resources among a common group.

In this visual representation, this economy is organized into discrete families, sub-classes, and example companies. To access the full directory of 9000+ companies visit the Mesh Index, at meshing.it/companies managed by Mesh Labs.

By Jeremiah Owyang
@Jowyang

With input from:

Neal Gorenflo (@gorenflo).
Lisa Gansky (@instigating).
Shervin Pishevar (@sherpa).
Mike Walsh (@mwalsh).
Brian Solis (@briansolis).
Alexandra Samuel (@awsamuel).
and Vision Critical (@visioncritical).

Design by Vladimir Mirkovic www.transartdesign.com
May 2014. Creative Commons license: Attribution-NonCommercial.

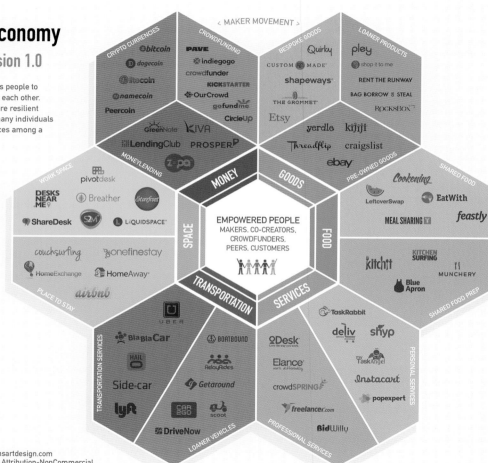

< MAKER MOVEMENT >

CRYPTO CURRENCIES
bitcoin · dogecoin · litecoin · namecoin · Peercoin

CROWDFUNDING
PAVE · indiegogo · crowdfunder · KICKSTARTER · OurCrowd · gofundme · CircleUp

BESPOKE GOODS
Quirky · CUSTOM MADE · shapeways · THE GROMMET

LOANER PRODUCTS
pley · shop it to me · RENT THE RUNWAY · BAG BORROW & STEAL · ROCKSBOX

MONEYLENDING
GreenNote · KIVA · LendingClub · PROSPER · zopa

PRE-OWNED GOODS
Etsy · yerdle · kijiji · Threadflip · craigslist · ebay

SHARED FOOD
Cookening · LeftoverSwap · EatWith · MEAL SHARING · feastly

WORK SPACE
pivotdesk · DESKS NEAR ME · Breather · Storefront · ShareDesk · S2M · LiQUIDSPACE

SHARED FOOD PREP
kitchit · KITCHEN SURFING · Blue Apron · MUNCHERY

PLACE TO STAY
couchsurfing · onefinestay · HomeExchange · HomeAway · airbnb

MONEY

GOODS

SPACE

FOOD

EMPOWERED PEOPLE
MAKERS. CO-CREATORS. CROWDFUNDERS. PEERS. CUSTOMERS

TRANSPORTATION

SERVICES

TRANSPORTATION SERVICES
UBER · BlaBlaCar · HAIL · Side-car · lyft

LOANER VEHICLES
BOATBOUND · RelayRides · Getaround · CAR2GO · scoot · DriveNow

PROFESSIONAL SERVICES
oDesk · Elance · crowdSPRING · freelancer.com · BidWilly

PERSONAL SERVICES
TaskRabbit · deliv · shyp · my TaskAngel · Instacart · popexpert

KEY MARKET FORCES

SOCIETAL DRIVERS
- DESIRE TO CONNECT
- SUSTAINABLE MINDSET
- POPULATION INCREASE

ECONOMIC DRIVERS
- FINANCIAL CLIMATE
- UNTAPPED IDLE RESOURCES
- STARTUPS HEAVILY FUNDED

TECHNOLOGY ENABLERS
- INTERNET OF EVERYTHING
- MOBILE TECHNOLOGIES
- SOCIAL NETWORKS

CROWD™ COMPANIES

www.crowdcompanies.com

THE NEW OPPORTUNITIES FOR SHARING

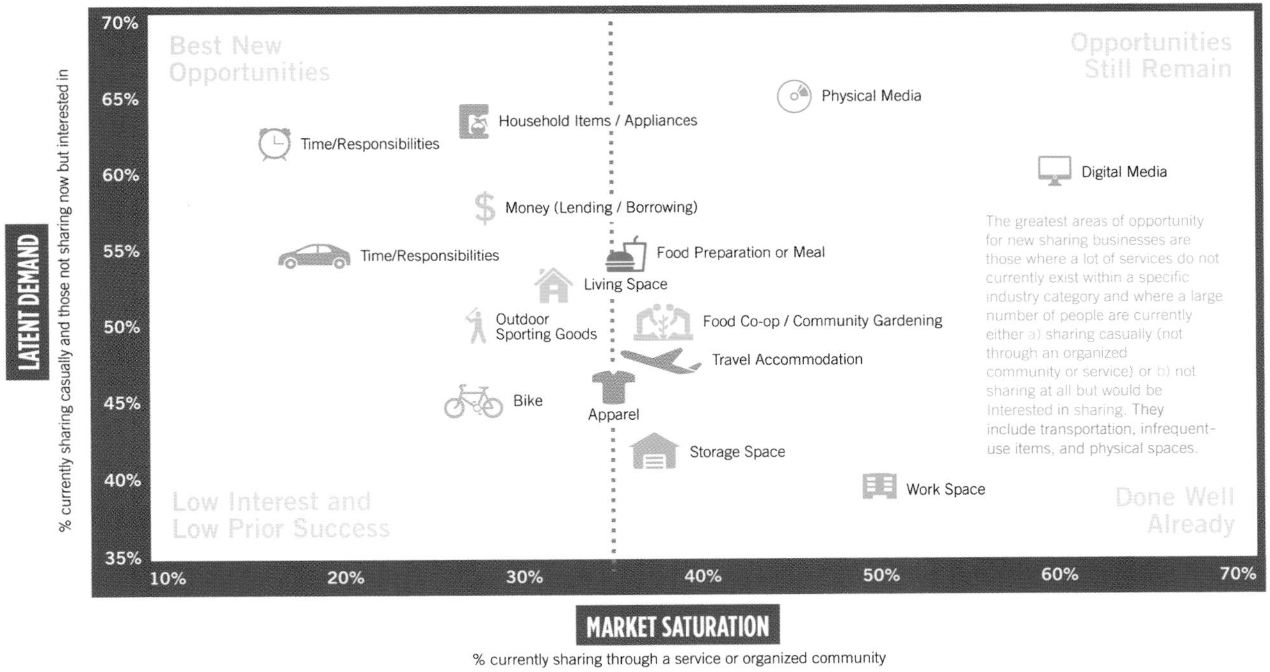

LATENT DEMAND
% currently sharing casually and those not sharing now but interested in

Best New Opportunities

Opportunities Still Remain

- Physical Media
- Household Items / Appliances
- Time/Responsibilities
- Digital Media
- Money (Lending / Borrowing)
- Time/Responsibilities
- Food Preparation or Meal
- Living Space
- Outdoor Sporting Goods
- Food Co-op / Community Gardening
- Travel Accommodation
- Bike
- Apparel
- Storage Space
- Work Space

Low Interest and Low Prior Success

Done Well Already

The greatest areas of opportunity for new sharing businesses are those where a lot of services do not currently exist within a specific industry category and where a large number of people are currently either a) sharing casually (not through an organized community or service) or b) not sharing at all but would be interested in sharing. They include transportation, infrequent-use items, and physical spaces.

MARKET SATURATION
% currently sharing through a service or organized community

PARTICIPANTS' IDEAS FOR NEW SHARING MODELS

Knowledge (multilateral sharing)

"Community college 2.0: provide some sort of structure that lets people let other people know what they know and what they want to learn. If you can get enough people together, everyone is both student and teacher."

–Male study participant, 29, Salt Lake City, UT

Skills and Services (micro-funding)

"… a sort of bounty hunting service for open source projects, where people in need would invest into certain features/fixes with (smaller amounts of) money. Bounties would therefore accumulate and developers would profit by providing solutions."

–Male study participant, 24, Ljubljana, Slovenia

Material Items (multilateral bartering)

"… person A needs something that person B has, and person B needs something that person C has, and person C needs something that person A has—except that this service would be free, completely based on bartering."

–Female study participant, 56, Ithaca, NY

Composite Model

"I'll walk your dog while you're away; you water my plants; I'll give you baby toys I don't need anymore; you loan me your lawn mower. I think this kind of interaction is part of community ties and support networks that used to develop naturally and spontaneously and need some encouragement now."

–Female study participant, 56, Ithaca, NY

Figure 3.10

CREATIVE INDUSTRIES

HERITAGE

Cultural Sites
Archeological sites, museums, libraries, exhibitions, etc.

Traditional Culture Expressions
Arts and crafts, festivals, and celebrations

ARTS

Visual Arts
Painting, sculpture, photography, and antiques

Performing Arts
Live music, theatre, dance, opera, circus, puppetry, etc.

MEDIA

Publishing and Printed Media
Books, press, and other publications

Audiovisuals
Film, television, radio, other broadcasting

FUNCTIONAL CREATIONS

Design
Interior, graphic, fashion, jewellery, and toys

Creative Services
Architectural, advertising, creative R&D, cultural, and recreational

New Media
Software, video games, digitized creative content

APPLYING THE SIX FORCES
TO YOUR STARTUP

Awareness of these powerful forces of change is not enough. Established companies are notoriously bad at finding new ways to take advantage, partly because they are so busy managing the day-to-day business. The key is to make these forces come to life for you and your colleagues, and then use them in your startup disrupt.

Use the questions below to jumpstart your discussions. Look for ways to unlock new business value from the Six Forces—and avoid being late to the game.

- **Regarding the Six Forces:** What ways can we leverage these emerging forces that we're not capturing now? Can we deliver this as part of our capabilities?

- **Brainstorm:** What possible new uses for the Six Forces might we be missing that could benefit our customers? Try to come up with at least 10 additional wacky and far-fetched possibilities that your organization might pursue. Have fun.

- **Ask:** What do we need to change (stop doing, sell off, close down, abandon, etc.) in light of these forces?

- **Consider:** What do we need to start embracing (consider, purchase, investigate and research, etc.) to capitalize upon each of the Six Forces?

  - How do we need to position ourselves differently in our markets?

  - What new capabilities or services might we start offering customers (internal and external) to ride these tidal waves of change?

  - Which of the six have the most promise/potential for our organization and why?

  - What startups should we consider purchasing to jumpstart our embrace of the Six Forces?

  - How can we innovate to take full advantage of these driving forces of technological and social change?

The Six Forces of Change will create new winners and take out laggards faster than ever before. The discoveries and innovations you develop in response to these trends could change your game, but only if you seize the day.

The Startup Equation

$$((En(Id))+So)^X+((Cu(Te+Ce))Br)^X+(((Fn(Sa+Ma))Sc)In)^X$$

Foundation   Experience   Growth

• THE ELEMENTS

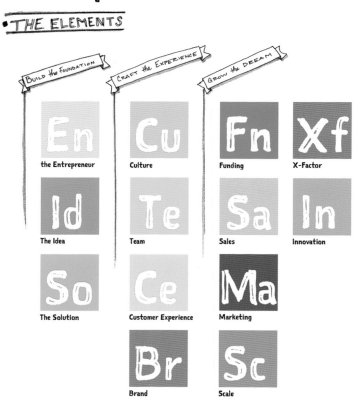

BUILD the FOUNDATION

En — the Entrepreneur

Id — The Idea

So — The Solution

CRAFT the EXPERIENCE

Cu — Culture

Te — Team

Ce — Customer Experience

Br — Brand

GROW the DREAM

Fn — Funding

Sa — Sales

Ma — Marketing

Sc — Scale

Xf — X-Factor

In — Innovation

Your time is limited, so don't waste it living someone else's life.

—*Steve Jobs*

The Startup Equation

THE EQUATION STRUCTURE

Many books try to get you to subscribe to how they think you should start and grow your business. We know that one size doesn't fit all. Just like you, your business has its own personality. However, we believe that it's possible to craft an equation that fits your business perfectly, no matter what type of business you plan to start. Whether it's a SaaS platform or a food truck, there are specific modules or "elements" that every business will have in them. But those elements might look slightly different depending on the type of business. The Startup Equation allows you to plug in the elements that are the most relevant to *who* you are as an entrepreneur, the *type* of business you're looking to start, and how you're looking to *grow* it, if at all.

It's also important to know that even as you grow and change, so will your business. What may work for your business in the first two years may not be relevant in year three. By adopting the equation that matches your business, you'll have an adaptable structure that supports you every step of the way.

To make the equation easier to understand, we've broken it into three parts:

1. Building the Foundation
2. Crafting the Experience
3. Growing the Dream

Each section has elements that are vital to every business. Let's get started by breaking down the sections.

BUILDING THE FOUNDATION

Before you can build a business, *you need to lay your foundation*. You will note that in this group of equation functions are three primary functions—**Entrepreneur (En)**, **Idea (Id)** and **Solution (So)**. These next few chapters will dive deep into this part of the equation and their respective elements with the aim of showing you what elements might work for you so you can build the foundation of a custom Startup Equation that works for you.

Foundational Equation Functions

We start with this section of the equation because in order to launch your startup, you first you need to understand who you are, what skills you bring to the table and why you want to start a business (**Entrepreneur (En)**). Then you multiply that times the concept or vision you have for the business (**Idea (Id)**). Together they are combined and applied to how you will actually build your startup (**Solution (So)**).

They each have two sub-groupings that contain the elements for that function of the equation. The first equation function, **Entrepreneur (En)**, helps you understand what Personality Type fits you and the Approach you take to it. After getting a feel for yourself as an entrepreneur, you will explore the **Idea (Id)** for your startup through the various Core elements and refine them with Generation elements. This will lead to defining the **Solution (So)** that includes the Business Model elements and the Approach elements to build a minimum viable product and refine how your startup will position itself to maximize its chances for success.

CRAFTING THE EQUATION

Now that you have begun to build the foundation, *you must craft an amazing experience*. You will note that in this group of equation functions are four primary functions—**Customer Experience (Ce)**, **Team (Te)**, **Culture (Cu)** and **Brand (Br)**. We will explore how it is not only important

to build a product and put it out there but also to craft an experience within the company and the way customers perceive and experience the company too.

Crafting the Equation Functions

A business is only as good as the experience. This rule applies to both employees and customers. We look to this section of the equation to find the answers that will help you dig in and craft the experience that you want people to have when they choose your business. First, look inward to find who should be part of the startup's Core and Extended **Team (Te)** and then explore ways to build company **Culture (Cu)** through various Core and Additive elements. Then we explore what makes a great **Customer Experience (Ce)** through first covering the various Programs and Testing elements. All of this is multiplied or rather amplified by building a stellar **Brand (Br)** experience leveraging the Identity and Senses that communicate the experience that customer and employee should expect from the company.

GROWING THE DREAM

Once you have worked on building the foundation and crafting the experience of your startup, what comes next? The next and what many would consider *the toughest phase is growing your dream* beyond you and your initial startup phase. For some this could entail automating things better so your lifestyle business can run smoothly while you take some much needed vacation. For others it will be about taking those early adopters of your great product and the team that helped get you there to that billion dollar exit you have always dreamed about.

You will note that in this group of equation functions are six primary functions—**Funding (Fn)**, **Marketing (Ma)**, **Sales (Sa)**, **Scaling (Sc)**, **Innovation (In)** and **X-Factors (Xf)**. These next few chapters explore how startups grow, scale and innovate as well explore using the intangible "X-Factors" that power the entire equation and truly are those elements that can't be created but must exist in some way for a startup to achieve success.

Growing Equation Functions

A successful business only has value if you can go away from it for a little while and it runs without you. We look to this section of the equation to find the answers that will help you grow and scale your startup to the height of success and maintain that momentum. First, we explore the Core and Model **Funding (Fn)** elements that are available to startups based on their goals and size. We then look to more operational functions with **Marketing (Ma)** Programs and Channels to attract customers as well as the **Sales (Sa)** Channels and Campaigns to close and retain them. Those elements are then multiplied by Core and Measurement **Scaling (Sc)** elements which all are in turn multiplied by the Method and Engine elements to drive continuous **Innovation (In)** in your startup. Finally, the entire equation with all of the functions is amplified by our "eXponent" or **X-Factors (Xf)** through the Core and Additive elements which underlie and drive the startup to success.

THE PERIODIC TABLE FOR STARTUPS

When we reviewed all the elements needed for the Startup Equation, it was clear that we needed a structure that would let you see all the elements at once and in relation to each other. What better way to show that relationship than in a periodic table. You'll note that the elements grouped by colors correspond to the major functions in the equation. Each element will be described in the upcoming chapters.

THIS IS A LIVING DIAGRAM

It is important to note that *this periodic table of startup elements is a living, breathing thing*. Does it account for every single thing you'll encounter as an entrepreneur? Have we discovered every element? Nope. Consider this a guide. This is the bare bones of what you'll encounter as you start and grow your business. As the world changes organically, so will these elements. But for today, they represent a great start.

This is Startup Alchemy

When you have the right startup elements, you can create magic. The beauty of this equation's fluidity is that it allows you to play with the elements until you can build an equation that fits you. It will fit who you are and what you want your business to become. Will it change? Of course, because you'll change and because businesses grow and evolve in ways that are hard to imagine. But this equation will help you keep that alchemy balanced as things pivot so that no matter what, you never lose the magic. The chapters ahead will dive in further to each element group and it is important to remember that this book should become an old friend, one that you continually turn to for advice on this wild adventure. **Let's get started.**

$$((En(Id))+So)^X+((Cu(Te+Ce))Br)^X+(((Fn(Sa+Ma))Sc)In)^X$$

| Foundation | Experience | Growth |

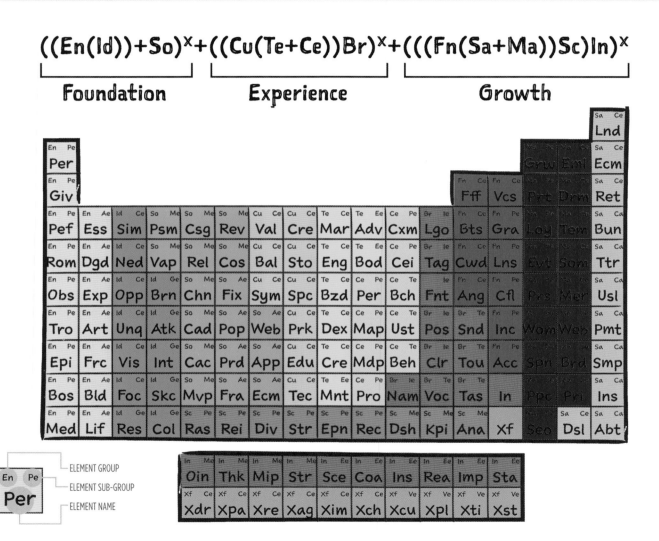

ELEMENT GROUP
ELEMENT SUB-GROUP
ELEMENT NAME

FOUNDATION ELEMENTS

En ENTREPRENEUR (EN)

ENTREPRENEUR PERSONALITY TYPE ELEMENTS
The Perfectionist (Per)
The Giver (Giv)
The Performer (Pef)
The Romantic (Rom)
The Observer (Obs)
The Trooper (Tro)
The Epicure (Epi)
The Boss (Bos)
The Mediator (Med)

ENTREPRENEUR APPROACH ELEMENTS
The Essentialist (Ess)
The Do Gooder (Dgd)
The Expert (Exp)
The Artist (Art)
The Franchisee (Frc)
The Builder (Bld)
The Lifestyle (Lif)

Id IDEA (ID)

IDEA CORE ELEMENTS
Simplicity (Sim)
Need (Ned)
Opportunity (Opp)
Uniqueness (Unq)
Vision (Vis)
Focus (Foc)

IDEA GENERATION ELEMENTS
Research (Res)
Brainstorming (Brn)
Attack Solution (Atk)
Intersections (Int)
Sketching (Skc)
Collaboration (Col)

So SOLUTION (SO)

SOLUTION MODEL ELEMENTS
Key Problem, Solution and
    Metrics (Psm)
Value Proposition (Vap)
Customer Segmentation (Csg)
Customer Relationships (Rel)
Solution Channels (Chn)
Competitive Advantage (Cad)
Customer Acquisition Cost (Cac)
Minimum Viable Product (Mvp)
Revenue/Profit Model (Rev)

SOLUTION APPROACH ELEMENTS
Fixed Space (Fix)
Pop-Up/Mobile Space (Pop)
Physical Product (Prd)
Franchises (Fra)
Online Presence (Web)
Mobile App (App)
E-Commerce (Ecm)

EXPERIENCE ELEMENTS

Cu CULTURE (CU)

CORE CULTURE ELEMENTS
Values (Val)
Balance (Bal)
Symbols (Sym)
Creativity (Cre)
Stories (Sto)

ADDITIVE CULTURE ELEMENTS
Spaces (Spc)
Perks (Prk)
Education (Edu)
Technology (Tec)

Te TEAM (TE)

CORE TEAM ELEMENTS
The Marketer (Mar)
The Technical
    Engineer/Hacker (Eng)
The Biz Developer or Hustler (Bzd)
The Domain Expert (Dex)
The Creative or Designer (Cre)

EXTENDED TEAM ELEMENTS
The Mentors (Mnt)
The Advisory Board (Adv)
The Board of Directors (Bod)

Ce CUSTOMER EXPERIENCE (CE)

CUSTOMER EXPERIENCE PROGRAM ELEMENTS
Customer Experience Personas (Per)
Customer Journey Map (Map)
Customer Experience Design and
    Prototyping (Pro)
Customer Experience
    Management (Cem)
Customer Experience Insights (Cei)

CUSTOMER EXPERIENCE TESTING ELEMENTS
Benchmarking (Bch)
Usability Testing (Ust)
Behavioral Targeting (Beh)

Br BRANDING (BR)

BRAND IDENTITY ELEMENTS
Name (Nam)
Logo (Lgo)
Tagline (Tag)
Font (Fnt)
Positioning (Pos)
Colors (Clr)

BRAND SENSES TESTING ELEMENTS
Voice (Voc)
Sounds (Snd)
Touch (Tou)
Taste/Smell (Tas)

GROWTH ELEMENTS

Fn FUNDING (FN)

FUNDING CLUSTER ELEMENTS
Friends/Family (Fff)
Crowdfunding (Cwd)
Angels (Ang)
Venture Capital (Vcs)

FUNDING PROGRAM ELEMENTS
Grants (Gra)
Loans/Microloans (Lns)
Cash Flow (Cfl)
Accelerators (Acc)
Incubators (Inc)

Sa SALES MIX (SA)

SALES CHANNEL ELEMENTS
Direct Sales (Dsl)
Landing Pages (Lnd)
E-Commerce (Ecm)
Retail (Ret)

SALES CAMPAIGN ELEMENTS
Bundling (Bun)
Test Trial (Ttr)
Upselling (Usl)
Promotions (Pmt)
Samples (Smp)
Inside Sales (Ins)
A/B Testing (Abt)

Ma MARKETING MIX (MA)

MARKETING PROGRAM ELEMENTS
Growth Hacking (Grw)
Partners (Ptr)
Loyalty Programs (Loy)
Events (Evt)
PR (Prs)
Word of Mouth (Wom)
Sponsorship (Spn)
PPC (Ppc)

MARKETING CHANNEL ELEMENTS
SEO (Seo)
Email (Eml)
Direct Mail (Drm)
Telemarketing (Tem)
Social Media (Som)
Merchandising (Mer)
Website (Web)
TV/Radio Broadcast (Brd)
Print (Pri)

Sc SCALE (SC)

SCALE PROGRAM ELEMENTS
Risk Assessment (Ras)
Reinvestment (Rei)
Diversification (Div)
Streamline (Str)
Expansion (Epn)
Recruit (Rec)

SCALE MEASURE ELEMENTS
Dashboards (Dsh)
KPIs (Kpi)
Analytics (Ana)

Xf X-FACTORS (XF)

X-FACTOR CONSTANT ELEMENTS
Drive (Xdr)
Passion (Xpa)
Resilience (Xre)
Agility (Xag)
Imagination (Xim)
Charisma (Xch)

X-FACTOR VARIABLE ELEMENTS
Curiosity (Xcu)
Place (Xpl)
Timing (Xti)
State of Mind (Xst)

In CONTINUOUS INNOVATION (IN)

INNOVATION METHOD ELEMENTS
Open Innovation (Oin)
Design Thinking (Thk)
Managed Innovation Process (Mip)
Strategic Foresight (Str)

INNOVATION ENGINE ELEMENTS
Scenario Planning (Sce)
Corporate Assets (Coa)
Customer Insight (Ins)
Organizational Readiness (Rea)
Disciplined Implementation (Imp)
Strategic Alignment (Sta)

• THE ELEMENTS

BUILD the FOUNDATION   CRAFT the EXPERIENCE   GROW the DREAM

En	Cu	Fn
the Entrepreneur	Culture	Funding
Id	Te	Sa
The Idea	Team	Sales
So	Ce	Ma
The Solution	Customer Experience	Marketing
Br	Sc	
Brand	Scale	
	Xf	
	X-Factor	
	In	
	Innovation	

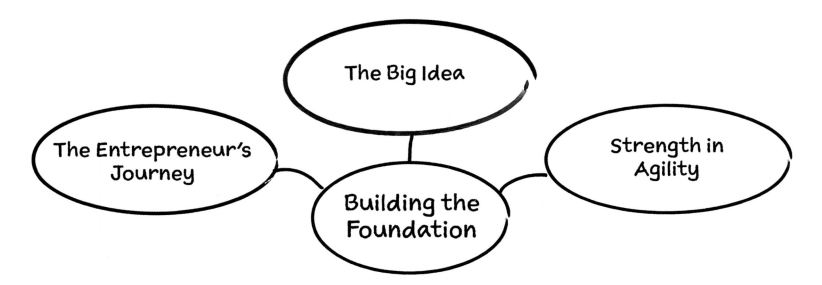

Before you can build a business, *you need to lay your foundation*. You will note that in this group of equation functions are three primary functions—**Entrepreneur (En)**, **Idea (Id)** and **Solution (So)**. These next few chapters will dive deep into this part of the equation and its elements with the desire to show you what elements might work for you so can build the foundation of a custom Startup Equation that's right for you.

How This Part of the Equation Works

The foundational elements in this section of the equation are the bedrock of any business. The way this part of the equation works is ((Entrepreneur × The Idea) + The Solution).

We start with this section of the equation because in order to launch your startup, you first need to understand who you are, what skills you bring to the table and why you want to start a business (**Entrepreneur (En)**). Then you multiply that by the concept or vision you have for the business (**Idea (Id)**). Together they are combined and applied to how you will actually build your startup (**Solution (So)**).

Entrepreneur (En) Elements

In Chapter 5, you'll dive into what entrepreneurial persona fits you and the approach you need to take based on your current commitments. The two entrepreneur element sub-groups are *Personality* and *Approach*. Though your approach may change as new chapters unfold, your personality type will most likely stay the same.

Idea (Id) Elements

You cannot have a business without a business idea. In Chapter 6 you will explore how to develop and refine your idea with two element sub-groups: *Core* and *Generation*. Within each business idea you should be able to identify a core reason for why you want to start this business.

Solution (So) Elements

After refining your idea, you should have a business you want to start. In Chapter 7 you will explore two element groups. These are *Models*, which covers how the business will function and build its first product, as well as the *Approaches* that can be used to position the startup in the right places but also to pivot it as its viability is tested with customers.

So let's get started . . .

BUILDING THE
FOUNDATION

En
the Entrepreneur

Building a Great Entrepreneur

Finding the Leader Within

Entrepreneurs, Know Thyself

No MBA Required

Plan to Succeed, Not Win

PERSONALITY ELEMENTS

the Perfectionist

the Giver

the Performer

the Romantic

the Observer

the Trooper

the Epicure

the Boss

BOSS

the Mediator

APPROACH ELEMENTS

the Essentialist

the Do-Gooder

the Expert

the Artist

the Franchisee

the Builder

the Lifestylist

Original Sketch by Kate Rutter

Opportunity is missed by most people because it is dressed in overalls and looks like work.

—Thomas Edison, Inventor

The Entrepreneur's Journey

Though being an entrepreneur is fun, it's also a ton of work. It means a lot of hours and many late nights for many years. It's a path that requires dedication and should be chosen only after a lot of thought. Building something great takes time and energy.

You might even be a little scared. That's OK because fear can be a good motivator, but don't let it deter you from your goal. If you're going to do something special, then you'll need passion to keep your motor running. This same passion will also help attract customers.

Dave McClure of 500 Startups, knows all about starting a company or two and making them successful. But he also has no delusions about what it takes to be an entrepreneur.[1]

Now please don't get me wrong . . . I'm not here to dump all over your enthusiasm for building a startup. Nor am I saying there is anything

bad about wanting to make money, or wanting to be your own boss, or to valiantly attempt to defy the odds and create the next Google or whatever.

But I DO hope some of you young-ass whippersnappers get your heads out of your collective asses and get a little more practical about what you're likely to encounter should you decide to do your own startup. And a little more real about what you may face at the end of a rough hand of poker.

To wit: the first time I tried to do my own business, it took 7 years of hard work, below market pay, near bankruptcy (2 or 3 times), broken friendships, damaged relationships, credit card debt up to my ears, ridiculous stress, several missed opportunities for big paydays as a grunt at Microsoft, Intel, Netscape, or Yahoo, all in exchange for a piddly-ass half-million acquisition that barely got me enough cash to

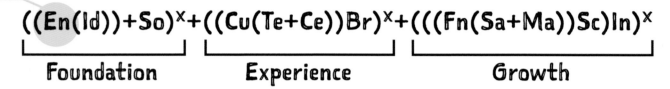

$$((En(Id))+So)^X+((Cu(Te+Ce))Br)^X+(((Fn(Sa+Ma))Sc)In)^X$$

Foundation   **Experience**   **Growth**

We start the equation with the entrepreneur. She is the one with idea and where this all begins. No two entrepreneurs are alike, and we group our elements into personality types and their approach.

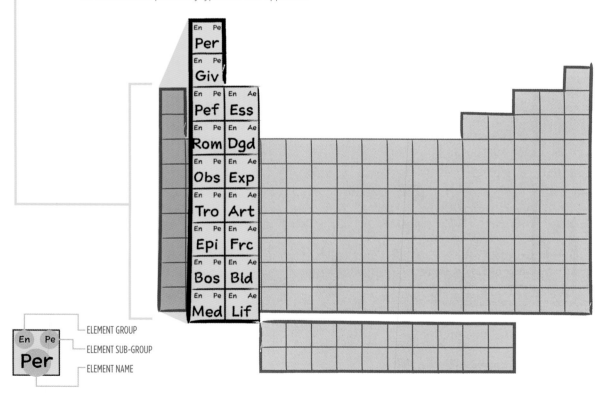

En	Pe
Per	

En	Pe
Giv	

En	Pe	En	Ae
Pef		**Ess**	
Rom		**Dgd**	
Obs		**Exp**	
Tro		**Art**	
Epi		**Frc**	
Bos		**Bld**	
Med		**Lif**	

En	Pe
Per	

— ELEMENT GROUP
— ELEMENT SUB-GROUP
— ELEMENT NAME

ENTREPRENEUR (EN) PERSONALITY TYPE ELEMENTS

No two entrepreneurs are alike. However, they share some common and dominant traits in their personality. Most entrepreneurs will self-identify with one or more of these elements.

The Perfectionist (Per)
Works towards perfection; Avoids error; Conscientious; Hates schedules & deadlines. Great Critical Powers; Leads by example; Prefers Doing Over Feeling

The Giver (Giv)
Wants to gain approval; Feels pride in being needed; Grows by discovering what they want. Craves freedom; Works for the respect of people.

The Performer (Pef)
Loves the spotlight; The instant expert; Captain of winning team. Heart is in the work.

The Romantic (Rom)
Wants creativity; Craves freedom; Called to emotionally intense lines of work. Attracted to what is missing; Competitive.

The Observer (Obs)
Likes boundaries; Watches life as an observer; Values unemotional decision making. Minimalist; Values emotional control; Extremely productive when in a decision-making role.

The Trooper (Tro)
Strong analytic powers; Comes alive under adversity; Clearly focused CTAs; Ambivalent about visible success. Thrives on adrenaline; Asks hard questions; Skeptic.

The Epicure (Epi)
Wants to keep energy up; Experiences joy, options and ideas; diffuses fear. The world is full of possibilities; Spontaneity; Positive future.

The Boss (Bos)
Concerned with injustices; Lusts for life; May see compromise as weakness. Defending the innocent; Setting boundaries; Enforcing the rules.

The Mediator (Med)
Maintains neutrality; Cannot say 'no'; Relaxes friction. Structured and Keeping the peace.

ENTREPRENEUR (EN) APPROACH ELEMENTS

Every entrepreneur has a different set of things they want to accomplish with their business. Most entrepreneurs will self-identify with one of these approaches to starting their business.

The Essentialist (Ess)
These entrepreneurs are starting a company out of necessity. They could have lost their job or need more income coming into their household.

The Do Gooder (Dgd)
These entrepreneurs want to change the world in their small way. Their #1 focus is figuring out how to make the largest social impact. Money is secondary to them.

The Expert (Exp)
These entrepreneurs are experts within a field and have decided to take that expertise to start something of their own. They are the lawyers, architects, and programmers of the world.

The Artist (Art)
These entrepreneurs identify themselves as artists and artisans first. Their #1 focus is to create. The business side of things may not come easy to this type, but it is a necessity in order to continue to do their art.

The Franchisee (Frc)
These entrepreneurs usually come to a business that has already worked out its systems, much like a franchise. They prefer knowing that a system works and that it is profitable. They are low-risk entrepreneurs with money as a priority.

The Builder (Bld)
These entrepreneurs are the opportunity seekers. Once they see an opportunity, they seize it to help it grow. These people are born entrepreneurs. It is in their blood. They are most likely to be serial entrepreneurs.

The Lifestyler (Lif)
These entrepreneurs love the idea of living the entrepreneurial lifestyle and are living to grow their businesses large enough to maintain that lifestyle.

put a down payment on a small condo in SF. Sure it was a good lesson in learning how to [NOT] run a business, but it was a HARD goddamn lesson. And one I'm pretty sure I never want to repeat. The fact that I still wanted to try and go back out and do another startup AFTER that first effort is prime evidence that I'm either crazy, stupid, or both.

Now, Dave has an interesting and colorful perspective, and his second startup was joining PayPal, so that was a good choice in long run for who he is and what type of entrepreneur he wanted to be. And that is at the heart of the self-discovery you need to do.

This is where the **Entrepreneur (En)** function of the Startup Equation comes into view.

BUILDING A GREAT ENTREPRENEUR

So what makes a great entrepreneur? Strong leadership skills? Good education? Previous experience? Motivation to see things through? It depends.

In a recent study of 549 founders,[2] Duke University sought out what demographic and psychographic factors great entrepreneurs share. A few things stood out:

- **They were supersmart in high school.** We're not talking college or grad school, but high school. Most people around the world get a high school education and many can't go to college because of some factor (usually money), but it doesn't mean they aren't some of the smartest people.
- **They have some industry experience under their belt.** While there are many young entrepreneurs with very little job experience, most have six to fifteen years of experience. This means they've gotten out there and know different job roles, have tried a few different companies, and see the startup opportunity as a next step.
- **Many are married and have a least one child.** The media impresses upon us that today's entrepreneurs are in their twenties and have the lifestyle to go all in, but that isn't really the case. They usually have experience and want to build something that's great. They often look to their family to keep them motivated.

- **They're motivated to build a company and create wealth.** While the thought of "doing a startup" can sound sexy, great entrepreneurs want to build something great. Of course, they would like to receive financial reward for their efforts, but most of the time they aren't in it for the money.

When it comes to building great entrepreneurs, Jason Henreichs is familiar with the process on both sides of the journey. Having been first an entrepreneur and then an investor with a great venture capital group for years, he is now helping others learn the ropes of working in a startup as a Managing Partner at the Startup Institute. We spent some time with him and asked him about entrepreneurship and becoming a great entrepreneur. Here are some of his insights:

SEQ: Can you recall an experience early in your life that really made you decide you wanted to be an entrepreneur?

Henreichs: Actually, it comes down to the lazy factor. When I was younger, I had grown up in a small town of less than 10,000 in southern Wisconsin. We had empty lots around us, which my dad didn't like, so my job was to mow the five empty lots so that the weeds wouldn't get in his yard. I hated the fact that that basically meant every day, after morning swim practice, I had to mow an entire bumpy lot. I asked my dad one day, I said, "So, am I getting paid to mow these lots or am I getting paid to keep the weeds down?" He said, "You're getting paid to keep the weeds down." That fall, I kept the seeds from my jack-o-lantern, and the next year, I planted two lots in pumpkins, knowing that the vines would provide the cover and I wouldn't have to mow. I would just have to water once a week and that was pretty easy.

It was going all well and good until I realized I was having a bumper crop of pumpkins. My dad said, "So, what are you going to do with all of the pumpkins?" I was like, "Oh. Man! What am I going to do with all of these pumpkins? This is kind of a problem!" He took me down to the local grocery store, the IGA. They paid me three cents a pound for all of the pumpkins I brought in. Granted, my dad charged me for renting the truck to move all of the pumpkins, but I ended up making over $500. As far as I was concerned, that was not only $500, that was hours of my summers not spent pushing a mower. That was my first entrepreneurial adventure and I've been hooked every since.

BUILDING A GREAT ENTREPRENEUR Figure 5.3

This information is based off the research project Global Engineering and Entrepreneurship done by Duke University. 549 company founders were surveyed from the United States.

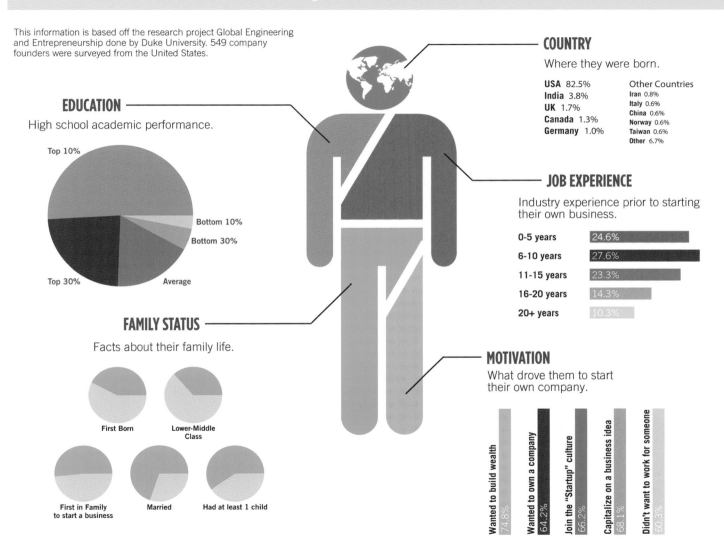

EDUCATION
High school academic performance.

Top 10%
Bottom 10%
Bottom 30%
Top 30%
Average

COUNTRY
Where they were born.

USA 82.5%	Other Countries
India 3.8%	Iran 0.8%
UK 1.7%	Italy 0.6%
Canada 1.3%	China 0.6%
Germany 1.0%	Norway 0.6%
	Taiwan 0.6%
	Other 6.7%

JOB EXPERIENCE
Industry experience prior to starting their own business.

0-5 years	24.6%
6-10 years	27.6%
11-15 years	23.3%
16-20 years	14.3%
20+ years	10.3%

FAMILY STATUS
Facts about their family life.

First Born
Lower-Middle Class
First in Family to start a business
Married
Had at least 1 child

MOTIVATION
What drove them to start their own company.

Wanted to build wealth 74.8%
Wanted to own a company 64.2%
Join the "Startup" culture 66.2%
Capitalize on a business idea 68.1%
Didn't want to work for someone 60.3%

SEQ: Do you think entrepreneurship is something that is built into you or do you think it can be taught?

Henreichs: I think it absolutely can be taught and it should be taught. We need to break out of the mindset that everyone needs to be a founder. Everyone needs to learn in a new economy, to be entrepreneurial. I think we need to do a better job of teaching that being an entrepreneur does not mean you sit in a garage and you come up with apps. There are plenty of those and that is all well and good, but the bulk of entrepreneurship is actually working at a startup that you did not found.

SEQ: What elements do you think make a great startup?

Henreichs: To me, a great startup boils down to the entrepreneur. Because great entrepreneurs, before they even build great products, they build great teams. They are going to work together. If they're going to have any chance of success, they're building a team of co-founders.

FINDING THE LEADER WITHIN

As entrepreneurs and investors, there's something that's abundantly clear to us and most people in the startup world: Entrepreneurs are natural leaders even if they don't realize it. When we hear the term leadership, it's easy to think of presidents and big company CEOs, but leaders are those who shine and show the way forward. Great entrepreneurs exude what Jeremiah Owyang calls the *Four Traits of Effective Leaders*.[3]

Having a Clear, Shared Vision

Great entrepreneurs have singular, unshakable vision. They clearly communicate their vision as a driving passion that inspires the entire company to share their vision and to make it their own. They're not the ones steering the ship, nor are they the ones rigging the sails. They are the ones standing at the bow, pointing the way, and urging the team onward. *Where there is no vision, people go off in different directions.*

Making the Commitment to See It Through

Great entrepreneurs are committed to completing the mission and achieving the vision. Nothing can distract them, detain them, or deter them from reaching their goal. Their focus is on the goal, and they're determined to reach it. They must be able to say "No" to otherwise good ideas because they might divert them from the task at hand. *Where there is no commitment, the ship often wastes resources as commitments shift constantly.*

Enabling to Get the Task Done

Great entrepreneurs can't get the job done alone. They must enable others by equipping and empowering them to get it done. Instead of becoming a monarch, the most savvy may become a servant or ask their staff to think of them as their internal clients. Those who can't look like micromanagers, which destroys spirit, innovation, and scale. *Where there is no empowerment, people don't feel motivated to be proactive.*

Putting Accountability in Place

Everyone must be accountable to someone. The leader is accountable to customers to deliver the goods, to stakeholders to deliver the profits, and to employees to deliver direction, purpose, empowerment, inspiration, and reward.

Each member of the crew is accountable to the others to be as strong a link in the chain as the rest. Failure and success must be consistently rewarded in appropriate proportion to ensure that the ship stays on course. *Where there is no accountability, people do whatever is right in their own eyes.*

Someone who knows about finding the leader within is Scott Duffy. Scott Duffy is Founder & CEO of The Launch Project™, a company dedicated to helping millions of people around the world live their dreams through entrepreneurship. Scott began his career working for best-selling author and speaker Tony Robbins and founded Smart Charter, an online booking tool for private aviation, which was acquired by Richard Branson's Virgin Group. We had the opportunity to sit down with him and talk about entrepreneurship and launching a great company.

SEQ: When you build your businesses, do you have a philosophy on building great teams?

Duffy: I've learned there's really three types of people in every company. There's what I call *the visionary*. This is the person that's got the big ideas, and they're great at getting out there and they're great at selling the idea. I've learned that there's a second kind of person in a company that I just call *a manager*. The manager is someone that's great at creating processes. They're great at operating. Then there's a third type of person in every company, and I call this person *the sharpshooter*. This person is someone that's really awesome. They're really great at one specific thing.

The number one mistake I see entrepreneurs make when they build a team is they miscast themselves. They put themselves in the wrong role. They may be visionary, but they're trying to run the day-to-day operations of the business and that's just not going to work. They get themselves off on the wrong foot.

SEQ: What would you say an entrepreneur needs to consider in order to make sure that they're ready for any challenge that comes to them?

Duffy: The question is this: Who are the people that you have around you that aren't pulling you up but are trying to pull you down? Because it's so important as an entrepreneur that you're always around people that are going to help you grow, that not only buy into but help you to grow your vision and pull it forward. What I always say is, " A great place to start is just to clean the closet. Write down a list of all those people that you spend your time with and check and eliminate the people that aren't doing anything positive to help you move forward."

SEQ: What do you think are elements of great startups as they begin their launch?

Duffy: I think that one of the most important things with any startup business is to try and keep things simple. In any business there's a lot of moving parts and there are a ton of things that are going on every single day. It's important to keep things simple and really to take whatever your big idea is and get the simplest version out to market as soon as you possibly can, and get feedback on that particular product or service before you go out and you go too big.

What I say to you as an entrepreneur is this: I would say stay narrow and stay focused on one thing. Get that one thing out. Become excellent, become exceptional at collecting feedback and then build off of that.

ENTREPRENEUR, KNOW THYSELF

After talking to entrepreneurs around the world leading startups of all kinds, we began asking ourselves, "What traits might entrepreneurs share, but not have equally?" Do different types of entrepreneur exist? We found that the answer is definitely "yes." We started with an existing personality framework as our baseline to develop the entrepreneur personality types. The personality types on the following pages are inspired by Helen Palmer's Core Personality Types in her book *The Enneagram in Love and Work: Understanding Your Intimate and Business Relationships*.[4]

There are nine core personality types and one of them is *your* primary type. Take a look at Figure 5.4. Which one resonates with you the most? Don't worry if you feel as though traits from another type sometimes fit you. It's common to have a secondary type that you occasionally relate to. As you explore your personality type, think about how this impacts your leadership style and how critical it is to understand when forming your team and crafting a culture.

Your Approach to Business

At this point, you might have a strong sense of your entrepreneur type, but that's only one side of the entrepreneurial coin. The other side is how you approach your startup venture. Not all entrepreneurs are driven to create a huge, venture-backed startup with billion dollar potential. Some become entrepreneurs out of necessity because they were laid off (**The Essentialist (Ess)**) or just want to turn their expertise into a practice of their very own. Others are into the freedom and lifestyle the life can provide (**The Lifestyler (Lif)**).

These are just a few of the entrepreneur approaches. You can see the full list and description of each type in Figure 5.5. It's also important to know that the type of entrepreneur you are today can dramatically change in 5–10 years and that's OK. Just as people evolve, so do businesses.

Discover Your Unique Startup Path

There are many types of, and approaches to being, an entrepreneur. To help you discover your entrepreneur type, let's walk through a simple formula that you can use to figure out the first part of your Startup Equation.

NAME	PERSONALITY	QUALITY	FOCUS	BEST ENTREPRENEURIAL TYPE	OTHER
The Perfectionist	Works towards perfection; Avoids error; Conscientious; Likes schedules & deadlines	Practical; Great Critical Powers; Leads by example; Prefers Doing Over Feeling	Highest Standards; Crucial Points	The Expert; The Franchisee; The Builder	Be careful not to act out of anger; Is uncomfortable with ambiguity or multiple possibilities; Devoted to work for work's sake
The Giver	Wants to gain approval; Feels pride in being needed; Grows by discovering what they want	Humble; Craves freedom; Takes own identify from authorities who can support their efforts; Works for the respect of people	Relies on developing key people; Attracted to promising talent and new directions	The Essentialist; The Do Gooder; The Lifestylist	Be careful not to manipulate others to reach goals; Has boundary issues; Highly responsive to approval; Identifies client needs
The Performer	Loves the spotlight; The instant expert; Captain of winning team	Hope; Self-survival; Veracity; Polyphasic thinking	Heart is in work; Tunnel vision on task; Avoids Risk	The Expert; The Franchisee; The Builder	Be careful of self-deception; Machine-like achiever; expands and franchises out
The Romantic	Wants creativity; Craves freedom; Called to emotionally intense lines of work	Balanced; Competitive	Attracted to what is missing; Uniqueness	The Do Gooder; The Artist; The Lifestylist	Be careful not to alienate yourself from opportunities if they have already been done; Wants distinctive work; Flourishes in cooperative environments
The Observer	Likes boundaries; Watches life as an observer; Values unemotional decision making	Non-attached; Minimalist; Values emotional control; Extremely productive when in a decision-making role	Believes in knowledge over power; Compartmentalizes; Focused on Ideas	The Expert; The Franchisee; The Builder	Be careful of your need for predictability; Leads from behind closed doors; Does well as an adviser; Usually positioned as a thinker or analyst

NAME	PERSONALITY	QUALITY	FOCUS	BEST ENTREPRENEURIAL TYPE	OTHER
The Trooper	Strong analytic powers; Comes alive under adversity; Clear focused CTAs; Ambivalent about visible success	Faith; Courage; Thrives on adrenaline; Asks hard questions; Skeptic	High goals; Interpersonal relationships; Clarity	The Do Gooder; The Expert; The Builder	Be careful of inaction. It can lead to anxiety; Rallies with the underdog; Extremely uncomfortable when they have to compete on a daily basis
The Epicure	Wants to keep energy up; Experiences joy, options and ideas; Diffuses fear	Planning; Work; Seeks stimulation; Equalizes authority	The world is full of possibilities; Spontaneity; Positive future	The Essentialist; The Do Gooder; The Artist; The Lifestylist	Be careful of open-ended agreements; They may take on a life of their own; Can become insistent about practical ideas; Delightful to work with
The Boss	Concerned with injustices; Lusts for life; May see compromise as weakness	Truth; Control; No hidden agenda; Assumes leadership	Defending the innocent; Setting boundaries; Enforcing the rules	The Do Gooder; The Expert; The Builder	Be careful to see other points of view. If not, may miss something extremely valuable; Direct and assertive; What you see is what you get; Dedicated competitors
The Mediator	Maintains neutrality; Cannot say "no"; Reduces friction	Keeping the peace; Structured	Procedures; Simplicity	The Essentialist; The Franchisee; The Lifestylist	Be careful not to be too cautious about taking risk; Energized by productive routine; Looks for ways to simplify as many things as possible

NAME	DESCRIPTION
The Essentialist	These entrepreneurs are starting a company out of necessity. They could have lost their job or need more income coming into their household. Either way, this entrepreneurial type will rise in the next decade.
The Do Gooder	These entrepreneurs want to change the world in their small way. Their #1 focus is figuring out how to make the largest social impact. Money is secondary to them.
The Expert	These entrepreneurs are experts within a field and have decided to take that expertise and start something of their own. These entrepreneurs are the lawyers, architects, and programmers of the world.
The Artist	These entrepreneurs identify themselves as artists and artisans first. Their #1 focus is to create. The business side of things may not come easy to this type, but it is a necessity in order to continue to do their art. These individuals are artists taking control of their economic well-being.
The Franchisee	These entrepreneurs usually come to a business that has already worked out its systems, much like a franchise. They are not interested in having their name tied to a unique entity, but prefer knowing that a system works and that it is profitable. This entrepreneurial type is a low-risk entrepreneur with money as a priority.
The Builder	These entrepreneurs are the opportunity seekers. Once they see an opportunity, they seize it to help it grow. These people are born entrepreneurs. It is in their blood. This type is most likely to start a company, build it to a specific point, and then move on to another venture. This entrepreneurial type is the most likely to be a serial entrepreneur.
The Lifestylist (The Micro)	These entrepreneurs love the idea of living the entrepreneurial lifestyle and are living to grow their businesses large enough to maintain that lifestyle. These entrepreneurs may piece together their business through capitalizing on their own skill set or personal assets. This entrepreneurial type will also have more than one project running, which may include a consultative practice.

Personality+Approach=Startup Path

As an entrepreneur you will discover your own path, so we won't waste your time detailing every possible combination (there are 63ish). However, let's review a few to get the gears turning:

The Epicure (Epi) (Personality Type) + The Do Gooder (Dgd) (Approach)
This entrepreneur type is all about social good with a desire to make a positive change for those around them. They might build a nonprofit, start a yoga studio, or even create a cause-focused website.

The Observer (Obs) (Personality Type) + The Builder (Bid) (Approach)
This entrepreneur type could take the path of a software startup founder. Focused on a vision and their primary goal is to build a minimum viable product (MVP). They usually don't stay for the full duration of the company and let professional management take over so they can move onto the next venture.

The Romantic (Rom) (Personality Type) + The Lifestyler (Lif) (Approach)
This entrepreneur type could take the path of letting their creative juices flow by freelancing and choosing the projects they take. They're not out to build a massive business, but one that gives them the freedom to work on great projects, pay the bills, save for retirement, and most importantly, gives them flexibility to spend time with family.

EXERCISE: Discover Your Personal Entrepreneurship Approach and Type

Know Thyself: Before you become an entrepreneur, you must first examine who you are as a person and how you handle situations. Ask yourself the following questions:

1. How do you view the world?
2. What is your relationship to authority/authoritative figures?
3. How would you describe your personality?
4. Name 5 of your strengths.
5. Name 5 of your weaknesses.
6. What is your leadership style?
7. How do you handle stress?

Based on your answers, go through each of the personality elements and see if you can find the one that best suits you. Please note that you will have personality types that are secondary, but there can be only one primary type that you identify with.

Approach: Before starting a business, you must know how you want this business to relate to your life. Some people are looking to be lifestyle entrepreneurs. Some are builders who can start businesses but then have to hand them over in order for that business to continue to thrive. In order to find the right equation for success, do this exercise to find the right approach for you at this point in your life:

What is important to you? List your interests. List your passions. Your answers may inform what type of approach best fits you. What you are committed to will help you figure out your approach. Here are some questions to guide you.

1. **How frequently do you finish projects?** We all start things, but do you normally finish them? Answering this will help you to understand if you are truly looking to see a business through, from start to finish.
2. **Why are you starting a business?** Is starting projects in your blood or are you doing this out of necessity?
3. **Are you more about building things or maintaining things?** Some people are better at starting things. Some have trouble starting them but can put them up and see them to the end. Knowing where you fit in that mix will help you decide which approach is right for you.
4. **Describe your comfort level with risk?** Some approaches have much more risk involved. Go into detail about what you are comfortable with and where you draw the line.

(continues)

5. **How much time are you willing to commit?** Becoming an entrepreneur and building your business will take up time and the time demanded will determine which approach feels right to you.

6. **Where will you be 3 years from now?** Where you see yourself in 3 years will be eye opening when thinking about what you are starting and what you would like it to organically become.

Answering these questions truthfully will allow you to really look deep into yourself and figure out what is *really* important in your life before you begin building your business.

Passion Projects vs Life's Calling

When I was five years old, my mother always told me that happiness was the key to life. When I went to school, they asked me what I wanted to be when I grew up. I wrote down 'happy'. They told me I didn't understand the assignment, and I told them they didn't understand life.

—John Lennon

Remember how we said it takes a ton of work to succeed as an entrepreneur? Some of you aren't ready for it, at least right now. And that's OK. Although you may have a passion for the work and business you want to pursue, you need to ask yourself a tough question: *Do I really want to spend the next five-plus years living and breathing this business?*

Many times, we do not start businesses around what we love because what we love may change over time. Instead, many people start businesses with the goal of solving a problem. The spur may also be something that keeps them up at night or gets them excited, but the underlying goal of building a business isn't dependent on someone's passion.

So even though it's possible for passion projects to become businesses, consider digging deeper inside and asking yourself, "Why?"

- Why am I working on this?
- Why is it important to do this every day?
- Why must I share this piece of what I believe with the world?

Though you may not know all the answers right away, give yourself time to contemplate and digest the questions. Your answers may surprise even you.

Someone who knows about following their passion is Jennifer Lum. She worked at big companies like Verisign and helped Apple build out their iAd platform. She has been a tech investor and worked at various mobile startups. She followed her passion to create her own mobile company and recently founded Adelphic Mobile. We had a chance to meet with her at their HQ in Boston and talk about her experiences, following her passion and having focus.

SEQ: Can you think of any experiences that made you want to walk the entrepreneurial path?

Lum: I've always been interested in business and technology, I never was certain that I one day would want to be the founder of a company and build something from scratch. In fact I didn't come to that realization until I was transitioning out of Apple. That's when I realized that my passion absolutely lies in the early-stage environment. I've learned that I love being able to work with the team to get something off the ground. I love being able to put my hands in many, if not all, areas of the business. Just the challenge involved in creating something that hopefully will be quite meaningful.

SEQ: From your experience as a mentor, what do you think gives some of these startups a greater chance of success?

Lum: At the earliest stages of a company, I firmly believe that the real differentiator is the team, it's the people and having passion. The fact that not only are they extraordinary entrepreneurs and/or technologists but that they have an unfair advantage within the space that they are looking to attack to make something happen.

SEQ: When things are really limited, where should entrepreneurs focus?

Lum: I think depending on where the team is or where the entrepreneurs are in growing their business, ideally they have a plan that they're working toward, whether it be milestones for fundraising, product development, closing a deal, or handing product off to a customer. I think entrepreneurs should focus in the areas where they could create the most value for the business to go to the next level. To hit that next milestone or to close off that round of funding or to sign that next customer.

EXERCISE: Uncovering Your Passions

Are you unsure what you are passionate about or what type of business would keep your interest? Answer the following questions:

- What subjects did you love in school and why?
- Name three things people seek your help with.
- Name five things you could do for hours.
- What odd jobs have you done that people have paid you for?
- What are you doing when you are at your happiest?

Look at your answers and see what themes you come up with. The key is to identify what skills and activities you are naturally drawn to. Also, if there are activities or things people already come to you for, then they really may be your first customers.

NO MBA REQUIRED

In 1985, according to the Kauffman Foundation, about 250 college courses taught entrepreneurship. In 2008, 5,000 self-described entrepreneur courses were available at two- and four-year institutions in the U.S. Now nearly 400,000 students take college classes on entrepreneurship each year. With college costs on the rise, particularly within the United States, there's a growing debate about the need for an MBA when starting a business.

Let's look to the data for answers. In September 2011, *The Wall Street Journal* noted that "applications for two-year, full-time MBA programs that start this fall dropped an average of 9.9% from a year earlier. The decline marks the third year in a row that applications have fallen." So, if budding entrepreneurs are turning away from the traditional form of education, then how can they learn the necessary skills to run a business? If you're seriously considering the non-MBA route, here are three essential steps you'll want to follow.[5]

1. **Seek advice:** No matter your path, our experience strongly supports talking to as many entrepreneurs as possible, regardless of their business focus. When people decide to meet with you, be thoughtful and respectful of their time by preparing questions in advance.

2. **Learn skills elsewhere:** Though you need a certain knowledge base and skill set to start and to grow a business, you don't have to learn that knowledge in school. Based on your interviews, make a list of the skills that you need to learn. Then, see if your current network includes experts in each of these areas and ask if they're willing to teach you or have you as an intern.

3. **Test your knowledge and skills:** No matter how you decide to learn, plan to test your newfound abilities so you're ready for your startup. Depending on the skill, you can also offer to do related work for free in order to gain real-world experience.

PLAN TO SUCCEED, NOT TO WIN

When you start your business, it's easy to focus on winning a sector or beating the competition. While these goals make for good motivators, they're short term. If you want long-term success, we encourage you to learn these key insights as quickly as possible.

Failure is Part of the Journey to Success

We know—you don't want to fail. However, mistakes will happen, and you need to learn to fail fast. Learn from your mistakes and identify ways to improve how your business pursues innovation.

How to Create your Own MBA

① Set Clear Goals

→ Set clear learning goals with deadlines

→ Work backwards to create monthly benchmarks

② Focus!

Focus on areas where you need the most help!

③ Include Core Classes

- Accounting
- Finance/Economics
- Ethics
- Systems Thinking
- Strategy
- Marketing
- Leadership

④ Beat Your Competition Learn Other Skills

#1

▲ Other Languages
▲ Design Thinking
▲ Persuasion

⑤ Create Your Team

- Primary Advisor
- Mentors
- Educators

GO TEAM!

→ Establish Goals with them

⑥ Map Out Your Curriculum

⑦ Ways to Learn

★ Online
- MOOCs
- YouTube
- edx
- Udemy
- Coursera

★ Audit a Class
★ Interview Experts

★ Become an apprentice
— Be an apprentice at a different compnay every month
— Focus on your weakest areas

⑧ Build Valued Relationships

→ Learn from others
→ Join clubs & organizations
→ Go to field-specific events to recruit help
→ Give back

WELCOME

⑨ Remember...

★ You customize your plan to you
★ Be realistic
★ Have your team create projects and deliverables for you

Ja-Naé Duane
@TheSunQueen
2013

We're not alone in making this recommendation. Jim Kim, the President of the World Bank Group, also supports the approach of failing fast, as he outlined in transcribed notes from his presentation in December 2012 at LinkedIn headquarters.[6]

In the last decade, many international leaders have put great emphasis on measuring results and learning from success and failure. At the Bank, the challenge now is to develop tools that accelerate our ability to learn from both positive and negative experiences in development. I'm convinced that revolutionary advances in communications and information processing, when linked to an enlightened approach to failure, can help transform our pursuit of ability to achieve development results, even in the poorest countries.

To help China, South Africa, and all of our member countries, the World Bank Group will be setting up what we're calling *delivery knowledge hubs*, which will begin by collecting and distributing case studies of both success and failure in tackling the most important development challenges from throughout the world.

Learning from failure is hard, complicated work. But all leaders could be well served if they admit what they don't know and learn from their own and others' experiences. We at the World Bank Group stand ready to work with leaders in both the public and the private sector to learn from success and failure. To take a page out of Google's playbook, if we "fail fast and learn fast," we will have a much better chance to end extreme poverty and build shared prosperity in every corner of the world.

You Need to Get Tough

According to Steve Blank and Bob Dorf, the authors of *The Startup Owner's Manual*, 90 percent of new products fail, and entrepreneurs who have failed have a 20 percent success rate with their next venture. Few people are born with resilience, so take heart that it's something you can learn through your own experiences.

Entrepreneur Jia Jiang knows rejection well. In 2012, he decided to improve his resilience by getting rejected as often as possible. He ran a 100 Days of Rejection Therapy campaign. The concept was simple. Each day he set himself one task or request that he expected to come with a rejection. One request included cutting in line to improve his odds of getting a meeting with President Obama.[7]

But why did he put himself out there knowing he'd get rejected? Jiang argues that "by exposing ourselves to rejection, we can desensitize ourselves to it and help conquer the fear. We can make bold decisions without letting the fear cripple us. Courage is essential in entrepreneurship and a corporate career, both of which I've done."

You can do something similar by looking for opportunities to ask the tough questions that will lead to hard answers. By making yourself and your company open to tough feedback, you'll have an easier time dealing with and learning from failure.

GETTING READY . . .

Becoming an Entrepreneur starts with knowing yourself and what you really want out of building a business. No two people are the same. Most people assume that when you start a business you are supposed to have it all "figured out." Luckily, you have this book and some time to figure out things, which gives you the chance to explore. To prepare you for building your unique Startup Equation, make sure you complete the exercises in this chapter. They are to be used to discover a little more about yourself and the type of business you would like to build.

- Discover Your Personal Entrepreneurship Approach and Type
- Uncovering Your Passions

The Idea

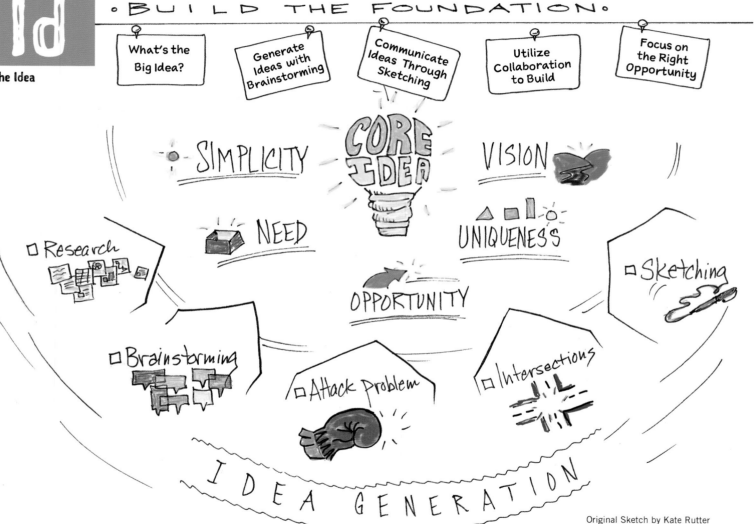

○ B U I L D   T H E   F O U N D A T I O N ○

What's the Big Idea?

Generate Ideas with Brainstorming

Communicate Ideas Through Sketching

Utilize Collaboration to Build

Focus on the Right Opportunity

SIMPLICITY

CORE IDEA

VISION

NEED

UNIQUENESS

OPPORTUNITY

□ Research

□ Sketching

□ Brainstorming

□ Attack Problem

□ Intersections

I D E A   G E N E R A T I O N

Original Sketch by Kate Rutter

CHAPTER 6

If at first the idea is not absurd, then there is no hope for it.

—Albert Einstein

The Big Idea

Simple, clean design was an obsession of Steve Jobs. His interest in design began with the style of architecture where he grew up and his love of the houses developed by Joseph Eichler. In an interview with his biographer, Walter Isaacson, Jobs shared his thoughts about Eichler's designs.

> "His houses were smart and cheap and good. They brought clean design and simple taste to lower-income people." His appreciation for Eichler-style homes, Jobs said, instilled his passion for making sharply designed products for the mass market. "I love it when you can bring really great design and simple capability to something that doesn't cost much," he said as he pointed out the clean elegance of the Eichlers. "It was the original vision for Apple. That's what we tried to do with the first Mac. That's what we did with the iPod."

There are times when we're driven by a concept, much like Jobs was by simple design. Sometimes there's the lightbulb moment when you experience a stroke of genius and an outward burst of "Aha!" Then there are times when an idea doesn't pop.

You may know that you want to start a business, but you're not sure what type of business or even if your idea is a unique one. This chapter will guide you through ways to formulate and test your ideas. No matter what your idea may be, in order for it to have longevity it needs the following elements:

- **Simplicity (Sim):** Any idea needs to be so simple that a child could explain it to someone.
- **Need (Ned):** Your idea has to serve a need for its customers, otherwise, what is the point?
- **Opportunity (Opp):** In order for the idea to make headway in the marketplace, there has to be an opportunity for this type of idea.
- **Uniqueness (Unq):** What does your idea have that no other idea out there has? What makes it unique?

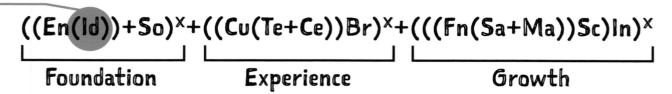

$$((En(Id))+So)^X+((Cu(Te+Ce))Br)^X+(((Fn(Sa+Ma))Sc)In)^X$$

Foundation   Experience   Growth

What is a great business without a great idea? This part of the equation takes the Idea as a multiplier with the Entrepreneur. There are core elements that are the essence of the great idea and ways to generate the one great idea that will start your new business.

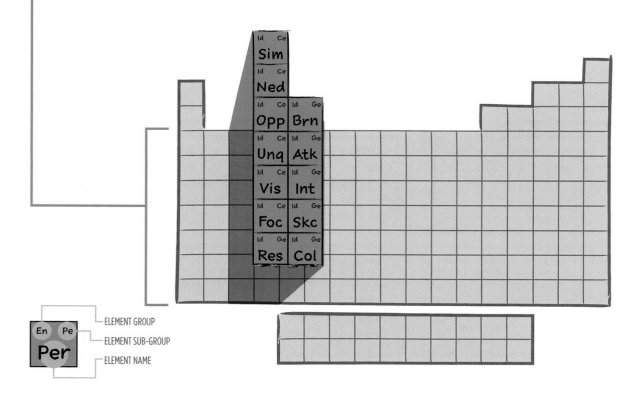

ELEMENT GROUP

ELEMENT SUB-GROUP

ELEMENT NAME

IDEA (ID) CORE ELEMENTS

These are the elements that are the essence of a great idea. Ideas should be simple and meet a certain need. This means that the unique opportunity has the focus and vision to be successful.

SIMPLICITY (Sim)
In the vein of "Keep It Simple Stupid," simplicity rules the day. Isn't a great idea, at its core, a very simple concept? As you evaluate your business idea, use simplicity as a baseline to keep you honest.

NEED (Ned)
Great ideas are great ideas, but in many cases, the need isn't clear…yet. Sure, people will cite Steve Job's philosophy: "People don't know what they need until you show them." But few people can build a successful business that way. If you're con-vinced people need your idea then you need to make the case for why.

OPPORTUNITY (Opp)
From need we move directly to opportunity. At this point, you transition from an idea to a viable business. Seeing that a yet unaware market exists that needs your product is the opportunity to create your business.

UNIQUENESS (Unq)
Every entrepreneur, including us, will reach a point when they believe they've got a "great idea" first, just as we did. We guarantee that somewhere else on the planet someone else also has or has had a similar idea. However, what you do with that idea and how you connect the need, the opportunity and eventually the execution will make your version unique.

VISION (Vis)
Vision consists of one part foresight and one part showmanship. Your vision will communicate a grand plan to inspire those who wish to embark on this journey with you. Vision can keep everyone grounded but focused on the bigger goal of building a business.

FOCUS (Foc)
No great idea is without vision but it must have focus in order for people to take action and carry out your vision.

IDEA (ID) GENERATION ELEMENTS

Idea generation requires setting up a creative space where people can say anything, show excitement, experience failure, and take risks without judgment. The goal? Allow new ideas to come to life. Idea generation will be a part of your business from the beginning.

RESEARCH (Res)
The type of information you gather will depend on the type of product or service you plan to sell. You can use research, for example, to assess market potential, complete a competitive analysis, determine pricing and create product positioning.

BRAINSTORMING (Brn)
Brainstorming combines a relaxed, informal approach to problem solving with creative thinking. It motivates people to come up with thoughts and ideas that might, at first, seem a bit out there or even outright crazy.

ATTACK PROBLEM (Atk)
You're more likely to find a solution by focusing on the problem you want to solve. Start by attacking the solution in terms of your product/service features, the benefits to customers, the personality of your company, key messages you'll relay, and the core promises you'll make.

INTERSECTIONS (Int)
Great ideas often come from the intersections created when people with different backgrounds and different mindsets collide. You can encourage these intersections by bringing together different groups within the company.

SKETCHING (Skc)
We're naturally drawn to visuals and sketching allows you to capture ideas to communicate concepts quickly, overcoming linear learning and language barriers.

COLLABORATION (Col)
Collaboration is the secret to a thriving business. Bringing people together exponentially improves the chances for developing refined ideas and better results that everyone can get behind.

- **Vision (Vis):** An idea (and its owner) needs to have a vision of how the idea will change the world.
- **Focus (Foc):** If an idea does not have focus, then it will eventually cease to exist.

These core elements are vital to building your Startup Equation. But don't worry if you don't know how your idea can have all of these things or even if you have your idea at all. From **Brainstorming (Brn)** to **Researching (Res)**, this chapter will help solidify your idea into a substantial one that you can begin to build for the marketplace.

WHAT'S THE BIG IDEA?

Every great business starts with a great idea. From that idea springs a vision, and from that vision comes the opportunity to make your business a reality. We have ideas all the time, but it's how we validate them and,

Accidental Great ideas

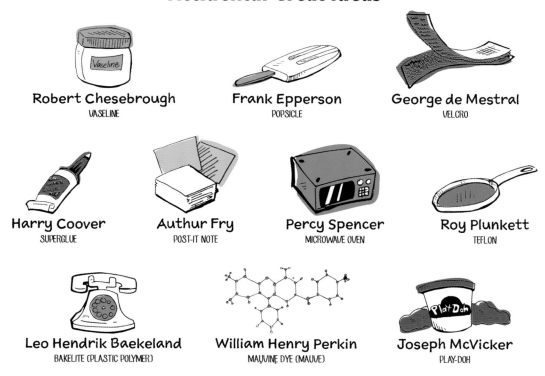

Robert Chesebrough
VASELINE

Frank Epperson
POPSICLE

George de Mestral
VELCRO

Harry Coover
SUPERGLUE

Authur Fry
POST-IT NOTE

Percy Spencer
MICROWAVE OVEN

Roy Plunkett
TEFLON

Leo Hendrik Baekeland
BAKELITE (PLASTIC POLYMER)

William Henry Perkin
MAUVINE DYE (MAUVE)

Joseph McVicker
PLAY-DOH

Figure 6.3 **Accidental Great Ideas**[1]

BE PASSIONATE ABOUT IT

Do you have enough passion for solving this problem to work on it for many years? While money may be a great motivator, it won't be there to get you through the dark times of being an entrepreneur.

KEEP IT SIMPLE

Start by solving a small problem for one customer that you can build on. Big ideas start from somewhere small and grow into radical and disruptive innovations.

ONE REVENUE STREAM

Focus on cultivating one revenue stream to begin with. Being able to identify and develop that will give you the power to build and create new ones. Without at least one, your startup idea will sink.

SHORTEN THE STEPS TO REVENUE

Keeping the number of steps to a minimum for earning revenue will decrease complexity. Visualizing how many stakeholders are involved will aid in helping you to see the bigger picture.

KNOW YOUR CUSTOMER

From the beginning it is absolutely necessary for you to know your customer and the problem that you are solving for them. This will help ensure you are truly answering a need that exists through a customer that will use the solution.

KNOW THE MARKET

Knowing the market helps you to become an expert in the space while developing a strategic vision and direction for your startup. Learn what is current and always remain up-to-date on your industry.

TAKE PART IN A LARGE ENOUGH MARKET

Just like Goldilocks, you must find a market that is just right with a robust enough size. You don't want to take part in a space that is too small nor do you want to enter one that is too large and overwhelming.

HAVE YOUR SECRET MIX

What is your secret mix? How are you providing a new and unique value to what already exists? Whatever makes you special will differentiate you from the competition and open new opportunities.

TEST AND RETEST

Testing and retesting will give you insight into your product or service's breakdowns and successes. Iteration will allow you to attack these problems in new ways through advancement and refinement.

SHARE YOUR IDEAS

Sharing your idea will help you gain feedback and new perspectives on your concept. Talk to others and be open to what they have to say. "…If it's original, you will have to ram it down their throats."

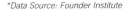

*Data Source: Founder Institute

ultimately, how we execute them that determines whether we say something like, "I had this great idea for a business, but I never acted on it, and six months later I saw someone do it," versus, "I had this great idea and started a business that changed my life." Fear of the unknown and an inability to execute will kill even the greatest business idea and vision.

Throughout her childhood, Ja-Naé and her father would constantly come up with inventions and entrepreneurial ideas that they were sure the world wanted or needed. It started one day in the parking lot of a grocery store. The wind picked up and started pushing shopping carts into cars. "There needs to be a way to protect cars from getting damaged," said Ja-Naé's dad. They began brainstorming and sketching out potential solutions.

After some brainstorming, they both agreed that a simple rubber bumper that jutted out beyond the carriage would make contact with a car first and protect it from dings. Ja-Naé wanted to build a prototype, but her dad didn't have time since he had his own budding startup. Needless to say, they both kicked themselves when they started seeing a very similar design on grocery carriages three years later. If only they had acted, right? How many times has this happened to you? You had a great idea, but you weren't sure if it would work or whether it was worth pursuing.

Many think that idea generation qualifies as an art form. In reality, idea generation is messy. It requires setting up a creative space where people can say anything, show excitement, experience failure, and take risks without judgment. The goal? Allow for new ideas to come to life. Your entire business is built on ideas.

In the vein of "Keep It Simple, Stupid," **Simplicity (Sim)** rules the day. Isn't a great idea, at its core, a very simple concept? As you evaluate your business idea, use simplicity as a baseline to keep yourself honest. If you're unsure whether your idea is simple enough, run it by someone outside your industry or even a kid. If they don't understand your idea, then retool it until they do.

If you have an idea, you may find that it has some serious holes. You don't have to scrap the whole idea, but **Research (Res)** will give you insights on how to rework it. Using these insights, it's time to bring your team together and turn to brainstorming to discover an alternative. To get

you started, we've pulled together some different strategies to help you generate ideas.

Identify the Problem You Want to Solve and Set the Objectives

Every business is built on the foundation of solving a problem and identifying a **Need (Ned)**. Sometimes we build businesses from problems we have faced ourselves. And sometimes we see **Opportunities (Opp)** within the market (or even an opportunity to create a market). If you are looking to start a business, then finding the problem you want to solve is critical. If you are unsure of where to start, ask yourself the following:

1. What frustrations are you personally experiencing as a customer or user in the industry you're interested in? You will find that some of the best ideas come from trying to solve problems that affect us personally.

2. What should companies be making or selling that they just are not doing yet? Is this something that customers would want today if they had the option to buy it?

3. What have you experienced as a consumer in this industry? How would you do business differently? What changes would you make?

Once you know what problem you are trying to solve for, you can use the following tools to generate ways to solve these problems for your potential customer. And to be honest, you may not even know which problem you would like to solve yet because there are so many. That's OK, too. Feel free to use the following to guide you along that path as well.

GENERATE IDEAS WITH BRAINSTORMING

A great way to generate ideas is through **Brainstorming (Brn)**. You can approach **Brainstorming (Brn)** two ways: as an *individual* or as a *group*. Group brainstorming offers a more effective environment for generating ideas, but several studies show that individual brainstorming produces more—and often better—ideas than group brainstorming. When you brainstorm on your own, you don't have to worry about other egos or opinions. You can be freer and more creative, too. However, you may not develop ideas as completely when you brainstorm on your own because you don't have the wider experience of others to draw on.

Individual brainstorming proves most effective when you need to solve a simple problem, generate a list of ideas, or focus on a broad issue. Group brainstorming can offer a more effective environment for solving complex problems. So even if you do not have a team or a group, put together a small group of individuals you trust in helping you come up with the right **Vision (Vis)** and **Focus (Foc)** for your idea.

To get your team's creative engine running at top speed, we've put together seven great ways to generate ideas in a group brainstorming session.

This type of creative brainstorming falls under the **Attack Problem (Atk)** element. The first time through sets up bringing your team together to discover a solution. It will take time, and it won't be easy, but if you focus on what you want to achieve in your brainstorming sessions, they'll be even more effective.

It reminds us of a story that David Kelley, the founder of renowned design firm IDEO, shared in an interview. He talked about wanting to design a coffee cup that cyclists could use while riding. You could describe what he wanted in a few ways: spill-proof coffee cup lids or bicycle cup holders. But a much better description sets a clear objective: Helping bike commuters drink coffee without spilling it or burning their tongues.

It's a cool, easy-to-understand example of an objective and clearly lays out what IDEO needs to achieve to measure success—helping bike commuters who drink coffee, want to avoid spills, and would prefer not burning their tongues. Diving to that level of detail *before* brainstorming about ways to design the cup holder significantly improves the chance that IDEO will succeed.

EXERCISE: Idea Generation with Brainstorming

To get you and possibly your team in on the flow of getting to that great idea, start with these idea generation steps using brainstorming:

1. **Try to generate solutions individually.** Before moving into group brainstorming sessions, insist that your team come to the table with their own solutions. As we discussed earlier, it's not uncommon for people participating in a group brainstorming session to get stuck on someone else's solution and overlook other great ideas that could be better.

2. **Build on the ideas of others, let the ideas flow, and don't judge.** You never know where a good idea will come from, and you need to provide a creative space that's comfortable for the group and encourages people to say what's on their minds without fear of judgment. It also means we encourage people to question and challenge the status quo so we can move to an even better place. Support the wild ideas because they can often be the foundation for creative leaps. When you speak during a brainstorming session, try to use *and* instead of *but*. You want to aim for as many new ideas as possible. In a good brainstorming session, your group could come up with a hundred ideas in sixty minutes.

3. **Stay focused and allow one conversation at a time.** Keep the discussion on target, otherwise you'll go beyond the scope of the problem you want to solve. Revisit the objectives set out when the session started. They can help you manage a group brainstorm where many conversations are the norm. However, remind your group that each member deserves the attention of the group and capture what everyone has to share.

4. **Be visual.** In brainstorms, we love using colored markers (Sharpies are the best!) to write on different colored Post-it notes that we stick on a wall. Nothing gets an idea across faster than drawing it. It doesn't matter if you're an artist! It's all about the idea behind your sketch. We'll discuss the elements of **Sketching (Skc)** and **Collaboration (Col)** in more detail next. *(continues)*

If you're not familiar with brainstorming, then it can sometimes be difficult to let go and allow yourself to explore. Be kind to yourself as you experiment, and allow yourself to do it in spurts. Remember, there are no wrong ideas. Just more complex ones. So look for the **Simplicity (Sim)** in every idea to help you get started.

EXERCISE: Fine-Tuning Your Idea

When coming up with a business idea, it is very easy to get bogged down in the minutiae. Here are a few exercises to fine-tune your idea:

1. **Identify Patterns:** Go through your brainstorming notes and begin to identify patterns. What continuously comes up? What stands out to you? Identify what you keep coming back to.

2. **Ask "What if . . . ":** If you are unclear about an aspect of your idea, start to ask questions. We prefer "What if?"

   a. What if we launched this as an app instead of a website?

   b. What if we focused on moms instead of dads?

   c. What if we tested a physical location with a pop-up store?

   By asking the questions, you allow yourself to explore possibilities that might not have come up otherwise.

3. **The One Thing:** Identify the one problem you are trying to solve for people. Write it down and describe it in 5 words or less.

   Coming up with your idea and distilling it down and simplifying it are completely different things. Allow yourself to dig in and then test your new version on someone who doesn't know your business.

EXERCISE: Unique Snowflake

Once you have an idea that has become more simplified, it is important to identify where this idea fits into the broader ecosystem and what makes it truly unique so that can you can build it and scale it. Answer the following questions:

1. Does your idea fit as an application to an existing product or service or does it act as a hub for other products?

2. Does your idea lower the barrier to entry within your product market (through cost, convenience, etc.)?

3. Does the market you're in already have competition or are you the only one in the field?

4. Do you fit into a market category or are you creating one?

5. How are you *changing* your market with this idea?

   Even if you are building something that is the first of its kind, knowing what the function of your idea is and what makes it unique will help you to build a business around it.

COMMUNICATE IDEAS THROUGH SKETCHING

Sketching (Skc) goes back to the time when we were kids, and many of us still leverage sketching to communicate a concept when we jump up to the whiteboard. As you'll see in Figure 6.5, sketching offers great opportunities to explore, discuss, and compare ideas while getting feedback.

One of our favorite books is *Back of the Napkin* by Dan Roam. In his book, he writes that if you can draw these shapes (see Figure 6.6) you can sketch and visualize your idea.

We're naturally drawn to visuals, but we're taught linear, verbal thinking in school. To begin capturing your ideas and concepts, follow what Dan calls "The 6x6 Rule." There are six ways we communicate visually and six ways to show it. So, in that spirit, we have a visual tool in Figure 6.7 to show them to you.

The Purpose of Sketching

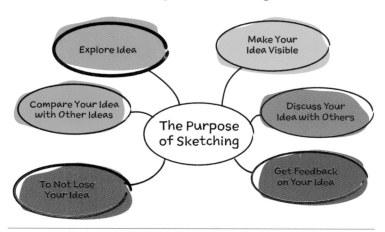

Figure 6.5 **The Purpose of Sketching**

How Can I Use Sketching?

As you move through the idea phase, your sketching can become a go-to tool for communicating ideas. It doesn't stop with your ideas. Sketching serves as an excellent tool for exploring business models, developing financial reports, refining product design, or reorganizing teams.

Someone who sketches a ton is C. Todd Lombardo, a Principal Innovation Catalyst at Constant Contact. His role there is to help drive innovation internally and externally in the organization and he does that through internal Innovation Jams, as well as through Innoloft, a Small Business Innovation accelerator program. If there is someone who lives and breathes ideas, it's this guy.

SEQ: Can you talk about the process you use at Constant Contact to generate new ideas?

Lombardo: We have a number of different ways to do that. One way is we democratize it, and we have something called an Innovation Jam. It's a lot like a startup weekend. You pitch an idea on Friday, you form a team, you build your idea, you work on it, you go out and validate it with your customers, and it is judged on Sunday.

Another way is we do them through Design Sprint. Let's say someone won one of the categories of an Innovation Jam. We could do something called the Design Sprint, and Design Sprint's a way to really dig deep and just unpack that idea and see if there's any business value to it.

We spend a lot of effort on that research phase of going out and face-to-face interviewing with people who might have this problem. This is a way for us to inexpensively, but still deeply and thoroughly, vet out these ideas.

SEQ: What, in your opinion, makes a great idea?

Lombardo: When somebody hears it, they make the connection. As soon as you talk about it, people go, "Oh, my God, that's a great idea," and so there's a resonance element of it.

There's also an element of, it has to solve some kind of need or problem and it could be a perceived need. It doesn't necessarily have to be a, "My car's broken. This is going to fix it," but it could be something more of a perceptual or emotional need. It doesn't only have to be a functional need.

SEQ: How do you feel about techniques like brainstorming and sketching to work through an idea?

Lombardo: Brainstorming has to be done carefully. I think brainstorming has to be done first, individually. You have to think, then you can bring together your ideas. First, if you do it as a group, you've got to have some individual time to think about it yourself and really ponder the problem. Carve out that mental space and say, yeah, I'm going to think about this for a while.

The mindset at this point has to be immensely curious. Almost everything coming out of your mouth should be in the form of some question so that you really understand what they're trying to accomplish with the ideas they came up with.

SEQ: What do you think is the secret to creating the collaboration during the idea process?

Lombardo: You've got to have a "safe" environment and your surroundings do matter. One of the reasons why you see companies like Google and Facebook heavily investing in a "cool office space" is because they've realized it promotes that creativity. IDEO's been doing this for decades before any of these other companies have because they've known it.

UTILIZE COLLABORATION TO BUILD

As we went to school and learned to "play well with others," we started to understand that it's a lot easier when many people get united behind what they want to happen. Sure, there are people only out for themselves, but the true players, the smart ones, know that **Collaboration (Col)** and winning together makes for friends on the way up and creates a greater chance of success in the long run. So, yes, learning this skill matters.

What does it take for collaboration to work? After several years studying the issue, we've discovered five behaviors that are key to making collaboration productive.

1. **Respect:** Don't even try to collaborate if you don't respect your potential collaborator. It won't work.

2. **Tolerance:** Collaboration is messy. But that's also what makes it useful. In the best circumstances, you and your collaborators get caught up in the fun of creating and working toward the bigger vision by putting aside your differences.

3. **Excitement:** If collaborating feels like a chore, then you might be in the wrong business or just on the wrong team. You want to feel excited that you have the opportunity to co-create with talented colleagues.

4. **Focus:** Nothing annoys people more than vague, open-ended, or loosely directed brainstorming. When you collaborate always have specific end goals in mind: a prototype, a website, a creative brief, etc.

5. **Appreciation:** Collaboration needs to be fed with large doses of "thank you" and "great job." Validation boosts our enthusiasm and helps us deal with a process that takes time. Make a point of routinely thanking your colleagues and acknowledging breakthroughs or interesting ideas.

Many times, it's better to have more than just one person working on an idea and bringing it to light. When we allow ourselves to have a healthy collaboration, we remain open to the idea that there's a different perspective available to solve the same problem. You may not always agree with your collaborators, but be willing to agree to disagree with them. That healthy tension is where great ideas are born. Use it.

FOCUS ON THE RIGHT OPPORTUNITY

From agreeing there's a need, you can move directly to identifying the **Opportunity (Opp)**. It's at this point where you transition from an idea to a viable business. The opportunity becomes the gateway to meeting the need for your target market. Learning that an as-yet unaware market needs your product means an opportunity exists to create your business.

> You can have brilliant ideas, but if you can't get them across,
> your ideas won't get you anywhere.
> —*Lee Iacocca*

EXERCISE: Focusing on the Right Opportunity

Finding an idea to start a business from is not an easy task. Many people start businesses to solve a problem.

1. Make a mind map of all the things that bug you within the industry you are looking to go into.

2. Who else has done what you want to do? Even if you do not know these people, find three people who have done what you are seeking to do. It doesn't matter if they've achieved it in another field.

3. Don't reinvent the wheel. Once you have mind mapped what bugs you, begin to make connections between who is currently trying to solve those problems and where they are falling short, in order to find gaps in the industry and create opportunities.

4. Then, brainstorm ways to connect those opportunities and what they might look like as a business.

5. Make a list of every connection you have within the industry that you want to join. After making that list, make another list of your questions. Before you get started, you need to arm yourself with as much information as possible.

Based on the number of opportunities and the ways of putting them together, you'll be able to tell whether you're building the platform for something bigger or a complement to something that already exists. Decide whether you want your business to be the hub or the spoke of a wheel. You can be one, but you can't be both.

GETTING READY . . .

Ideas are fleeting unless we decide to make them into something. With practice, we can get better at identifying the great ideas and put our full entrepreneurial weight behind them. At this point in your startup journey you probably have a good idea of what you want your business to be and how it might be different and valuable. Take a step back and run through the concepts in this chapter to see which elements help the most.

The following are exercises to help you solidify your ideas and direction. Again, these are just guideposts for you on the journey to create the right Startup Equation for you.

- Idea Generation with Brainstorming
- Fine-Tuning Your Idea
- Unique Snowflake
- Focusing on the Right Opportunity

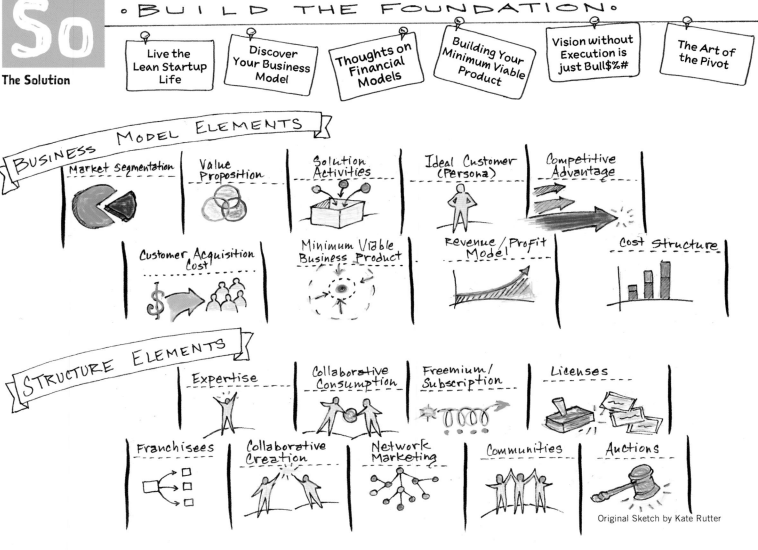

So

The Solution

∘BUILD THE FOUNDATION∘

Live the Lean Startup Life

Discover Your Business Model

Thoughts on Financial Models

Building Your Minimum Viable Product

Vision without Execution is just Bull$%#

The Art of the Pivot

BUSINESS MODEL ELEMENTS

Market Segmentation

Value Proposition

Solution Activities

Ideal Customer (Persona)

Competitive Advantage

Customer Acquisition Cost

Minimum Viable Business Product

Revenue/Profit Model

Cost Structure

STRUCTURE ELEMENTS

Expertise

Collaborative Consumption

Freemium/ Subscription

Licenses

Franchisees

Collaborative Creation

Network Marketing

Communities

Auctions

Original Sketch by Kate Rutter

CHAPTER 7

Not long ago, the term 'business model' was not exactly on the tip of everyone's tongue. Then, in the early to mid-1990s, 'business model' became a catchphrase that described how a company makes money or saves money.

—*Marc Ostrofsky*

Strength in Agility

An idea is only good if it's executable, with a repeatable and scalable business model behind it. Many first-time entrepreneurs do not get it right when they go out on their own and try to build a business. When Bill Gates was in high school, he launched one of his first ventures, Traf-O-Data, a traffic counter. The target market was local government. Unfortunately, the company failed when the state of Washington started offering counters to cities for free, wiping out his business.

Another successful entrepreneur who didn't start out as a success is Peter Thiel of PayPal. Clarium Capital, his hedge fund, managed $7 billion in assets. But following a series of bad investments, the fund lost 90 percent of its value. Needless to say, Thiel has since done quite well with PayPal (the most successful online payments system) and his early investment in Facebook.

Both examples prove that everyone makes mistakes, and though you may think you have the right business model (or business, for that matter), it may not be the right one for you or your target market. Agility is king in your search for the right solution that makes your business fire on all cylinders.

A recent study done by Harvard Business School's Shihar Ghosh looked at 2,000 startups over the last ten years, and the results showed that 75 percent fail. It's a striking number, but the message is clear—the odds are not in your favor, so you must be agile to explore the solution your business will provide, and over time, test its viability in the market. This is where the **Solution (So)** function of the Startup Equation comes into view.

When creating a business model for your idea, structure elements like **Key Problem, Solution and Metrics (Psm)**, **Value Proposition (Vap)**, **Customer Segmentation (Csg)**, **Customer Relationships (Rel)**, **Minimum Viable Product (Mvp)** and **Revenue/Profit Model (Rev)** you will absolutely want to include in the mix. They will help you understand

75

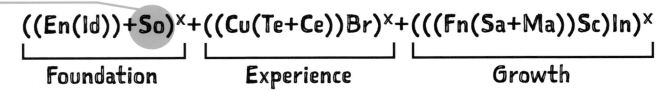

$$((En(Id))+So)^X+((Cu(Te+Ce))Br)^X+(((Fn(Sa+Ma))Sc)In)^X$$

Foundation   Experience   Growth

As we move through the third major function of the "Foundation" part of the equation, we have learned about ourselves and our approach to the business and then come up with our great idea. Now is the time we work through what the business model we create to succeed.

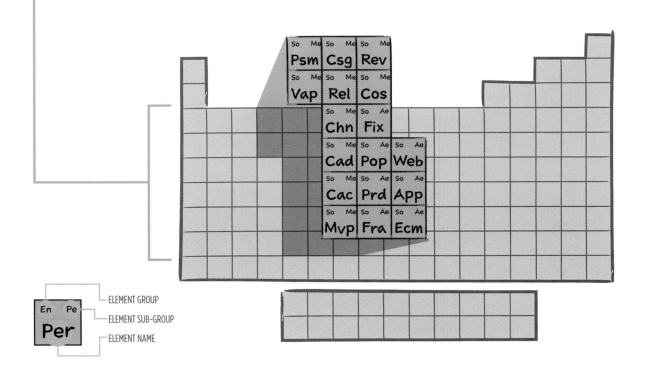

ELEMENT GROUP
ELEMENT SUB-GROUP
ELEMENT NAME

SOLUTION (SO) MODEL ELEMENTS

These are the elements that comprise the business model of our solution. The model looks at markets, customers, minimum viable products and financial models.

Key Problem, Solution and Metrics (Psm)
These are the partners, resources and activities that are key to supporting your business and making it successful.

Value Proposition (Vap)
This is the value you deliver to the customer by solving a specific problem they have with a certain product or service.

Customer Segmentation (Csg)
You must know who you are creating value for, who your most important customers are, and what the archetypes and personas of your ideal customer are.

Customer Relationships (Rel)
This is about getting, keeping and growing customers. Which relationships have been established, how are they integrated with the business model and how much do they cost the business?

Solution Channels (Chn)
It is through channels that you reach customers. Look at how others reach them now. Which is most cost efficient and works for you?

Competitive Advantage (Cad)
You understand your competitor's differentiation as well as yours and have the ability to win over customers based on various advantages.

Customer Acquisition Cost (Cac)
As you begin to understand your customer channels, you must refine the cost at which you acquire customers to improve the cost structure of your business.

Minimum Viable Product (Mvp)
A minimum viable product is the minimum solution required to launch and to test whether if you are solving your customer's specific problem and satisfying their need.

Revenue/Profit Model (Rev)
Here you focus on what customers are really willing to pay for the value you are providing. It involves pricing tactics to discover your best revenue model.

Cost Structure (Cos)
These are the important costs inherent to your business that include acquisitions, key resources and activities that affect your profitability.

SOLUTION (SO) APPROACH ELEMENTS

These are the elements that leverage a specific approach for the business. You may have more than one approach in your strategy but you will probably start with just one.

Fixed Space (Fix)
This is a physical space that is in a fixed location and used for retail activities. Examples of this type of approach are retail stores, restaurants, or offices.

Pop-Up/Mobile Space (Pop)
This is a space that is mobile and can be either temporary or "popped up" for a certain period of time. Examples include seasonal shops, pop-up stores, food trucks, street team marketing stands.

Physical Product (Prd)
This is a manufactured physical product that you provide for sale to customers.

Franchises (Fra)
This is business model that can be either part of your strategy to expand your business or an existing business franchise that you purchase.

Online Presence (Web)
This is an online presence for your business and in most cases would consist of a website that contains information about your business (e.g., services, team, contact info).

Mobile App (App)
This would be a mobile application used on mobile devices (e.g., smartphone, tablet) with a specific purpose. This could be an application you sell as a revenue stream or one you provide as part of your business offerings.

E-Commerce (Ecm)
This is a focus on selling products online through a digital storefront. It consists of an online store, a digital shopping cart and electronic payment. The e-commerce element usually leverages the online presence and mobile app elements.

the pillars of your business model and the solution you will design for your own startup equation.

You will also need to consider the approach elements sub-group you use to power your startup and reach customers, which includes things like **Pop-up/Mobile Retail (Pop)**, **Physical Product (Prd)**, **Mobile App (App)** and **E-commerce (Ecm)** among others. We will expand on both sub-categories of elements later in this chapter to help you craft your business model.

LIVING THE LEAN STARTUP LIFE

In the last few years, we've seen a new process appear that reduces the risk of starting a company. It's a methodology called *the Lean Startup*, and it favors experimentation over fancy planning, actual customer feedback over internal opinion, and intuition and iterative design over the traditional "do it all now" development. Developed by entrepreneur and author Eric Ries, he devoted an entire book to the concept, and we highly recommend you add it to your library.

As a starting point and connection with this book, the Lean Startup is a core component of the **Solution** elements because it provides you with great techniques to build out your **Solution Model** and test your **Solution Approach**. When you look at elements like **Value Proposition (Vap)**, **Competitive Advantage (Cac)**, and **Minimum Viable Product (Mvp)**, these are part of the Lean Startup and key building blocks as you craft your unique Startup Equation.

Lean Startup Basics

One of the critical differences between existing companies and startups is that the former execute business models while startups look for theirs. The Lean Startup makes this distinction less of an issue: businesses search for a repeatable and scalable business model. No matter what type of business you're starting—food truck, consulting firm, software company—the following Lean Startup key principles will help you as you build your Startup Equation.

1. **Founders summarize their solution in a framework called a Business Model Canvas.** Instead of writing a business plan and engaging in months of planning and research, use a visual representation or canvas to begin building your startup.

2. **Founders use the Customer Development ("Get Out of the Building") approach to test their solution**. Start by asking potential users, purchasers, and partners for feedback on all the elements of the business model (e.g., features, pricing, channels). It's about speed and taking a minimum viable product (MVP) to them and using the input to refine and start the cycle again.

3. **Founders practice Agile Development to build their solution and use it in conjunction with the Customer Development approach to test the MVP.** Agile Development originated in the software industry, but its principles can apply to almost any business. At its core, the goal is to eliminate wasted time and resources by developing a product iteratively and incrementally.

You can see in Figure 7.3 that the Lean Startup approach requires experimenting and iterating, with failure providing a pathway to success. As you work through the **Solution** elements consider that each element is related to the Lean Startup and its related Customer Development Process and Business Model Canvas. Each of these elements are key to crafting your own unique Startup Equation.

DISCOVERING YOUR BASE BUSINESS MODEL

As you begin to formulate your solution, you may be asking yourself if you need to form a business plan. Probably not, but you do need to come up with fundamental pieces that incorporate the core solution elements we talked about earlier.

Forming Your Mission

We're firm believers that before you set out on a journey, you need to have focus and know your purpose. With all of the companies Steve has built or advised, he pushes to form a mission before diving into the business model. Entrepreneur and author Guy Kawasaki likens this process to creating a mantra by using a few words to describe the essence of what your company does. We prefer to use the term *mission* because it implies

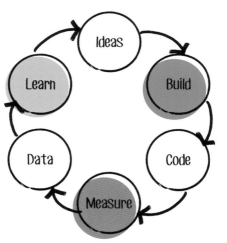

EXPERIMENT

EXPERIMENTS ALLOW YOU TO MINIMIZE FAILURE WHILE MOVING FORWARD

ITERATION

IMPROVES DEVELOPMENT AND MAXIMIZES LEARNING

FAILURE

IS THE KEY TO SUCCESS!

	LEAN	TRADITIONAL
STRATEGY	Business Model Hypothesis-driven	Business Plan Implementation-driven
NEW-PRODUCT PROCESS	Customer Development Get out of the office and test hypothesis	Product Management Prepare offering for market following a linear, step-by-step plan
ENGINEERING	Agile Development Build product iteratively and incrementally	Agile or Waterfall Development Build the product iteratively, or fully specify the product before building it
ORGANIZATION	Customer and Agile Development Teams Hire for learning, nimbleness, and speed	Departments for Function Hire for experience and ability to execute
FINANCIAL REPORTING	Metrics that Matter Customer acquisition cost, lifetime customer value, churn, viralness	Accounting Income statement, balance sheet, cash flow statement
FAILURE	Expected Fix by iterating on ideas and pivoting away from ones that don't work	Exception Fix by firing executives
SPEED	Rapid Operates on good-enough data	Measured Operates on complete data

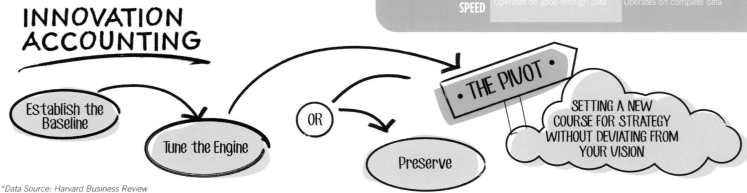

INNOVATION ACCOUNTING

Establish the Baseline

Tune the Engine

OR

Preserve

• THE PIVOT •

SETTING A NEW COURSE FOR STRATEGY WITHOUT DEVIATING FROM YOUR VISION

*Data Source: Harvard Business Review

direction and purpose. Whatever you call it, this statement explains in short and clear terms why your organization exists.

Next, craft short statements about what makes you stand out from the competition (**Competitive Advantage (Cad)**) and why customers will choose your business over others (**Value Propositions (Vap)**). This step will get your mind geared up for the task of figuring out a business model and helping your team focus on the mission you want to accomplish with your company. After you put your answers and statements together, a mission will emerge around your business idea. The next set of steps will help you craft your business model.

Starting with the Business Model Canvas

One you know what you stand for, it is time to figure out your business model. To fully develop your model, you may find the Business Model Canvas useful. This tool helps organizations have strategic conversations about elements of their business model. It's not only for the new startup. Your business can also use it to find new opportunities.

Alexander Oserwalder created the Business Model Canvas in 2010 based on an evolution of his 2004 Ph.D. thesis research about business model ontology. You can see the results in Figure 7.5.

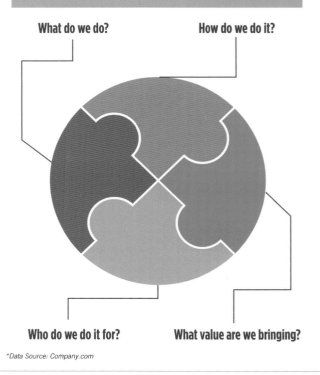

FORMING YOUR MISSION

What do we do? How do we do it?

Who do we do it for? What value are we bringing?

Data Source: Company.com

Figure 7.4 **Forming Your Mission**

Leveraging the BASE Board

After much research into the Business Model Canvas, we felt strongly that some components needed refinement and many things were just missing. This is not to disparage the original Business Model Canvas, but to evolve it in a manner that is more holistic to serve what startups and entrepreneurs need to consider today. Dr. Oserwalder was generous enough to release the Canvas via Creative Commons so people could share it, tweak it and hopefully evolve it. This is why we used it as a component

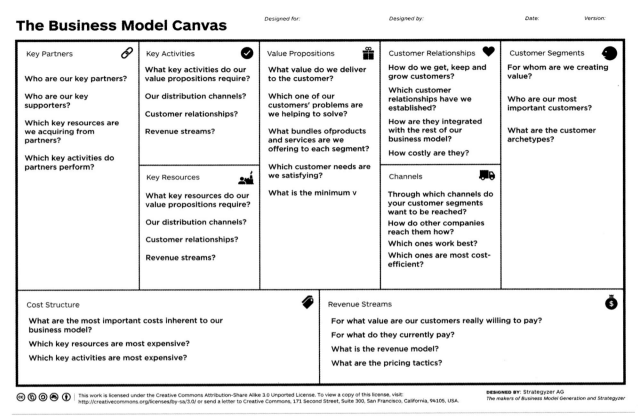

The Business Model Canvas

Designed for: Designed by: Date: Version:

Key Partners

Who are our key partners?

Who are our key supporters?

Which key resources are we acquiring from partners?

Which key activities do partners perform?

Key Activities

What key activities do our value propositions require?

Our distribution channels?

Customer relationships?

Revenue streams?

Key Resources

What key resources do our value propositions require?

Our distribution channels?

Customer relationships?

Revenue streams?

Value Propositions

What value do we deliver to the customer?

Which one of our customers' problems are we helping to solve?

What bundles of products and services are we offering to each segment?

Which customer needs are we satisfying?

What is the minimum v

Customer Relationships

How do we get, keep and grow customers?

Which customer relationships have we established?

How are they integrated with the rest of our business model?

How costly are they?

Channels

Through which channels do your customer segments want to be reached?

How do other companies reach them how?

Which ones work best?

Which ones are most cost-efficient?

Customer Segments

For whom are we creating value?

Who are our most important customers?

What are the customer archetypes?

Cost Structure

What are the most important costs inherent to our business model?

Which key resources are most expensive?

Which key activities are most expensive?

Revenue Streams

For what value are our customers really willing to pay?

For what do they currently pay?

What is the revenue model?

What are the pricing tactics?

Figure 7.5 **Business Model Canvas**[1]

to build the Business Approach & Structure Elements (BASE) Board. The BASE Board is intended to provide a graphical guide to evolving a business approach and related products/solutions. It includes the following modules in four connected groups (Envisioning, Assessing Opportunity, Evolving Strategy and Operations) and is shown in Figure 7.6.

Before you start: *Before we dive into breaking down each section you will want to print a copy or draft the rough structure on a whiteboard. You will also need lots of Post-it notes and ways to record the result and decisions.*

Important to Note: *Though the components and considerations herein are by no means exhaustive, they should help guide your thinking, inquiry and strategy development. So let's begin our review of the Board.*

Envisioning

This hearkens back to Chapter 5 and Chapter 6 and the **Entrepreneur (En)** and the **Idea (Id)** functions of the equation, respectively.

Me: This is related to the Entrepreneur (En) part of the equation that we discussed in Chapter 5. You will want to know your personality type and approach element from that part of the equation. Questions to consider:

- What are my motivations/interests?
- What are my strengths/weaknesses?
- How do these all play into this effort?
- Where do I see myself as an entrepreneur in five years?

My Idea: This is related to the Idea (Id) part of the equation that we discussed in Chapter 6. We discussed the core elements that make up an idea and the generation elements that foster the process of creating and refining your idea. It's about setting your vision down on paper and outlining what it is your startup is looking to achieve. Remember, a good idea is only the beginning and is not enough. All strategy must be developed with a bias for implementation. Also, do not try to qualify your perception or desire regarding your idea. Deal with the realities you determine. In some cases you may discover that your idea does not represent an opportunity. This should motivate you to adjust your original vision to something from which you can build a business. Questions to consider:

- What is my idea?
- How did I get this idea?
- Is this idea something I am passionate about?
- What is my company name?
- What do I want customers to think about my company?
- What do I envision my company will become in five years?

Assessing Opportunity

After you have envisioned the idea and the core vision of the startup, you must move quickly to assess the opportunity. If there is a market, there's most likely competition existing in another form.

The Opportunity: Here are the questions to consider as you develop the opportunity:

- What does our business do?
- How will we make money? (What is our product/service)

- What trends support our business?
- What do others think of this idea?

The Market: Here are the questions to consider as you evaluate the market for your opportunity:

- How big is the potential opportunity?
- What should be our initial market focus?
- Who is our real competition? Why?
- Who are our customers?
- What do we know about them?
- Why would they buy our product/service? (Features, Benefits, Value)
- How will we reach them?
- Other customer segments/revenue streams?

After you have identified the opportunity and market, you will need to do research on the market and opportunity to understand your **Competitive Advantage (Cad)**. Perform a SWOT analysis (Strengths, Weaknesses, Opportunities and Threats) and talk with the team to help identify how you should differentiate yourself from competitors and win customers. You will also need to get a sense for what resources you will need to deal with the SWOT analysis. Here are questions to consider for each part of the SWOT analysis:

Strengths: What are the strengths of our company? Our people? Major revenue streams? Special Sauce?

Weaknesses: Internal weaknesses? Lacking skill sets? Resources? Negative perceptions? Place in the race?

Opportunities: Hot market or trend? Unique niche/hole in the market? Changing business climate or customer needs?

Threats: Timing? R&D Time? Money? Competition? Market conditions? Change in laws/government policy?

Necessary resources: Finally, you will have to make some estimates on the resources needed to execute on this opportunity. Here are questions to consider related to the resources you will need:

- What skills/people do we need?
- What partners do we need?
- What money, facilities and/or equipment do we need?
- What strategy help do we need (marketing, financial, other)?

Evolving Strategy

Evolving strategy is about defining how you go to market with your startup, including things like sales strategy, marketing campaigns, and product messaging, as well as your operations, financial processes and how you will go to market.

Company Goals: This is related to the Idea (Id) part of the equation that discusses your vision and mission. These goals are what you want to achieve with the business and build from the vision and mission. Here are the questions to consider:

- What do we want to achieve? Why? How? For whom?
- What is our mission statement?
- How will this goal translate to our value proposition? Business operations?

Value Proposition: This is also related to the Idea (Id) part of the equation that discusses your vision and mission. It connects the vision and mission with the goals to focus on the specific **Value Proposition (Vap)** you deliver to the customer by solving a specific problem. Here are the questions to consider as you work to create the value proposition for your startup:

- What is our value to our customer?
- What is our stated value proposition?
- How is this value driven by our goals/mission?

Marketing, Sales and Go-to-Market Strategy: This is related to the Marketing (Ma) and Sales (Sa) part of the equation that we cover in Chapters 13 and 14, respectively. While they are covered later in the book, here are some questions to consider now:

- Who are our customer segments? How will we reach them?
- What type of relationship do we want with them?

- How will our marketing and sales operations support our goals and desired customer relationships?

Operations and Financial: This is related to both the Solution (So) part of the equation where we dive into financial models later in this chapter as well as the funding chapter that supports your ongoing operations. We consider financials and operations to include **Revenue/Profit Model (Rev)** and **Cost Structure (Cos)**. The **Revenue/Profit Model (Rev)** focuses on what customers are really willing to pay for the value you're providing, and it involves pricing tactics to discover your best revenue model. For **Cost Structure (Cos)**, there are important costs inherent in your business, including acquisition costs, key resources, and activities that affect your profitability. Here are the questions to consider as you construct the operations and financial strategy for your startup:

- Where will our company be based?
- How will our management be structured?
- What permits or licensing do we need?
- Where does our revenue come from?
- How much money do we need to get started?
- How much do we need to achieve critical mass?
- How does money flow through our business?
- What are our cost centers? Profit centers?
- Even through we are just getting started, what is our exit strategy? Investor buy-back? Acquisition? IPO?

Operations

Even though we mentioned Operations in the previous section, the discussion was focused on the strategy you propose to execute on. This final section of the BASE Board will seem familiar because many of the components are from the original Business Model Canvas. As we stated earlier, this is a great tool shared with the world via Creative Commons, and we have decided to include what we consider relevant at the proper stage for consideration by the entrepreneur designing a business.

Key Activities, Players & Partners: To get your operations running at full steam, you need a baseline of the key activities, partners and players. Key activities include **Problem, Solution, and Metrics (Psm)** that will create a foundation of measurement. Key players include the partners, resources, and required activities to make your business successful. Here are some questions to consider:

- Who are the key people in our company? What are their strengths?
- Who are our key partners? What value do they bring to our company?
- How do we deliver value to the customer?
- What activities accomplish our goals? Development (Creative, R&D)? Production? Promotion?
- Are these activities daily? Occasional? Seasonal?

Customer Segments & Relationships: The next parts of your operations that you must detail out are **Customer Segmentation (Csg)** and **Customer Relationships (Rel)**. For **Customer Segmentation (Csg)**, you must know who you're creating value for, the identity of your most important customers, and the archetypes or personas of your ideal customer. For **Customer Relationships (Rel)**, it's about getting, keeping, and growing customers by reviewing what relationships have been established, how they integrate with the business model, and how much they cost the business. Here are some questions to consider:

- Is there "low hanging fruit" we can immediately capture with our product/service?
- Do we appeal to the mass market? Just a niche? Are we national? Local?
- What type of relationship do we want with our customers?
- What do we want them to think about us? Feel about us?
- How will our company's operations accomplish this?

Channels: This is about how you use **Solution Channels (Chn)** to reach customers. Look at how others reach them now, assess what's most efficient, and weigh which ones work for you. With the **Solution**

Channels (Chn) you will apply the Approach elements of the **Solution (So)** part of the equation. Here's a breakdown of those approaches:

- **Fixed Retail (Fix):** A fixed location for your business.
- **Pop-up/Mobile Retail (Pop):** A temporary or mobile location for your business.
- **Physical Product (Prd):** A manufactured product to sell.
- **Franchise (Fra):** A business model that can become or already is a franchise.
- **Online Presence (Web):** A presence on the Internet, most commonly a website.
- **Mobile App (App):** A mobile application as a product or platform for your products/services.
- **E-commerce (Ecm):** A web-based digital storefront.

In a perfect world, you would be able to launch as many approaches as possible when starting your business. And both of us have seen many businesses fall flat on their faces by doing so. In order to see which approach to start with, ask yourself the following questions:

- How can we reach our customers?
- What messages do we need to convey? How do they change over time?
- How do we introduce ourselves? And how do we maintain the relationship after the sale?
- Do I need a physical location to start selling or can I start with a temporary one?
- Is the core thing I am selling a physical product? If so, what is the leanest way I can build it in order to start testing the concept and making money?
- Is my business model one that can be easily replicated and sold?
- Do I absolutely need an online presence to start generating revenue?
- Do I absolutely need a mobile application to start or can I test my business idea another way?

SOLUTION ELEMENT EQUATION DESIGN (SEED) BOARD Figure 7.6

THE STARTUP EQUATION BUSINESS MODEL CANVAS

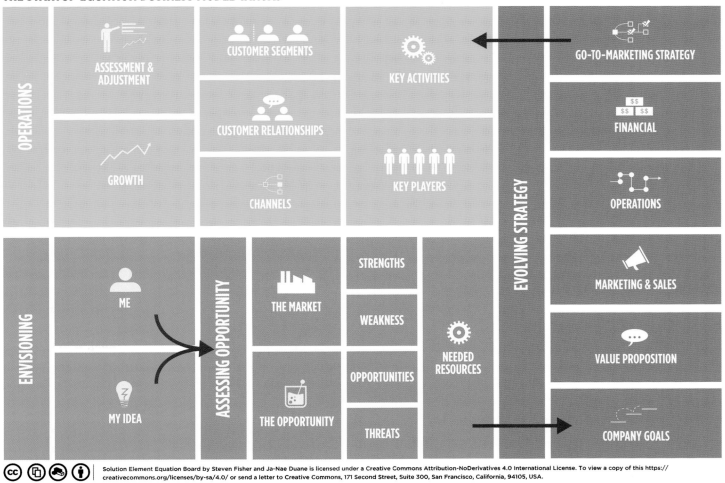

DESIGNED BY: Steven Fisher and Ja-Nae Duane
The creators of The Startup Equation

Additional Sources: Karl Baehr, Alexander Osterwalder

Growth: This relates to the **Scale (Sc)** function of the equation and helps address a key factor in your startup's life – what will the business look like long term? Here are some questions to consider:

- How do our goals, mission and value proposition translate to growth?
- How should we grow? Why? How fast? Where?
- Are there any immediate opportunities for growth?
- How will this growth be managed?

Assessment and **Adjustment:** This explores the metrics and measurement to refine and improve your company's performance. An example of a metric is **Customer Acquisition Cost (Cac)** where once you begin to understand your customer channels, you must refine the cost to acquire customers so you can improve the cost structure of your business. Over time this will help you chart a path for growth and scale to achieve success. Here are some questions to consider:

- How will we monitor and assess what we do?
- What measures will we employ for our key activities?
- How will we handle customer issues? Questions? Complaints?
- How will we handle problems? PR? Communications with Stakeholders?
- How often will we review company performance?

Many times we want to come out of the gate with everything perfect. But that is the best way to lose thousands of dollars. Instead, ask yourself the hard questions and keep your initial approach as lean as possible.

EXERCISE: Craft Your Own BASE Board

The principles, concepts and frameworks we just reviewed are covered in this book but as a preparation exercise complete the following:

- Review the Diagram earlier in this chapter - "Lean Startup Model Explained"

- Review the Business Model Canvas basics covered in this book and in greater detail in the book *Business Model Generation* by Alexander Osterwalder.
- Review the Business Approach & Structure Elements (BASE) Board on the following page and using this section and the descriptions on the diagram build out your own on paper or on a white board.
- **Before you start:** *Like we said before, before you dive into breaking down each section you will want to print a copy or draft the rough structure of the BASE Board on a white board. You will also need lots of Post-it notes and ways to record the result and decisions.*

Exploring BASE Model Scenarios

As you begin to test your BASE Board design, you may want to begin to explore some popular structures or "scenarios" used by startups. We have outlined below what we consider the most common in use today:

- **Expertise:** This business model leverages the expertise of you and your co-founders, like a consulting or professional services business.
- **Collaborative Consumption:** The model of collaborative consumption (e.g., the sharing economy) is about leveraging what you own to create income from underutilized resources. Uber and AirBnB use this model.
- **Freemium/Subscription:** In many cases, people want to use your service before buying. Startups provide a free version that attracts people with the goal of moving customers to a paid, premium version of the product. Examples of this model include Freshbooks and Dropbox.
- **Licenses:** When your business model licenses the intellectual property of someone, usually an inventor, it takes that license and transforms it into a viable business. Under Armor and 180s Apparel use this model.
- **Collaborative Creation:** This model leverages thousands of people to solve a certain problem, a portion of a larger problem, or

build/improve a product. Linux, Wikipedia, and Threadless have adopted this model.

- **Network Marketing:** Network marketing, also known as multi-level marketing (MLM), has proven a successful model for some large companies. The sales force is compensated for sales they personally generate and for the sales of other salespeople they recruit. It's a cornerstone of this model as demonstrated by companies like Amway, Herbalife, and Pampered Chef.
- **Communities:** Businesses using this model leverage the power of social ties to deepen experiences and encourage consumers to share common interests, activities, and the offerings that support them. Social networks and opinion sites like Facebook, Twitter, Yelp, and TripAdvisor make use of this model.
- **Auctions:** Making use of supply and demand curves to create a marketplace, this model supports people bidding on products and services they need. Companies like eBay and Live Auctioneers paved the way for businesses to use this model online.

Your business model may not leverage any of these models, but it's important to have a good understanding of these basic models to help you weigh all your options. We will dive into these "scenarios" at the end of the book when we bring the equation together and show how they are put into practice.

EXERCISE: Selecting some Solution Structures to Test

In preparation to create your BASE board you should decide on the structure for your startup. Work through the following questions to identify this strategy:

1. Which scenarios might apply to my business?
2. Is there more than one scenario that will work? Will it be complementary? Will it be part of a tiered strategy?
3. Which structures will work with my startup?

Once you have decided on these, make note of them and put them aside for use at the end of this book when you build your own Startup Equation.

THOUGHTS ON FINANCIAL MODELS

Do you need a financial model, too? Yes and no. Financial models are always wrong, but it's important to create one anyway. We know that sounds provocative, but financial modeling is more about the thought process than the model itself. During our walkthrough of the BASE Board design we discussed this process in the Evolving Strategy cluster on the BASE Board. The Financial building block included relevant **Solution** elements like **Revenue/Profit Model (Rev)** and **Cost Structure (Cos)**. Customers are really willing to pay for the value you're providing. It also involves pricing tactics to discover your best **Revenue/Profit Model (Rev)**. Then there's **Cost Structure (Cost)**, which includes important costs inherent to your business, including acquisition costs, key resources, and activities affecting profitability.

So, what is a financial model?

- It's a discussion about what you believe will happen.
- It's an assessment of your realism (e.g., revenues and costs).
- It's a statement about your assumptions.
- It's a way to visualize how your business actually works.

A financial model is not:

- All about the numbers.
- A hockey stick.
- A waste of time.

Simple financial models are about three things: **cash** (how much do you have), **expenses** (how much you spend), and **revenue** (how much money you make and how you expect to make money). To build the financial model for your startup, we've pulled together a five-step process for you:

Step 1: Understanding the Drivers of Revenue

- How much does your company make?
- What affects how much your company makes?
  - If you make money from users, how much does revenue increase as growth occurs?

- If you sell goods, how does cost of goods impact revenue as you grow?
- What's a reasonable and logical calculation for customer conversions?
- Know that expectations of early-stage revenue isn't the primary driver.

Step 2: Understanding the Drivers of Expenses

- What do you need to spend money on?
  - People
  - Marketing
  - Operations
- What affects how much your company spends?

Step 3: Income Statement

- Create an income statement showing profits/losses for a specific period.

Step 4: Balance Sheet

- Create a balance sheet to take a snapshot of your company at one instant in time.
- Start by building the right side (i.e., Total Liabilities and Total Equity) and then the left side (i.e., Total Assets); the left and right sides should be equal.

Step 5: Cash Flow Statement

- Cash is king. The cash flow statement is most important to a startup because it will tell you whether you can do essential tasks, like pay employees and the bills.

As you answer these questions and build these financial elements, it's easy to get overwhelmed. Take it one step at a time. There are a ton of templates available to get you started. If you're unsure about anything, reach out to your network. They can help fill in the blanks.

Financial Modeling Do's and Don'ts

- **DO** the income statement first, followed by the balance sheet.
- **DO** stay conservative with your assumptions.
- **DO** underpromise and overdeliver.
- **DO** spend time thinking about what drives revenues and expenses.
- **DO** give yourself room to iterate the business before you run out of money, with a cushion to raise additional funds when 3-6 months of cash remain.
- **DON'T** justify early financial decisions with inflated forecasts.
- **DON'T** project negative cash. Raise enough equity or debt to cover losses.
- **DON'T** forget to look at the model and update it monthly with real numbers.

Remember that creating a financial model forces an entrepreneur to outline in detail how a business works. It highlights how a company creates its products, how users and customers find and use its products, and how those processes create revenues and expenses. The end result provides a set of operational metrics, financial statements, and the "financial equation" of your business.

EXERCISE: Create Your First Financial Model

After you have worked through the previous exercises to create your SEED board along with your approach and structures, you will need to put some real numbers behind it. Here are some things you can do to get started on your financial model:

1. **Focus on expenses:** You've probably spent a great deal of time thinking about your product, users, marketing, and even the exit. All of these things involve costs, so start your financial model by estimating your expenses.

2. **Outline how the product or service is built, marketed, sold and delivered:** Create your revenue plan with a concrete, bottom-up look at what's required to take your product or service from a plan to the customer. Your financial model will vary depending on the type of business and business model.

3. **Analyze your assumptions and your market. Benchmark your projections:** Start digging into what your model means. How big is the market for your product or service? Who are the competitors and what size of the market do they control? How big a market do you think you'll need in three months, six months, and one year?

4. **Create detailed financial statements:** Depending on your current stage, you may need to create more detailed financial statements. These statements can include a balance sheet, cash flows, financing structure, and capitalization table. This will require a bit of finance and accounting knowledge. You can always search the web for financial model templates, plus talk to other entrepreneurs, potential investors, and consultants.

Ultimately, you can only learn by doing. One other piece of advice: Don't hire someone just to build a financial model. Get an advisor, a mentor, an investor, and build a model together. It's the startup version of being taught how to fish. Then, go fish.

BUILDING YOUR MINIMUM VIABLE PRODUCT

Minimum viable product (MVP) means different things to different people. So let's start with what we mean. Eric Ries provided one of the earliest definitions of MVP:

> A Minimum Viable Product is that version of a new product which allows a team to collect the maximum amount of validated learning about customers with the least effort.

We want to refine and expand this definition a bit. An MVP is the minimum solution required to launch and test if you're solving your customer's specific problem and whether it's satisfying their need. An MVP has three key characteristics:

- It has enough value that people are willing to use it or buy it initially.
- It demonstrates enough future benefit to retain early adopters.
- It provides a feedback loop to guide future development.

As you can see in Figure 7.7, a business can leverage that feedback to create an improved, minimum viable product for the next round of customer feedback. We believe that after some brief rounds of this show-and-tell, you'll have an MVP.

What qualifies as an MVP? Here are a few examples from the *Ultimate Guide to MVPs* that might apply to your business.[2]

- **Explainer Video:** An explainer video is a short video or animation that walks through what your product does and why people should buy it.
- **Landing Page:** A landing page quickly communicates the value of your offering, addresses objections, and calls the visitor to action. But wait a second. Isn't a landing page a marketing tool? Sure, but it's also an MVP. The landing page validates your **Value Proposition (Vap)**.
- **Wizard of Oz MVP:** A Wizard of Oz MVP involves putting up a front that looks like a working product, but you manually carry out product functions. It's also known as "flintstoning."
- **Concierge MVP:** Instead of providing a product, you start with a manual service, but not just any service. The service should consist of exactly the same steps people would follow using your actual product.
- **Piecemeal MVP:** This strategy is a blend between the Wizard of Oz and Concierge approaches. Again, you emulate the steps people would go through using your product as you envision it with existing tools.
- **Raise Funds from Customers:** This is a special case of "sell it before you build it." The basic idea is simple. Launch a crowdfunding campaign on platforms like Kickstarter, IndieGoGo, and RocketHub.

With a successful crowdfunding campaign, you earn a tribe of early adopters and raving fans. Of course, crowdfunding will not work for just any type of product.

- **Single-Feature MVP:** Some of the most successful applications started out with a simple feature. Remember Google and Dropbox when they started? It's interesting that these two remain relatively the same as when they first launched.

The whole point of the MVP is to avoid burning money on a product no one will use. Get creative and think hard about what minimum thing you can do now to make sure you don't waste money. But how do you choose?

EXERCISE: Creating Your MVP

Now it's time to figure out your startup's MVP. Answer the following:

- Define the Minimum Viable Product for your own startup.
- How will you go about testing the functionality of your MVP?
- What would you consider success?
- Can the MVP fail to meet the criteria?
- Can you remove any features?

As you begin diving into your MVP, consider the following:

1. **Set a VERY, VERY clear goal for yourself.** There's a certain energy that comes when starting a business. Usually a person gets amped up and wants to jump in head first to get started right away. That energy is infectious and amazing on so many levels. Keep it, but give yourself a direction in which to jump. You can do that by setting very clear goals. Then, set a date and time to complete for that goal. The clearer the goal, the better.

   For example, in order to test my MVP, I will reach out to twenty people who support me by October 24, 2015, at noon. Having a very specific goal allows you to know what you're working towards, as well as helping you find ways to move towards that goal. Add in three small actionable steps to take towards achieving this goal and have the first one be asking your network for help.

   Also, as you set these goals, add in metrics for yourself. You can't know what you're trying to achieve unless you've decided what to measure.

2. **Use your network.** Each of us has a network. This network can consist of family, friends, colleagues, and social connections. If there are things that you need or if you require help finding your direction, then all you have to do is ask. You may be saying to yourself, "I would love to, but if I ask, then I'll look like a failure." Actually, it's quite the opposite. When we get vulnerable and utilize the people within our network, we're strengthening that relationship and allowing for people to feel like they're a part of building your company with you. People will be more invested and will want to see you succeed if they feel a connection to you and your business.

   There will also be times when your network does not have the answer or the resource you need. If that's the case, have them reach out to their network on behalf of you. For every person you know and are connected to, they have at least a dozen people in their network. You never know what might come from just asking.

3. **Listen.** There's an old saying: "You have two ears and one mouth for a reason." We never have all the answers. By taking the time to listen to feedback from clients, customers, employees, and partners, we can allow ourselves to identify problems quickly, as well as their potential solutions.

Interesting exercise, isn't it? Once you have understood what your MVP is and what a successful test looks like, then you are ready to reach out to your network and start testing. Spending the extra time now will save you time and money later.

MVP EXPLAINED Figure 7.7

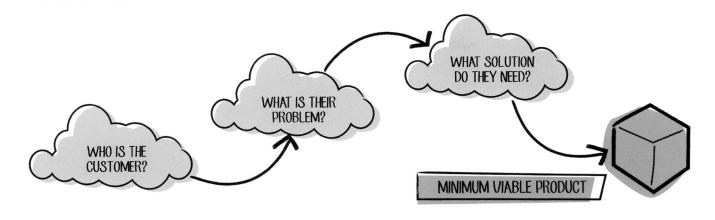

WHO IS THE CUSTOMER?

WHAT IS THEIR PROBLEM?

WHAT SOLUTION DO THEY NEED?

MINIMUM VIABLE PRODUCT

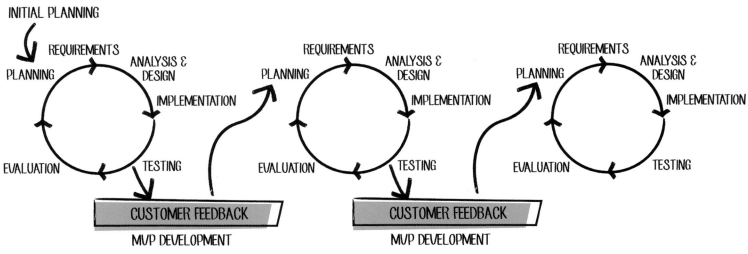

INITIAL PLANNING

REQUIREMENTS
PLANNING
ANALYSIS & DESIGN
IMPLEMENTATION
EVALUATION
TESTING

CUSTOMER FEEDBACK

MVP DEVELOPMENT

REQUIREMENTS
PLANNING
ANALYSIS & DESIGN
IMPLEMENTATION
EVALUATION
TESTING

CUSTOMER FEEDBACK

MVP DEVELOPMENT

REQUIREMENTS
PLANNING
ANALYSIS & DESIGN
IMPLEMENTATION
EVALUATION
TESTING

*Data Source: Harvard Business Review

VISION WITHOUT EXECUTION IS JUST BULLSHIT

The difference between a dreamer and an entrepreneur is the entrepreneur actually goes and does it. This level of execution begins with things like a minimum viable product. It also requires developing a process to get customers. This is known in the startup world as the Customer Development Model (CDM).

Originally described by Steve Blank in his book *The Four Steps to the Epiphany*, Blank defines CDM as "a set of objectives and milestones that are meaningful for a startup." In practical terms, Blank's model is a way of questioning the assumptions underpinning a startup by systematically testing them in the marketplace. The CDM process consists of four distinct but connected steps.

1. **Customer discovery:** Focus on understanding your customers, their problems, their preferences, and their buying behavior.
2. **Customer validation:** Develop a replicable sales process, an essential step in scaling a business.
3. **Customer creation:** Generate demand, and identify and tease out potential customers.
4. **Company building:** Focus on building your organization to scale and executing the business plan.

At this stage, you'll focus your energy on the first two stages: customer discovery and customer validation. This is related to the Startup Equation Elements **Customer Segmentation (Csg)** and **Customer Relationships (Rel)**.

You'll notice that several items in Figure 7.8 have been discussed in this chapter. In coming chapters, we'll address the sales and marketing roadmap as well as scaling the organization, which involves the latter two stages of **Company Creation** and **Company Building**.

THE ART OF THE PIVOT

What happens when you realize that the original business model isn't working as planned? Sometimes entrepreneurs will immediately blame their staff or the economy. More often than not, however, if something

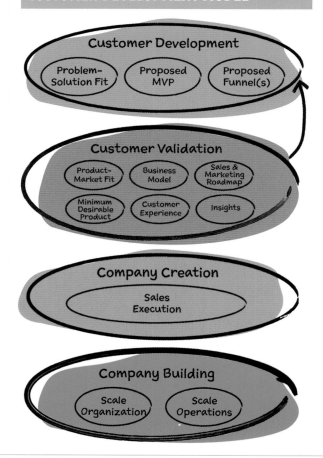

Figure 7.8 **The Customer Development Model**

isn't working, then it may only require tweaking and reconfiguring your business model. Look again at Figure 7.8.

The first two stages, customer discovery and customer validation, are all about tweaking, particularly the validation stage, as it shows when you must alter or modify the direction you're taking. *In other words, a pivot.* Here are some common pivot points that your startup may need.[3]

- **Customer Pivot:** Your business does not exist without a customer base. The sole objective of every company is to address the needs and problems their customers face. If you're not doing that, then you're not actually running a business.

- **Technology Pivot:** When building an app or a platform, it's sometimes hard to scrap the way the technology works. But startup success is less about the technology that you or your engineers create and more about solving a problem as you learn more and more about your customer base.

- **Product Pivot:** You may have a product that really speaks to your customers, but what happens when that need no longer exists? Just because you're known for one product now doesn't mean that you'll always be known for that product.

- **Market Segment Pivot:** There are times when you have the right product, but the wrong customer base, so you make a market segment pivot. Usually a key indicator is that the customers you're targeting aren't buying your product.

- **Revenue Model Pivot:** Sometimes the price is right. Other times, it's hindering your ability to actually make a profit. If you're having difficulty making money, look at your revenue model.

Allow yourself to take a hard look at your business and then match it against each of these pivots. You may find that everything is working out better than expected and that's fantastic. If not, see if one of these pivots makes sense for you.

Interview with an Entrepreneur: Mike Troiano, Actifio CMO

Mike is one of those guys you like instantly and wouldn't mind having a beer with to talk about pretty much anything. When we asked him for a title or one line bio, we got "marketing guy, entrepreneur, lyrical gangsta. Actifio CMO." Yep, that pretty much sums up Mike.

SEQ: Mike can you recall any early experiences that shaped you as an entrepreneur?

Troiano: I learned a lot from my first attempt. In retrospect, I was much more interested in starting a company (which is fun) than in building a business (which is hard). The latter is about selling, about getting out there to engage the world with your product or service in such a way that corrupts your initial vision with the external reality. That process requires a balance of conviction and flexibility that rarely comes in the same individual.

SEQ: When was there a time when you failed? What did you learn from it?

Troiano: I was the CEO of a company called Matchmine, a business focused on media discovery. We failed when we tried to build that business from the technology out, instead of from the opportunity back. That mistake was mine, and it cost a lot of really good people their jobs. I will never make it again.

GETTING READY . . .

At this point in your startup journey, you probably have a good idea of what you want your business to be and how it might be different and valuable. Take a step back and run through the concepts in this chapter to see which elements help you the most. If you want your business to succeed, then you, yes *YOU*, have to begin somewhere. Make sure you complete the following exercises located throughout this chapter to get yourself ready to build your own unique Startup Equation.

- Forming Your Mission
- Craft Your Own SEED Board
- Identifying Your Business Approach and Structure
- Create Your First Financial Model
- Creating Your MVP

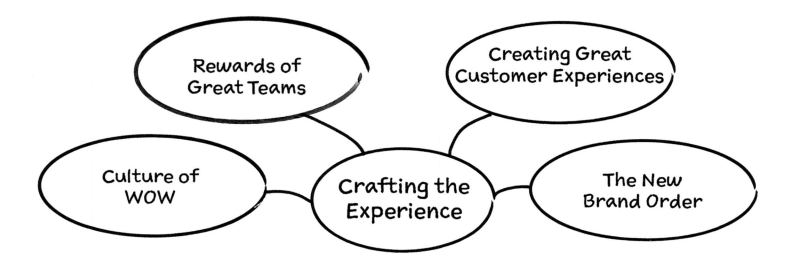

Now that you have begun to build the foundation, *you must craft an amazing experience*. You will note that in this group of equation functions are four primary functions—**Customer Experience (Ce)**, **Team (Te)**, **Culture (Cu)** and **Brand (Br)**. These next few chapters explore how it is not just important to build a product and put it out there but to craft an experience within the company and the way customers perceive and experience the company too.

The Way This Part of the Equation Works

A business is only as good as the experience. This rule applies to both employees and customers. We look to this section of the equation to find the answers that will help you dig in and craft the experience that you want people to have when they choose your business.

Culture (Cu) Elements

Building company **Culture (Cu)** requires more than having Bourbon Fridays and flextime. It's about aligning every employee with the company's mission and values with the goal of empowering them as evangelists for the brand. In Chapter 8, we will explore the sub-groups of *Core* and *Additive* elements that can help embody your culture and give people something to believe in.

Team (Te) Elements

Great leaders build companies with the support of great, long-term **Team (Te)** members. Sometimes that means actually leading and sometimes it means knowing when to step away and let people do their jobs. In Chapter 9, we'll explore how to find the best members for your *Core* and your *Extended* that will support your business even through the toughest of times.

Customer Experience (Ce) Elements

As technology evolves, so does the way we create a way to engage with our **Customer Experience (Ce)**. In Chapter 10, we will help you tackle this challenge and walk through the element sub-groups of *Programs* and *Testing* that you can use to find what works for you and your business.

Brand (Br) Elements

Brand (Br) plays a vital role in every business. The brand you adopt tells people how to engage with your business and if you're a good match. In Chapter 11, we'll explore the element sub-groups of your brand *Identity* and how you leverage brand *Senses* to consistently deliver an experience that will keep your customers coming back for more.

So let's get started . . .

CRAFTING THE EXPERIENCE

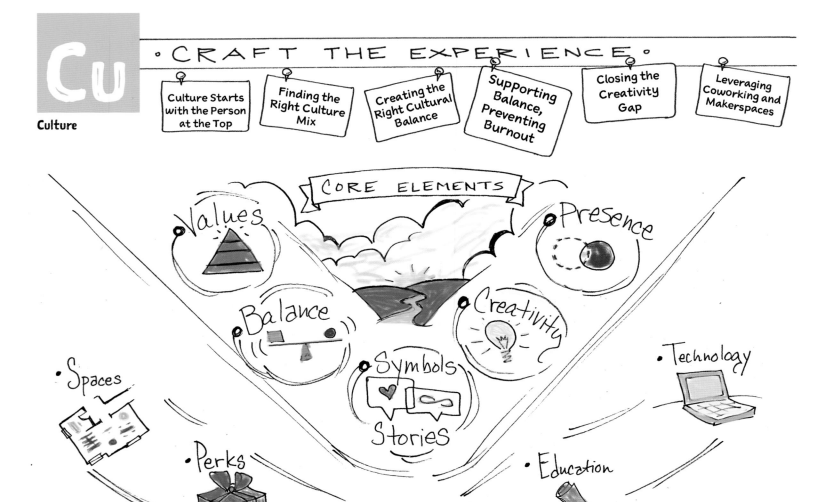

Culture Starts with the Person at the Top

Finding the Right Culture Mix

Creating the Right Cultural Balance

Supporting Balance, Preventing Burnout

Closing the Creativity Gap

Leveraging Coworking and Makerspaces

CORE ELEMENTS

Values

Presence

Balance

Creativity

Symbols
Stories

Spaces

Technology

Perks

Education

Additives

Original Sketch by Kate Rutter

CHAPTER 8

Your brand is your culture.

—*Tony Hsieh*

Culture of Wow

Richard Branson is no ordinary entrepreneur. He dropped out of school at fifteen, and despite suffering from dyslexia and attention deficit disorder, went on to found Virgin Group, a business empire that includes more than 370 different companies. He embodies the Culture of WOW.

In an interview with *HR Magazine* in 2010, Branson stated, "I started Virgin with a philosophy that if staffs are happy, customers will follow. It can't just be me that sets the culture when we recruit people. I have a really great set of CEOs across our businesses who live and breathe the Virgin brand and who are entrepreneurs themselves."

Anyone can build this type of brand loyalty. But once you have your solution figured out, you have to become dedicated to developing a meaningful cultural experience and finding the right fit for the fans who believe in you and your startup. In this chapter, we'll explore some of the cultural elements needed to build this loyalty and help you start building your Culture of WOW.

As you develop your Culture of WOW, there are specific elements that you will need to incorporate into your equation:

- **Values (Val):** The basic elements of how we work and the beliefs tied to that work.
- **Balance (Bal):** Making sure that there is an even distribution of weight and importance among areas of your startup and within people's lives.
- **Symbols (Sym):** Items that represent the values of your startup.
- **Creativity (Cre):** The ability to use imaginative ideas.
- **Stories (Sto):** Narratives that can be used to communicate on behalf of your startup.

As we go through the chapter, we'll walk through how you can find each of these elements for your startup and the right mix of elements for your team.

CULTURE STARTS WITH THE PERSON AT THE TOP

What separates startups from existing companies? Culture plays an integral role. At startups, a fun and exciting culture often becomes a

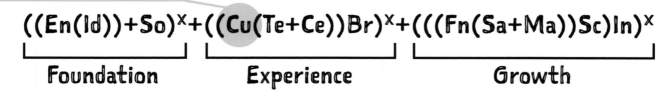

$$((En(Id))+So)^X+((Cu(Te+Ce))Br)^X+(((Fn(Sa+Ma))Sc)In)^X$$

Foundation **Experience** **Growth**

Great businesses begin with that one great idea, and there are some key characteristics in what makes a great idea. One of those aspects is the culture you embrace for your startup. In our Startup Table of Elements, we separate Culture (Cu) elements into two categories: Core and Additive.

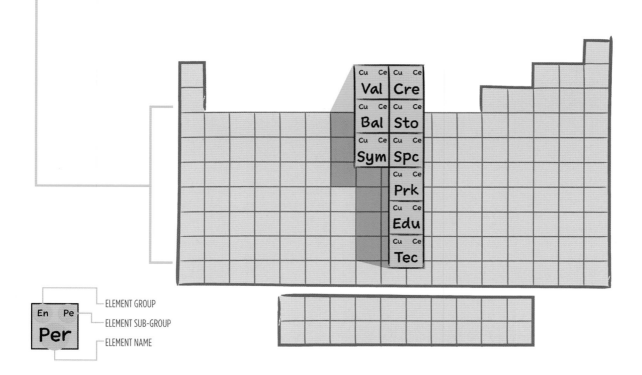

ELEMENT GROUP
ELEMENT SUB-GROUP
ELEMENT NAME

CORE CULTURE (CU) ELEMENTS

Core culture elements are the fundamental essence and underlying value in what makes a company's culture. Healthy core culture helps increase the productivity and growth of an organization.

Values (Val)
Your business will eventually need a set of core values to give your company an internal guide to live by, preferably something actionable that's easy for people to understand

Balance (Bal)
Many entrepreneurs talk about having balance, which can be setting deliberate boundaries or seamlessly integrating work life with your personal life.

Symbols (Sym)
Symbols represent the values of a company and can act as a calling card and can come in many shapes and forms, including logos and phrases.

Creativity (Cre)
Work environments should be designed to empower creative thought. Creativity needs to be embedded in your culture. Creativity fosters innovation.

Stories (Sto)
Stories are a direct, proactive way to learn new information because we're required to engage to understand them.

ADDITIVE CULTURE (CU) ELEMENTS

Core culture elements are the fundamental essence and underlying value in what makes a company's culture. Healthy core culture helps increase the productivity and growth of an organization.

Spaces (Spc)
Space is a way to inspire collaborative and social work, while also creating areas for individual work and processing of information.

Perks (Prk)
Personal creative benefits to motivate your employees, spark creativity in the workplace and help the organization move forward.

Education (Edu)
You never stop learning and it is important to have that constant educational thread running through your culture, so that skill sets can increase and morph with the changing tides

Technology (Tec)
We look to technology to be our research assistant, the center of our businesses, and our brain trust. It can also help us communicate.

cornerstone, but one that adapts to the team. The creation of a great culture, however, doesn't happen magically. It takes dedication and a desire to invest in improving the lives of every employee.

Tony Hsieh, the founder of Zappos, knows a thing or two about intentionally building a Culture of WOW from the top.[1] Zappos may have started out as a company known for selling shoes, but it's now equally well-known for its culture. It took time for that to happen. Much of what Tony learned came through his first company, LinkExchange. In a *TechCrunch* interview with Kevin Rose, Tony offered this advice:[2]

> From the beginning, company culture was always important. Is this someone I would choose to hang out with or grab a drink with, if we weren't in business? If the answer was no, we wouldn't hire them.

Much like a family dynamic, your business will eventually need a set of **Values (Val)** to give your company an internal guide to live by, preferably something actionable that's easy for people to understand. Identifying your company's mission is also key because it serves as a beacon for easy reference when you need to confront the question, "What's the reason for my company's existence?"

Companies like Zappos and HubSpot built their culture around their core values and even let people go when if it becomes apparent that the mission and values don't align with an employee. If you reach a point where you think your company needs an established set of values, don't force the issue. Chances are you already have values that dictate how you work, but you haven't articulated them yet. We suggest working backwards.

Observe how you do things. Then, think about why you do them. Now you've got a good idea of your values. It doesn't hurt to get input from other people. Often the people in your company can recognize the daily practices and articulate why you do things a certain way.

The Relationship Between Space and Culture

New paradigms of knowledge, education, creation, and technology have changed the way we work and interact. We now share knowledge and create content collaboratively in a variety of environments. Even though the world is our sandbox, a startup's physical space remains crucial for fostering its creative identity and trust.

Vince Pan, the founder of Boston-based Analogue Studio, knows a lot about how to design space to fit a culture's values. We had a chance to ask him how he designs great spaces that fit the business and the people. What follows is our Q&A with him.

SEQ: How do you think office design impacts or affects the company's culture?

Pan: Obviously, we feel it's important. There's a few different ways that we feel it affects organizations. One is at a very basic level. How you set up your desks says a lot about who you are and how you work and how you relate to one another. What we find a lot of times is that when you inherit a space, you just start to work in it. Young organizations, they've got a million things going on, and it's not one of the top-of-mind things, but just thinking about how you're placing key members, how you're placing new team members, how you are organizing yourselves and furniture matters.

SEQ: When entrepreneurs get ready to think of their own space and what kind of culture they should create, what should they keep in mind?

Pan: Generally, the number one thing that we ask is where's the communal space? Where is it and how do you use it? How's it integrating into the flow of things, because it can be the heart of an organization or it can just be the place where nobody goes depending on where you put it.

EXERCISE: Setting Your Core Values

Before you can ask anyone else to believe in you or your business, you need to know what it is that YOU believe in. A company's values can seamlessly combine with people's individual values. This approach changed everything for Zappos and can work for you, too. Start with these steps:

1. **Break stakeholders up into small groups.** These groups can be founders, managers, or anyone who sets the tone for a cohort within your company.

2. **Ask them to share their personal values.** Send them each an email asking them to define in a short phrase the 3-5 key values that guide them personally. Feel free to emphasize that you're looking for the things that define who they are.

3. **Look for themes.** Go through the responses and find themes or repeated values. Then, narrow the list down to the 10 values shared by the most people.
4. **Take time to reflect.** Meet with your small groups and reflect on the results. Then collectively brainstorm how you can begin to implement and test these values within your culture.
5. **Share the love.** Once you have a game plan in place, share the process and the findings with your company, and how you're going to test these shared values.
6. This level of transparency and collaboration will show that you are firmly committed to having people get to know and trust one another.

Then ask the following questions:

1. **What are your beliefs about yourself?** What can't you live without? Do you believe that chocolate pudding should flow freely through the streets on Fridays? Write down 10-20 things that you believe in as a person.
2. **What are your beliefs about the company?** Why did you start this company? What should this company stand for? Why should people buy from you? Make a list of 10-20 things that you believe make this company special.
3. **Where do you see overlap?** Now, take a look at both lists and circle the common answers. Look for those to be your guideposts.
4. **What are the top 3-5 values?** From this list, pick 3-5 values that you want your startup to support. They will be the starting point for your Culture of WOW.

EXERCISE: Unlocking Your Core Values

It's not always easy to identify the core values of your company. At first, they may look like one thing, but as the company grows, those values may change as the culture changes. Though you may want them to stay the same, it's natural and healthy for them to adapt. From the personal values exercise, now focus on the stakeholders and the broader values (Val) you will need to determine and work through these questions:

- What is our company's broader purpose?

- What impact does our company want to make on the world?
- What do we want be known for?
- How do we want to treat employees?
- How do we want to treat customers?
- Why do we act the way we act and do the things we do?
- What is most important to our employees?
- What is most important to our stakeholders? Exceeding customer expectations?
- What is most important to our customers?

Based on those answers, consider the values and ethics that are needed to help you achieve your broader impact on the world and the people who are helping you. By setting the bar together, you empower others to focus on what's important, while giving them a sense of ownership and accountability. This should focus you on creating a list of core values (Val) that your company will stand behind and create an enduring culture.

FINDING THE RIGHT CULTURE MIX

How is startup culture defined and what makes a startup great? Corey McAveeney, founder of Kulturenvy, evaluates startup culture and helps companies craft their individual cultural mix. We sat down with her to talk about startup culture and her journey as an entrepreneur.

SEQ: What is startup culture and how is it different from corporate culture?

McAveeney: Startup culture is a shared set of values, practices, behaviors, and beliefs that manifest at companies in the startup environment or companies that have outgrown the startup moniker, but are striving to maintain the high impact, high energy, and cohesion of a high-growth team. People want to contribute to something meaningful, and the tradeoffs they're willing to sacrifice are different from what previous generations sought from their careers.

SEQ: Why is it important to measure your startup culture?

McAveeney: Focusing on the effectiveness of various startup culture aspects helps companies realize outcomes previously thought to be unattainable. Startup culture analysis looks at what tools you use to communicate, develop relationships, and how individuals' behaviors influence team performance and dynamics. This information, along with a customized strategy, helps a team see the potential of its unique culture and its impact on daily operations and long-term outcomes.

Use Symbols (Sym) and Stories (Sto) to Craft Your Culture

Symbols (Sym) are one of the most dynamic tools an entrepreneur can use to help build their culture. They represent the values of a company and can act as a calling card, sort of like membership in a secret club. Symbols can come in many shapes and forms, including logos, phrases, success stories, and images. Entrepreneurs who intentionally introduce symbols into company culture do so with the intention of building something bigger than themselves.

We're also told that we should tell stories. Why do stories matter to your business and your company culture? **Stories (Sto)** are a direct, easy-to-understand form of communication.[3] When we read or hear a story, our brains absorb the plot as we try to make sense of it. It's a proactive way to learn new information because we're required to engage to understand the story.

> In a world where people have a lot of choices, the story may be the deciding factor.
> —*Nick Morgan*

When people talk about your company, they want to share things that are relatable and repeatable. By sharing stories with your team, and encouraging them to share stories, too, you're helping people both in and outside your business identify with your company and share the company's values and essence in a meaningful way.

EXERCISE: Honing Your Company Story

When asked how you started your business, you want to tell a story that grabs people's attention, while showcasing how you help solve your customers' problems. Here are three ways to hone your story:

1. **Write it down.** Write down your story as you would tell it to someone. Use your voice, and focus on being clear and as brief as possible.

2. **Identify your add-ins.** There are two vital things usually missing from every first draft of the founder's story: the emotion and the why. People connect with stories through emotion. Try telling your story in a way that stirs emotions while explaining why you started your company.

3. **Don't be afraid to streamline.** Many stories are too long. Details important to us may not be important to the listener. Read over your story, and you'll likely see some fat you can trim from your story. If you need a little extra help, then record yourself or read it to a friend for some feedback.

Remember, a story can make or break a person's connection to your startup. Give them something to believe in.

Utilize Perks (Prk) in the Right Way

Personal needs motivate most people. To truly engage individuals, look for ways to offer people something they value. Startups often can't afford huge monetary rewards or everyone taking time off to go to Costa Rica for a week. But you can come up with creative benefits to motivate your employees, spark creativity in the workplace, and help the organization move forward. **Perks (Prk)** are a fun, simple tool to help with that very thing. We're talking simple benefits like a Thirsty Thursday or allowing dogs at work. Look for ways to engage your employees that don't require big financial commitments.

Leverage Technology (Tec) and Education (Edu) as Weapons of Mass Retention

Technology (Tec) plays a big role in our startup culture and shapes our attitudes about when it's appropriate to use it. As a result, our increasing comfort with technology has led to a startup culture focused on innovation while larger, slower-moving companies have struggled to adapt. Companies like Blackberry, who have dealt with this struggle, find themselves left out in the cold and unable to transition.

As an entrepreneur, you will never stop learning. You will wear many hats at the same time and may have to learn on your feet. However, by making it a point to educate yourself about what's most important in each area of your business, and doing it efficiently, you can make your business a success.

Even as your startup grows into a small business, your team's desire to continue their individual **Education (Edu)** will be crucial. As trends and industries change, it's even more important to have that constant educational thread running through your culture, so that skill sets can increase and morph with the changing tides. Of course, education comes in many forms. Whether you choose formal classes like those found on Lynda.com or an informal option like a mentorship, find the right mix of education that supports your efforts and your team's efforts to stay ahead of the curve.

CREATING THE RIGHT CULTURAL BALANCE

We all make hiring mistakes. It's a common mistake to hire someone who seems similar to you. You're often looking for balance, and hiring your twin doesn't provide that balance. Depending on your industry, it can prove challenging to get good people, but it's worth the effort to get the hire right the first time. So instead of hiring another version of you, we suggest look for the following qualities:

1. **Complementary Skills:** You don't need someone who has your exact skill set unless you plan to take a sabbatical or you expect this person to take your place.

2. **Willing to Disagree:** Some of the most amazing breakthroughs come when your opinions are challenged. By building a team with different perspectives, you'll boost the potential for idea generation and add constructive criticism to the discussion. If your employees don't feel comfortable speaking up and offering valid feedback, you can't support an innovative culture.

The Hiring Gut Test

Over time, you'll need to practice relying on your gut. It's easier said than done. We've all probably had a moment when we didn't know how to trust our gut or believed it's wrong. It took us a long time to trust our guts.

For instance, during new employee interviews, Ja-Naé discovered that she'd feel an initial reaction that was quickly followed by an immediate, secondary reaction that *seemed* much stronger. So, she went with that second reaction.

"Of course," said Ja-Naé, "Every time I followed that second reaction and jumped in head first, it turned into a disaster." However, once she found a way to trust her gut, Ja-Naé still wondered if she missed an opportunity to hire the next superstar. "The key for me was focusing on my initial impressions and incorporating a method for evaluating a candidate against what I knew the company needed." We've discovered three ways to help you identify potential candidates so you can learn to trust your gut.

Invite Others to the Hiring Process

Even if you're a company of one, bring in at least two trusted colleagues to assist with the process. It allows you to see how candidates interact with other people and shows you how others interview.

Test Your Candidates

Anyone can learn your business, but not everyone comes with the skill set and ability to fit your company culture. Start by creating a 3–5 question test that immerses candidates in your culture and provides a chance to demonstrate their abilities. Provide scenarios they may encounter in their potential job to see how they tackle a problem.

Measure on Passion and Potential

Many things can be learned, but passion cannot. As you explore candidates, identify their passions and if they align with your company's values. But how do you measure passion? As part of the hiring process, assign a small, test project related to your company. Then, look at two things: (1) the results of the project and (2) how the candidate approached the project. Did they reveal an inner drive that you can tap and direct? If so, you've found someone you can nurture who will help build your business.

You may have heard the saying that not everyone auditions well. The same is true with interviews. Use your gut to weed out the "absolutely nots," then, test run the candidates who show potential, but you're just not sure of. You may be surprised at what you discover when you give someone a chance.

Culture Snapshot: Fresh Tilled Soil

Fresh Tilled Soil, a Boston-based creative services firm that prides itself on bespoke or custom-built applications, worked with Kulturenvy to develop a stellar culture. Corey McAveeny describes them as "a small team with impressive ambition. They're able to move in fast due in large part to their culture. It's not a culture they manufactured overnight."

Defining Respectful Boundaries

The lines can blur when you're an entrepreneur. When Ja-Naé started Wild Women Entrepreneurs, she started it with three friends. Then came the problem. How do you tell a friend you don't think they're working smart enough?

Ja-Naé's decision didn't have long-term consequences, but it did highlight that hiring friends comes with issues. Of course, it's not automatically a mistake to hire someone you have a personal relationship with (after all, we're married and writing this book together). However, it requires setting boundaries and benchmarks that everyone agrees to. Here are three ways to find the perfect balance:

1. **Set Parameters:** Before you ever have that first conversation with a friend about working together, know your limits. How will you handle mistakes? Know and accept where your lines are before you try to draw the line with anyone else.

2. **Set Standards:** You may want to treat everyone equally, but it's sometimes impossible. One time, Ja-Naé served as Director of Marketing at a startup whose CEO hired his mother-in-law as a graphic designer, but she reported to Ja-Naé. You can guess whose opinion the CEO supported and which startup is now trying to fund raise again.

   If you bring on a friend or family member that reports to someone else, make it clear their direct boss has the final say. If this person reports to you, remove all ambiguity by setting specific expectations.

3. **Set Benchmarks:** Not everything is quantitative, but many jobs have quantitative aspects. Settle on mutually agreed benchmarks. Then, if performance issues arise, you both have a foundation for that conversation. Also, we've talked about hiring friends, but what about a business romance?

   We've seen it happen over and over. As the owner, you need to be extremely careful. People have lost their businesses over a fling. If

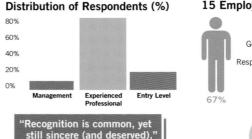

KULTURENVY PROFILE: FRESH TILLED SOIL

WORKPLACE CULTURE

Distribution of Respondents (%)   **15 Employees Surveyed**

Management — Experienced Professional — Entry Level

Gender of Respondents

67%   33%

"Recognition is common, yet still sincere (and deserved)."

"Whenever an employee has achieved a milestone (launched a major project, received press, praise, or recognition from a client, or gone the extra mile for a client or an internal project) management shares this with the entire team. This happens via company-wide email or a weekly company meeting, and also in more informal settings."

73%

Of respondents "Strongly Agree" they have a healthy work-life balance (the remaining 27% "Agree" they have a healthy work-life balance)

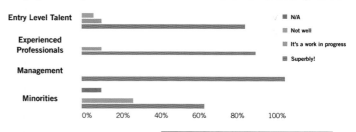

Employee Perception – Fresh Tilled Soil Can Retain the Following Talent:

Entry Level Talent — Experienced Professionals — Management — Minorities

- N/A
- Not well
- It's a work in progress
- Superbly!

0%   20%   40%   60%   80%   100%

73% of respondents "Strongly Agree" that they identify easily with the company mission.

"We have frequent interactions beyond that required for work alone. I attend frequently, and most employees attend with enough frequency to indicate that they enjoy it rather than think of it as an obligation. Everyone has a good time."

* Data Source: Kulturenvy LLC

Figure 8.3 **Kulturenvy Culture Profile: Fresh Tilled Soil**

you're truly in love, do yourself and the other person a favor and put an agreement in writing. It sounds cold, but don't underestimate the cost of a business romance gone bad.

SUPPORTING BALANCE, PREVENTING BURNOUT

Pursuing an entrepreneur's life means needing to consider the difficulties that tend to come with this choice. Among entrepreneurs, the question of balance comes up often. Though many entrepreneurs talk about having **Balance (bal)**, they don't explain how to make it a priority when the list of to-dos gets really long.

The balancing act is different for everyone, but equilibrium is possible even for you! Some entrepreneurs set deliberate boundaries while others seamlessly integrate their work life with their personal life (if such a thing exists). Many entrepreneurs only manage a haphazard home life while forging full steam ahead professionally. It's very easy to lose yourself in the process. However, if a balance isn't found, you'll burn out.

When you feel your productivity slowing, spend twenty minutes doing something else. Ja-Naé will read, break out her sketchpad, or head to the piano. Find activities that help you reenergize so when you come back to that list, you're ready to tackle it again. While Ja-Naé relies on more "mental" activities, Steve turns to yoga and running to center and calm him. He's also started meditating, another option that's known to calm and focus the mind. Identify 3-5 activities that reenergize you and help you find that internal balance.

What ways can you add balance to your company and culture? Both you and your team will need it to stay sane.

It's Not About You—It's About Them

Many CEOs and founders think they are their culture. While they may set the tone for their employees, other important dynamics exist. When you build something from the ground up, it's hard to see the forest for the trees.

EXERCISE: Crafting Your Startup Culture

When starting a business, it's easy for a culture to organically evolve without even thinking about it. However, you want to make sure that you're establishing a culture that you and your employees can support. Here are a few steps to help you get started:

1. **Observe:** What does your real culture look like versus what you think it looks like? How do people engage with each other? Where do people gather? What do people avoid? Make a list of everything that you observe. Once you have that list, go through and identify:

   - Observed patterns
   - Natural leaders/influencers
   - Vital behaviors that lead to results
   - Obstacles that block a culture change

2. **Set a Goal:** After you've observed what your real company culture looks like, set a small, specific goal for yourself. How do you want to change your company culture? Start small to avoid overwhelming others, which may stop you from achieving your goal.

3. **Recruit Help:** Acknowledging that it's not just about you will help you extend your reach and include others in your efforts to implement the culture you want. This process can also help you see issues that you may be too close to see otherwise. Encourage and empower others to expand your vision.

CLOSING THE CREATIVITY GAP

What if you could do your best thinking at work? If you're like most people, work rarely provides the time or creative space to think. Most work environments aren't designed to empower creative thought. Think about that paradox.

Organizations turn to employees for new ideas or products, but most employees feel their work environment stifles creativity. Many large organizations implement their own **Creativity (Cre)** strategies. Others turn to startups for elements that can be scaled. The physical surroundings and a culture of trust and innovation aren't the only aspects of a thriving creative culture. There's also the reality that startups are inherently closer to failure and willing to take risks more established organizations won't.

However, the shocking results of Adobe's 2012 State of Create highlight a gap between workplace expectations and the reality of creativity.[4] Only one in four employees believe they live up to their own creative potential. The remaining 75 percent said they face growing pressure to be productive, but not creative, at work.

These staggering statistics make it apparent that the "creativity gap" is growing, and we need to take action. With employees hungry for creative opportunities, managers can support innovation and ignite workplace creativity with three small, but powerful, moves you'll want to embrace because it's time to close the gap.

EXERCISE: **Closing the Creativity Gap**

Allowing creativity to be a core element in your culture mix is a great way to come up with original ideas and new ways to go to market. The following steps will help you close the creativity gap within your own startup.

1. **Set Clearly Defined Goals:** Make sure the goal has a measureable outcome and a deadline. It's not compelling to say, "I want everyone to come up with new ideas." However, what if you said, "I want twenty people to submit new product ideas by December 31, 2014, at 12:00 p.m." See the difference? A clear goal engages us and helps others understand what you want to achieve.

2. **Create Intersections:** Great ideas often come from the intersections created when people with different backgrounds and different mindsets collide. The key is to find them, encourage them, and use them to your advantage. Look to see what intersections already exist. It may be the office kitchen or lounge, maybe even someone's desk. Observe where people congregate naturally and use those spaces to help inspire more intersections that support your goals.

3. **Reward Failure—Strategically:** During her live cooking show, Julia Child often made mistakes and left ingredients out. Production budgets were tight, so she had only one shot each time. But when she made a mistake, she'd laugh about it and alter the recipe. Her creative confidence not only humanized her brand, but also demonstrated that making a mistake can still lead to good things.

To encourage creative risk, consider rewarding failure—strategically. Make a list of 3-5 ways you can do the following:

- Encourage the execution of ideas
- Only reward a failure the first time and require that a person learn from it
- Only hire people who are upfront about their failures and willing to learn from them

Everyone fails from time to time but you can use those moments to explore and reward **Creativity (Cre)** whenever possible, including creating an open innovation loop. This approach empowers creative risk and helps people feel their ideas are valued.

LEVERAGING COWORKING AND MAKERSPACES

How we work now doesn't look like it did fifty years ago. For the most part, the cubicle is dead. We no longer "go" to work. It's often all around us, both a good and bad thing. You may not have experienced it directly, but you've probably heard of telecommuting, telework, or online work. Ever-improving technology blurs the lines between our professional and personal lives. At the same time, our work is less routine and more focused on outcomes.

As a result, motivated people come together to foster collaborative work based around results. It's given life to the idea of coworking and makerspaces, concepts we introduced in Chapter 3.

Entrepreneurs use **Spaces (Spc)** as a way to inspire collaborative and social work, while also creating areas for individual work and information processing. As companies evolve, so do the working dynamics within that company. Build a flexible space so that you and your employees can rearrange it to adapt to your immediate needs.

Coworking spaces usually offer modern, uber-efficient environments where mobile professionals can make connections and collaborate on creative projects. The collaborative nature of the coworking community embraces a project-oriented work model. The physical density of coworking spaces allows talented professionals to come together in mutually beneficial ways and often spawns startups that bring this sharing mindset to the new global economy.

Makerspaces are similar to coworking in that people gather at physical locations, share resources and knowledge, work on projects, and network. But they differ because people physically build something in these spaces.

A makerspace provides the tools and room to build in a community environment. The makerspace often gets associated with fields like engineering, computer science, and graphic design.

Spaces like these increase the odds of making more connections, which in turn makes it easier for ideas to grow and spread. In the most recent Global Coworking Survey, the data shows that 71 percent of participants reported a boost in creativity since joining a coworking space, while 62 percent said their standard of work improved.

Your Coworking or Maker Space Checklist

As coworking grows, so have the available models. Before, all you would see were '90s-style cube farms. Now you'll find collaborative spaces, open-floor plans, and fridges holding gallon-sized energy drinks.

Higher up the coworking pyramid are the curated communities, like LaunchPad in New Orleans, Workbar in Boston, Indy Hall in Philadelphia, Google Campus in London, and The Hub, which has locations around the world. They're designed to encourage cross-pollination.

According to Eze Vidra, the head of Google Campus in London, more than 1,000 entrepreneurs come through every week. It's becoming ground zero for the London tech scene with old warehouses morphing into coworking spaces and funky startup offices.

In order to get started here is a checklist of things to look for/ask about when evaluating a coworking or maker space:

1. **Cost:** Do they have a free day you can test out? Do they have different packages to fit your needs and your growth? This includes permanency—can you use the same desk or space everyday? Is it hard to get a seat? Do you have to pack up your stuff everyday?

2. **Hours of Business:** You may not need a space 24 hours a day but do they have access (e.g. keycard) available when you want to work?

3. **Facilities:** How many outlets are next to each workspace? What are the Internet capabilities? Do they have IT procedures to handle IT issues? Do they have printing services? Dedicated mailbox? If you are looking at Makerspaces, do they have the equipment you need for your projects? Training classes for the equipment?

4. **Comfortable Seating/Desk Options:** You need good seating options, and that includes desk options, like standing desks.

5. **People:** You left the work-from-home/coffee shop to remove the isolation, and these are people that, even though you may not work with them, will interact and you'll get to know.

6. **Networking/Education:** One of the great things about coworking is community. Heck, that is what the "co" part of coworking stands for, and most coworking/makerspaces have classes and networking events to bring the members together but also bring the outside community in to see the space and engage the larger community.

7. **Surroundings:** What is the style of the space? Does the "vibe" fit your style? What are your lunch options? Do they have lunch as a perk? What is your commute like? Public transportation options?

8. **Culture Perks:** Many spaces have perks that contribute to the surroundings but also contribute to the culture and appeal of the space. This can include, coffee machines, microbrew taps, and soda but it can also include partnerships with companies to bring in things to try.

9. **Privacy:** Most coworking is an open space, but you might want to use conference spaces or places to make private phone calls (phone booths/rooms) and even private offices if your work is sensitive or you have a few people that you want to have in one place.

GETTING READY . . .

Building a Culture of WOW doesn't happen by accident. It takes commitment to build something greater than just a company. Make sure you complete the following exercises in this chapter as you prepare to build your own unique Startup Equation.

- Unlocking Your Core Values
- Setting Your Core Values
- Honing Your Company Story
- Crafting Your Startup Culture

Te

Team

CRAFT THE EXPERIENCE

- The Single Founder vs Co-Founding Team
- How to Find The Right Co-founder
- Recruiting the A-Team
- Leveraging Great Mentors and Advisors
- Building and Leveraging Great Advisory Boards
- Crafting a Stellar Board of Directors

MENTORS · Designer · Marketer · Hacker · Expert · Hustler · ADVISORS

Original Sketch by Kate Rutter

CHAPTER 9

The main ingredient of stardom is the rest of the team.

—*John Wooden*

Rewards of Great Teams

Francis Upton. John Kruesi. Charles Batcheldor. Ludwig Boehm. While we're familiar with the great inventions that changed the world, and perhaps even know the names of the main inventors, it required amazing teams to make these ideas reality. And those names we listed to start? Francis Upton was a Princeton-trained mathematician. John Kruesi was a Swiss clockmaker. Charles Batcheldor was an English machinist. Ludwig Boehm was a German glassblower. All of these men had varied backgrounds, yet they were all a part of the same team dedicated to one purpose.

They were all attracted to a quiet town in New Jersey called Menlo Park by a force of nature: Thomas Edison. We know Edison was brilliant, but his inventions, like the light bulb and phonograph, came to life because he had a great team. Edison's gift for bringing the right people together allowed him to tap into their special skills and turn his vision into a steady stream of workable products.

Francis Upton purchased the mechanical instruments and Batcheldor's dexterous hands threaded the carbon filament into the bulb that Boehm then turned into a vacuum space. Through the efforts of five men, the world was introduced to the electric light bulb on October 22, 1879.

Looking back through history, we can find many great stories of great teams. The Mac team at Apple. The Ford Taurus team in Detroit. The Lockheed Skunkworks team. All of them had superstars working alongside one another revolutionizing their industries.

When you build your founding team, look for people who offer a mix of the following types. We consider each type important, but recognize

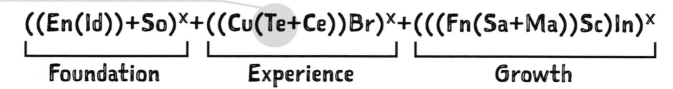

$$((En(Id))+So)^X+((Cu(Te+Ce))Br)^X+(((Fn(Sa+Ma))Sc)In)^X$$

Foundation	Experience	Growth

As we continue to build our company and craft the experience, no great company exists without a great team. It is more important than your product. These people are your work family and can make the company a success or contribute to its downfall.

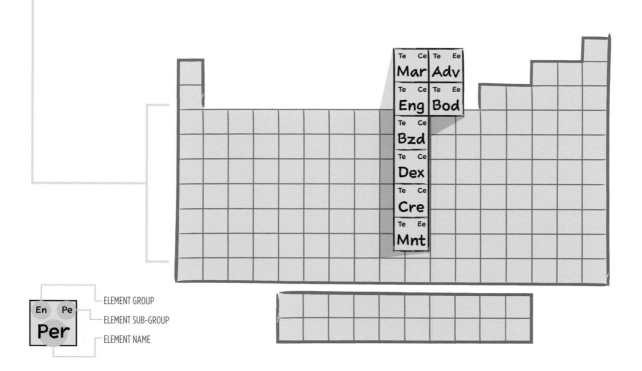

ELEMENT GROUP
ELEMENT SUB-GROUP
ELEMENT NAME

CORE TEAM (TE) ELEMENTS

You never want to hire yourself. That is boring and a recipe for disaster. These are the general types of team members who might be some of your co-founders and definitely part of the core team.

The Marketer (Mar)
Marketer excels at communicating and knows how to engage customers.

The Technical Engineer or Hacker (Eng)
A strong scientific and/or technical background means the Technical Engineer usually takes the lead on developing the product.

The Biz Developer or Hustler (Bzd)
Making a startup successful requires customers. The Biz Developer will close the deal.

The Domain Expert (Dex)
The Domain Expert brings to the table experience and knowledge of your industry that other founders lack.

The Creative or Designer (Cre)
The Creative can visualize the possibilities, translates the vision into wireframes and creates experiences to build or code.

EXTENDED TEAM (TE) ELEMENTS

These are your trusted circles that have experience to guide you and provide the oversight to make you successful. They are the mentors, advisors and board of directors that your company will leverage in their startup equation.

The Mentor (Mnt)
Mentors are the powerful allies that are there for you and provide advice, perspective and guidance that transform you.

The Advisory Board (Adv)
These are the experts with particular knowledge that lend credibility and time in exchange for upside and ownership in your success.

Board of Directors (Bod)
These are the group that the CEO reports to who provide fiduciary oversight and guidance to protect the shareholders' assets and ensure that they receive a decent return on their investment.

that it may take time to add more people to your team who demonstrate these qualities.

- **The Marketer (Mar):** When we think of great teams, we immediately identify the person who takes the role of lead evangelist and engages people. The **Marketer (Mar)** excels at communicating and knows how to engage customers.

- **The Technical Engineer or the Hacker (Eng):** Many startups have a technical founder/co-founder. A strong scientific and/or technical background means the **Technical Engineer (Eng)** often takes the lead on development.

- **The Biz Developer or Hustler (Bzd):** The *Marketer* can weave the message that captures their attention, but the **Biz Developer (Bzd)** closes the deal. A charismatic personality gets people to commit their money and attention to the startup. Most founders discover some of this element in themselves.

- **The Domain Expert (Dex):** Much like the Technical Engineer, your startup needs someone that knows the space, but with a different perspective. The **Domain Expert (Dex)** offers experience and industry knowledge other founders lack. You may discover this role fits people on your advisory board perfectly.

- **The Creative or The Designer (Des):** You might think of marketing when you think of the **Creative (Des)** role, but it goes beyond taglines and logos. The *Creative* co-founder can visualize the possibilities and translate the vision into wireframes for the *Technical Engineer* to build or code. This co-founder brings a much-needed design perspective to building and launching your product/service.

In this chapter we'll dig into finding team members and how to work with them.

THE SINGLE FOUNDER VS CO-FOUNDING TEAM

What is a founder? Some people define it differently, but for our purposes, let's agree on a definition of a founder in the context of a startup. From the many ways people try to define it we propose *"Founders are people who create, invest, and execute ideas by transforming them into startups."*

Conventional wisdom suggests that your startup needs a co-founder. We hear it often. Accelerators and venture capitalists (VCs) love founding teams. Of the single-founder startups Noam Wasserman studied, he found that only 16.1% got funding.[1]

Among investors, you'll find a general bias against startups with only one founder. It's assumed that one person can't do it alone, but that assumption creates a paradox. While two people may share a vision, many a startup idea came from one person whose vision and drive then attracted others to the startup.

It's also assumed that one person can't be excellent at marketing, sales, technology, and running the business simultaneously. Based on these realities, if you plan to pursue outside investments, you may get taken more seriously if you're joined by a co-founder. That said, the push for a co-founder often comes more from investor fear than legitimate concerns about a single founder's abilities. We've started companies individually and with co-founders. Both options come with positives and negatives.

Going it alone can help keep you focused, but if you need to scale quickly, you might find the solo path difficult. Of course, many startups want to stay small, and a single founder can work fine in these situations. Going it alone also means less accountability. Eventually, however, the time will come to hire employees, and if you want your business to grow, you'll need to hire people smarter than you. Then, you'll need to trust them to fail and succeed, otherwise you'll hit a point where you can no longer grow your business and manage the day-to-day operations by yourself.

Steve's dad had a successful business for thirty-five years and loved to share great sayings about business, but one in particular had a lasting impression. "If you can't go away on vacation, and things don't run, you haven't created anything of value." You don't want to get locked in the mindset of, "They can't run things without me."

On the flip side, when you run a business alone, you're for the most part, alone. As a single founder, you won't have anyone that shares your burden and understands your fears and frustrations.

The Co-Founder Paradox

Let's assume you've decided to bring on a co-founder or two. What does that really mean? Well, it's a lot like dating. You have no idea how things will work out at the end. You just need to keep putting yourself out there until you find the right fit.

Adding co-founders also represents a vote of confidence in your startup. With co-founders, you show other potential team members that your idea convinced the smartest people you know to join you on this adventure. One of Steve's dad's other great sayings addressed the issue of money and ownership. "It's better to have 20 percent of a $50 million dollar business then 90 percent of a $200,000 business." So don't let the fear of losing out on ownership stop you from seeing the benefit of bringing in co-founders.

So, How Many Co-Founders?

We're reluctant to set a hard number on this question. We've seen great companies succeed with three or more co-founders, and many readers of this book will go on to create companies with multiple co-founders. However, our experience suggests that too many co-founders can lead to friction. While conflict isn't guaranteed with multiple co-founders, it does seem more common. It can lead to wasting time and money, so getting the number right from the beginning benefits everyone. Because things change, we strongly recommend what we call a Founders Prenup.

The Founder's Prenup

In the United States, people getting married have the option to sign a prenuptial agreement clearly outlining what each person will receive if the marriage ends, including specific clauses regarding forfeiture or voiding of the agreement (e.g., infidelity). It can simplify things later because it requires a discussion of complicated issues ahead of time and makes things easier if the relationship stops working.

It's hard to ignore the similarities between a marriage and the relationship you have with a co-founder. Let's walk through a potential scenario. Assume you start a company with a good friend and split ownership 50/50. Of course, if it becomes the next Google or YouTube, you'll always stay friends. But we'll add a twist. What if your co-founder isn't a good friend, but instead someone you brought on as the **Technical Engineer (Eng)** and you're the **Biz Developer (Bzd)**?

You met through your network and think you have good working chemistry that balances the other person. But in reality 99.99% of companies do not become the next Twitter. In fact, instead of becoming an overnight success, it's taking longer to gain traction, and there are bills to pay. Between the two of you, how do you decide who gets to take a full-time job elsewhere while the other keeps working on the new business?

Does the partnership stay 50/50? What if you have to make tough calls on cutting costs, development deals, and fundraising and you can't agree how to proceed? What if your perfect match doesn't turn into a great co-founder like you expected?

As we discussed earlier, these issues grow exponentially with multiple founders. Again, great companies with three-plus founders can succeed and exist without destructive friction. However, you'll increase your odds of success by tackling some of the issues in advance with a Founders Prenup.

HOW TO FIND THE RIGHT CO-FOUNDER

When looking for a co-founder, it's suggested that you put together a co-founder pitch to help with the vetting process. You'll do it before you ever meet a potential co-founder. While you don't need an investor-level presentation at this point, the following structure will help others understand what you expect from a co-founder.

- Who are you?
- What are you best at?
- Founder's FAQ
- Conclude with your pitch

Founder's Frequently Asked Questions:[2]

- If you had a great idea and co-founder, how soon could you quit your job?
- Will family and friends support you living with the uncertainty of a startup?
- Can you live without a paycheck for up to a year?
- How much of your own money are you willing to invest as a co-founder?
- Imagine we crash and burn in six months. What would you do next?
- What hobbies do you have to take your mind off work?
- Do you consider yourself punctual or tardy?
- What are your biggest professional weaknesses?

So you ask the questions and think you've found a potential co-founder, but how do you know if it will work out? The best way to discover if you can work together is to work together. We suggest setting a discrete task to execute together in one week. You'll get a chance to see your potential partner in action. The result will either validate your choice or make you think twice.

We've gone this route a few times—asking someone to work on a project—and gotten the response, "Will I be compensated?" It's understandable, but this response may point to more of a consultant mindset than potential co-founder. The burden does rest on you to make it a realistic project so people don't feel like you're taking advantage of them. Working together to build some basic financial spreadsheets or a few wireframes makes sense. Building a complete financial model or a website does not.

During your test project with your potential co-founder, you'll want to consider:[3]

- Little things about a person that repeatedly frustrate you
- What gets promised versus what gets delivered
- How this person manages time
- The overall commitment to real work
- Do you have fun working with this person

RECRUITING THE A-TEAM

Let's test your knowledge of TV trivia and see if you know this one:

In 1972, a crack commando unit was sent to prison by a military court for a crime they didn't commit. These four men promptly escaped from a maximum-security stockade to the Los Angeles underground.

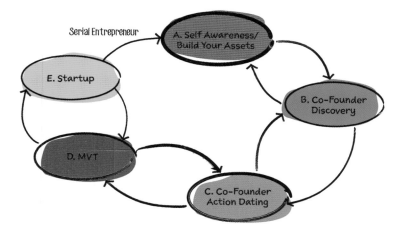

The Co-Founder Development Cycle

Serial Entrepreneur

A. Self Awareness/ Build Your Assets

B. Co-Founder Discovery

C. Co-Founder Action Dating

D. MVT

E. Startup

The A-Team went off the air in 1987 (still wanted by the government), but television has yet to produce a better blueprint for team building. The key elements that made the A-Team so effective? A cigar-chomping master of disguise, an ace pilot, a devilishly handsome con man, a mechanic with a Mohawk, and an amazingly sweet van. Sweet van aside, each member had specific complementary skills with clear ways to contribute, as well as a leader to define the vision and set goals that strive towards the success of that vision.

You'll want to build your own version of the A-Team and create your minimum viable team (MVT) to move your startup closer to success. Here are a few steps to guide you along the way.

Building Your Minimum Viable Team

As you launch and grow your startup, you'll begin to pull your team together. But, how do you figure out the best team mix for right now? Researchers Frank Nouyrigat and Marc Nager from Startup Weekend identified a common trend in that community that didn't really surprise anyone. Founders have a hard time attracting and validating great co-founders.[4] The same holds true for team members.

These results motivated them to come up with an approach called the minimum viable team (MVT). It takes its cues from Steve Blank's *Customer Development* and Eric Ries' *Lean Startup* methodologies by proposing a *capable* team. This group represents the minimal team required to start and grow the company. They also suggest an initial list of questions to help you get through the MVT process:[5]

- Is your team the smallest possible?
- What ideas could you develop with your team's competencies?
- Who do you need to add or remove to get your MVT?

To get started, seek out other places with a high concentration of potential candidates. What competencies do you need most? Perhaps you need a technical co-founder. If so, tech meetups are a logical place to start looking. Recognize that this is not a trivial exercise. It takes time and patience to find the right match.

Nouyrigat and Nager also recommend setting a weekly goal of meeting ten potential candidates. We won't call them dates, but you get the idea. One of the challenges you'll face most often involves geography. You may not be physically close to other possible co-founders. In this situation, you have two choices: (1) become the leader in your community and get everyone together, or (2) move to a place more aligned with your startup. Of course, you can start a company anywhere in the world, but as a startup economy goes, some places are more optimal than others.

If the answers come back positive, you can move from dating your potential co-founder to bringing someone on officially. Now that you've got a co-founder in place, it's time to recruit the rest of your MVT while keeping in mind the important elements that will drive team stability (e.g., roles, equity dilution). Once you have your A-Team and know you can execute, you can then focus on the product, the market, or the fit.

Design Your Minimum Viable Team or MVT

In order to get your best and minimal "A-Team" ready to get your startup going you will need to start with the following:

1. What do you think the initial size of the team should be?
2. Review the types of team members covered earlier in this chapter.
3. Decide if this is going to be a solo or co-founder(s) structure.
4. Draw different organizational charts for the following milestones:
   - Decide who needs to be on board to build the initial concept
   - Decide who needs to be there for the launch
   - Decide who needs to be there for the initial growth phase

You should have at this point drafted out three stages of your startup and if/when co-founders come into the picture as well.

Hiring Friends and Family

We've hired both friends and family with results ranging from good to absolutely horrible. You might think that friends and family will provide inexpensive labor. That labor may come with a far bigger price, so do the following:

- Be clear with the objectives and accountability for their role.
- Be explicit in the terms of hiring and firing.
- Don't set them up as a direct report; keep at least one layer between you.
- If they try to go around their manager, refer them back to their manager and make it clear that it's unacceptable to jump the line.

Hiring someone close to you can work. Steve knows from direct experience. When he started his first company, Steve hired his sister, Laurie, an incredibly organized and a fantastic operations person. Plus, he trusted her with the books and many of the day-to-day tasks.

Social Recruiting

In our experience, and perhaps yours as well, we've determined that personal relationships lead to the best jobs and talent connections almost every time. The reason is that rapport and trust has already been established. People are more likely to do business and help those that they have a connection with.

However, sometimes you need to reach beyond your immediate network to build a startup team. Social networking platforms represent one of the best places to look for talent, no matter what your age. Places like LinkedIn, Twitter, and even Facebook will give you a starting point. However, if you really want to work with people you like, respect, and trust to do the job, stay focused on people two to three degrees separated from you and your immediate network.

Exercise: Strengthening Your Network

A network is only as strong as the relationships in it. Many people will ask and ask, and not give anything back in return, but that's no way to keep a connection. Here are three ways to strengthen your network:

1. **Give to Three People Each Day:** Make a list of 75-100 people in your network. Then make a point to give or do something for three of

them each day. It doesn't have to be big (e.g., a thank-you card), but you perform an act of service.

2. **Make a List of Your Needs:** Most people do not want to be bombarded with people asking favors. However, if you have a specific need, then find the person who may be able to help you the best and ask them. If they cannot help you, then ask them if they know someone who can.

3. **Stop Selling:** Many people look at their network as a way to sell, but they're really your extended team. They can make and break your company. Build them up in the same way you would build up members of your startup team.

Recognizing Your Limitations

Let's face facts. We cannot do it all (or have it all). Trust us, we have both tried. Recognizing your limitations and embracing the potential of powerful teams can liberate you. Once you take the leap and begin building a team you can trust, you'll see parts of the company run completely on their own without requiring your day-to-day input. That's what it means to scale and grow a successful startup.

> You have to get along with people, but you also have to recognize that the strength of a team is different people with different perspectives and different personalities.
>
> —*Steve Case*

Hiring a Team of Rivals

While we don't suggest hiring people who hate you, we do think you should build your startup team with an eye on diverse opinions and complementary values to help propel your company. You'll want to do the same thing as your company grows, and you add people to the team. Hiring like-minded people, but who have a different perspective, will benefit your company. Plus, looking for complementary as opposed to your twin will help you form a team that gets things done versus searching for lightening in a bottle.

> Remember teamwork begins by building trust. And the only way to do that is to overcome our need for invulnerability.
> —*Patrick Lencioni*

Essential Qualities of a Great Startup Team

You've selected co-founders and built a great team. Now what? We've discovered that the truly great teams always have a noble cause. They have extreme clarity about what they want to achieve, live by simple rules, and hold each other accountable.

- **Great teams always have a noble cause.** These teams were not just building companies; they were revolutionizing industries and changing the future. Think about how you can build around something bigger than the company.

- **Effective teams drive engagement.** Engaged employees are those who care about the organization, are willing to give extra effort, and will own problems. People will engage when they receive regular, peer-to-peer recognition, and understand how the work of their group affects the larger organization.

- **Their performance is driven by team, not company, loyalty.** Here's one of our biggest findings, and CEOs hate it. People are more loyal to their teams than to their companies. After all, we love our countries, but aren't we more loyal to our families? It's our nature to band together in small teams for support and encouragement. Great leaders know this and don't fight it. They keep teams together longer (it's a fallacy that team productivity drops off after a few years) and even move great teams together instead of moving stars around.

- **Great teams simplify.** We found that the best teams live by sets of simple rules and hold each member accountable for honoring those rules. We culled the various rules down into the three that were most common: (1) Wow, (2) No Surprises, and (3) Cheer.

Dealing with Dysfunction

For those of you unfamiliar with the term, dysfunction happens when your team doesn't work well together. We might have to deal with a little to a lot of it. The question you need to ask is, "Will you be the awesome startup team that puts the 'funk' in dysfunction or the unhappy startup team that puts 'dis' in dysfunction?"

During the last fifteen years, Steve's held a variety of leadership roles. He's built teams of all shapes and sizes. Part of that process now includes making the bestseller *Five Dysfunctions of a Team* by Patrick Lencioni required reading for all his direct reports. It's a breakthrough book that will make you say, "Of course that's what I should do." Even better, it shows you how to do it well. We set the same goal for this book.

Lencioni does an excellent job of drawing lines from teams who need to achieve results, but fail to do so if they aren't working together. Teams have to promote a winning dynamic, and there isn't room for big egos. While Lencioni covers many different concepts in *Five Dysfunctions*, we've highlighted his core concept in a sketchnote. He takes a cue from Maslow's Hierarchy of Needs (i.e., physiological, safety, love/belonging, esteem, and self-actualization) and created a five-stage pattern of actions that lead to team dysfunction.

1. **Absence of Trust:** It's the biggest barrier to team success, and you need trust to establish a strong foundation for a good organization. A team that doesn't trust will conceal their weaknesses and waste time and energy managing this misbehavior. They fail to tap into the skills of the team.

2. **Fear of Conflict:** Few things are more frustrating than yes-men and women telling you what you want to hear. It's productive to debate company behaviors, processes, services, and products.

3. **Lack of Commitment:** Healthy teams will have debate and conflict. However, once a decision gets made, everyone gets behind it.

4. **Avoidance of Accountability:** It seems like many teams at big companies get away with avoiding accountability in spite of the structure and rules. However, a lack of team-member accountability can kill a small startup.

5. **Inattention to Results:** When teams try to focus on fifty different things, they're not really focused on anything. It's a harsh reality, but easily distracted teams will fail to grow and so will your company.

The Five Dysfunctions of a Team

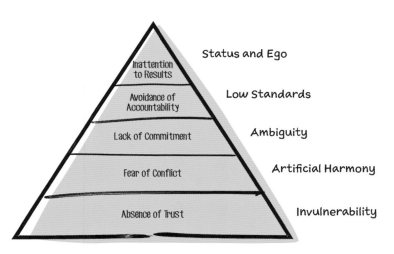

LEVERAGING GREAT
MENTORS AND ADVISORS

Having a great **Mentor (Mnt)** can be a transformative experience. In the strictest sense, mentoring is a one-to-one relationship between an experienced professional who shares knowledge, skills, and experience with a less experienced professional to assist in a specific aspect of a career or company.

Yes, your core team is critical, but most first-time founders don't fully understand the value of having mentors, like an **Advisory Board (Avd)** and a **Board of Directors (Bod)**. You may have never had these resources before, and even if you have, you might not know how to get the most from this extended team.

Throughout our careers, we've had a few mentors, some for specific aspects of our career that we wanted to develop and refine. Certain mentors

were there every step of the way. Steve often turns to his father for mentoring on how to run a business. His advice, encouragement, and respect for the value of money and people made Steve a successful entrepreneur.

Mentors and Startups

We all need great mentors. Mentoring can help entrepreneurs in many ways. But don't confuse mentors with advisors. Mentors give their time and help freely, usually because they like you and believe in you. Advisors offer specific, subject-matter expertise, and they're compensated for their work and advice to add skills that you can't afford and don't need on a full-time basis in your startup. We'll discuss advisors more in the next section, but first, let's address building mentoring into your startup.

So what should entrepreneurs expect from their mentors? If you're a mentor to others in your company, here's a great mentor manifesto that David Cohen of Techstars wrote up based on his observations of many startups.

The Mentor Manifesto

- Be Socratic.
- Expect nothing in return (you'll be delighted with what you do get back).
- Be authentic; practice what you preach.
- Be direct.
- Tell the truth, however hard.
- Listen.
- The best mentor relationships eventually become two way.
- Be responsive.
- Adopt at least one company every single year.
- Experience counts.
- Clearly separate opinion from fact.
- Hold information in confidence.
- Clearly commit to mentor or not.

WHAT IS MENTORING?

Mentoring is a **one-to-one relationship** between an experienced professional (**mentor**) who shares their knowledge and experience with a less experienced professional (mentee) to assist in their career progression.

Mentee
Embark on the exercise only when you can make the commitment to prepare, attend meetings and take action after meetings. A mentee needs to be capable of clear self-assesment and to look honestly at their strengths and weaknesses as these form part of the discussion with the mentor.

Mentors
Mentors commit to a mentee for a set period and invest time in getting to know the mentee, their capabilities, interests, and ambitions. The mentor will be knowledgeable in their field and pass on wisdom gained through their own business experiences.

The mentor explores with the mentee their current career situation, what they wish to achieve, and how they go about doing this but does not prescribe solutions or career routes.

HOW THE MENTOR HELPS

Career Introductions	Corporate Understanding	Problem Solving	Overcome Hurdles	Explore Work Methods	Career Planning

*Data Sources:
1. Pew Public/Private Ventures Impact Study 1995
2. Benefits of Mentoring 2007 by Triple Creek Mentoring Software (3creek.com)
3. Volunteer rates by state 2010 (volunteeringamerica.gov/rankings.cfm)
4. Volunteering in America 2007 and Volunteers Mentoring Youth 2006 (nationalservice.gov)

PLANNING AND INSIGHT

Mentoring is about long-range career planning or strategic business challenges. The mentor provides support and advice that enables the mentee to forge ahead with their ambition. In the mentoring relationship, the mentee actively manages the two-way process of exploration and discussion, making the most of the highly experienced professional at their disposal.

Get to Know Each Other and Build Trust

The mentoring partners agree:
• Duration of the mentoring period
• Contact plan – e.g., regular meetings, contact
• Frequency of contact • Length of meetings
• Location of meetings • Content of meetings
• Expectations of each other

Mentoring in Business
Research on mentoring in the workplace shows significant positive impact in four major areas of business:

Retention
 77% Companies who reported that mentoring increased retention.

 20% Employee turnover reduction with mentoring.

 35% Employees who do not receive regular mentoring look for another job within 12 months.

Promotion
 75% Executives say mentoring plays a key role in their careers.

 70% Women of color who had a mentor received a promotion.

 The more mentors a woman has, the faster she moves up the corporate ladder.

Productivity
 88% Productivity increase for managers when mentored.

 24% Productivity increase for managers when training alone.

 95% Mentoring participants say the experience motivates them to do their very best.

Development
 60% College and grad students list mentoring as a job criterion.

 35% CFOs say the top benefit of a mentor is having a confidant.

 Workers with mentors earn $5K-$22K more annually than those who do not.

- Know what you don't know.
- Say I don't know when you don't know—it's preferable to bravado.
- Guide, don't control.
- Teams must make their own decisions.
- Guide but never tell them what to do.
- Understand that it's their company, not yours.
- Accept and communicate with other mentors that get involved.
- Be optimistic.
- Provide specific, actionable advice; don't be vague.
- Be challenging/robust but never destructive.
- Have empathy.
- Remember that startups are hard.

As your startup grows and you make plans to scale, you should work with the team member or outside firm that handles human resources to set up a formal mentoring plan. Jumping into a startup, people need to learn a lot about many things at once. You can see from Figure 9.5 the significant and positive impact that mentoring has on retention, productivity, promotion, and development.

EXERCISE: Finding a Mentor

You may be thinking, "Great! I know I need a mentor, but how do I go about finding one?" Here are three steps to finding the right mentor for you:

1. **Know What You're Looking For**: Many times, we know that we want or need help, but we're unclear about what we need help with.
2. **Start with Friends and Family:** Tell your network who you're looking for and why. They can then reach out to their network to help find someone right for you.
3. **Reach Out:** Do some research as to who within your community might have the expertise that you need. Then, reach out to them. Let them know your story and what you need. The worst they'll say is, "No." But more than likely, they may be willing to give you a bit of their time.

BUILDING AND LEVERAGING GREAT ADVISORY BOARDS

Now that you have a starting point for your mentors, let's talk about advisors (**Avd**). You look to an advisor for specific, subject-matter expertise. Advisors are compensated for their work and advice. They also add a level of credibility to your startup without requiring the fiduciary duty or commitment required in a **Board of Directors (Brd)**, which we will talk about in a minute.

What kind of advisors will you need? Here are some examples.

- **Accountants:** As a service provider, they have a certain responsibility to stay objective, so compensate them with cash first and some stock options (not equity).
- **Lawyers:** Employee and founder agreements and contracts are only a few of the services you'll need. And intellectual property attorneys? Having a great one can make all the difference since they can help you get through the IP process successfully.
- **Technical Experts:** These expert advisors are the real-life equivalent of rocket surgeons. They know an aspect of your business intimately, sometimes have industry recognition, and add credibility to your startup.
- **Business Leaders:** Business leaders are experts in their own right with the ability to advise your startup from many different angles. If they like your idea, they might consider joining the company. Besides offering varied skill sets, these advisors can help you practice your investment pitch, work on your financial model, help with recruiting talent, and so many more things.

You may identify other key advisors for your startup, but these four advisor types will play a key role in the future success of your business. Now, building and leveraging a great **Advisory Board (Avd)** requires finding advisors who get what you're doing and want to be involved. At this point, your startup needs people skilled at certain things, but you can't afford to staff a full-time position. Look to your advisory board to gain access to these skills at a manageable cost at certain points in time.

How do you compensate an advisory board? At a startup, offering advisors 0.25-0.5 percent of common stock is standard, but it depends, in part, on the financial value of their advice, the frequency of their advice, and if you offer cash compensation in addition to stock. When it comes to service providers, they need to maintain objectivity, so compensating these advisors with stock can be a gray area, but many startups still do it. In most situations, we recommend compensating these advisors with cash (if you can afford it) to avoid a conflict of interest.

When you need the guidance of experts or business leaders, you can expect a different conversation. These advisors are interested in your startup and will want to invest their time and resources in you. And while they believe in you, they'll want some skin in the game. The number of shares rarely matters.

CRAFTING A STELLAR BOARD OF DIRECTORS

Mention the phrase **Board of Directors (Brd)** to the average person, and it usually brings up images of annual reports full of nicely dressed men and women smiling congenially around a mahogany table. Now, ask the entrepreneur to describe a board's responsibilities for their startup and very few can offer a definitive answer.

In the United States, the primary responsibility of a board of directors is to protect the shareholders' assets and ensure they receive a decent return on their investment. In some European countries, many directors feel that it's their primary responsibility to protect the employees of a company first and the shareholders second. In these social and political climates, corporate profitability takes a back seat to the needs of workers. Your country might fit these responsibilities, but it could differ so we would invite you to do some research on your local country's laws and protocols.

Five Things to Consider When Building Your Startup Board

Many new entrepreneurs ask us what they should do when they're trying to form their first board of directors. In situations where entrepreneurs raise funding, these investors will require a board seat, but there will be some open slots that should be filled. Consider these five things when you're trying to build your board of directors:

1. **Get the Right People on the Board.** Board members can be great resources who provide support, knowledge, and access to unique professional networks. Unfortunately, not all board members offer such value. One should be highly aware to avoid the five types of dysfunctional board members as defined by Jack and Suzy Welch: (1) The Do-Nothing, (2) The White Flag (avoids confrontation), (3) The Cabalist (driven by personal agenda), (4) The Meddler (dwells on details), and (5) The Pontificator (talks for sake of talking).[7] Also, appoint at least one independent director who's loyal to the company only.

2. **Get Alignment Regarding the Board's Role.** Boards of directors have many fiduciary and legal responsibilities. Still, boards often have additional roles, correlated with the startup's business stage. At early-stage startups, members should support the management (without micro-managing it) and provide advice on product decisions or provide access to recruiters, customers, and investors.

3. **Build a Diverse Board.** Start with listing the skills and experience needed from the board (e.g., product design, customer acquisition, partnerships, user experience, great network). While not a showstopper, you should be cautious and potentially reject solid candidates whose skills and experience are common within the board in favor of candidates who possess the missing skills and attributes.

4. **Avoid Too Many Board Members.** For a startup, a ten-person board will rarely be as engaged and helpful as a smaller one. Further, the logistics (i.e., getting everyone together) becomes exponentially more complex. Fred Wilson from Union Square Ventures thinks a board of five members is ideal, but recommends no more than seven board members (two founders, one to three VCs, and one to two other

industry professionals). In order to avoid this issue, you should negotiate the number of future board seats entitled with investors in the shareholder's agreement.

Startup Board Compensation

One question entrepreneurs often struggle with is how the board members should be compensated. While every situation is unique, there are some good rules of thumb that entrepreneurs should keep in mind—if only as a starting place. Identifying the various director categories can help. The vast majority of startup directors fall in four categories.

- **Insider Directors:** Startup founders and managers
- **Independent Directors:** Independent members of both the entrepreneurial team and the investors; typically bring some "value add" to the table, most often in the form of knowledge, connections, and/or reputation in the business space the startup is targeting
- **Professional Investor Directors:** Represent institutional venture capital investors in the deal
- **Angel Directors:** Often the most problematic in terms of figuring out compensation, these directors are also angel investors

Let's start with the easy ones, the insider and professional investor directors. These folks should get nothing. The insider director is already compensated adequately for their role in building the company, and serving as a director is a reward in and of itself.

Professional investor directors generally don't get any compensation for serving on the board of directors because such service is part of their basic job description. In fact, most institutional venture capital funds will have their own rules prohibiting these directors from receiving personal compensation from portfolio companies.

Independent directors, in the startup context, will generally get something like a quarter point (0.25%) to two points (2.0%) of equity, vesting over two years—or perhaps three or four years in exceptional cases.

We wish we could tell you that these figures for independent directors are written somewhere in stone, but they're not. They are based

solely on doing our own startups and being in and around the venture capital and high-impact entrepreneurship space for the last fifteen years.

The last, but perhaps most problematic category of startup directors is the angel director. Compensation for angel directors is one of those issues where the right answer and the actual answer rarely match. While it can vary, our experience suggests that an angel director really falls in the same category as the professional investor director—they don't receive compensation. Many angel investors see board service for a portfolio company differently (or at least they say they do). When they do, our advice to entrepreneurs is to push hard on this one.

You probably noticed that we didn't discuss cash compensation because any startup director that has done their homework should know that startups can't afford to pay directors up front. If a potential director doesn't know that, run the other way. It's worth it to note that the no-cash compensation rule does not apply to reasonable, out-of-pocket expenses, which are often reimbursed.

This section would be incomplete if we didn't mention a unique, independent director we like to call the Superstar. In this case, many things we mentioned as rules and recommendations might have to be thrown out the window. If Richard Branson (founder of Virgin Group) is so excited about your startup that he's willing to be on the board of directors, well, personally, we would be sorely tempted to accept just about any deal he put on the table.

Someone who really knows about putting teams together is a serial entrepreneur we mentioned earlier: Brad Feld. Brad did 40 angel investments between 1994–1997. He also co-founded or helped start companies and firms such as Mobius Venture Capital, Foundry Group, FG Press, and Techstars. We had a chance to talk to him about building and scaling startups.

SEQ: You have built two great companies and funded many others. What are the methods or techniques key to successfully scaling a company?

Feld: Team, team, team. The big miss for most founders is that you have to constantly be upgrading your team, especially your leadership team. People who were effective in a certain role at a specific size might or might not scale. This doesn't mean they should necessarily leave the company, but you've got to be really focused on building, and scaling, the team throughout the life of the company. Oh, and remembering that it's always really hard.

SEQ: When companies scale prematurely, what do you think are contributing factors to their failure?

Feld: Jacking the burn rate way up before you've figured out product/market fit. Hiring too big of an executive team that wants to manage, but doesn't know how to actually grind out the work. Getting confused about what "success" means and scaling ahead of various success points.

SEQ: You have worked with hundreds of startups. Are there common elements in what makes a great startup team?

Feld: Obsessive focus on the product. Brutal honesty with teammates. Humility.

SEQ: When entrepreneurs are just starting out and resources are limited, where should the entrepreneurs focus their time?

Feld: Product, product, product. Make something people love.

GETTING READY . . .

Great teams can transform your company. From the founding team to scaling up, it's critical to find the right mix. Here are some parting thoughts on how to get you on your way to finding the right team for your Startup Equation:

1. **Prioritize:** It is very easy to look at the long-term vision of your business and realize that you need help. Take a look at the skills exercise you did earlier in the chapter and then take a look at your core product/service. Based on your needs, prioritize which teammate/co-founder you should go after first. You'll get the focus you need to home in on the right people for your A-Team.

2. **Decide:** You may or may not be wondering whether or not you should start looking for co-founders. It's a big decision, but you need to decide how you want to steer the ship. There is no right answer to

this question, just the right answer for you, your time, and your resources. This is your adventure. You choose.

As you get ready to build your own unique Startup Equation make sure you complete the following exercises in this chapter:

- Which Member of the Startup Team Are You?
- Design Your Minimum Viable Team, or MVT
- Strengthening Your Network
- The Shape of Things to Come
- Finding a Mentor

Customer Experience

° CRAFT THE EXPERIENCE °

Everything Starts with the Customer

The Six Disciplines of Great Customer Experiences

Discovering the Customer Journey

Building a Minimum Delightful Product

Customers as Partners

Leveraging Benchmarks, Testing and Customer Insights

PROGRAM

TESTING

Referrals · Reviews Testamonials

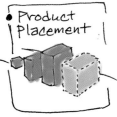

Feedback

Customer Advisory Panel

Product Placement

BEHAVIORAL TARGETING

USER TESTING

FOCUS GROUPS

SITE SURVEYS

Original Sketch by Kate Rutter

CHAPTER 10

Everything starts with the customer.

—Louis XIV

Creating Great Customer Experiences

So many startup books focus on the idea of build and iterate, but it's only half of the story. From the beginning, your startup needs to think about delivering a great customer experience. Early customers can provide valuable feedback and generate word-of-mouth to spread your story. You're too late if you wait to reach out to customers until the first day your product goes live.

Throughout this chapter, we'll dive into elements that you can use to craft the ultimate customer experience for your startup. The elements are divided into two core groups: *Program* and *Testing*.

This includes elements such as **Customer Experience Personas (Per)** and **Journey Maps (Map)** that explore your customer needs and behaviors. It also includes building **Prototypes (Pro)** and collecting **Insights (Cei)**.

Program

- **Customer Experience Personas (Per):** These are your ideal customers. These personas include demographic and psychographic information.
- **Customer Journey Map (Map):** This map brings you through the journey of touch points that a potential customer will go through in order to buy your product or service, as well as the touch points when using your product/service.
- **Minimum Delightful Product (Mdp):** A version of your minimum viable product that users absolutely love.
- **Experience Design Prototype (Pro):** A sample or model of a product or process used to test its viability and usability.
- **Customer Experience Management (Cxm):** A strategy that focuses the business operations and processes around the needs of the customer.
- **Customer Experience Insights (Cei):** A program that collects, measures, and manages customer insights

As we walk through these elements, you'll find that some make sense to embrace now and others will make more sense as you grow your company. These elements will help you meet customer expectations today and get your startup to the next step.

There's no denying we're in the age of the customer. However, you don't have to fear customers or their opinions. You and your team have the opportunity to craft the experience you want for your customers.

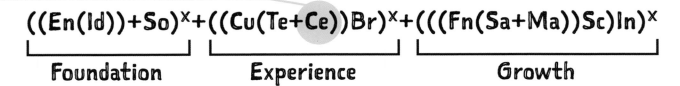

$$((En(Id))+So)^x+((Cu(Te+Ce))Br)^x+(((Fn(Sa+Ma))Sc)In)^x$$

Foundation   **Experience**   **Growth**

As you take your idea to develop a product that is viable, you must drive toward creating something that is desirable and useful. It is within the customer experience that you can transform something from being merely useful to being fun to use on a daily basis. In our "Startup Table of Elements" we separate Customer Experience (Ce) elements into two categories – Program and Testing.

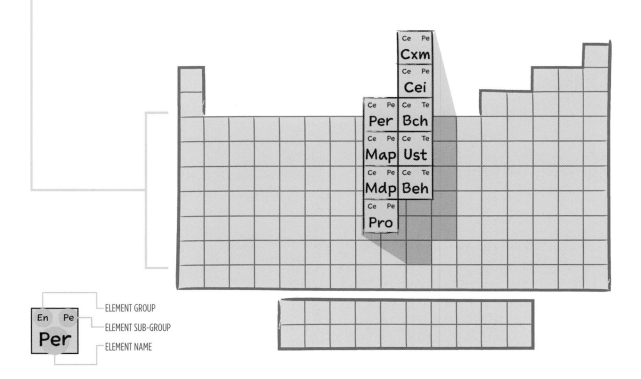

ELEMENT GROUP
ELEMENT SUB-GROUP
ELEMENT NAME

CUSTOMER EXPERIENCE (CE) PROGRAM ELEMENTS

To make the leap from incremental improvements to breakthrough transformation, companies must routinely leverage a set of sound, standard practices. This program has a number of elements to reinforce this standard.

Customer Experience Personas (Per)
These are your ideal customers. They are the people who will buy and use your product. They will also provide the necessary feedback to make your products and the customer experience better. A persona program includes investigative techniques like surveys, stakeholder interviews and contextual inquiry,

Customer Journey Map (Map)
The customer journey map is an oriented graph that describes the journey of a user by representing the different touch points that characterize his interaction with the product or service. Understanding the customer journey includes activities like competitive analysis, task analysis and journey maps.

Minimum Delightful Product (Mdp)
Beyond building a Minimum Viable Product (Mvp) it actually has to be useful and have people want to use it. Viability isn't enough for small business software, services, hardware, or retail and consumer products. Delightful products get adopted faster, encourage better word of mouth, and trigger better satisfaction. Users fall in love with delightful products.

Customer Experience Design and Prototyping (Pro)
A prototype is an early sample, model or release of a product built to test a concept or process or to act as a thing to be replicated or learned from. It can be in physical or digital form and leverages techniques such as sketching, wireframing and 3-D printing.

Customer Experience Management (Cxm)
Customer experience management (CEM or CXM) is a strategy that focuses the operations and processes of a business around the needs of the individual customer. It represents the discipline, methodology and/or process used to comprehensively manage a customer's cross-channel exposure, interaction and transaction with a company, product, brand or service

Customer Experience Insights (Cei)
Customer insight programs collect, measure and manage customer insights and feeds them back into the customer experience, either through immediate action or longer-term strategy. This includes programs such as the Voice of the Customer and a Customer Advisory Panels.

CUSTOMER EXPERIENCE (CE) TESTING ELEMENTS

Testing your customers' experience requires changing your perception of how they interact with your company. A customer-centric approach adds value to your company and helps differentiate your business from your competitors. These elements help you understand what customers actually experience on the site and which elements most impact overall satisfaction.

Benchmarking (Bch)
Understand how usable your product or service is by having a representative set of metrics and using confidence intervals to generate a reliable benchmark. It also includes comparative benchmarks using the same tasks on competitive applications.

Usability Testing (Ust)
As you gain a better understanding of your customer channels, you can lower your acquirement costs with usability testing. There are many components to usability testing including card sorting, tree testing, eye tracking, focus groups, A/B testing, surveys, interviews, contextual inquiry and heuristic evaluations.

Behavioral Targeting (Beh)
Behavioral Targeting refers to a range of technologies and techniques used to increase the effectiveness of their products. A more targeted experience will naturally be more interesting to a user and provide an improved customer experience. Behavioral data can also be combined with other user information such as purchase history to create a more complete user profile.

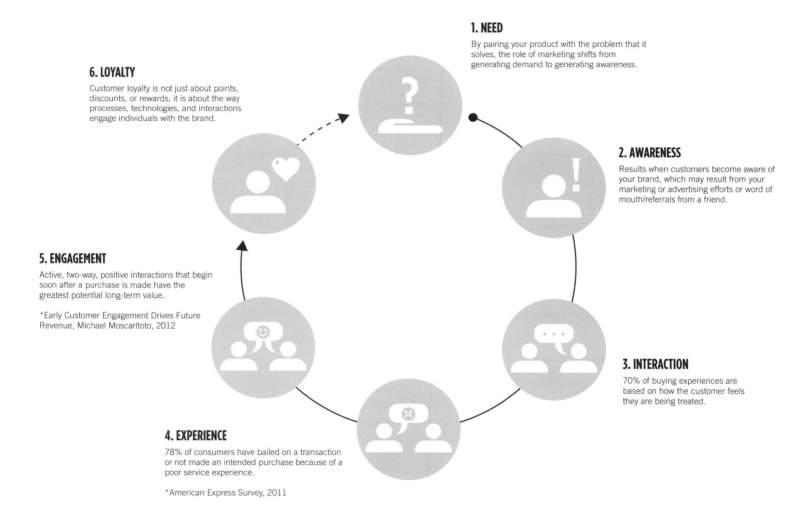

1. NEED

By pairing your product with the problem that it solves, the role of marketing shifts from generating demand to generating awareness.

6. LOYALTY

Customer loyalty is not just about points, discounts, or rewards; it is about the way processes, technologies, and interactions engage individuals with the brand.

2. AWARENESS

Results when customers become aware of your brand, which may result from your marketing or advertising efforts or word of mouth/referrals from a friend.

5. ENGAGEMENT

Active, two-way, positive interactions that begin soon after a purchase is made have the greatest potential long-term value.

*Early Customer Engagement Drives Future Revenue, Michael Moscarltoto, 2012

3. INTERACTION

70% of buying experiences are based on how the customer feels they are being treated.

4. EXPERIENCE

78% of consumers have bailed on a transaction or not made an intended purchase because of a poor service experience.

*American Express Survey, 2011

When Ja-Naé started Wild Women Entrepreneurs, she started with the goal of helping women entrepreneurs find resources to help them with their businesses. The reality? Ja-Naé didn't yet know where to find those resources herself. At the time, she was an opera singer who wanted to help some really deserving women succeed. However, the fact that she didn't know how to raise venture capital or even find a babysitter didn't faze her.

Ja-Naé knew she didn't need to know all the answers. She just needed to reach out to her customers for help finding them. So, when it came time to help Julie in Kentucky find venture firms in the state that she could pitch, Ja-Naé just started asking. She asked her personal network and reached out to the other ladies in Wild WE. Not only was she able to help Julie, but she was also able to create a list of firms across the United States for her ladies to access.

EVERYTHING STARTS WITH THE CUSTOMER

According to Wikipedia, "Customer experience (CX) is the sum of all experiences a customer has with a supplier of goods and/or services, over the duration of their relationship with that supplier. This can include awareness, discovery, attraction, interaction, purchase, use, cultivation and advocacy. It can also be used to mean an individual experience over one transaction; the distinction is usually clear in context."[1]

> Customer Experience is the path to more recommendations. Organizations need to view a good recommendation as an outcome from a good experience.
> —*Forrester Research*

Your startup should think early on about how to leverage CX as a strategy to focus business operations and processes around the needs of the individual customer. It represents the discipline, methodology, and process used to comprehensively manage a customer's cross-channel interaction with a company, product, brand, or service.

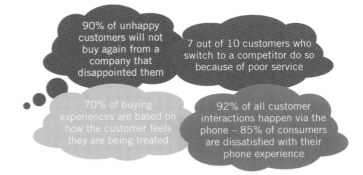

WHY CUSTOMER EXPERIENCE MATTERS

You can't not have an experience! Individual customers decide whether they have had a good or bad customer experience. This impacts their future buying decisions and whether or not they will recommend us to friends or family.

WHAT IS CE AND WHY DO I CARE?

90% of unhappy customers will not buy again from a company that disappointed them

7 out of 10 customers who switch to a competitor do so because of poor service

70% of buying experiences are based on how the customer feels they are being treated

92% of all customer interactions happen via the phone – 85% of consumers are dissatisfied with their phone experience

Eighty percent of companies believe they deliver a superior customer experience, but only eight percent of their customers agree.

Think about a recent example in your own life where you were the customer and you had a bad experience...

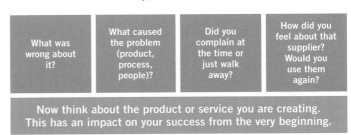

| What was wrong about it? | What caused the problem (product, process, people)? | Did you complain at the time or just walk away? | How did you feel about that supplier? Would you use them again? |

Now think about the product or service you are creating. This has an impact on your success from the very beginning.

Data Source: Harvard Management Update, January 2010

Figure 10.4 **Why Customer Experience Matters**

THE SIX DISCIPLINES OF GREAT CUSTOMER EXPERIENCES

To make the leap from incremental improvements to breakthrough transformation, companies must routinely perform a set of sound, standard practices. In the report, "The Path to Customer Experience Maturity," Kerry Bodine, Vice President and Principal Analyst for Forrester Research, discussed the forty essential practices they've collapsed into a framework called the Six Disciplines of Customer Experience:

1. Customer experience strategy
2. Customer understanding
3. Design
4. Governance
5. Measurement
6. Culture

Collectively, the six disciplines represent the most important things that the best companies do to be great at customer experience. *Fast Company* published a helpful article with an abbreviated description of each of these disciplines:[2]

- **The Strategy Discipline:** "It's a set of practices for crafting a customer experience strategy, aligning it with the company's overall strategy and brand attributes, and then sharing that strategy with employees to guide decision-making and prioritization across the organization . . . [It's] critical because it provides the blueprint for the experience you design, deliver, manage, and measure."

- **The Customer Understanding Discipline:** "Create[s] a consistent, shared understanding of who customers are, what they want and need, and how they perceive the interactions they're having with your company today."

- **The Design Discipline:** "Envision and then implement customer interactions that meet or exceed customer needs. It spans the complex systems of people, products, interfaces, services, and spaces that your customers encounter in retail locations, over the phone, or through digital media."

- **The Measurement Discipline:** "[Quantifies] customer experience quality in a consistent manner across the enterprise and deliver[s] actionable insights to employees and partners."

- **The Governance Discipline:** "Help[s] organizations manage customer experience in a proactive and disciplined way . . . It holds people accountable for their role in the customer experience ecosystem and helps keep bad experiences from getting out the door."

- **The Culture Discipline:** "Create[s] a system of shared values and behaviors that focus employees on delivering a great customer experience . . . think of it as the way you shape what your employees do when you're not in the room."

Take a look at the "Six Disciplines" sketchnote drawn by Kate Rutter for the Service Experience Conference in 2012. It maps the six disciplines and how they work in practice. Review the sketchnote and think about how your organization would use these disciplines in its everyday customer experience.

From User Experience to Customer Experience

One company that has built its reputation on crafting stellar customer experiences for their customers is Fresh Tilled Soil. Here is what CEO Richard Banfield had to say about discovering that right mix for themselves:

SEQ: What's your philosophy on that concept and what you guys do here at Fresh Tilled?

Banfield: I think we do a lot of things. The most important thing is that we are creating a company. Day to day, we build websites and web applications and mobile applications for our clients, but what we're really doing is building a company of people. If you think about that work at your company, it's companionship, it's a group of individuals that share a vision.

We've had only one person leave in the last two years. We have almost zero staff turnover. I don't know of a single company both in our industry and beyond it that can say the same thing. The reason is because we care. We really care about building a company that's taking care of the people that are a part of that company.

SEQ: What are your thoughts on how brand experience and customer experience are connected or how they aren't?

Banfield: I think they're connected. I think the mistake that a lot of us have made in the past is thinking that you can define a brand through some kind of identity creation and then push that identity creation across into the marketplace with the hope that you're going to build an experience on top of that.

What we've discovered, of course, is that it's the reverse. You build an experience, and from that experience comes your brand. Your brand is

CUSTOMER EXPERIENCE VS USER EXPERIENCE Figure 10.6

USER EXPERIENCE

User Experience focuses largely on the research, design, and development of a project.
• The goal is to build a better experience around the product or service.
• This can include mobile and desktop apps, websites, or other digital interfaces.
• This can also include non-digital materials such as paper or marketing collateral.

YOUR BRAND

CX

UX

CUSTOMER JOURNEY

CUSTOMER EXPERIENCE

Customer Experience explores the overall experience that a customer can have across each touch point of the brand.
• This includes communication and interaction points such as email, phone, or person.
• This can include both digital interaction and physical face-to-face.
• The goal is to identify problematic areas that could produce a bad customer experience.

USER EXPERIENCE DESIGNER

Can take a human-centered approach and better support commercial objectives (near-term and long-term) and not just balance usability and delight. The feasibility of a business is based on on-going customer engagement, not just lowered learning curves.

YOUR BRAND

Customers have the ability to engage with your brand across a variety of different channels from in-store to web, phone, or media while receiving a consistent experience across all platforms. Your channels should interact with one another which provides the opportunity for UX and CX to work together

CUSTOMER EXPERIENCE DESIGNER

Can define experiences that extend beyond the purchase of a product or service. To ensure feasibility of a business, customers must remain engaged, and this requires thinking across all stages of the relationship and looking for ways to add or increase value.

what people say outside the room behind your back when you're not there. Building that experience is essential to fulfilling the brand goal.

DISCOVERING THE CUSTOMER JOURNEY

Though you have already created an MVP, and your business model is on track, we challenge you to think very carefully about this question: *Who are my ideal customers?*

- What do they want?
- What are the steps they take to engage with my product?
- What happens after they buy?
- How does the company service their needs and keep them happy so they come back and also rave about how awesome we are to friends and family?

You can work through all of these questions by discovering the journey customers take with your business. We'll show you how to do just that.

Starting with User Personas

The first step in understanding the customer journey is to understand who qualifies as an ideal customer. You can accomplish this task by creating **Customer Experience Personas (Per)**. These personas represent your ideal customers. A persona program includes the following investigative techniques:

- **Survey:** Surveys are an affordable way to identify your users, what they want, what they do, what they purchase, where they shop, and what they own.
- **Market Segmentation:** Once you have some good survey data, you'll want to turn it into meaningful clusters. This process will help group needs and wants into specific segments and at what point they care the most in the buying process. It's about demographics and key differentiators.
- **Competitive Analysis:** If you think you don't have competition, you haven't done enough research or you probably don't have something people want. Understand the market, find out what similar companies

do in your market, and look to similar industries. What features do you share? What delights customers? You can use industry benchmarks to help create a baseline.

- **Contextual Inquiry:** This process observes users in their workplace or home and attempts to solve problems and accomplish goals by looking to identify unmet needs and understand the tasks they perform. Contextual inquiry, while time consuming, can be incredibly revealing.
- **Stakeholder Interviews:** An amazing amount of information already exists in different company departments. Don't simply interview the "most important" or "highest paid people" in the company. Your results will be limited and probably not useful. Use a structured interview to ask customer support, QA, development, marketing, and sales to find out what to build, what to fix, and what to cut.

You can start with personas even before you work on your business model, but if you don't have a clear path on the business model, your personas will turn out untargeted. As a result, you'll waste your time in a constant state of revision.

Proto-Personas Can Be Enough for Right Now

The web contains many examples of persona diagrams, and it could be an endless exercise in making really cool charts with all the data of your users. Ultimately, you need enough good data so you have a way to focus as you build your business and begin to craft the customer experience for your business, including creating proto-personas to help you focus on building your product. Jeff Gothelf, who co-wrote the book *Lean UX*, describes proto-personas as "a variant of the typical persona, with the important difference that they are not initially the result of user research."[3]

EXERCISE: Proto-Personas

Proto-personas are ad-hoc personas built to represent the archetypal "people" you believe will be your customers now and in the future. You should stress to your team that these archetypes are not scientifically proven. They're here as a reference point. *(continues)*

Developing your product can be very expensive – it often requires significant capital and resource investments. This is where you can incorporate proto-personas into your design process.

Proto-personas are ad-hoc personas built to represent the archetypal "people" you believe will be your customers now and in the future. Doing a proto-persona exercise takes about two days. The first part requires a few hours. Your goal is to look at the company from the customer's point of view. Then, articulate who the customers are and what needs they have that impact the company. You should stress to everyone involved that these archetypes are not scientifically proven. They're here as a reference point for your team. They help build your product, plan the roadmap, and aid with decision making.

They're drawn in four quadrants, and you'll note in the Proto-Persona Framework diagram below they're mapped as follows:

STEP 1:
Have each person sketch on a piece of paper a proto-persona they think represents the buyer of the product.

STEP 2:
After each team member creates their own proto-persona, they each present in front of the group their persona and take questions as to why this person is appropriate for the business.

STEP 3:
Then, you do successive rounds where people incorporate their ideas or decide which elements are better. The goal is to try and find common elements and consolidate personas until you have three to five proto-personas that work. After that part is done, the team determines where each persona is positioned on five different spectrums.

HOW PROTO-PERSONAS ARE MAPPED

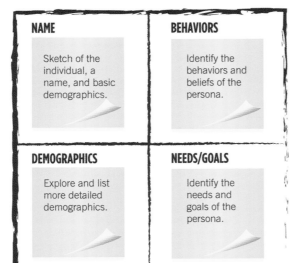

A PROTO-PERSONAS WITH EXAMPLE INFORMATION

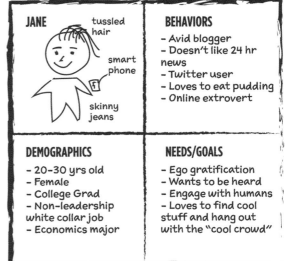

Data Sources: http://uxmag.com/articles/using-proto-personas-for-executive-alignment, http://www.dtelepathy.com/blog/philosophy/how-to-make-proto-pesonas

Doing a proto-persona exercise takes about two days. The first part requires a few hours. Your goal is to look at your startup from the customer's point of view. Then, articulate **who** the customers are and **what** needs they have that **impact** the company.

Within the Proto-Persona Framework, there are four quadrants mapped out as follows:

- The top-left quadrant is for a sketch of the individual, a name, and some basic demographics
- The top-right quadrant is for behaviors and beliefs of the persona
- The bottom-left quadrant is for demographics
- The bottom-right quadrant is for needs and goals

The first step is to have each person sketch out a proto-persona they think represents the product buyer. After each team member attempts to create their own proto-persona, they present their persona to the group and take questions on why this person is appropriate for your business.

Next, do successive rounds where people incorporate feedback and decide which elements are more important. The goal is to find common elements and consolidate personas until you have three to five proto-personas that work. Finally, the team determines where each persona is positioned on five different spectrums.

Once you have your group of proto-personas done, it's time to map their journey with your company.

The Customer Journey Map

The **Customer Journey Map (Map)** helps you build a better understanding of how your customers interact with your company and your brand. When used properly, it forces you to consider every channel, product, and touch point that characterizes your customer's interaction with your product or service.

Your *Customer Journey Map* builds on the proto-personas you created and dives deeper into the customer's needs objectives, perceptions, and motivations. It can reveal paths to purchase by giving you insights that increase your chances of success while identifying the potential barriers and pain points in the customer experience.

> **EXERCISE: Experience Mapping the Customer Journey**
>
> On the following pages, we've laid out a framework for creating your own *Customer Journey Map*. There are six things that smart companies include in their map:[4]
>
> 1. They define a clear, compelling value proposition for customers
> 2. They know the journeys that matter and why they matter
> 3. They continuously innovate the end-to-end journey experiences
> 4. They use journeys to reinforce front-line culture
> 5. They optimize processes and systems to ensure consistent delivery
> 6. They use journeys to define a metrics and governance system

BUILDING A MINIMUM DELIGHTFUL PRODUCT

An MVP is one of the most popular ideas to emerge from the Lean Startup movement. It reduces the chances that you'll build a product customers don't want. Think of it as a broader methodology that gathers qualitative and quantitative customer and user research throughout the development process.

But it's time to ask the question: Will this product delight my customers? You won't know for sure until you put something out there and start testing. It's also true that an MVP might work initially, but it simply isn't enough to succeed. Our goal is for you to build a product that's both viable and delightful. Delightful products get adopted faster, encourage stronger word of mouth, and trigger better satisfaction. Users fall in love with delightful products. Your real goal is to build more than a MVP. Build a **Minimum Delightful Product (Mdp)**.

What Does It Take to Build an Mdp?

Three areas must come together:

- **Whole Product Approach:** You design your product as a whole instead of feature by feature. It's a combination of user experience and functionality that makes a product wonderful.
- **Elegant Design:** Think of Google's simple search box or how apps fade on a mobile phone. Elegant design is delightful.
- **Focused Quality:** Simply put, when something is done, it's done and should work without problems. It may not have all the functionality you want, but what does exist needs to work well.

Minimum Delightful Products (Mdp) and Prototyping (Pro)

A great way to create your **Minimum Delightful Product (Mdp)** is through an **Experience Design Prototype (Pro)**. A prototype is an early sample, model, or release of a product built to test a concept or process or to act as a thing to be replicated or learned from. It can be in physical or digital form and leverages techniques such as sketching, wireframing, and 3-D printing.[5]

Advantages of Prototyping

There are many advantages to protoyping. Here are just a few:

- **Reduced Time and Costs:** Prototyping can improve the quality of requirements and save money versus if it was done later in the development cycle.
- **Improved and Increased User Involvement:** You have a great opportunity to talk to the users and see how they interact with your prototype to reduce the cost and give the customer what they really want.

While there's no hard definition for what constitutes a prototype, they generally fall into five categories:[6]

Proof-of-Concept Prototype

A proof-of-concept prototype tests some aspect of the intended design without attempting to simulate the visual appearance exactly, the choice of materials, or the intended manufacturing process. Such prototypes can "prove" a potential design approach like range of motion, sensors, and architecture. These models can help identify which design options will work and if additional development and testing is necessary.

Form Study Prototype

This type of prototype allows designers to explore the basic size, look, and feel of a product without matching the actual function or exact visual appearance of the product. This prototype helps assess ergonomic factors and provides insight into visual aspects of the product's final form. They may even be hand-carved or machined models from easily sculpted, inexpensive materials (e.g., urethane foam).

User Experience Prototype

If the prototype needs to invite active interaction and support user-focused research, a company will produce a user experience model. The goal isn't to address possible aesthetic treatments, but to represent the overall size, proportions, interfaces, and articulation of a promising concept. This type of model allows early assessment of how a potential user interacts with various elements and the overall user experience.

Visual Prototype

This version will capture the intended design aesthetic and simulate the appearance, color, and surface textures of the intended product, but will not function like the final product. These models work well for market research, executive reviews and approval, packaging mock-ups, and photo shoots for sales literature.

Functional Prototype

Also called a working prototype, this model attempts to simulate the design, aesthetics, materials, and functionality of the finished product. A functional prototype may be scaled down to reduce costs.

Look at the prototyping process as something that is iterative and core to your product development process. It helps you craft the user experience that ultimately forms a basis for the overall customer experience.

4 STEPS TO UNDERSTANDING THE CUSTOMER JOURNEY

   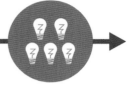

KNOW THE CUSTOMER

Examine customer interactions and the behavior they display across the various touch points and channels of their journey.

MAP THE JOURNEY

Take your data and findings and transform them into a map that follows your customer's journey.

TELL THE STORY

Use your map to build compelling stories across touch points and channels to create understanding.

LET THE MAP GUIDE

Let the map be your guide for developing new insights and finding new ways to provide a better experience for your customers.

The Activity
The process of mapping a user's experience is collaborative and co-creative that visualizes a holistic exploration of the customer. The end result is an artifact called an *experience map*.

The Artifact
The experience map provides support for guiding your strategic moves while also presenting a rich guide for understanding the entire journey of your customers.

ELEMENTS OF A JOURNEYMAP

TOUCHPOINT

A point of interaction between a person and any agent or artifact of an organization. These interactions take place at a certain point in time, in a certain context, and with the intention of meeting a specific customer need.

CHANNEL

A medium of interaction with customers or users. Print, the web, mobile, voice calls, and brick and mortar locations are all common channels for reaching out to and interacting with customers. A channel defines the opportunities or constraints of a touch point.

Data Source: Adaptive Path

THE FRAMEWORK OF AN EXPERIENCE MAP

The components of this framework are: the lens, the customer journey model, and the takeaways.

The moment you conceive of a plan to map the customer journey, you need to chart a course to actionable results. The takeaways signal which way you are recommending the organization head next. Your takeaways could include:

• Strategic insights
• Recommendations
• Design principles

Takeaways are typically added to the map late in the process, once you have begun to pivot from understanding the current state of your customer experience to envisioning the future state. There are different takeaways you could include, but they should answer the questions "So what?" and "What now?"

More: http://adaptivepath.com/ideas/the-anatomy-of-an-experience-map

WHAT'S IN A CUSTOMER EXPERIENCE MAP?

There are six dimensions and three components of experience the map should capture. These represent important reference points for features of the service design – e.g. how the service is found, who uses it, what they're looking for, what information they use, who and what is of most help etc. By capturing these experiential aspects we ensure the customer's voice is represented as the service is designed and implemented.

6 Dimensions: These dimensions help extract content for the map and generate conversation during the mapping. The responses help in considering what is to be recommended in the design.
• Time/duration
• Interactivity
• Intensity
• Breadth/consistency
• Sensoral/cognitive triggers
• Significance/meaning

3 components: These represent the key content of the map itself. Simply put, what people:
• Think
• Do
• Use

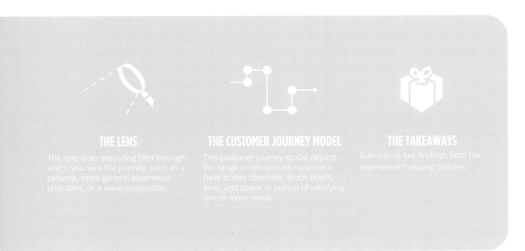

THE LENS
The lens is an overriding filter through which you view the journey, such as a persona, more general experience principles, or a value proposition.

THE CUSTOMER JOURNEY MODEL
The customer journey model depicts the range of interactions customers have across channels, touch points, time, and space in pursuit of satisfying one or more needs.

THE TAKEAWAYS
Summarize key findings from the experience mapping process.

BUILDING BLOCKS OF A JOURNEY MAP

Understanding the customer's behavior can be complex, but doing so provides you with rich information on how your customers will interact with your brand over time. The firm Adaptive Path has broken down the process into a series of helpful building blocks to guide you in getting started. The process relies on two areas of focus: Research and Discovery. They rely on a foundation of Doing, Thinking, and Feeling.

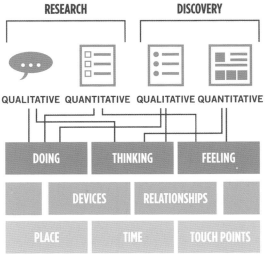

DOING
What actions is the customer taking to meet their needs? What is key in their behavior?

THINKING
How do your customers evaluate their experience? What is it that they expect?

FEELING
What emotions do they have along their journey? What are their highs and lows?

CUSTOMERS AS PARTNERS

When you begin building relationships between your business and customers, understand that there are really two ways to create that relationship.

1. **Staying Casual:** You have something a potential customer may need. You make the sell and an exchange or two may follow, but that's it. They may adore your product or service, which you appreciate, but the connection stays casual, leaving room for competitors to sweep in at any time.

2. **Building a Partnership:** Instead of settling for an amicable relationship without much expected from either side, build a real partnership with your customers. How can you foster a partnership? Here are three building blocks to help you build a partnership with your customers:

   - **Solve Real Problems:** Customers must deal with an overwhelming number of choices. Don't provide only another choice. Provide a solution. Listen to your customers so you can understand what they truly need. Ask more questions if needed because your customers' problems aren't likely to be your problems. Prioritize small changes that could solve your customer's problem.

   - **Be Transparent:** People buy from companies they trust. Building that trust starts with you. Commit to being as transparent as possible with your customers. Share your story and allow people to know why you started your business. If something goes wrong, admit it and let them know how you'll fix the issue.

   - **Run Beta Tests:** Who better to help with the beta test of your product or service than real customers? Many customers appreciate the invitation to provide this kind of help. Beta testers often end up investing a ton of time in you and your business. Bring your customers into your inner circle and reward them for their efforts and support.

A company that's built its customer experience through partnerships is Behance. Behance is a company dedicated to organizing the creative world. We had a chance to chat with co-founder and Head of Design, Matias Corea to see how they did it:

SEQ: When you were doing Behance with Scott, as you were going along, did the original idea change a lot?

Corea: At the beginning, I think ideas are always blurred. Even if you think they're sharp, they're not, because I have yet to see something that was identical at the moment of conception and when it becomes successful.

Think about the biggest platforms, Facebook, Twitter, Digg, Behance. Products themselves always transform, and evolve, and improve, and some of them completely change into other businesses. For us, I think something that never changed was empowering creative, but we found a way to do it more efficiently by trial and error.

SEQ: Was there a tough decision required to change the direction?

Corea: I think the hard decisions we had to make are around focus and resources. We threw all those lines into the sea to see which ones pulled and slowly, the hard decision was to sell products and parts of our business. Why? Because every time you have one of those lines, you're putting attention, you're putting energy, and you're putting resources in them. The hardest part of building a business is actually knowing and the hard decision is knowing what you have to keep and what you have to let go.

Building a Customer Experience Management (CXM) Program

To support and provide some focus around all of your efforts to work with your customers and improve your product, you should build a **Customer Experience Management (CXM)** program. A CXM creates alignment between groups and focuses the operations and processes of a business around the needs of the individual customer. This is an ongoing, transparent program that represents the discipline, methodology, and/or process used to comprehensively manage a customer's cross-channel exposure, interaction, and transaction with a company, product, brand, or service.

> **EXERCISE: Outline Your Customer Experience Management (Cxm) Framework**
>
> On the following page is a CXM Program Framework example. It is separated into three parts: (1) the Framework Alignment, (2) the Customer Experience, and (3) the Framework Implementation. There are a few things to keep in mind with this program flow.
>
> The Framework Alignment is there for you to audit and map processes to align with the organization. The Customer Experience looks at the various touch points used in the Framework. Framework Implementation is focused on mapping the program to customer insights and feedback along with metrics (e.g., KPIs) that track action and success.

Testing the Customer Experience

Testing your customers' experience requires changing your perception of how they interact with your company. A customer-centric approach adds value to your company and helps differentiate your business from your competitors. Plus, you'll end up with a customer experience so epic and unique that you'll only add to the pool of customer evangelists from the very beginning of your business.

We suggest designing your testing around these five tips:

1. Know what matters to your customers because it informs risk-based testing.

2. Keep any promises you make. Can you test these promises?

3. Spot potential problems and fix them!

4. Communicate clearly and simply to test your communication (e.g. error messages).

5. Take responsibility when things go wrong and test the fix processes, too.

Checking In with the Customer Development Process

We started Chapter 7 with the introduction of the Customer Development Model that Steve Blank came up with in his book *Four Steps to the Epiphany*. Let's revisit this diagram to check-in with your progress. At this point, you should be in the Customer Validation phase with a validated business model.

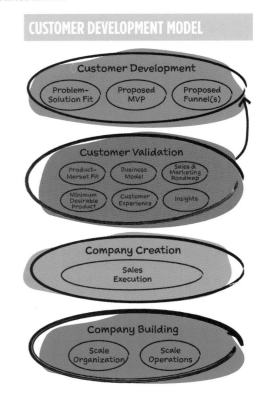

CUSTOMER DEVELOPMENT MODEL

Customer Development
- Problem-Solution Fit
- Proposed MVP
- Proposed Funnel(s)

Customer Validation
- Product-Market Fit
- Business Model
- Sales & Marketing Roadmap
- Minimum Desirable Product
- Customer Experience
- Insights

Company Creation
- Sales Execution

Company Building
- Scale Organization
- Scale Operations

FRAMEWORK ALIGNMENT
First-time and periodic activities to gain a holistic view of the Customer Experience and align the Customer Experience Management Framework.

Customer Experience Lifecycle Audit

Experience Lifecycle Audit
Audit of the Customer Experience Lifecycle that covers all channels, internal and external, between customers and the company beyond the Customer Lifecycle.

Mapping
A map of the Customer Experience Lifecycle is established and various interactions prioritized in terms of business importance and impact on customer experience.

Customer Research

Multi-channel Insights
Different research methods are used to gain deeper insights into customer needs and what constitutes customer value at different channels.

Segments and Value
Customer segments are identified based on psychographics and particular attention is paid to understanding emotional value.

Organizational Alignment

Process of Analysis
Analysis of internal processes to manage the customer experience, including cross-departmental information gathering and sharing.

Policy Alignment
Ensure processes, performance metrics, incentives, and training are aligned with Customer Experience goals across departments.

THE CUSTOMER EXPERIENCE
The start, middle, and endpoint of the Customer Experience Management Framework.

Experience Design

Designing the Interaction
Understanding of channels, customer value, and company processes is used to:
• Design the Experience at individual channels and touch points
• Create seamless multi-channel interactions for better experiences

Customer Experience Roles
Customer Experience is every department's responsibility.

Marketing
Communicates the differentiated customer value and brand promise. Also monitors customer feedback and opinion in public channels and respond accordingly.

Human Resources
Communicates the Customer Experience brand values and goals internally and ensures staff have the appropriate skills and mindset to deliver the Customer Experience.

*Data Source: Customer Input Limited 2011

FRAMEWORK IMPLEMENTATION

Structured enterprise-wide systematic collection and management of customer insights and the processes to feed them back into shaping the experience.

Mapping

The Customer Insights Program, which integrates the Voice of the Customer (VOC) is a collaborative effort between different departments. It may be managed by a dedicated Chief Experience Officer.

Ongoing Feedback

Feedback from different sources is shared across relevant department for action to be taken. This can include everything from call center enquires to social media discussions.

Periodic Research

A mix of research methods can be used to understand the overall customer experience with the company and that at specific channels.

KPIs

Customer Experience KPIs are used to measure experience improvements and set experience goals.

Immediate Action

Feedback is passed on to the relevant departments for immediate action. For example, PR may respond to complaints in social media, or reported issues with a product can be sent to development for immediate fix.

Business Decisions Process

Insights are factored in at the core of business decisions. This can be in terms of:

- Branding and Marketing
- Sales or servicing processes
- Product or service enhancements
- New products or services

Website · **Point of sales** · **Advertisement** · **Products** · **Branding** · **Facilities** · **Social media** · **Call center** · **Business partners** · **Customer service** · **Service center**

Customer Experience

The experience is what happens when customers interact actively or passively with any channel.

Operations

To facilitate the delivery of Customer Experience by enhancing internal processes and back-end functions and to deliver it directly at multiple servicing and support channels.

Sales

Ensures sales people have the appropriate skills to understand and deliver customer value at each phase of the sales cycle; from recommending solutions that meet customer needs to post-sales follow-up.

Research & Development

Understand customer value through customer research and the Customer Insights Program and integrate it at the core of the company's products or services.

You should be working on your minimum desirable product, and in the event of a major revelation that requires a pivot, taking steps to adjust your business as you go. You should also be thinking about your sales and marketing roadmap. The customer personas and journey maps will help you create a strong roadmap and related programs. We'll do a deeper dive of those things in the upcoming chapters.

LEVERAGING BENCHMARKS, TESTING AND CUSTOMER INSIGHTS

To understand the usability of your product or service, you need a representative set of metrics to generate reliable **Customer Experience Benchmarks (Bch)**. You're ready to benchmark if you have at least a functioning beta and understand the usability of your product or service from your customer experience work. Jeff Sauro, the founder of Measuring Usability (a quantitative research firm), has a great list of benchmarks for user experience. They offer a starting place if you're having trouble finding a starting point:[7]

- Task Completion Rate
- Net Promoter Score—Consumer Software and Website versions
- System Usability Scale (SUS) Score
- Task Difficulty
- Speed of Use

These benchmarks will eventually include comparative benchmarks using the same tasks on competitive applications. Comparative benchmarks look at things like how difficult are the same tasks on the competitive applications you identified. To measure, recruit some users then use core metrics like completion rates, time, and task difficulty. It will be eye opening to see the strengths and weaknesses of your product.

Start a User Testing Program

Businesses that provide an engaging, hassle-free customer experience are the ones that convert browsers into buyers and first-time buyers into repeat customers. For the online business, the first step towards improving conversion and customer retention rates is to understand what customers experience on the site and which elements most impact overall satisfaction. But it's impossible to predict customer experience without reliable, interpretable data from real people interacting with the site. This is where **Customer Usability Testing (Ust)** becomes critical. Here are some examples of different testing:

- **A/B Testing:** Design and improvements don't stop once you've gone live. A/B testing is a simple way to test changes against the current design and determine which ones produce positive results. You can test forms, buttons, copy, images, and prices. Don't be afraid to test wild-card ideas.

- **Multivariate Testing:** If you're in a hurry or like to test multiple scenarios and combinations of things, you can do multivariate testing on a live website or simulate the experience in a development environment using attitudinal data instead of actual purchases.

- **Surveys:** We mentioned surveys a bit earlier. They're tried and true. You can go paper or digital. You can find out things like whether users are recommending your website or product. You can use the results in your comparative benchmarking. What is also great about surveys is that you can include open-ended comments that add dimension to the quantitative data you're gathering.

Your Data Reveals Behaviors and Better Ways to Target

Using a range of technologies and techniques, you can increase the effectiveness of your products through **Customer Behavioral Targeting (Beh)**. There are three primary dimensions:

- **Customer Acquisition:** The main goal of your product, especially at its initial release, is the acquisition of new customers. An intuitive, considerate customer experience leads to better conversions. By following the consumer's interests, patterns, and behaviors, you effectively reach consumers in a natural fashion.

- **Branding Reinforcement:** We'll get to branding in Chapter 11, but after you've acquired a customer, you need to keep up the conditioning of consumers' perceptions of your brand and increase awareness, recall, and equity over time so when they're ready to come back, they know exactly who to go to: you.

- **Customer Retention:** Think like Amazon and pull together your user data to achieve a deeper understanding of customer predispositions. You can then provide recommendations and offers that map back to those needs to improve the experience even before they ask you how.

Leveraging Customer Insights

You will note in the earlier diagram for the *Customer Experience Program* the right side is focused on gathering customer insights. The **Customer Experience Insights (Cei)** program collects, measures, and manages data to feed back into the customer experience, either through immediate action or longer-term strategy. This includes existing customer programs such as the Voice of the Customer and a Customer Advisory Panel, which are shown in diagrams on the following pages.

Insights Inform Decisions

A **Customer Experience Insights (Cei)** program provides you with data to inform a variety of business and design decisions. Below are some of the things that great insights can address for your startup as it continues to grow:

Business Strategy Issues

- Do users understand the site's value proposition? Do their perceptions of the value proposition change after site usage?
- Does the actual customer experience stay consistent with brand positioning? Does it stay consistent with the offline brand?
- How does user experience on the site compare with competitors' sites?
- After interacting with the site, are users likely to come back? Why or why not?
- What features are users expecting to see on the site?
- Does a particular type of user (e.g., novice users, power users) react differently to the site? What special needs do particular groups have?

Design Issues

- Can users accomplish critical tasks, like searching and registering? If not, why?
- At what point in the process of pursuing specific tasks do users fail or give up? Why?
- Do users notice and make use of particular features on the site?
- How much time and effort does it take to accomplish critical tasks? How can this best be reduced?
- Do users read and make use of information provided? Do users have enough information?

GETTING READY . . .

At this point in your startup journey, you're exploring how to craft a stellar customer experience. To get started you should work through the following exercises:

- Define your **Customer Experience Personas (Per)** with a Proto-Persona Exercise
- Outline the **Customer Journey Map (Map)** with an Experience Mapping exercise
- **Prototype (Pro)** Your **Minimum Delightful Product (Mdp)**
- Outline Your **Customer Experience Management (Cxm)** Framework
- Set the **Customer Experience Benchmarks (Bch)** you wish to measure
- Start a **Customer Usability Testing (Ust)** Program
- Identify the **Customer Experience Insights (Cei)** to improve the customer experience

LEVERAGING A CUSTOMER ADVISORY PANEL

(Source: Wikipedia)

A customer advisory panel is a group of existing customers convened on a regular basis to advise company management on industry trends, business priorities, and strategic direction. It is different from a focus group in that its membership is made up of senior executives from customer companies, not product users. Topics of discussion tend to be more strategic than tactical.

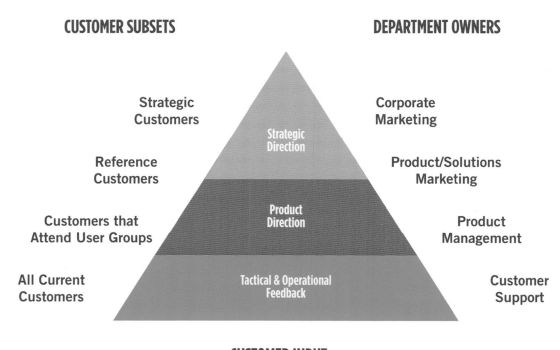

CUSTOMER SUBSETS		DEPARTMENT OWNERS
Strategic Customers	Strategic Direction	Corporate Marketing
Reference Customers		Product/Solutions Marketing
Customers that Attend User Groups	Product Direction	Product Management
All Current Customers	Tactical & Operational Feedback	Customer Support

CUSTOMER INPUT

*Data Source: Wikipedia, Forrester Research, Inc. 2007, Temkin Group 2011

CUSTOMER INSIGHTS WITH CUSTOMER ADVISORY PANELS AND VOICE OF THE CUSTOMER PROGRAMS

Running a Voice of the Customer (VOC) Program

The Voice of the Customer program is a market research technique that produces a detailed set of customer wants and needs, organized into a hierarchical structure, and then prioritized in terms of relative importance and satisfaction with current alternatives. Voice of the Customer studies typically consist of both qualitative and quantitative research steps. They are generally conducted at the start of any new product, process, or service design initiative in order to better understand the customer's wants and needs, and as the key input for new product definition, Quality Function Deployment (QFD), and the setting of detailed design specifications.

LEVELS OF THE VOICE OF THE CUSTOMER

	Description	Used to:
Relationship tracking	Survey customers at regular intervals (e.g., quarterly, annually) on how they feel about the company. Use simple metrics such as likelihood to repurchase, or likelihood to switch companies.	• Set long-term corporate goals and track overall progress • Focus investments in key areas that correlate with improvements
Interaction monitoring	Survey customers after key interactions to determine how satisfied they are with both the results and the processes.	• Spot problematic trends • Provide detailed feedback to/about frontline employees • Trigger an immediate response to events like negative feedback from a key customer
Continuous listening	Sample frontline customer interactions on a regular basis by listening to call center conversations, reading emails, chat logs, or blogs, or by visiting stores/brances.	• Identify early signs of problems • Understand the emotional side of customers' issues and concerns
Project infusion	Systematically include definitions of target customers' needs within project plans for tools like design personas and requirements documents.	• Keep projects focused on the needs of specific customer segments • Align investments on a core set of customer experience improvements
Periodic immersion	Periodically get executives to spend significant time interacting with customers and frontline employees.	• Identify obstacles encountered by employees • Question the status quo about business rules and processes

20 LEADING AND EMERGING PRACTICES FOR VOICE OF THE CUSTOMER PROGRAMS

VoC Discipline	Leading and Emerging Practices
Detect	1. Social media integration 2. Contact center insight extraction 3. Frontline feedback solicitation 4. Unstructured feedback expansion 5. Strategic sampling
Disseminate	6. Consultative supporting 7. Role-based reporting 8. Insight alerting 9. CRM integration 10. VoC community building 11. Customer callback institutionalization
Diagnose	12. Customer journey and segment analysis 13. Diagnostic capacity creation 14. End-user drill-down enablement
Discuss	15. Ongoing cross-functional participation 16. Clear executive involvement
Design	17. Customer collaboration 18. Promoter activation
Deploy	19. Experience release planning 20. Iteration planning

Brand

CRAFT THE EXPERIENCE

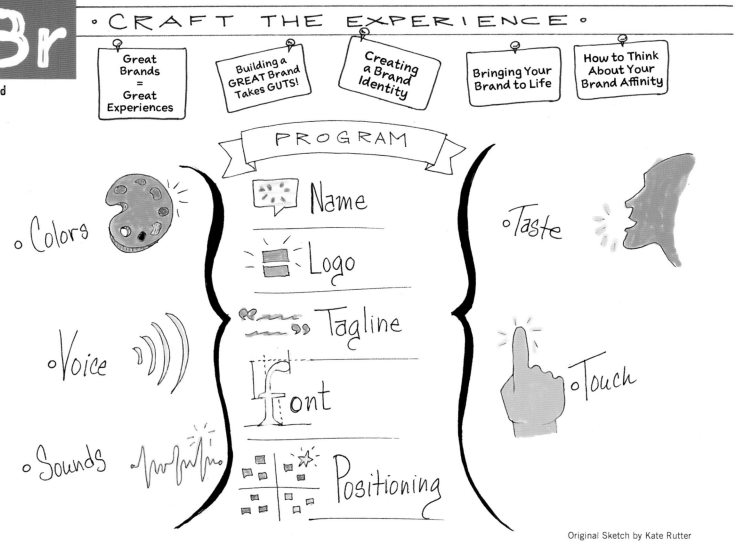

Great Brands = Great Experiences

Building a GREAT Brand Takes GUTS!

Creating a Brand Identity

Bringing Your Brand to Life

How to Think About Your Brand Affinity

PROGRAM

- Colors

- Voice

- Sounds

Name

Logo

Tagline

Font

Positioning

- Taste

- Touch

Original Sketch by Kate Rutter

Authentic brands don't emerge from marketing cubicles or advertising agencies.
They emanate from everything the company does . . .

—*Howard Schultz*

The New Brand Order

When Ja-Naé and her team started Wild Women Entrepreneurs (Wild WE), they all agreed to make sure they created a place where women entrepreneurs felt safe to be themselves and talk about their failures as well as their successes. So, they set off to make sure every piece of branding conveyed to the entrepreneurial members that this was "their community." No BS, no suits, no pretense. Just real women starting real businesses while living real lives. This passion and consistency of brand is what allowed Wild WE to grow to fifty-five chapters in seven countries in under a year.

This section of the book began with "The Customer Experience" which voices the message that without a great experience, your company will fail. The continuation of that message is shaping a brand for your company that lives beyond your four walls and captures the essence of your company. Almost every startup uses their product as their message,

which is just dead wrong. Leading with your brand and its essence will help you create a whole world around it, if done right.

GREAT BRANDS = GREAT EXPERIENCES

Brand is one of those words everybody uses, but it's the unsung hero of a startup. Sure, brands can be sexy, but everyone seems to focus on their product MVP and getting "traction." Branding, however, is a cornerstone element of the Startup Equation. When most startups assess their priorities, branding often gets put on the to-do list closer to launch.

Your startup needs to be think about branding from the start. As an entrepreneur, you should view your brand as the emotional response to what you provide your customers. Your startup is branding itself from the very moment you ask a friend or family member to support your idea.

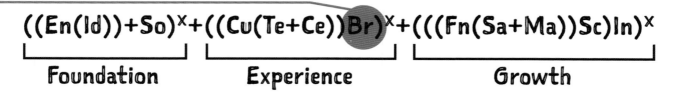

Foundation Experience Growth

Branding is one of the most important aspects of any business because it is the foundation of how you will communicate about your company. It is the promise of your brand and how people will psychologically connect with your company. From the creation of your logo to your single word equity, these elements will help you figure out where to start.

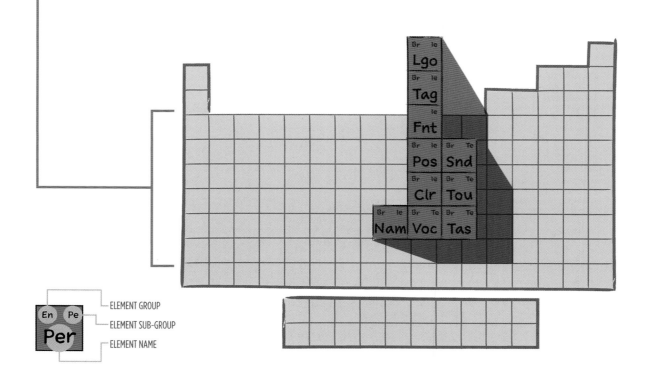

ELEMENT GROUP
ELEMENT SUB-GROUP
ELEMENT NAME

BRAND (BR) IDENTITY ELEMENTS

The brand identity is the representation of your company's mission, attributes, values, strengths, and passions. Having a strong brand identity fosters customer loyalty through clarity. People will know who you are and what you stand for. This allows them to choose whether or not to align with your business. Here are some of the brand identity elements to be aware of:

Name (Nam)

Names are quite powerful. Each one has a distinct difference. Some debate that getting your company name right is the most important aspect to branding. We will let you decide that yourself.

Logo (Lgo)

Your company logo is your symbol. It's one of the first things someone will see when they visit your website or looks at anything with your name on it. A unique logo is one of the main ways people remember your company.

Tagline (Tag)

A really great tagline conveys a company's uniqueness with personality. The most memorable taglines connect on with customers on an emotional level and illustrates what your company does.

Font (Fnt)

Typography plays a key psychological role in how people view your brand. The typeface matters because of its power to create a sense of recognition and trust between you and your customers. The logo, the typeface within it, and all of your branding identity elements all go hand in hand.

Positioning (Pos)

A brand's positioning is a one or two sentence statement that clearly identifies what your unique value is to your customer and what your brand promise is to them. That promise may be about how you differ from the competition or why your customers should care. No matter what, it sets the expectation in the customer's mind.

Colors (Clr)

The color of your brand is an essential character in your company. When choosing a color to represent your brand, it goes way beyond personal preferences. Color is the very first perception customers will have of your company, and with that comes an immediate emotional response to your company.

BRAND (BR) SENSES TESTING ELEMENTS

When creating your startup, you want to brand it so that it sticks in people's minds. It is not about just your product or service, but about the experience you create and that includes all 5 senses. But using sensory branding, you invoke an emotional response from your customers and this can mean the difference between acquiring new customers or not.

Voice (Voc)

Your brand voice is not what you say, but how you say it. This encompasses more than the words you choose. It encompasses their rhythm and their pace. A brand's tone of voice should be distinctive, recognizable and unique. Your brand's voice will inform all of its written copy, including its website, social media messages, emails and packaging.

Sounds (Snd)

A sound that is associated with your startup can be a jingle, a unique voice, a theme song, or familiar beep. It doesn't have to be extravagant, but it has to be unique to you.

Touch (Tou)

People pay close attention to product design. Tactile aspects can improve usability and customer satisfaction. How a product feels matters almost as much as its functionality in the consumer's mind. Physical proximity to product is elemental to purchase decisions.

Taste/Smell (Tas)

The sense of smell is a powerful tool, and can trigger emotions that aren't exactly defined, as well as evoke memories. When people smell, it has a distinctive attachment to an object or place. The sense of smell emotionally affects humans up to 75% more than any other sense. The combination of smell with taste invites people to engage multiple senses at once.

One startup in Boston knows how important it is to evoke that emotional response through its brand and it's Roxy's Grilled Cheese. When asked about starting a business and the importance of branding, here is what Founder, James DiSabatino had to say:

SEQ: How did you go about starting Roxy's and what was your motivation beyond creating it?

DiSabatino: I became an entrepreneur because I had to. It's really that simple. I can't work for someone else, the same way some people can't eat peanuts. But at the same time, I didn't want to do anything that anyone had done before in Boston. I'm sure a lot of people dream of things like this, but it clicked for me in 2010, shortly after finishing Emerson and having traveled the world a few times with my brother's band, *The Carrier*.

While traveling Europe, we would arrive in cities with incredible spreads of food. But the constant thing we got in every country was an abundance of cheese and bread. I made a joke saying that I would love to make cheese sandwiches for a living, and then I realized that I could. Not only that, I could do it out of a food truck, something that no one had done before in Boston. It was a case of personal need meeting opportunity.

SEQ: What is the secret sauce in Roxy's branding?

DiSabatino: Authenticity. It's equal parts aggressive and sophisticated, I think. It's congruent with how we run our business.

SEQ: Which branding elements were core to getting Roxy's up and running?

DiSabatino: It was important to me that our branding evoke the same emotional response as the experience of dining with us. It's D.I.Y but driven by hospitality. We were creating a world class concept, so we needed world class branding, even if it's a bit off-kilter at first look.

Some will argue that you don't need to worry about branding, and they'll point to tech companies like Amazon, Dropbox, or Facebook to make their point. True, these companies used good PR, viral marketing, and word of mouth, but despite the arguments otherwise, they were communicating a brand message from the beginning. So many startups seem to profess that their product is their message. After building products for two decades, we're convinced this approach is plain wrong. There will be many who argue with us, but let's look at the evidence.

BUILDING A *GREAT* BRAND TAKES GUTS!

Like your personal relationships, you discover that brands (including yours) have different dimensions. Erik Roscam Abbing of Zilver depicted these dimensions in the graphic "Brand and Customer Relationship Model."[1] He also added marketing and product development into the mix to make the model more holistic.

Roscam Abbing broke the model into four dimensions or quadrants with clear connections between each.

1. The Organization (Purple): Your company
2. The Consumer (Orange): Your user/customer
3. Brand Reflection (Blue): Your internal discussion
4. Brace Action (Green): Your brand as a driver for creativity and innovation

Your brand's maturity can change how someone relates to it. We compare it to the different approach you use for a new customer versus a customer you've had for years. Your brand experience is not one size fits all.

Asserting Your Brand Through Value and Customers

There are strategy gurus who suggest that business strategy comes first. However, we argue that if your strategy doesn't focus on value and customers, you're on shaky ground. To bring your brand to life, you must define a few things to establish your brand experience.

First, brands are built over time. As a startup you compete on brand. Once a relationship exists based on the exchange of value (e.g. products, services), your brand begins to accrue meaning either intentionally or unintentionally.

Second, brands are a promise of what the customer values and what the business offers to the customer. Branding elevates ideas from being visual identifiers that provide value to expectations about the value itself.

THE FLOW OF BRAND AND EXPERIENCE

The figure below shows how brand and experience flows between the customer and your business.

There are three primary building blocks of connecting brand and experience.

1. Brand—who you are as a business and what you stand for.

2. Product services—actual value customers are paying for in the first place

3. Engagement experience—where when and how you interact with customers

These building blocks help translate the brand into engaging value and reinforce brand meaning through the real experiences of real people.

UPSTREAM FLOW

The upstream flow from customers begins with the experiences they have around value with the products and services you offer, from initial awareness through to purchase and use. If there is real value, you can strengthen the perception of the value by paying attention to relationships and allowing customers to add their own meaning to the brand.

DOWNSTREAM FLOW

The downstream flow from the business begins with the definition of brand. When done correctly brand is a guide for the value propositions of the products and services offered by the business. If it all goes well customers perceive this value as the business intended.

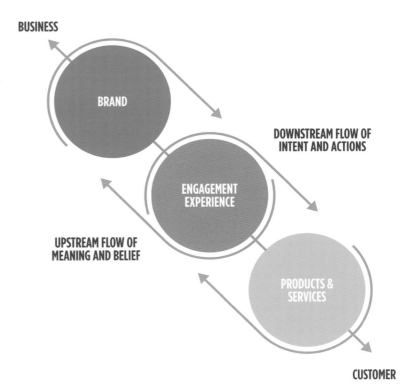

*Data Source: Newbery, Patrick and Farnham, Kevin, Experience Design: A Framework for Integrating Brand, Experience and Value, 2013, p76

HOW GREAT BRANDS AND GREAT EXPERIENCES CONNECT

Great experiences are predicated on the idea that a brand is connected to value and is perceived by the customer to have real meaning and true benefit to the business. In this integrated framework diagram we see four components:

1. **Brand concept and value pillars**—This is used to convert the basic essence of the brand from abstraction into actionable areas that inform what kind of value can be created for customers.

2. **Brand attributes**—Your company's brand attributes transform the brand from a shallow static identity system that is largely used for consistent recognition into the DNA that can be used to guide the development of artifacts, behaviors and qualities of the experience.

3. **Products and services**—This covers how your company meets the needs of customers in ways that provide real value.

4. **Customer journey**—As discussed in the previous chapter, this connects the stages of engagement and qualities of experience that customers have with your brand.

Data Source: Newbery, Patrick and Farnham, Kevin, Experience Design: A Framework for Integrating Brand, Experience and Value, 2013, p168

BRAND AND CUSTOMER RELATIONSHIP MODEL Figure 11.5

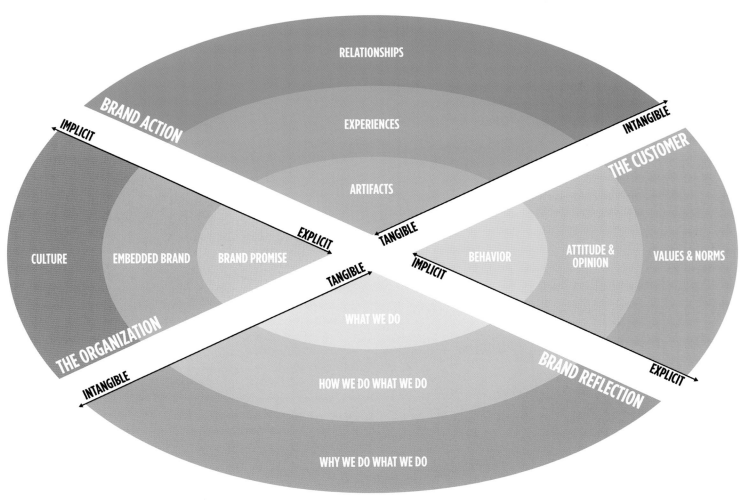

RELATIONSHIPS

BRAND ACTION

IMPLICIT

EXPERIENCES

INTANGIBLE

THE CUSTOMER

ARTIFACTS

EXPLICIT

TANGIBLE

CULTURE   EMBEDDED BRAND   BRAND PROMISE

IMPLICIT   BEHAVIOR   ATTITUDE & OPINION   VALUES & NORMS

TANGIBLE

WHAT WE DO

THE ORGANIZATION

INTANGIBLE

HOW WE DO WHAT WE DO

BRAND REFLECTION

EXPLICIT

WHY WE DO WHAT WE DO

*Data Source: Erik Roscam Abbing, 2009

Third, companies are no longer their own brand; customers own the brand. This is thanks to technology and the social web. Value is increasingly based on experience and how that matches up with the expectation set by the brand.

The Importance of a Brand

Why does your brand matter? Because all our brains work roughly the same way. Humans like to take data and try to decode a meaning behind the data. Through your brand, you can motivate behavior by supplying data that our brains will want to decode. You can then watch and figure out why people react the way they do. The really great brands figure this process out quickly and understand how to get in the minds of their customers. Figuring out your branding allows for people to connect with your company in a way that aligns with their values and needs.

A brand represents your visible promise to the world about your company. It's also how people will perceive your company. It's critical to your business to make sure you have the right brand and elements. We won't walk through a complete branding session, but we'll highlight the elements that deserve priority. Generally, these branding elements fall into two element groups: *Identity* and *Senses*.

CREATING A BRAND IDENTITY

Brand identity speaks to the totality of the brand. At minimum, this includes:

1. **Name (Nam):** The right name can influence buyers and become a staple of your company's entire image.

2. **Logo (Lgo):** Once you have your name and tagline, it's time to represent your brand visually. A logo offers the most impactful way to visualize a brand. The best logos offer a distinctive, but simple image of your brand. A great logo in one image conveys the meaning of the brand and the message that accompanies it.

3. **Tagline (Tag):** A tagline usually comes from your positioning statement. Your positioning statement defines your unique selling

proposition. Your tagline is a quick and effective way to communicate your purpose.

4. **Font (Fnt):** Font selection is a key component in successful communications. Your typography needs to work as part of the overall brand design.

5. **Positioning (Pos):** Successful brands appear both relevant and important to the consumer. They also prove memorable because they alone hold a unique position.

6. **Colors (Clr):** Colors mean many things to different people. Your brand color palette will have a visceral and profound effect on everyone who sees it.

On the next few pages you will complete the following exercises:

1. Name Your Brand

2. Craft the Essence of Your Logo

3. Craft a Tagline for your Startup

4. Draft Basic Brand Positioning

Brand architecture refers to the relationship between brands the company owns and uses. The vertical axis of the matrix is a spectrum of a branded house versus a house of brands.

The horizontal axis of this framework speaks a bit more to the qualities of the market that customers should perceive in the brand's value. You could view this as a rollup of the brand attributes or criteria for developing and prioritizing attributes. From pragmatic and tangible to idealistic and aspirational, you need to make sure your customers agree with the values you've identified for your brand and startup.

If your startup desires to be a house of brands, then each member brand must have a clear and intended value perception. Whether the brands relate to one another depends on whether a given customer is likely to buy from more than one brand and how the value delivered relates to the other brands.

Pulling in the Senses

Sensory branding leverages all five senses to connect your customers and potential customers on a much deeper level. By taking a holistic approach, you are helping your customer have a deeper emotional connection to your brand. These elements add authenticity, distinctiveness, and compelling brand stories.

To create a holistic brand strategy, you will want to:

- Understand the core equity of your brand
- Identify your brand's true "sense"
- Align this with customers' desired emotions and feelings
- Craft integrated messages you want to send
- Decide the channels you plan to use and the senses you intend to tap into within each element of your brand

BRINGING YOUR BRAND TO LIFE

The brand you build can take on a life of its own and become a living entity separate from you and your team. Like people, brands have a personality, a soul, belief systems, aspirations, and ambitions. Brands also have the ability to inspire and change lives. This brand essence connects to the underlying idea that it's important for the business to help the customer understand the value the business creates and how it relates to customer needs and perceptions.

In addition to a brand's essence, there are brand attributes. These qualities help characterize the brand as it's expressed through touchpoints between the business and customers. They should also be applied to the quality of the interaction that anyone has with the brand. By defining your brand's attributes, you'll set a standard that supports long-lasting relationships between your brand and customers. As a result, you establish an emotional connection between your company and real people, a connection that creates an experience.

Then, through our limbic brain, we recall those experiences and the feelings associated with them. If you've done right by your brand, people will recall your great brand and connect it to great experiences. It's a win for both you and your customers.

> **EXERCISE: The Emotional Connection**
>
> It's one thing to talk about it, but it is another to find that emotional connection with your customers. Here are a few questions to ask yourself and your team:
>
> 1. What are we passionate about?
> 2. What motivates us?
> 3. What are we the most proud of?
>
> By answering these questions, you can begin to build out the emotional connection that is meaningful and should be conveyed at all times. Someone who knows about bringing passion to a brand is Jeff Hayzlett. Jeff was the Chief Marketing Officer of Kodak before going out on his own. From building the Kodak brand to building his own brand, Jeff spoke to us about what the essence of brand is all about.

SEQ: You joined Kodak in 2006 and you were pretty keen to help reinvent the brand. What were the first things that you did to get a handle on like understanding their brand identity?

Hayzlett: One, the company itself had a great brand identity, it was just unfortunately the wrong one for where they were going. If you look at the company as it was back in 2006-2010, it's a B2B company. That was their future as a business to business, but they were known as a consumer company. Most people would think of Kodak and still think it's a consumer company, it's a film company, it's a camera company and they're so far from that. They weren't able to make the transition.

SEQ: What do you think it means be a great brand?

Hayzlett: I think most people get the word *brand* confused. It's the iconic representation of ownership. Then we transferred that over to the brand

Choosing a name may not seem like the biggest challenge your company faces, but the right name can influence buyers and become a staple of your company's entire image. The most notable brands of the world understand that a name should never be chosen on a whim—it must be carefully planned and selected with purpose.

THE THREE APPROACHES

There are three common approaches that companies use to name their businesses. Each style offers benefits and drawbacks depending on the goals of the company.

"   "      ABC+D=NAME

The Blank Slate:
Choosing a broad and abstract company name that doesn't indicate what the business actually does.

The Direct Approach:
Choosing a name that describes exactly what the business does.

Coining a Name:
Making up a new word for the company name doesn't currently exist in language.

Example: Apple, Inc.

Example: Burger King

Example: Skype

COINING A NAME

When a company decides to coin a new word for their name, they do so with intent. Most coined names were chosen because they say something about the company.

Using Prefixes & Word Segments:
Coined words can convey a message by using common prefixes or suffixes.

Combining Relevant Words:
Combining two words that describe what your business does can produce an original name that explains what you do.

Painting an Image:
Companies who thrive on how customers see their products often use words that trigger images and shape perception.

Example:
ACURA uses "acu" to express precision.

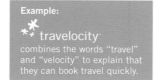
Example:
travelocity
combines the words "travel" and "velocity" to explain that they can book travel quickly.

Example:
ALIENWARE
HIGH-PERFORMANCE GAMING SYSTEMS
creates a futuristic, otherwodly image of its product with its name.

*Data Sources: entrepreneur.com, members.boston.com namelab.com, sba.gov, pnas.org

COGNITIVE FLUENCY

Regardless of the approach a business takes, science shows an easy name is usually the way to go.

Cogntitive fluency is a study in psychology that measures how easy it is to think about something.

Psychologists have found that shares in companies with easy-to-pronounce names *significantly outperform* those with hard-to-pronounce names.

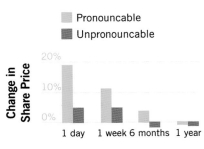

Duration From Initial Offering

Psychologists believe that the early brain likely evolved the preference for easy names and avoidance of unfamiliar ones as a survival mechanism.

In other words, if it is familiar, it hasn't eaten you yet.

MAKE COGNITIVE FLUENCY WORK FOR YOU

Since cognitive fluency can influence the way people behave with their wallets, professional business namers warn companies against choosing non-fluent names. There are always exceptions, but most **recommend avoiding** initials, words from a language foreign to the main target market, words that can be pronounced in several different ways, and words that are difficult to pronounce.

DECIDING ON A WINNER

Sometimes businesses come up with several possible names and gut instinct isn't enough to choose the winner. How do they choose the best name? Testing:

Focus Groups:
Gather a group of volunteer consumers and ask them to record how they feel about the potential, what each name makes them think of, etc.

Opinion Surveys:
Distribute surveys about your product and the potential names that could be associated with it, and see which ones participants respond positively to.

Graphic Elements:
Try combining different graphics, fonts, and logos with your names to see how the name appears when stylized for branding.

Market Testing:
Run some ads using one name, and other ads using another. Let the customers pick the winner with their wallets.

...BUT A BRAND PROCESS

Thinking about designing a logo? *Smashing Magazine* put together a thorough process for undertaking this task.

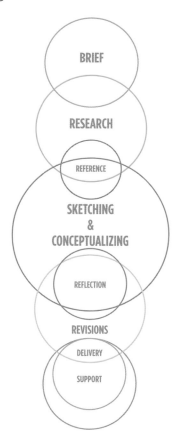

Data Source: Smashing Magazine

Design Brief: Create a design brief before designing your logo. Be clear about the desired outcome so you have a specific benchmark to reach.

Research: Interview partners or employees to gather their thoughts about the brand and what concepts the logo should convey. Also, conduct some industry research and see how others have done it. See what's worked and what hasn't. It is your job to be a problem solver first, then a designer later.

Reference: Look at current styles that may relate to the design brief you put together. Don't copy what others are doing, but recognize elements or trends that you like and your reasons for liking them. It will give you a helpful reference point.

Sketching and Conceptualizing: Now, for the fun part. It's time to get creative. Based on your brief and research, begin to sketch and conceptualize at least 25 different logos (yes, 25). This will allow you to truly explore without getting stuck on one idea or style. You may be surprised where your brainstorming takes you.

Reflection: After spending so much time in the design process, let it go for a bit and reflect. Put your concepts away for a few days and return later with a fresh perspective. It will give you time to show your work to others and get their feedback on the initial concepts.

Revisions and Positioning: Once you have had time to reflect and solicit feedback, go back and revise your concepts based on the suggestions you've received.

Presentation: It is one thing to create a great logo, but it is another thing to present it in the right light. Remember that when you are presenting your brand (logo or not), it is about the feeling you are trying to invoke and the experience you are creating for someone. Presentation is key.

CRAFTING A TAG LINE Figure 11.8

BRAND EXPERT PETER THOMSON PROVIDED SOME SAGE ADVICE ON CHOOSING A TAGLINE FOR A STARTUP:

"The most important thing to ask is where your tagline will be used. Is it going on the back of your business cards? On the signage outside your office? If you are a startup with a quirky name then you will be using your tagline locked-up below your wordmark as part of your logo. Let's be honest, you want a tagline hanging under your logo because your name doesn't have enough industry recognition (yet) for people to instantly know what it is that you actually do. In this case, the audience for your tagline is people who are already shopping for what you have, but don't yet know whether or not you sell it."

1. A tagline is not about you, it's about the pain you solve
Imagine that your customer's pain makes them like a group of people walking around with a big padlock around their necks. They are looking for a key to unlock their particular padlock. A practical and pragmatic tagline might be boring but if it explains what you do clearly enough then it can help sell widgets.

2. A tagline is not your brand essence
BMW's brand essence is Driving Excellence but they have never used it as a tagline. They have used all sort of variations ranging from "Driving's Car" to "Driving Joy" through to the perrenial "Ultimate Driving Machine". But none of these external taglines fully revealed their secret brand essence. The reason that great companies don't wear their heart on their sleeve is that an internal brand essence is about what your vision is for the impact that you will have on the world. Don't try and make your tagline convey the deepest secrets of your company or be a manifesto for changing the world.

3. A tagline is not your features and benefits
If you're asking your tagline to close a sale for you then you are being premature. You don't need to get your audience all the way to a purchase based only on the tagline. You only need your audience to be interested enough to want to find out more. The goal of a tagline is to stimulate interest. Stick to being specific about the industry you serve and the pain you solve.

*Data Source: Peter Thomson

4. A tagline doesn't need to cover everything you do
Bad taglines are a shopping list of things that a company sells. Pick whichever service you are best at, gets the best margin, or that best defines your position in the market. A tagline should help you focus.

5. A tagline is not a vague promise about the outcomes you sell
If your tagline has the words "solution" or "profit" in it then you have made a grave error in the psychology of how people buy products. If you try to sell only the outcome then your tagline will be too vague to be useful. The old advertising adage that you should "Sell the hole, not drill" only works if people know what "drills" are. If your startup is in a new category then people may not know that they want a "hole" yet. Your tagline just needs to convey what you do, not why.

6. A tagline does not have to be unique
Never kill a tagline because "it could just as easily apply to our competitors". For startups, a tagline similar to your competitors' probably means that your tagline is doing a good job of describing your industry. The uniqueness of your corporate personality will probably mean that the right tagline will still be different from your competitors'. However, your tagline is not there to differentiate you, that is the job of your brand name, key messages, and brand services.

EVALUATING YOUR BRAND

Jack Trout coined the term brand *positioning* in the early 80s. A brand's "position" is the place it occupies in the customer's mind. All brands have a position in the consumer's mind. The idea is to have it be great and viewed positively. Successful brands appear both relevant and important to the consumer. They also prove memorable because they alone hold a unique position. Use your brand positioning to convey the values and the essence of the brand, not just the core message. This approach will help you create a long-term strategy that you can tweak and pivot from as the brand organically grows.

	EXISTING PRODUCTS	NEW PRODUCTS
EXISTING MARKETS	1 BRAND RELEVANCE	2 BRAND EXTENSION
NEW MARKETS	4 BRAND EXPANSION	3 BRAND DIVERSIFICATION

BRANDED HOUSE	
PRAGMATIC	IDEALIST/ ASPIRATIONAL
HOUSE OF BRANDS	

FRAMEWORK #1 – ANSOFF GROWTH MATRIX (BRAND EDITION)

The Ansoff Growth Matrix is often used in corporate strategy. We have modified it for use with your brand strategy. You start in the upper left and move clockwise. It can help you understand whether your brand remains relevant and can be used in all the quadrants assuming that each quadrant represents a specific scenario of how your company and a customer group would interact.

FRAMEWORK #2 – BRAND ARCHITECTURE MATRIX

Brand architecture refers to the relationship between brands the company owns and uses. The vertical axis of the matrix is a spectrum of a "branded house" vs a "House of Brands". The horizontal axis of this framework speaks a bit more to the pragmatic or aspirational qualities of your brand that customers should perceive in the brand's value. You could view this as a rollup of the brand attributes or criteria for developing and prioritizing attributes.

Data Source: Newbery, Patrick and Farnham, Kevin, Experience Design: A Framework for Integrating Brand, Experience and Value, 2013, p168

BRAND POSITIONING EXAMPLES

The diagram to the right applies the Brand Architecture Matrix and explores paths companies who were once startups themselves have taken with their brand positioning.

A parent company owns and is in charge of a series of brands that can act independently of one another.

HOUSE OF BRANDS

P&G

ENDORSED BRANDS

A series of brands that are endorsed and promoted by a larger organization.

Marriott.

These are brands that are additional products or services that build upon the parent brand and its value.

iPad iPhone

SUB-BRANDS

A Branded House is a series of brands that are arranged and built around the parent company.

Virgin

BRANDED HOUSE

Data Source: Hanover Research and Brand Architecture

BRAND COLORS AND THEIR MEANING Figure 11.10

Why do companies like Coca-Cola or Red Bull use red as their primary color in comparison to Starbucks or John Deere who use green? Colors mean many things to different people. It can even spur a variety of emotions depending on your gender. Also, cultures around the world can view colors very differently. Here are a few examples of what colors mean to different cultures:

China
The color of brides, good luck, celebration, summoning
Cherokees
Triumph, success
India
Purity
South Africa
Mourning color
Western
Excitement, love, passion, stop
Hebrew
Sacrifice, sin
Japan
Life
Christian
Sacrifice, passion, love

European
Soothing, "something blue" bridal tradition
Cherokees
Defeat, trouble
Iran
Mourning, color of heaven and spirituality
China
Immortality
Hinduism
The color of Krishna
Judaism
Holiness
Christian
Christ's color
Middle East
Protection
Worldwide
"Safe" color

European
Happiness, hope, joy, cowardice, hazards, weakness
Asia
Imperial, sacred
China
Royalty, nourishing
Egypt
Mourning
Japan
Courage
India
Merchants
Buddhism
Wisdom

China
Health, prosperity, and harmony
Japan
Life
Ireland
Symbol of the entire country, Catholics
U.S.A.
Money
Western
Spring, new birth, go, Saint Patrick's Day, Christmas (with red)

European
Marriage, angels, doctors, hospitals, peace
Japan
Mourning, white carnation symbolizes death
China
Mourning, death
India
Unhappiness
Eastern
Funerals

European
Mourning, funerals, death, rebellion, cool, restfulness
China
Neutral color
Thailand
Bad luck, evil, unhappiness
Judaism
Unhappiness, bad luck, evil
Australian Aboriginals
Color of the people, ceremonial ochre

6 COLOR TIPS FOR WEB DESIGN

TIP ONE
Remember the importance of contrast

TIP TWO
Don't get carried away with color

TIP THREE
Use white space wisely

TIP FOUR
Be careful when using light texts on dark backgrounds

TIP FIVE
Emphasise important items with bold colors

TIP SIX
Make sure your colors fit the mood

Data Sources: helpscout.net/blog/psychology-of-color, colorcom.com/research/why-color-matters, KISSmetrics

The hue and the intensity of the color can make a big difference, too, again, dependent on gender. But no matter the hue, both genders tend to pick blue as their favorite color.

Your brand color palette will have a visceral and profound effect on everyone who sees it. Recent research conducted by the Seoul International Color Expo revealed that people make a subconscious judgment about a person, environment or product within 90 seconds of initial viewing. Of those assessments,62-75% are based on color alone. It's vital to pay attention to the colors that you use to represent your brand and how people connect with them.

Not sure where to start when choosing your brand colors? Here are a few steps to get you started:

Know Your Industry
Certain colors work better with specific industries. For example, if you were to open an organic food store, you may want to have a hue of green in your brand. Green in western culture signifies organic, spring, birth, nature. Most organ-ic brands have elements of green within them. Do some research to see what's working for your competitors.

Know Your Customers
Your brand colors are not about what you like, but what your customers will respond to. If you're targeting women, then having strong, primary hues won't fly for most of them. Create a few sample logos and use people you know that fit your target audience persona as a beta group. They will let you know what works for them.

You again go into quite a bit of detail for this one. I'd suggest breaking out the choosing colors section separately...

Completing the visual portion of your branding represents a big achievement. However, more than looks make up your brand. When crafting the brand experience, you'll want to incorporate all the senses. Most successful brands deliver when it comes to feeling and emotion, including:

We comprehend everything around us through our senses. They are directly linked to the limbic part of the brain that is responsible for our...

By incorporating the other senses, you are reaching the limbic part of the brain that connects our feelings, memories, and emotions.

Testing the Senses
The use of such a memorable key of branding should absolutely be used within your branding. But how does one come about identifying a scent for their brand? Here area few things to do:

Consider Your Brand Personality
First, go back to your brand personality and ask yourself if your brand had the personality of "sincerity," what would fit? Maybe warm, oven-baked cookies? Real estate agents use them and their scent all the time during open houses to try and sell a home. What scents will fit your brand personality?

Brainstorm
Brainstorm: With your brand personality in mind, brainstorm all the various memories and emotions that you associate with that type of personality. Make a list. Bring in others to help. It's better to start with a long list of potential options, than only one or two that may not work.

Test
Use that test group of friends, family and customers that you have turned into evangelists to help you narrow down what might be the right fit. Have each of them record their recollections and see if you can narrow it down to one smell.

* Data Source: slideshare.net/NonstopdesignZona/sensory-branding-13012274, fastcompany.com/1555211/10-most-addictive-sounds-world, brandessence.com.tr/en/koku_bilimi.html, wpp.com/~/media/SharedWPP/Marketing%20Insights/Reports%20and%20Studies/coley_futuresense.pdf

of a company and lot of people think it deals with your look and feel and those things, but it really deals with the promise delivered.

What promise do you deliver to your customers? I don't think most companies, especially younger companies or more immature companies, spend enough time on the essence of the brand. What is the promise you're delivering and then how do you carry that forth in your design guidelines, your energy in the way you describe the company?

HOW TO THINK ABOUT YOUR BRAND AFFINITY

Think of a brand that you love and feel absolute loyalty to and ask yourself the following questions:

1. Why is it your favorite?
2. Why do they have your loyalty?
3. As prices go up, how much would the price have to go up before you switched to another brand?
4. What other causes would force you to change brands?

Understanding why your loyalty to a brand will help you get into the mindset of your customers. This alignment will help you focus on providing value in customer relationship. It will also help you focus on your brand's current position and strategize how to get to where you want to go through *valued-based engagement*.

Whatever side of the branding argument you fall on (e.g., to start early or wait), here are a few more things to think about. Write out your answers below:

- Reaching your target audience: Who is your target audience? Does your brand identity relate to them? How?
- Social media: Who in your startup is using social media? How do they use it? Does it align with your brand values?
- If potential customers/users had to walk away and describe what you do (i.e. word-of-mouth) to someone else, what would they say about you? What would you want them to say?

- If you were to be interviewed by publications and media outlets, how would you answer the interviewer's questions? What's your sound bite message to the public?
- What does your website—often the first interaction point users will have with your brand—say about your business?

This general sense of your branding mix will help you reach out and get the funding that you need for your startup, which we will chat about in the next chapter.

At this point in your startup journey, you probably have a good idea of what you want your business to be and how it might be different and valuable. Take a step back and run through the concepts in this chapter to see which elements help.

If you want your business to succeed, then you, yes YOU, have to begin somewhere. Here are a few action items to get you going and building your brand:

- Name Your Brand
- Craft the Essence of Your Logo
- Craft a Tagline for your Startup
- Draft Basic Brand Positioning
- Tapping Into Your Emotional Connection

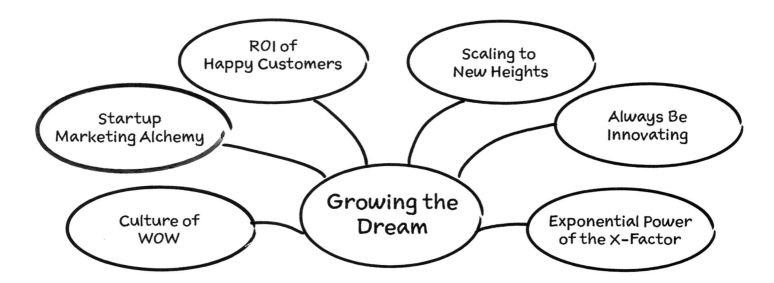

Since you have worked on building the foundation and crafting the experience of your startup, the next and what many would consider *the toughest phase is growing your dream* beyond the initial startup phase.

The Way This Part of the Equation Works

We look to this section of the equation to find the answers that will help you grow and scale your startup to the heights of its success and maintain that momentum.

Funding (Fn) Elements

Finding ways to finance that business and building a sustainable financial model are essential to getting **Funding (Fn)**. In Chapter 12 we explore the *Core* and *Model* elements so you'll get a better sense of available financing resources and potential models for your business.

Marketing (Ma) Elements

With **Marketing (Ma)** you can emphasize the value of your company to both potential customers and existing ones. In Chapter 13 we explore the *Program* and *Channel* elements that will work on little to no budget, but can be sized up as more marketing dollars become available.

Sales (Sa) Elements

Running a successful business requires selling something to someone. **Sales (Sa)** is a fundamental piece of the complete equation. In Chapter 14 we explore *Channel* and *Campaign* elements that are best for your startup.

Scale (Sc) Elements

Not every business grows to the same size. The ability to **Scale (Sc)** depends on leveraging the right things at the right time. In Chapter 15 we explore the *Core* and *Measure* subgroups to help you along the best path best.

Innovation (In) Elements

In order to stay competitive and ahead, you must embrace continuous innovation. In Chapter 16 we explore the various *Method* and *Engine* elements like design thinking and strategic foresight to push the envelope.

X-Factor (Xf) Elements

Other factors can play a role in your success, too. In Chapter 17 we explore the *Constant* and *Variable* **X-Factors (Xf)** to help you along your entrepreneurial journey.

So let's get started . . .

SECTION

4

GROWING
THE DREAM

Fn

Funding

Picking a Funding Strategy

Leveling Up With Angels and VCs

The Art of the Pitch

Beyond Investors: Loans, Grants and Cash Flow

The Rocket Fuel of Startup Accelerators and Incubators

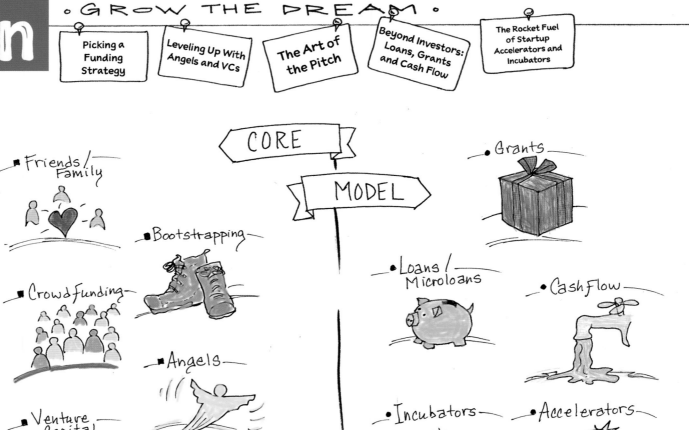

CORE

MODEL

- Friends/Family
- Bootstrapping
- CrowdFunding
- Angels
- Venture Capital
- Grants
- Loans/Microloans
- CashFlow
- Incubators
- Accelerators

Original Sketch by Kate Rutter

Profit is good.

—Dr. Karl Baehr

No Money, No Excuses

Building a startup will prove one of the hardest things you'll do. It can feel like Sisyphus pushing the rock up the mountain. Just when you think you're about to reach the top, you slide down to the bottom.

From friends and family to angels and crowdfunding, there are a number of opportunities to fit every type of startup. The biggest factor is knowing when to raise money, how much to ask for, and which funding types to pursue. You'll discover the funding journey rarely follows a straight path, and you may find opportunities in unlikely places. We'll discuss the wide range of funding elements within this chapter.

PICKING A FUNDING STRATEGY

Funding is an exercise in showmanship to convince people to part with their money so you can build something they hope will return their investment many times over. For most businesses, funding will need to be addressed at some point. Whatever tool you pull from the financial toolbox (e.g., friends and family, crowdfunding, venture capital, small business loan), make the most of it to help your company grow to the next level.

Picking a funding strategy depends on many factors. What type of business are you? How much do you need? Will you scale? How will you use the funds? And most importantly, what will you do with it? For many years funding was a familiar set of names—"friends and family," "angels," "the bank," and "VCs." In today's startup world, those opportunities still exist. Plus, there are new opportunities like crowdfunding and accelerator/incubator programs, and it costs less to start many types of businesses, something we'll cover in the next section.

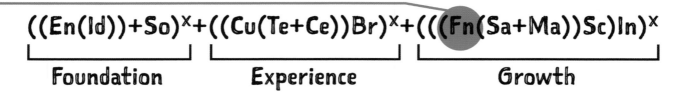

$$((En(Id))+So)^x+((Cu(Te+Ce))Br)^x+(((Fn(Sa+Ma))Sc)In)^x$$

Foundation   **Experience**   **Growth**

To help your company scale for growth, you might need to raise money. For many startups the term "Funding" is a daunting prospect with many questions—when to start, starting too early, how much funding do we need, how much equity to we give up, etc. To navigate the funding landscape we separate the funding elements into two group: Clusters and Programs.

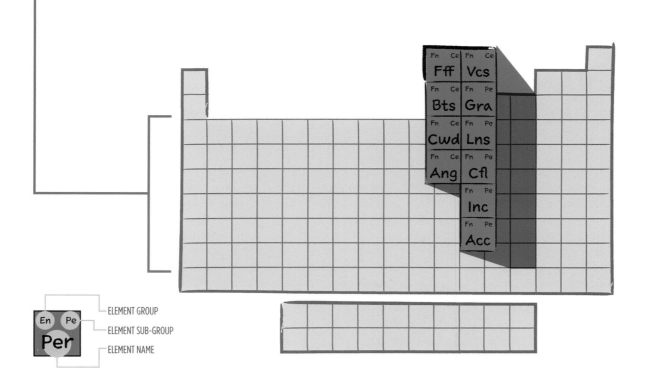

ELEMENT GROUP
ELEMENT SUB-GROUP
ELEMENT NAME

FUNDING (FN) CLUSTER ELEMENTS

The funding clusters are groups of individuals that help fund a business at various stages of its lifecycle. Some are more open and informal while others are formal and institutional. Not every startup would leverage all of these cluster types and some might not ever use any of them.

Friends/Family (Fff)
Friends and family can provide the seed capital to get you going until you can search out further funding.

Crowdfunding (Cwd)
Crowdfunding is the collection of finance to sustain an initiative from a large pool of backers—the "crowd"—usually made online by means of a web platform.

Angels (Ang)
Angels are high net worth individuals who invest their own money at early stages of a startup's life. They usually come in when higher amounts are needed to bring a company to the next stage when institutional funding is appropriate.

Venture Capital (Vcs)
Venture capital is from an institutional fund with limited partners who invest in start-ups with limited operating history, which cannot raise funds by issuing debt.

FUNDING (FN) PROGRAM ELEMENTS

This type of funding comes from the programs offered by organizations or your own internal operations. It can include government programs, banks or startup launch programs.

Grants (Gra)
Grants are non-repayable funds disbursed by one party (grant makers), often a government department, corporation, foundation or trust, to a recipient, often (but not always) a nonprofit entity, educational institution, business or an individual.

Loans/Microloans (Lns)
Loans are funding that is repayable in installments to the institution that provided the funds. Repayment is usually with an amount of interest to provide the lender with a return on their investment.

Cash Flow (Cfl)
Cash is king. This is the operating capital that comes from the cash generated from the business. It can be used as collateral to expand through loans and other debt instruments.

Accelerators (Acc)
An accelerator is a facility or a mentorship program for early stage startups. Accelerators have a competitive application process, and a company is accepted into the program based on its ideas and the team's potential.

Incubators (Inc)
An Incubator picks up where accelerators leave off. If an accelerator is similar to an undergraduate education, an incubator is like graduate school. Incubators focus on seed-funded startups on the cusp of rapid growth.

PICKING A FUNDING STRATEGY Figure 12.4

	BOOTSTRAPPED	TRUE ANGEL	SUPER ANGEL	VENTURE CAPITAL
Average Initial Investment Size	Whatever they can scrounge, re-invest profits as you go.	$10,000–$50,000	$50,000–$100,000 (individual super angels) $500,000–$1,000,000 collectively in an early round	$1,000,000+
Relationship With Entrepreneur	Self.	Family, Friend, Colleague.	Colleague, Knows Industry Expert, Credible Name.	Strictly business
Additional Value Beyond Money	Blood, sweat, and tears	Little to no involvement beyond cash investment	Involvement can be minimal to extensive. They provide industry-specific expertise and a broad network of connections.	Heavy involvement, extensive business coaching, potential future takeover of company.
Typical Reason for Investment	Desire for control, full equity, believe they can accomplish their goals on their own, and of course to re-invest business profits for continued growth.	They are friends with the entrepreneur and they have knowledge of the same industry.	They typically have multiple investments and are hoping that one of them goes huge.	They believe in the company's business plan and want to own a large piece of the company if it goes big.
Reasons Entrepreneurs Go to Them for Money	Because it is quick and easy to transfer money from you personal checking to business checking.	They have little involvement in the company, leaving the founder in control.	Generally okay with early exits, move lightning fast to fund, usually offer entrepreneur-friendly terms and don't demand control of the company. They offer social clout and often provide a vast network of industry "all-stars."	They offer large amounts of money, they will hold the entrepreneur's hand from beginning to end.
Reasons Entrepreneurs Dislike Their Type of Funding	It can limit the pace of growth and ability to scale up.	Money more investors need to be involved to get to $500k–$1 million in funding.	They may demand a large piece of the pie for what is a seemingly small cash investment. Some (but not all) may not get a lot of attention/input from super angels who are invested in hundreds of companies.	Often have to give up control of their own company, more pressure from investors to perform as they are sitting on your board.

*Data Sources: David Hauser, Co-Founder of Grasshopper Group

	BOOTSTRAPPED	TRUE ANGEL	SUPER ANGEL	VENTURE CAPITAL
Reasons for Investing	Believe in themselves and the idea, willing to risk personal savings and funds.	$10,000–$50,000	$50,000–$100,000 (individual super angels) $500,000–$1,000,000 collectively in an early round	$1,000,000+
Type of Companies They Invest In	Bold ideas hatched in the garage with the potential to change the world, or at least make a solid living.	Passion projects of friends, causes, or innovations they believe in.	Big baskets of early stage startups, often social applications or other consumer-oriented, web-based innovation.	Companies that have higher upfront R&D cost requirements such as biotech.
Portfolio/ Investment Strategy	They may have any number of other companies going at the same time depending on level of experience, i.e. first startup vs. someone who has sold three companies.	They have little to no overall portfolio strategy. They invest in what they know and love.	They spread their risk around by investing in a large amount of startups, hoping that one or two will make it big.	They have a very focused portfolio strategy with a fixed timeline depending on the type of funding.
How They Make Money	Make the company profitable!	More likely to have their portfolio return a loss without a coherent strategy, but of course some have the potential to invest in the right lottery ticket.	May pick up some cash on the convertible note carry, otherwise via a coherent portfolio strategy that allows for profitability based on a targeted number of acquisitions (big or small) i.e. 500 startups approach.	Interest carry, management fees along the way, big returns when a portfolio company goes public or is acquired.

A Benjamin and A Dream: Bootstrapping with $100

When many entrepreneurs start their businesses and they don't know where to begin, they do what Ja-Naé did with Wild Women Entrepreneurs: Bootstrap the business. Ten years ago, most entrepreneurs didn't have the option to **Bootstrap (Bts)** their startup. Today, the cost of building a company is a thousand times cheaper. With $100 and a dream, it's possible to start a company.

EXERCISE: Explore Bootstrapping

It's a great idea to assess what you need to start your business. Work through these steps to decide what you really need financially to start your business:

1. **Product:** Examine the main product/service your business will provide.
   a. Can I can create or build it myself? If not, can I bring on a co-founder with that skill set? *(continues)*

Asking these questions helps you think lean and learn what it really takes to get started. Remember: You don't need perfection to launch. You do need the ability to run on a skeleton crew that you can manage and maintain as you grow.

Up Close & Personal: Friends & Family

When it comes to starting your business, **Friends and Family (Fff)** may be the first place you check for startup funds. In many startup situations, *Friends and Family* can provide the seed capital to get you going until you can find angel investors or venture capitalists. However, the shortest route to funding may not be the best route.

While the people closest to you may want to invest in you, they're also unlikely to have enough investing experience to understand the risk. There's also the issue that this type of funding can lead to a sense of entitlement that investors should have a say-so in your company's direction. Carefully assess your options, and select *Friends and Family* who aren't interested in involving themselves in day-to-day operations.

Everybody into the Pool: The Power of Crowdfunding

Even with *Friends and Family*, you may still have a funding gap, but there's another option: **Crowdfunding (Cwd)**. *Crowdfunding* relies on financing from a large pool of backers usually made online through a web platform.

Of course, you might have access to other funding, like loans, angel investors, and venture capital, but if not, crowdfunding may prove a viable way to fill the gap while testing your initial concept/minimum delightful product and building an army of evangelists.

To get started with *Crowdfunding*, you'll need to put out a call for financial support, typically through services like Kickstarter, RocketHub, or IndieGoGo. Crowdfunding comes with a few risks. Some sites (Kickstarter) won't pass on the funds if your fundraising goal isn't met. Sites that don't require you to meet your goal (IndieGoGo) will charge a higher transaction fee. Other sites offer hybrid models (RocketHub), but you'll need to weigh the options and pick the best fit.

Keep in mind that crowdfunded financing isn't considered a loan in the traditional sense. In most crowdfunding campaigns, you need to prepare product offerings, discounts, or other incentives for contributors.

We had a chance to chat with CTO and co-founder of RocketHub, Vlad Vukicevic about crowdfunding.

SEQ: What's your philosophy on crowdfunding and entrepreneurship?

Vukicevic: One of our biggest underlying beliefs is that we shouldn't be the arbiter of what's right or what's wrong, in terms of crowdfunding ideas. We said that as long as it's legal, in good taste, you can launch on RocketHub. That open philosophy really built the foundation for that pivot or that extension. If we were closed off, we would've never seen this grand, much bigger opportunity within entrepreneurship, science, even components of philanthropy, in addition to the art world.

In terms of overall crowdfunding philosophy, we feel that in five years or so, crowdfunding will be a mainstream concept. It'll be another option, in terms of fundraising, particularly for the seed level. Anywhere from a few thousand up to $100,000.

LEVELING UP WITH ANGELS AND VCS

At this point, you might be past the idea stage and you've bootstrapped things for a while, but you need to hire people and move to production. At this point, you need more capital than you have on hand, and banks consider you too great a risk. You're left with two options: **Angel Investors (Ang)** and **Venture Capitalists (Vcs)**.

The Angels and the Demons

Today, angels can commonly be found at accelerator programs and demo days. But who really is an angel? **Angels (Ang)** are high-net worth individuals who invest their own money at early stages of a startup's life. They usually come in when higher amounts are needed to bring a company to the next stage when institutional funding is appropriate.

Traditionally, an angel investor comes to the table with at least $1 million in net worth. In exchange for capital, you provide convertible debt or equity in your company. Most angels invest anywhere from $25,000 to $500,000 USD. Higher numbers tend to involve multiple angels to spread around the risk. Angels usually close the gap between the friends and family round of funding we mentioned earlier.

The Lure and Myths of Venture Capital

Venture Capital (Vcs) funding involves institutional investments by limited partners (usually wealthy individuals and pension funds) who place their money in a fund to create a larger pool. That larger pool then invests in certain types of companies at specific stages of growth. The primary difference between angels and VCs involves the source of the funds.

Angels invest their own money, and venture capitalists manage money pooled from many people. Venture capital investments often require a ten-year horizon, on average, before investors see a return. Unfortunately, not all companies that receive VC funding achieve success.

Only 10–20% of VCs do well on their exit (e.g., IPO, acquisition). VCs and entrepreneurs need to carefully select startups and weigh the timing of their investments.

While you may have a great idea, if you're ahead of the curve or you're pitching a derivative (e.g., we are the AirBnb of . . .), then you may not get funding. We won't discuss the mechanics of how VC funds work, but failing to get funding isn't personal.

If you've ever tried to raise money, you may have noticed that there's a "no-fly zone" between what angels and VCs provide. Angel rounds are usually around $100,000 to $750,000. Venture capital investments start around $2.5 million USD and can go up to over $100 million USD. A few investors, like "super angels" or syndicates, will invest in that range, but realistically, for all the time and effort you put into the fundraising process, you really want to raise enough so you don't need to go back for more later. It could put your milestones at risk.

Due Diligence is for Quant Jocks

VCs need numbers before they'll commit. It involves running various scenario models on your company (e.g. discounted cash flow) to come up with a few different projections to help set the long-term valuation of your business and whether it's a good investment match for the fund.

THE ART OF THE PITCH

At the heart of attracting a strategic investment in your company sits the great pitch. A clear, concise pitch that articulates the problem you're solving also needs to highlight the upside of the investment. This gives you focus and clarity of message for whatever audience you are talking to about your company. *We know from experience: It's damn hard*.

Ultimately, it comes down to getting the point across fast enough to keep the person engaged so they stayed interested and motivated to take action. As an exercise, we recommend following Guy Kawasaki's 10-20-30 Rule of PowerPoint. "[A] PowerPoint presentation should have ten slides, last no more than twenty minutes, and contain no font smaller than thirty points."[1]

Crowdfunding is a term used to describe individuals coming together to support—and directly fund—projects by other individuals and organizations. For small businesses and startups, crowdfunding can be an engine for job creation and development.

THE EVOLUTION OF CROWDFUNDING

The concept of crowdfunding isn't entirely new. It's come about thanks to a progression of other funding ideologies.

Microfinance   Microlending   Peer-to-Peer Lending   Crowdfunding

THE NUTS AND BOLTS

Prospective and established small business owners can use crowdfunding platforms to jump-start their next project.

Donations, Philanthropy, and Sponsorship   Lending   Investment

THE PROS AND CONS

PROS

Platform also serves as a marketing tool.

Provides a forum for feedback on the project.

Relatively inexpensive way to raise funds.

CONS

Often limited on amount of funding you can raise.

Exposes project to the public, risking copycats.

Funds may be subject to securities regulation.

DOES IT WORK?

Popular site Kickstarter has put up some pretty impressive figures since its launch two years ago, but not all projects are successful.

At a Glance, As of April 2011

$53 Million	$40 Million	20,371
PLEDGED	COLLECTED	PROJECTS

SUCCESS RATES

43%	52%	90%	21%
of all projects are succesful.	of projects with one pledge succeed.	of projects that reach 1/3 of needed funding succeed	of projects don't receive any pledges.

Data Sources: crowdsourcing.org, startsomegood.com, Kickstarter, Mashable, BusinessInsider, LexisNexis

SNAPSHOT OF VARIOUS PLATFORMS

More crowdfunding sites are introduced every year. We take a closer look at a few of the popular options out there.

TYPE OF ORGANIZATION	Kickstarter	IndieGoGo	Pozible	RocketHub	Causes/Razoo/Crowdrise	StartSomeGood
U.S. 501(c)3s Only					●	
For-Profit Enterprises Only						
Allows Unincorporated Groups	●	●	●			●
Allows Both For- and Non-Profits	●	●	●	●		●
TYPE OF PROJECT						
Creative Projects Only	●		●			
Social-Change Projects Only					●	●
TYPE OF FUNDING						
Future Revenue Sharing						
All-or-Nothing Model	●		●			
Keep-What-You-Raise Funding Model		●		●	●	
Blended Tipping-Point Funding Model						●
OTHER						
Campaigns	●	●	●	●	●	●
Venture Profiles					●	●

HOW CROWDFUNDING WORKS Figure 12.8

STEP 1

An artist brings an idea/project to the Kickstarter team, and if approved, can set up a project page.

**ARTIST WITH
AN IDEA**

**KICKSTARTER
TEAM**

STEP 2: WHICH CATEGORY?

The project must fit into at least 1 of 15 categories: Art, Comedy, Comics, Dance, Design, Fashion, Food, Film & Video, Games, Journalism, Music, Photography, Technology, Theater, or Writing & Publishing.

STEP 3: RAISE MONEY FOR YOUR PROJECT

The project owner must set a goal amount and deadline for reaching the goal, and if they receive enough pledges to meet the goal, then they keep the money, but if they don't meet the goal, they don't get any money, and pledgers are not charged. This is called **"all or nothing"** funding or a **"threshold pledge system."**

STEP 4: SET REWARDS

The project owner sets rewards for various pledge levels; this encourages the community to sponsor various amounts based on the reward they want.

STEP 5: SHOWCASE YOUR PROJECT

The project owner creates a video to showcase their project and prove that they are who they say they are.

STEP 6: ENTER THE COMMUNITY

The project enters the Kickstarter community.

STEP 7: UPDATE YOUR INVESTORS

Throughout the project, the project owner must include updates to keep their investors posted on how things are going.

STEP 8: RECEIVE THE FUNDS

If the project owners meet or exceed their goal, they receive all of the funds minus 5% which goes to Kickstarter and 3–5% which goes to Amazon IF they are using Amazon payments to receive money.

* Data Sources: crowdsourcing.org, startsomegood.com, Kickstarter, Mashable, BusinessInsider, LexisNexis, en.wikipedia.org/wiki/Crowd_Funding, en.wikipedia.org/wiki/Kickstarter, google.com/ anning/site_profile?hl=en#siteDetails?identifier=kickstarter.com&lp=true

MAXMIZE YOUR CROWDFUNDING CAMPAIGN

Choose the Right Site for You
Some sites have a focus such as arts or nonprofits. Find the one that fits your business.

Set a Realistic Target and Time Limit
Asking for too much or too little can affect your project's chances of success.

Create a Campaign Video
A personal touch pays off. Projects with videos outperform those without by 125%.

Offer Rewards
Supporters may be more eager to back you if you offer a small incentive.

Connect with Friends and Family First
Begin with word of mouth among your inner circle, then promote your campaign on social media.

Post Regular Campaign Updates
Keep supporters engaged and maintain momentum.

- Build a ten-slide pitch deck following this format:
    - **Define the problem:** Hit them with the challenge out of the gate.
    - **Solve the problem:** How does your product/service solve the problem.
    - **Pick the business model:** How will you make money and scale?
    - **Define the competition:** How big is the market, who else is doing it, and how will you do it better?
    - **Name the team:** These are the members of your "A-Team."
    - **Outline the financials:** When will you be profitable? How will you spend the investment you're requesting?
    - **Explain the milestones:** What will the funding help you do? This is also a place to describe successes to build momentum and discuss prior examples of exits for companies like yours.
    - **Issue the call to action:** Quickly summarize the one-minute pitch and tell them what they can do to invest and get in on the opportunity NOW.
- Keep it to 20 minutes and use 30-point font. A presentation is a visual aid, not a crutch. We suggest adding images to reinforce your pitch.
- Find some time to practice your pitch with people you trust that give constructive feedback. Pick advisors or even friends who have experience with pitches.

BEYOND INVESTORS: LOANS, GRANTS AND CASH FLOW

Cash Flow (Cfl) is king. It's the operating capital that can be used as collateral to expand through loans and other debt instruments. Venture capital and angel investors might work for certain businesses, but they only cover a small part of the lending marketplace. In traditional small

(continued on page 189)

WHO ARE ANGELS?

Retired industry executives

People well versed in a specific industry

Individuals with the financial means to help new entrepreneurs

Angel investors contribute about **90% of seed capital** to aspiring businesses.

HOW TO WOO THEM: Nail the pitch Speak clearly Strong eye contact Dress well

WHAT ARE ANGELS?

Provide the financial capital for business start-ups

Act as mentors throughout the process

 $ **$** $

In 2011, angel investors gave a total of **$22.5 billion** to more than 66,000 entrepreneurial ventures.

WHERE TO FIND THEM

Word of mouth

Trade groups

Online investor networks

"My goal is to get **100 introductions** to get **10 meetings** to get **3 presentations** to close **1 deal.**"

Funding Criteria	Angels
Quantum of funds	Low
Cost of funds	High
Speed to get funds	Fast
Availability of options	Many
Ease of discovery	Hard
Due Diligence	Easy
Mentorship and Coaching	Great
Cost Support	None
Restrictive Terms	Minimal
Control you give up	Minimal
Business Development	Great

STAGE OF INVESTMENT
Average Stage of Company Receiving Investment

 39.2%
Seed/Startup

 40%
Early Stage

 18.5%
Expansion

 2.3%
Later Stage

60,000 Companies Per Year
They Invest in Approximately 60,000 Companies Per Year

60,000 Companies

80% of angel investments are seed or early stage investments

Data Sources: Carolyn M. Brown, Karen Axelton, Brent Bowers, Guy Kawasaki, SmallBusinessNotes.com, AngelreSources.org, WSBE.unh.edu/

$90,000
Average Angel Investor Annual Income

$750,000
Average Angel Investor Net Worth

$37,000
Average Individual Investment Per Venture

Angels Invest in 1 out of 10 Business Deals

47
Average Age of an Angel Investor

Angel Investments Created

106,400
New Jobs in 2012

That's 4 Jobs Per Angel Investment

59.2%
Increase

Active angel investors increased by 59.2% from 2002 to 2011 (from 200,000 to 318,480)

43.3%
Increase

Dollars invested increased by 43.3% from 2002 to 2011 (from $15.7 billion to $22.5 billion)

Healthcare
20.1%

Mobile and Telecom
14.9%

Consumer Products and Services
5.8%

Electronics
4.5%

Angel Investor Deals Made By Industry

Internet 31.2%

Other 23.5%

ANGEL INVESTMENTS IN:
2010 – $20.1 billion
2011 – $22.5 billion
Q1 and Q2 of 2012 $9.2 billion

All Angels Want: A Stake in a Successful Company
…usually a five to 25 percent stake in the business and perhaps an annual return of at least 15 to 20 percent over five years as well, depending on the scale of risk.

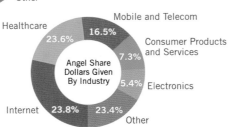

Healthcare
23.6%

Mobile and Telecom
16.5%

Consumer Products and Services
7.3%

Electronics
5.4%

Angel Share Dollars Given By Industry

Internet 23.8%

Other 23.4%

INSIDE THE INVESTOR'S MIND
Jeff Clavier Walks Through Early Investment Analysis

How do I feel about working with this team 5–7 years?

TEAM

Alpha Product Release

PRODUCT

TRACTION

Within 3 Years

MARKET OPPORTUNITY

I like everything so far, but what will it take to raise Series A 18 months from now?

VALUATION

The Ideal Combo

1 Developer
1 Designer
1 Business Expert

Too Many People

5 Founders

Lonely Journey, But You Can Do It

Solo Founder
(ex. minte.com)

Seen It Work

Married
(ex. Eventbrite)

Who Will Build?

All Business Experts

Alpha Product Release

Is there organic retention?

What's the user acquisition model?

Revenue Opportunities

Feedback from Early Users

Retention is Key

Unit Economics
Comparables
  LTV
  RVP
  rDAU
Rough Acquisition Costs
  SEM
  Facebook
  PPI

Enterprise (SaaS)

$10–$50M
Revenue

Consumer Product

10M–100M
Users

Is it expensive to build (ex. e-commerce marketplace)?

Are VCs interested in this type of product?

Okay, I'll Invest!

Traditional VC Expectation:
"I will lose 30% of my investments"

SoftTechVC's Result:
Lost about 20%

*Data Sources: Anna Vital, softtechvc.com, fundersandfounders.com

FUNDING

FOUNDER DILUTION

Who's Joining Us?

OTHER INVESTORS

FUNDS CONTACTED

Always Use Lawyers

COST OF FUNDING

Last as Long as You Can (Family and Friends)
Bootstrap
0–$100K

Lasts 12–18 Months
Seed
$1M–$1.5M

Lasts 2 Years
Series A
$3M–$5M

Series B
$8M–$15M

Incubators
5%–10%

Seed Round
Option Pool
10%–20%
Round
20%–25%

Series A
20%–25%

5–15 in Cap Table
1–3 uVCs
1 Traditional VC
(if you must)
Helpful Angels
(with expertise,
time, Rolodex,
syndication)

Don't Talk to Competitors

Pre-Marketing
5 Funds

While Fundraising
10 out life of
20–25 funds

Incorporation and Convertible Note
$5,000

Equity Round
$20,000
$30,000

Other Rounds
$30,000
$50,000

"I can sum it all up for you in my '3-Asses Rule'"

Jeff Clavier
Managing Partner, SoftTechVC

WHAT NEVER WORKS

IS IT WORKING?

140 COMPANIES FUNDED

85 Still Going on

25 Dead

30 Got Acquired
ex. Mint.com (x17 return)

DOES IT WORK?

SMART TEAM

KICK PRODUCT

BIG   MARKET

No Crisp Vision of Product

No Vision How to Acquire Users

Founder Says "In 5 years Google will buy us"

Will the Company Raise Series A?
Yes
Great!
No
Let's find a
soft landing:
Acquisition
Aquihire

At the early stages valuation does not show the true value of the company. It shows how much of the company investor gets for his investment.

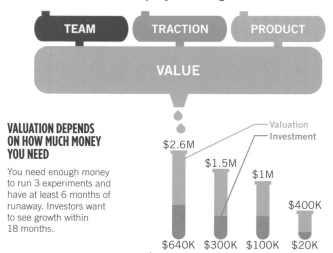

TEAM · TRACTION · PRODUCT

VALUE

VALUATION DEPENDS ON HOW MUCH MONEY YOU NEED

You need enough money to run 3 experiments and have at least 6 months of runaway. Investors want to see growth within 18 months.

— Valuation
— Investment

$2.6M
$1.5M
$1M
$400K

$640K $300K $100K $20K

VALUATION DEPENDS ON WHO YOU TAKE MONEY FROM

Micro-VC	Super Angel	Angel	Incubator
20%	16%	9%	5%

INVESTORS FIND SIMILAR COMPANIES

and figure out their valuation-to-revenue ratio—the "multiple." Then they multiply your company's revenue by that multiple.

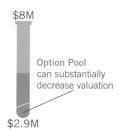

$8M

Option Pool
can substantially
decrease valuation

Similar Companies
Revenue : Valuation

Your Company
Your Revenue : x

$2.9M

HOW TO CALCULATE VALUATION

Find
Similar
Companies

v > r
How Many Times
Their Valuation Is
Bigger than Revenue?

$$\frac{\text{Enterprise Value}}{\text{Earnings or Users}} = \text{Multiple}$$

Calculate
the Multiple

$x?
Multiply Your Revenue
By the Multiple

DATE
Take Revenues
This Month, Year,
and Next Year

Calculate Best Case,
Worst Case, and
Base Case

Triangulate
the 3 Cases

Project When
the Startup
Will Exit

Discount Earnings by
the Time Value of Money

*Data Sources: Determining Valuation Multiples, AVC.com; the NASDAQ and NYSE listing requirements, ListingCenter.NASDAQomx.com; Halo Report, AngelResourceInstitute.org/halo-report; Anna Vital

HOW IS THE COMPANY DOING?

Acqui-Hire
The team is going strong, but the product is not taking off.

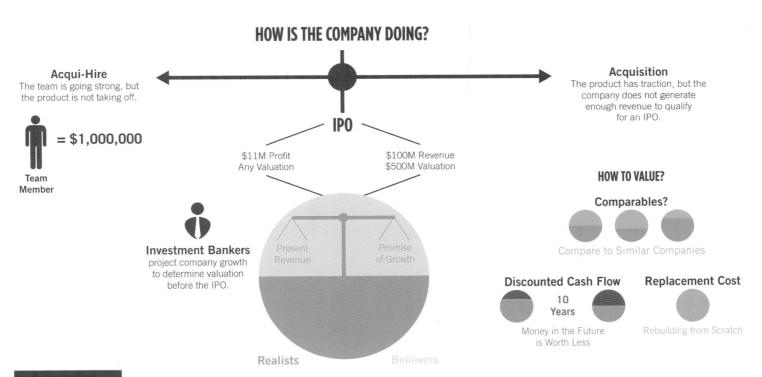

= $1,000,000

Team Member

Acquisition
The product has traction, but the company does not generate enough revenue to qualify for an IPO.

IPO

$11M Profit
Any Valuation

$100M Revenue
$500M Valuation

Investment Bankers
project company growth to determine valuation before the IPO.

Present Revenue

Promise of Growth

Realists

Believers

HOW TO VALUE?

Comparables?
Compare to Similar Companies

Discounted Cash Flow
10 Years
Money in the Future is Worth Less

Replacement Cost
Rebuilding from Scratch

WHY FINANCE?

	~Time	~Needed	Spent On?	~Valuation		~Seed Investor Gets		~Series A Investor Gets		~Series B Investor Gets		~You Get	
Gestation	9 mo.	$125K	MVP Design, Engineering, and Testing	$500K		25%						75%	
Commercialization	18 mo.	$1M	Sales & Production/ Engineering Support to Keep Up	$3M		20%		30%				50%	
Growth	18 mo.	$2.4M	Expanding Into New Segments/Locations, Brand, & Rebuild	$8M		14%		21%		30%		35%	
Trade Sale or IPO	18 mo.		Finding, Pitching, & Closing with Continued Growth	$20M	$100M	$2.8M	$14M	$4.2M	$21M	$6M	$30M	$7M	$35M

THE INVESTOR DUE DILIGENCE PROCESS Figure 12.13

FIRST MEETING

When I'm meeting a startup for the first time, my goal is to understand as much about the business and team as I can.

FOUNDERS/TEAM

How do the founders know each other? How do they interact with each other? Are they passionate? How qualified are they? What would it be like to work with them?

BUSINESS

In some form, I walk through the Business Model Generation framework: value proposition, key activities, key partners, major assets, channels of distribution, customer segments, cost structure, and revenue streams. Is the problem worth solving and if the startup succeeds, how valuable would it be?

GO TO MARKET

Can the company articulate their value proposition simply? Can the team explain how they will go to market? Do they have a good understanding of the competition?

THE ANGLE

What secret, what insight has the founding team made that the rest of the market hasn't yet realized? What discontinuity in the market can they leverage to win large shares?

AFTER THE FIRST MEETING

After a startup has left and I'm "doing diligence," I want to test some of the assertions made by the company.

MARKET SIZE VALIDATION

The first thing is to verify market size and whether it foots with the data the company presented. Then, I try to dig deeper into the nuances of the market. How concentrated is the market? What kinds of moves are the incumbents making and how do they change the market? How might a startup disrupt the market?

PITCH-IT-MYSELF TEST

I stop a few partners in the office and give them the pitch to test their reactions. I do the same with my wife. In a sense, I'm getting their cursory opinions and some skewed market feedback, but I'm also testing the pitch, the go-to-market, and the top level attractiveness of the company. It helps me think through a lot of the business and test my assumptions.

SIX DEGREES OF SEPARATION

I look up the founders on LinkedIn, send a few emails for references, and then wait to hear back on some initial reference calls.

*Data Sources: tomtunguz.com/breaking-down-a-typical-vcstartup-diligence-process/

SECOND AND THIRD MEETINGS

Follow up meetings are dedicated to metrics and the future.

PIPELINE

Let's get to brass tacks and some numbers. How many customers/users? How often are they using it? What are CAQ, LTV, and churn metrics? How do those compare with industry benchmarks?

PRODUCT ROADMAP

I know it's early and hard to forecast, but I'm looking to be convinced the founder has a good sense of where the company is going and why.

FINANCING PLAN

What are the major buckets of expenditures? How do they change over time? Is the revenue plan reasonable? What are the key metrics for the business?

INDUSTRY

I'll call a few friends in the industry who can help me better understand the dynamics in the sector.

ADDITIONAL MEETINGS/ FULL PARTNER MEETING

At this point, I'm really interested and I'm trying to understand the investment risks better.

KEY ISSUES ANALYSIS

After a founder has met several partners, I gather questions and dig deeper to answer them as best I can. If I don't have the material to answer the questions, I diligence some more: data, reference calls, and more meetings.

AFTER THE TERM SHEET

After the term sheet is signed, the lawyers step in.

LEGAL DILIGENCE

I'm interested in learning how well formed the company is, if there are any skeletons in the closet like fired co-founders or large debts or consultants who are owed shares or pending lawsuits. I'm also curious to see how a founder negotiates (though this comes through after the term sheet has been issued).

Each fund raising process is unique. Sometimes investors will have deep experience in a sector or know the team very well, both of which can accelerate the process significantly. But I hope this general outline sheds light on the key steps and questions answered in the fund raising process.

A VC term sheet provides the guidelines and provisions of an investment deal. It is the contractual document between investors and founders for raising capital and includes a set of major sections such as: the company's worth, who is on the board, who gets what, how are investments protected, and how much is set aside for a team.

VALUATION

A valuation is the calculated value of a company. The valuation is derived form the past performance of the company, its projected performance in the future, and the perceived worth of its intellectual property. The financial figure that comes from a valuation will help you figure out how much capital you should be seeking to raise and at what equity percentage the company might be worth.

Tip: Do your best to ensure you receive the most "fair" deal over the "best" deal for your company's valuation.

BOARD OF DIRECTORS

The board of directors is a guiding force for the company. Typically it is comprised of investors who put capital into the company and want to protect their investments.

Tip: Always try to ensure you have a balanced board for your company from industry experts to investors.

LIQUIDATION PREFERENCES

Liquidation preferences outline how your company is broken down, who gets what slice, and by how much. Liquidation preferences come into play during acquisitions and buyouts and the preferences provide the backbone for how shareholders receive their payouts.

Tip: Do not be too fancy with liquidation preferences, keep them as simple as possible and remember what might be given up early can be asked back later down the road.

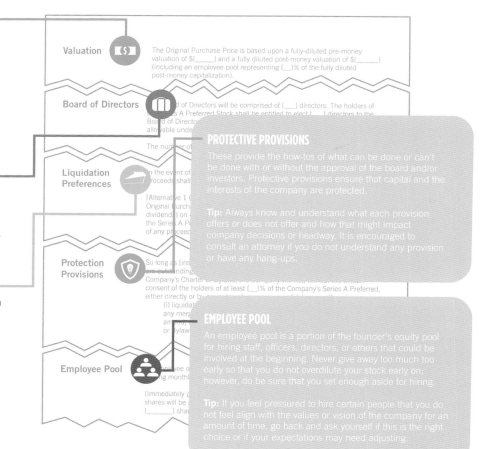

Valuation — The Original Purchase Price is based upon a fully-diluted pre-money valuation of $[_____] and a fully diluted post-money valuation of $[_____] (including an employee pool representing [__]% of the fully diluted post-money capitalization).

Board of Directors — d of Directors will be comprised of [__] directors. The holders of s A Preferred Stock shall be entitled to elect [__] directors to the Board of Directo allowable unde

The number o

Liquidation Preferences — n the event of roceeds shall

[Alternative 1 (
Original urch
dividend] on
the Serie A P
of any proceed

Protection Provisions — So long as [ins re o standing Company's Charter consent of the holders of at least [__]% of the Company's Series A Preferred, either directly or by
(i) liquida
any merg
am nd,
or ylaw

Employee Pool — yee o
g month

[Immediately p
shares will be
[_____] shar

PROTECTIVE PROVISIONS

These provide the how-tos of what can be done or can't be done with or without the approval of the board and/or investors. Protective provisions ensure that capital and the interests of the company are protected.

Tip: Always know and understand what each provision offers or does not offer and how that might impact company decisions or headway. It is encouraged to consult an attorney if you do not understand any provision or have any hang-ups.

EMPLOYEE POOL

An employee pool is a portion of the founder's equity pool for hiring staff, officers, directors, or others that could be involved at the beginning. Never give away too much too early so that you do not overdilute your stock early on; however, do be sure that you set enough aside for hiring.

Tip: If you feel pressured to hire certain people that you do not feel align with the values or vision of the company for an amount of time, go back and ask yourself if this is the right choice or if your expectations may need adjusting.

Data Source: OPENForum.com, Erika Napolitano, Jason Medelson, Foundry Group, National Venture Capital Association

business funding, there's also the option of small business loans, grants, lines of credit, peer lending, and receivables factoring.

Loans (Lns) are funding that is repayable in installments to the institution that provided the funds. Repayment is usually with an amount of interest to provide the lender with a return on their investment. These loans cover lines of credit, purchases, construction of new facilities, and capital to buy existing businesses.

Like loans, **Grants (GRA)** are designed to help a business grow. They come in two flavors: government and private. But unlike loans, grants are just that, granted to your company. You don't need to pay the funds back.

When your business has some history (usually two years), you can establish repayable lines of credit. Lines of credit are great debt instruments to support things like payroll, which must go out on time even if your clients pay late.

EXERCISE: Evaluating Your Funding Strategies

To evaluate your best funding options we suggest the following steps:

1. Just starting out and have a great idea? You might want to start with *Friends and Family*. You could also go with a seed fund if you have a successful track record.

2. Do you have a prototype or proof of concept? Maybe a customer or two? Seed funds or angels are options at this point in addition to *Friends and Family*.

3. Will you create a product/service that requires capital to get things created but you can deliver direct to early supporters? Take a look at crowdfunding.

4. Have you proved your business model and it's time to scale the business? Now venture capital is a great option.

5. If investor funding isn't an option, then consider loans, lines of credit, or grants.

6. If you've got *Cash Flow*, receivables factoring is an option to close the gap.

STARTUP ROCKET FUEL: ACCELERATORS AND INCUBATORS

Accelerators: A Global Initiative

Accelerators (Acc) are essential to the growth of entrepreneurial ecosystems because they provide a petri dish for innovation and create jobs. One of the best-known accelerators is Y Combinator (YC). YC provides seed funding, which is the earliest stage of venture funding and pays the expenses while a startup gets off the ground. Since 2005, YC has funded more than 460 startups, including Reddit, Disqus, Dropbox, Heroku, and Airbnb.

There are hundreds of accelerator programs around the world including other well known ones like 500Startups (USA), NewMe (USA), Springboard (UK), FounderFuel (Canada), Startupbootcamp (Europe—Amsterdam, Berlin, Madrid). There are also specialized accelerator programs:

- **Vertically Focused:** General accelerators like TechStars have proved that the model works. They've gone on to license their brand to other accelerators that focus on specific industry sectors or brands (e.g., TechStars Nike+ Accelerator). As a result, we see more vertical-focused accelerators like healthcare (e.g., Healthbox and Rock Health), clean tech (e.g., Surge and GreenStart), hardware (e.g., Lemnos Labs and Bolt), and even government (e.g., Code for America).

- **Not-for-Profit Accelerators:** Not all accelerator programs are for profit. Universities like the University of California, Berkeley, launched Skydeck, an engineering and MBA focused accelerator for digital businesses, in collaboration with Lawrence Berkeley National Laboratory and several other partners.

- **Soft-Landing Accelerators:** This is a newly evolving type of accelerator. Countries who have launched programs like this include Innovation House Norway, Mind the Bridge from Italy, Spain Tech Center, and the German Silicon Valley Accelerator to name a few.

Incubating Your Dream

The proliferation of accelerator programs has overshadowed a much older concept many have heard of: incubators. Unlike accelerators, incubators are more long term and permanent for a startup. Incubators

THE ART OF THE PITCH Figure 12.15

THE RULES OF THE PITCH

10/20/30

This format allows for more conversation before jumping right into the presentation. The discussion then becomes a part of the pitch.

THE 10 SLIDE PITCH

From VCs to partnership presentations, you'll need a deck that follows this basic structure and include relevant visual aids:

Slide 1 – Problem Definition
Slide 2 – How You Solve the Problem
Optional: Underlying Technology
Demo Product or Video of Example
Slide 3 – 50K Ft View of Company and Business Model
Slide 4 – Market Size
Slide 5 – Competition
Slide 6 – Team
Slide 7 – Financial Projections and Milestones
Slide 8 – Use of Proceeds
Slide 9 – Fundraising Process
Slide 10 – Summary/Next Steps and Call to Action

If this structure feels too formal, Steve suggests the alternative option of pitching like it's a stage play with three acts:

ACT 1 – Discussion
ACT 2 – The Pitch
ACT 3 – The Demo

1
2
3
4
5
6
7
8
9
10

*Data Source: Guy Kawasaki

THE 20 MINUTE PITCH

Guy's advice: "You should give your ten slides in twenty minutes. Sure, you have an hour time slot, but you're using a Windows laptop, so it will take forty minutes to make it work with the projector. Even if setup goes perfectly, people will arrive late and have to leave early. In a perfect world, you give your pitch in twenty minutes, and you have forty minutes left for discussion."

THE 30-POINT FONT

Guy's advice: "The majority of the presentations that I see have text in a ten point font. As much text as possible is jammed into the slide, and then the presenter reads it. However, as soon as the audience figures out that you're reading the text, it reads ahead of you because it can read faster than you can speak. The result is that you and the audience are out of synch. If "thirty points," is too dogmatic, then I offer you an algorithm: find out the age of the oldest person in your audience and divide it by two. That's your optimal font size."

THE 4 FOUNDATIONS OF DELIVERING A GREAT PITCH

CLARITY
Be clear and precise, clarity will always trump excess or persuasion

SIMPLICTY
Keep it simple and clean, trim the excess and simplify the language

PRACTICE
Practice makes perfect. Use your friends and family to prepare more

PASSION
Show that you care and that you believe in what you want to achieve while being memorable

can provide shared offices and services at a discount but incubation also includes hands-on management training, marketing support and, often, access to some form of financing.

- **Local Economic Development Incubators:** Non-profit in structure, they focus on job creation and economic development in the local area. This can also mean supporting particular target groups or industries to develop a cluster of businesses (e.g., service companies and high tech companies).

- **Academic and Scientific Incubators:** These non-profits focus on high-tech endeavors to help commercialize technologies. Their focus is usually on taking internal, institution projects prior to company creation. However, they also support external projects looking for commercialization.

- **Corporate Incubators:** These are for-profit incubators that are usually launched for high-tech endeavors. This kind of incubator also helps a company get access to new technologies, business models and markets that help them stay innovative and generate new revenue streams for the company.

- **Private Investor Incubators:** These are also for-profit incubators and usually bring in their portfolio companies that they have invested in to help them get a better start. They are usually high-tech and biotechnology startups and this type of incubator is focused on generating profits from the exits of these companies through acquisition or IPO.

Chris Schultz knows a few things about finance, funding, and launching companies. Chris is a serial entrepreneur who co-founded a collaborative workspace in New Orleans (Launch Pad), makes angel investments through Voodoo Ventures, and is currently working on a product called Niko Niko, a happiness tracker for teams that turns mood into actionable data for managers. We had a chance to get Chris' take on funding.

SEQ: Launchpad is your baby. How did you and your co-founders go about starting it? What was the motivation behind it?

Schultz: It was very organic birth. I had some extra office space, and I put that on Craigslist. I ended up having a couple of guys move in, and those two people ended up becoming the partners in Launchpad. We liked being able to work together and work through problems. So we opened Launchpad in 2009, and it had a great response.

SEQ: As an angel investor what do you looking for in a company?

Schultz: I look primarily at the founder, founding team, or co-founders. I don't have as strong a bias toward cofounding teams as some of the accelerator programs. I've had success with individual founders. At the angel level at the earliest stages, I think it boils down to the ideas or the business models. I have a bias towards founders that have deep industry experience. By deep I don't mean twenty years, it could be three or four years, but it needs to be some industry where they're starting the company. They also have the network customer contacts and understand the way the industry works.

SEQ: With limited resources, where should entrepreneurs focus?

Schultz: I have a bias of funding your company through customers and building a product that you can sell. You may not be able to fully fund your business, you may still need capital, but just the fact that you have customers is going to position you in a more interesting way for investors.

GETTING READY . . .

We covered a lot in this chapter. To get started with the **Funding (Fn)** part of The Startup Equation, make sure you complete these chapter exercises:

- Review *Bootstrapping* as an Option
- Build Out Your Pitch
- Select Funding Strategies that Fit Your Startup
- Evaluate Accelerator and Incubator Programs to support your growth

We will review this again in Chapter 18 when we connect all the elements of The Startup Equation and map these elements to your particular startup.

Marketing

GROW THE DREAM

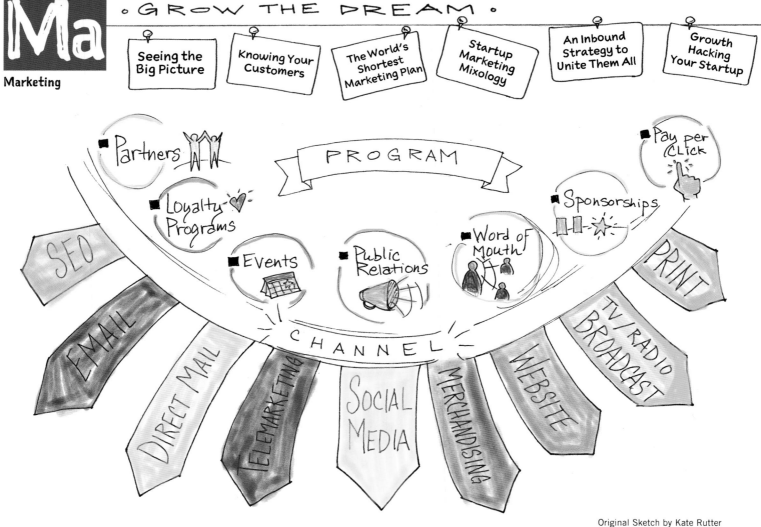

PROGRAM

■ Partners

■ Loyalty Programs

■ Events

■ Public Relations

■ Word of Mouth

■ Sponsorships

■ Pay per Click

CHANNEL

SEO

EMAIL

DIRECT MAIL

TELEMARKETING

SOCIAL MEDIA

MERCHANDISING

WEBSITE

TV/RADIO BROADCAST

PRINT

Original Sketch by Kate Rutter

CHAPTER 13

Doing business without advertising is like winking at a girl in the dark.

You know what you are doing, but nobody else does.

—Stuart H. Britt

Startup Marketing Alchemy

J a-Naé's drive to help millions of women fulfill their dreams of starting a business helped her start Wild Women Entrepreneurs (WWE), but it takes more than drive to succeed. It also takes marketing, but how do you market with zero budget?

Ja-Naé knew that her approach to marketing the Wild WE needed to focus on why she started the organization in the first place. Then, she got to work and experimented with every "free" resource at her disposal, eventually building fifty-five chapters in seven countries in less than nine months.

Though Ja-Naé found a solid marketing mix relatively fast, it's not always that easy for people. Sometimes it's hard to know where to start or the best channels for reaching your audience. In this chapter we'll go through the marketing elements that we've assigned to two major sections: *Programs* and *Channels*. *Programs* (like **Growth Hacking (Grw)**, **Partners (Prt)**, **Loyalty Programs (Loy)**, **Events (Evt)**, **PR (Prs)**, **Word of Mouth (Wom)**, **Sponsorship (Spn)**, and **PPC (Ppc)**) are the vehicles used to market, while the *channels* (**SEO (Seo)**, **Email (Eml)**, **Direct Marketing (Drm)**, **Telemarketing (Tem)**, **Social Media (Som)**, **Merchandising (Mer)**, **Website (Web)**, **TV/Radio Broadcasting (Brd)**, **Print (Pri)**) are places to find your audience. We will dive into the various elements of marketing and provide some exercises to help you identify the right elements for your equation.

SEEING THE BIG PICTURE

Too often we see people throwing stuff at the wall to see "what sticks" and skip the critical step of developing an effective marketing strategy. However, more than one startup has failed to understand its importance

$$((En(Id))+So)^X+((Cu(Te+Ce))Br)^X+(((Fn(Sa+Ma))Sc)In)^X$$

| Foundation | Experience | Growth |

Marketing your startup is about how you position it to satisfy your market's needs. The mix that you create is the set of controllable, tactical marketing tools that you'll need to produce a desired response from your target audience. This mix is what you build your marketing strategy from.

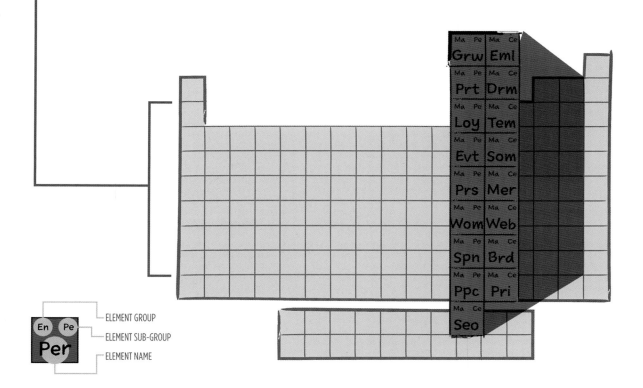

ELEMENT GROUP
ELEMENT SUB-GROUP
ELEMENT NAME

MARKETING (MA) PROGRAM ELEMENTS

A marketing program allows you to integrate your marketing mix to reach prospective customers and maintain your current customer relationships.

Growth Hacking (Grw)
Growth Hacking is a program with one absolute focus: growth. Every methods, tool, and tactic within this program is built around growing an area of your business.

Partners (Ptr)
A Partners program can be developed when one business can accomplish their goals more effectively by leveraging the complementary strengths of another. Partners can con-tribute to increase brand awareness, product distribution, and customer acquisition.

Loyalty Programs (Loy)
A Loyalty program is structured to encourage brand loyalty through encouraging buying behavior.

Events (Evt)
Events are programs that describe an experience created that targets customer needs and that can occur online or offline.

PR (Prs)
Public relations (PR) is the management of spreading information about your company, particularly through news outlets.

Word of Mouth (Wom)
A Word-of-mouth marketing program is when word about the company or a promotion spreads virally from person to person. Word-of-mouth is an unpaid marketing program.

Sponsorship (Spn)
Sponsorship is a program to promote company awareness through another company used primarily to obtain specific business goals. Sponsorship can be financially supported or through in-kind support.

PPC (Ppc)
A pay-per-click (PPC) program is a form of internet advertising where advertisers pay you when their ad is clicked on. Programs are usually set around specific key-words, a budget, and benchmarks.

MARKETING (MA) CHANNEL ELEMENTS

A marketing channel is an area a company can use to market their business through a set of activities in a process. A marketing strategy would encompass tactics and activities using a multi-marketing channel mix.

SEO (Seo)
SEO stands for "Search Engine Optimization" and is the method that impacts how well your website can be found when a person searches for it. SEO is an unpaid or organic way of boosting your website's visibility.

Email (Eml)
Email marketing is a way of reaching your current and prospective customers through their electronic inbox such as gmail, Yahoo or Microsoft Exchange.

Direct Mail (Drm)
Direct mail is the act of advertising directing to your prospective/current customers through the mail. The intent is to solicit an action from them.

Telemarketing (Tem)
Telemarketing is when a company cold calls a person on the phone unsolicited on behalf of your company in order to get them engaged in your company.

Social Media (Som)
Social Media is a set of virtual networks, websites, communities, and applications that allow for individuals to engage with one another and exchange information, thoughts, and ideas.

Merchandising (Mer)
Merchandising is when you sell your product or service through retail outlets. This can occur online or offline.

Website (Web)
A website is a location on the Internet that is focused on a company, person, place, topic, or a series of related items. A website normally has multiple pages and one domain name leading to it.

TV/Radio Broadcast (Brd)
TV or radio marketing is a form of broadcast advertising that gives visibility to your company by sending it out to the masses.

Print (Pri)
Print marketing is how you advertise your business through printed materials. The most common forms of print marketing are newspapers and magazines.

until they've spent a lot of time and money on stuff that doesn't stick. We've made this mistake, too, but we've also learned that a plan can help you achieve your goals and make the most of your available resources.

EXERCISE: Defining Clear Goals

To start, any strategy needs a defined, measurable goal. Before you do anything ask yourself this question: What is the ONE thing I want to accomplish and why is it important? Answers might include:

- Generate revenue
- Build awareness
- Shift brand perception
- Recruit new employees
- Create a customer service cycle

Once you know the one thing you want to achieve, set a clear, measurable goal with a specific date and time. As part of this process, define a specific reason for your goal. Why include the why? It makes it obvious to your lizard brain the importance of the action. Here are some examples:

- In order to find my first paying customer, I'll form a team of ten beta-testers by March 1, 2016.
- In order to build up my brand awareness, I'll partner with two charitable partners by May 20, 2016.

We strongly suggest making one overarching goal for your business for one year, even if you set smaller goals in support of the bigger one.

The Best Marketer is You!

Everyone has different skills. However, if you're starting or growing a business, you're likely the best marketer available for your company. When asked about your company, let your passion shine through. While people may not expect perfection in the beginning, they do want to see the creator's excitement about the new business.

KNOWING YOUR CUSTOMERS

In previous chapters, we've talked about the need to know your customers, and we can't stress enough the importance of customer research. Here are some key questions:

1. **Who** are you trying to reach? What is their gender? How old are they?
2. **How** do they spend their time online and offline?
3. **Where** are they online? Do they already congregate in specific places?
4. **What** are their fears? What motivates them? What would motivate them to buy your product or service?
5. **Why** would they buy from you? What type of education or information would they need to convert them into customers?

The answers to these questions will help you craft the right marketing mix. We had the chance to chat with someone who knows from experience why it's so important to know your customers. Humberto Matas, the Managing Partner of DesignIt Barcelona, has a passion for human-based design. His successful firm was acquired by DesignIt four years ago.

SEQ: What are your thoughts on how brand experience and customer experience are connected or not?

Matas: There are two ways of approaching the same goal. We use different terminology because there are different professionals with different backgrounds, but we're trying to aim for the same thing: to deliver relevant experience for the customers. The brand is no longer an image.

SEQ: If a startup is just starting, when do you think they should make brand a priority?

Matas: That's a very tough question. To me, following as a principle that brand is the consequence of your job. It's something that emerges from what you do. It's not something that you put on like a costume. There's a moment in the life of your company where you have reached enough clients and you have established enough internal processes to deal with your clients and your customers that you know that you have to do something to take care of the messages or the experience that you're delivering through those channels.

THE WORLD'S SHORTEST MARKETING PLAN

Once you set a well-defined goal, it's time to construct a plan. Everyone strategizes and plans differently, but the key is to find what works for you and your team. We've pulled together some popular, and proven, ways to help you get started.

We'll start with the World's Shortest Marketing Plan. Created by Kelly Odell, it gets down to business by focusing on the important stuff. You'll start by addressing the four Ps: Product, Price, Place, and Promotion. For each "P" you'll review how they relate to the six imperative questions: (1) What, (2) Why, (3) When, (4) How, (5) How Much, and (6) Who. No matter what marketing direction you pick, answering these questions will get you off to a fantastic start.

EXERCISE: SWOT Marketing Analysis

Next on the list: a SWOT analysis. At its heart, SWOT is a market research method. It's a great tool to use when trying to understand who you are as an entrepreneur, your brand's strengths and weaknesses, and why your target audience should choose you.

SWOT stands for:

- Strengths
- Weaknesses
- Opportunities
- Threats

STARTUP MARKETING MIXOLOGY

Once you have a marketing plan that fits your current needs, it's time to dig in and plan your overall marketing strategy. However, when time is valuable (and rare), you'll want to consider options that help you save time and money.

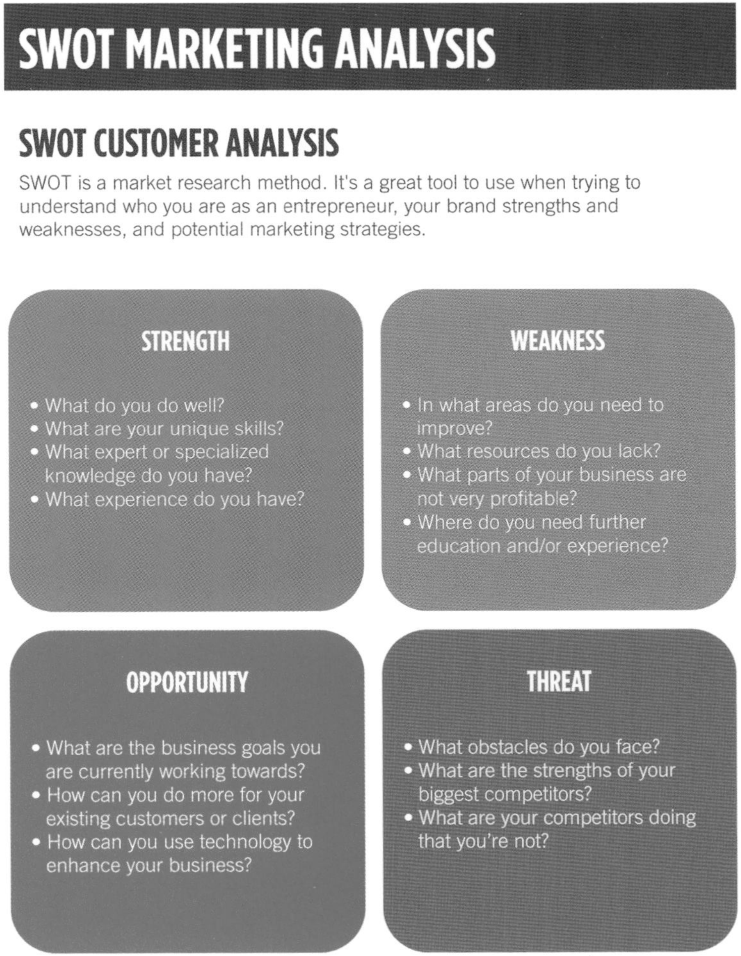

SWOT MARKETING ANALYSIS

SWOT CUSTOMER ANALYSIS

SWOT is a market research method. It's a great tool to use when trying to understand who you are as an entrepreneur, your brand strengths and weaknesses, and potential marketing strategies.

STRENGTH
- What do you do well?
- What are your unique skills?
- What expert or specialized knowledge do you have?
- What experience do you have?

WEAKNESS
- In what areas do you need to improve?
- What resources do you lack?
- What parts of your business are not very profitable?
- Where do you need further education and/or experience?

OPPORTUNITY
- What are the business goals you are currently working towards?
- How can you do more for your existing customers or clients?
- How can you use technology to enhance your business?

THREAT
- What obstacles do you face?
- What are the strengths of your biggest competitors?
- What are your competitors doing that you're not?

Figure 13.5 **SWOT Marketing Analysis**

THE PLAN WITHIN A PLAN Figure 13.3

BUSINESS PLAN

STRATEGIC MARKETING PLAN

MARKET RESEARCH			TACTICAL MARKETING				

BUSINESS MISSION & VISION	MARKET SEGMENTATION AND TARGETING	COMPETITIVE ENVIRONMENT	DEFINITION OF OFFERING	MARKET POSITIONING & STRATEGY	MARKETING & SELLING MODEL	PRODUCT LAUNCH	OPERATIONS & ORGANIZATION	FINANCIAL ANALYSIS
Define Mission & Vision **Business model** - Acquisitions, Liscenses & Partnerships needed **Market Entry Strategy** - Major Barriers to Entry - Alternative Strategies	**Market Segmentation** **Identification of Target Segments & Customers** **Confirmation of Customer Needs (Voice of the customer)**	**Identifiy and Profile** - Primary Competitors (SWOT) - Secondary Competitors (SWOT)	**Prioritize Customer Needs** **Description of Offering** **Pricing Strategy** **Validation Testing**	**SWOT** **Unique Selling Propsition (USP)** **Market Entry Strategy** - Major Barriers - Alternative Strategies - Objectives **Critical Success Factors**	**Sales and Channel Strategy** **Sales Force Organization** **Sales Metrics & Incentives** **Brand Strategy** **Advertising & Promotion Strategy**	**Time-frame & milestones** **Potential rists/bottlenecks** **Key success factors** **Marketing Action Plan (MAP)**	**Organizational structure** **R&D and Operations Model** - Degree of vertical integration - In-house vs. Outsource **Human Resources** **Culture & Management Style** **Business System & Processes**	**Financial Model** - Cost Structure - Projected Revenues & Profits by Segment **Investment Requirements & Financing Strategy**

MONITOR/EVALUATE RESULTS/REVISE

Data Source: Aistrup Consulting © 2010

THE WORLD'S SHORTEST MARKETING PLAN Figure 13.4

	WHAT?	WHY?	WHEN?	HOW?	HOW MUCH?	WHO?
PRODUCT	What products do you need?	What need does it fill?	When do you need it?	How will the product fit the need?	Product cost, Volume to be sold, etc.?	Customer segments to be targeted?
PRICE	What price will you sell for?	Why is that the right place?	How long will that price be valid?	How will the price develop over time?	How much sales and margin will be created?	Different prices for different segments?
PLACE	How will products be distributed?	Why choose these channels?	When do customers choose different channels?	How will we create or enter these channels?	What are the costs/benefits of these channels?	How do different segments use different channels?
PROMOTION	What types of promotion will be used?	Why choose these activities?	Timing, launch, lifecycle, etc.?	How will the promotions be executed?	Costs/benefits of the promotions?	Target groups for various promotions?

Data Source: Kelly Odell

We recommend you follow these five steps to build your marketing strategy:

1. **Unique Selling Proposition (USP):** A fundamental piece of the marketing plan, entrepreneurs regularly overlook the USP. It captures the "why" for people buying from you and not your competitors. When pitching:

   - Explain how you solve a holistic problem for your target audience
   - Highlight the distinct benefits of a relationship with you over your competitors
   - Make a promise or guarantee that no one else in your industry offers

   Once you have these items, condense everything down to one, brief sentence. That explains the "why" for your company.

2. **List Your Benefits:** While you're at it, list all of your benefits. Everything from being first to market to stellar customer service, goes on the list. These benefits will help guide you no matter the marketing channels you pick.

3. **Decide Product/Service Positioning:** Your positioning will determine how your product/service is viewed by customers, and ultimately, the success of your business. We suggest using the following framework:

   - For (your target customer or market)
   - Who (give a compelling reason to buy/what is there need)
   - Our product/service is a (product/service's placement within a new or existing market)
   - That provides [key benefit(s) that directly addresses the reason to buy from you]
   - Unlike (primary competitor offering same benefit)
   - Our product/service (key difference or point of differentiation in relation to the specific target customer)

   One great example is Harley Davidson's positioning statement:

   The only motorcycle manufacturer
   That makes big, loud motorcycles
   For macho guys (and "macho wannabes")
   Mostly in the United States
   Who want to join a gang of cowboys
   In an era of decreasing personal freedom.

Ready to try? Use this template to help build your own.

Figure 13.8 **Positioning Statement Generator**

4. **Decide on Your Marketing Budget:** Whether you have $5,000 or nothing, it's absolutely essential to know what financial resources you're putting towards your marketing. Unfortunately, we can't claim there's one default amount. Some say ten percent of your overall budget, while others say up to fifteen percent.

That said, as you look at your overall budget, we recommend planning on at least seven percent. Then, look where your customers go. Even if you're only spending one percent on marketing, take the time to pick the right channels.

Then, after you spend it, track it to gauge the success of a campaign or channel. And track more than brand awareness Key Performance Indicators. Go through the entire sales funnel to see where you need to spend more next time.

5. **Decide on Your Marketing Methods:** With so many marketing channels available, it's very easy to bleed money. But how do you know where your target audience congregates?

- **Ask:** It doesn't hurt to ask. If you're just starting out, reach out to your network and explain the type of persona you want to reach. If you already have customers, then start with your beta-testers and your evangelists.

- **Research:** One of the first things Ja-Naé did when starting WWE was to learn about demographic and psychographic behaviors. It helped her understand what was important to her potential audience.

- **Create Segment Tests:** After you've done research, do some small segment testing to find your audience sweet spot. Allow yourself to experiment in order to find the right audience for your brand.

Also, it's important to note that when you're first starting out, you'll rarely have the capital to be everywhere at once. Make informed decisions on where to start and how much effort to spend in each place.

Programs and Channels

A marketing strategy gets broken into two core pieces: *Programs* and *Channels*. *Programs* are a set of customer-based activities that help you achieve your marketing goals. *Channels* are the places to move these programs so that your target audience sees them and, hopefully, engages with them.

Picking The Right Program Elements to Begin

Every company has different marketing resources available to them. However, figuring out which programs your business should use isn't an easy task. It can take some testing to get the right mix for where you are today.

Creating Experiences

A large part of marketing is creating the right customer experience that both sets an expectation of your brand but provides a level of trust and value that your customers cannot get elsewhere. Here are some elements that can help:

- **Loyalty Programs (Loy):** We've talked a lot about crafting the customer experience. But for good reason. To acquire a new customer, it costs a business about 5-10 times more than selling to an existing one.[1] And based on a report by Manta and BIA/Kelsey, a repeat customer spends sixty-seven percent more on a sale than a new customer does.[2] **Loyalty programs (Loy) a**re structured to reward customer buying behavior. Make sure you're providing real value to your customers with rewards that make sense.

- **Events (Evt):** When crafting your brand experience, connecting your customers with one another is a great way to build evangelists. One way you can do that is through **events (Evt)**. They allow you to get face-to-face with your customers (even if it is online) and create something that encompasses all their senses. However, doing *events* can be a daunting task and costly, if you are not careful.

- **Sponsorship (Spn):** *Sponsorship* marketing is usually tied to a specific purpose or a campaign in order to reach a wider audience. You can either be a sponsor of a program or event where you know your target audience will be engaged, or you can offer sponsorships for you and your business. There are pros and cons to both and no matter how you slice it, it's about creating a win for you, a win for the partnering company, and a win for the customer.

Getting the Word Out

Some marketing programs focus more on the communication of the brand. These elements include:

- **Pay-Per-Click (PPC):** *Pay-per-click* is an online, advertising model used to drive website traffic. You can run a PPC campaign or program to bring brand awareness or promote a specific program, product, or service. It's also a great way to test product ideas and new forms of communication.
- **PR (Prs):** *PR* does double duty as a marketing program and helping you build relationships with journalists and reports. PR is about more than sending out press releases. It's also about syndicating your refined message through the relationships you build with the press. However, a PR program can be expensive and requires careful management.
- **Word of Mouth (Wom):** *Word of mouth* remains the most powerful form of marketing because people buy from brands that their friends and colleagues know and trust. However, while *word of mouth* marketing might get people in the door, it's up to you to keep them there.

EXERCISE: How to Build a Word of Mouth Campaign

According to Nielsen, ninety-two percent of people trust recommendations from friends and family more than all other forms of marketing, making *word of mouth* one of the most powerful marketing elements.[3] So, where do you start?

1. **Start with Friends:** The people in your life are already invested in who you are a person. Reach out to them and have them start advocating for you and your brand.

2. **Identify Influencers:** Each industry has a set of influencers. These are the people you want to tap into. Make a list of them and then reach out. You never know who will love your stuff and want to support your brand.

3. **Leverage Uniqueness:** No one really cares to share a product or service unless there is something interesting about it. Maybe it's your story. Maybe your product has a unique feature. Maybe you're doing something differently than everyone else. Whatever it is, THAT is what you should highlight and lead with.

Channels

Marketing channels are a way to distribute information about your brand and the marketing programs outlined earlier in this chapter, including:

- **Search Engine Optimization (Seo):** Used to improve a website's organic search results, *Search Engine Optimization (SEO)* focuses on increasing the visibility of your website and your content. No SEO means no organic traffic from search results. For a great resource, we recommend Moz.com. Rand Fishkin and the crew are the go-to source for SEO.
- **Email (Eml):** You probably receive some of this channel marketing in your inbox. *Email* is a great channel to stay in touch with your customers and to highlight new products and services. As of 2013, there are nearly 3.9 billion email accounts worldwide, with that number expected to increase to 4.9 billion by the end of 2017.[4] But, like every channel, do some research to confirm how your target audience prefers you use this channel.
- **Direct Mail (Drm):** Open your mailbox, and you'll likely see an example of *direct mail*. Though great for businesses who want to visually convey their brands, this channel can prove expensive as the price of postage increases.
- **Telemarketing (Tem):** *Telemarketing* helps you market your product or service by phone to potential customers. It can be a challenging channel because of Do Not Call regulations.
- **Merchandising (Mer):** *Merchandising* involves putting a product on a store shelf. Supporting *merchandising* activities include giving away samples, providing product demonstrations, and promoting special offers.
- **Website (Web):** Your *website* is your home on the internet. It's where people will come to find out about you, your brand, and what you stand for. *Websites* can include integrated ecommerce platforms, blogs, and other applications to enhance the visitor's experience. It's the gateway to helping people get to know you. So, always keep your *website* up-to-date and mobile friendly.
- **TV/Radio Broadcast (Brd):** *TV/Radio broadcasting* allows you to reach larger audiences within a geographical region. Spots can be sold

during different programming and the price will vary dramatically depending on whether it's "prime-time" programming.

- **Print (Pri):** *Print* advertising encompasses newspapers, magazines, and fliers. *Print* media, like TV and radio, is hard to track and depends largely on whether or not your target audience sees your advertising, and if they do, knowing what they read.
- **Social Media (Som):** *Social media* is more than just a place to connect with your friends. It's a communication channel that you can leverage when building your community to find evangelists and help with customer service.

AN INBOUND STRATEGY TO UNITE THEM ALL

Once you identify the channels that make the most sense for your audience and the marketing programs you want to launch, the next step is to craft an inbound marketing strategy. The goal? Helping your target audience find you.

Your target audience is inundated with advertising on a daily basis. There is absolutely no way to compete with all the noise if you're just starting out, no matter how much money you put behind it. However, inbound marketing helps you attract the most qualified prospects to your business. Here's how:

1. **Focus on solving problems for niche groups in your audience.** Within your target audience, there are a number of niche communities. By taking your content and focusing on them, you'll have more success creating diehard evangelists.
2. **Focus on the buying cycle.** As people find you, they'll be in different phases of the buying cycle. Providing great content helps answer questions throughout this cycle and overcomes obstacles stopping customers from committing.
3. **Deliver content valuable to your audience.** Your content should always be about your target audience, not your brand. Though there are times when you can pull back the curtain and show them your brand, people are inherently more interested in themselves and their needs.

- **Make It Useful:** Content should be educational, but feel free to spice it up and entertain them as well. We can all use a good laugh.
- **Make It Relevant:** Most people only care about themselves and their needs. So, when they're searching for something, they're looking for specific answers. Create that content for them.
- **Tell a Story:** Storytelling is a crucial way to get your target audience to remember your brand and your values. Our brains process by putting information into patterns and stories.
- **Make It Quality:** There's a lot of regurgitated crap out there, and people are tired of it. They want high-quality content. Customize it and pay attention to detail.
- **Make It Heartfelt:** People can smell a fake a mile away. People do not do business with brands. They do business with other people.

When focusing on your marketing and sales efforts, work smarter not harder. Build an inbound marketing machine that works with your time and budget. Find a consistent pattern that works best for you and help set expectations.

Someone who has done a great job on keeping that focus and building a platform of customers based on need and relevancy is Lewis Howes. This one-time All-American star in two sports now spends his time teaching others what he has learned and helping them to aspire to greatness. We had a chance to chat with him to truly understand his journey and how he got to where he is today.

SEQ: Lewis, thank you for being here. Let's start with how you evolved into your current role.

Howes: I was a two-sport, All-American in college as an athlete. Then, after an injury, I retired from arena football and started pursuing the business world to figure out how I was going to make a living, what I was going to do for the rest of my life, and what my purpose was going to be next.

I've focused on understanding people in general and connecting and interviewing a lot of influential, inspiring, amazing individuals. It's grown into a podcast called "The School of Greatness" and many other products, courses, and consulting along the way. I'm still building my

LAUNCHING IT

 DISTRIBUTING IT

 BUILDING ON IT

THE LAUNCH PAGE

Generating buzz around your launch page is imperative. Its effectiveness depends on your use of social media to attract attention and how you empower your site with social sharing options. Allowing visitors to tweet, link, share, and reblog your startup's content is important for creating early buzz and awareness.

THE SOCIAL PEOPLE

Social media is about being social and being able to connect with your customers and their advocates.

The power rests not just in the platform but in the people, connect with those most vocal and get their help to spread the word.

Some of these people may be important bloggers who are reviewing products, brands, or discussing relevant material.

70% 35%
of bloggers are discussing brands, products, and services organically | of bloggers are writing about brand reviews and product reviews

WHICH PLATFORMS ARE MOST USED?

 93%
BEST FOR:
Sharing, Conversation, Feedback

 78%
BEST FOR:
Sharing, Conversation, Feedback

 61%
BEST FOR:
Sharing, Conversation, Feedback

MAKE GREAT CONTENT

 +

In the land of the social, content is king. The quality of the content you produce will vastly improve the amount of interaction and interest as you push media outward. When you begin increasing quality over quantity the value, care, and capability to go viral also goes up.

DID YOU KNOW?

80% 50%

of online consumers are more likely to share and talk about the brands they love and follow? | of those are also more likely to persuade friends and family to purchase by being brand advocates?

Always keep an eye out for where buzz on social media is coming from. This helps you target your efforts and discover where your campaign might also be failing or lacking. Be sure to use and leverage what is working in your startup's favor.

MONITOR THE RESULTS

Simple analytics tools can help measure the impact of your marketing efforts. This not only helps you convert followers into customers but also helps to examine why a customer clicked or was interested.

WHAT CAN I USE TO MEASURE?

72%
Visitors & Sources of Traffic

63%
Network Size:
Followers & Fans

56%
Quantity of Commentary

50%
Sentiment or Quality of Commentary

*Data Source: EMarketer.com, MarketingSherpa.com, Forbes.com, Udemy.com

business and looking for ways to always improve and take everything to the next level.

SEQ: What was your initial journey and what were a couple of transformation points to get you to that level?

Howes: For the first two years, I had probably three key mentors I worked with on a weekly basis. I didn't have the skills in business that I needed coming out of football. I just started to create content online. I started helping people one on one. Then, I started to take them to small groups, just started to speak about it, about LinkedIn specifically.

The big aha moment was understanding that, as an entrepreneur, in order to scale myself, I can't be trading my time for dollars anymore and that's what I was doing. I was making a couple hundred bucks for a couple hour session, trading my time for teaching people about LinkedIn one-on-one.

It wasn't until I did my first webinar I made $6,200 in an hour speaking in front of about 500 people who were interested in learning about LinkedIn. At the end, I offered them an advanced training course where I made the $6,200 and that's when I was freaked out. I was blown away that I could actually leverage my time and my information and my skill set and convert it into sales and money for myself through this technology of having a group of people listen to me online at one time and then offer something at the end. For me it blew me away and it's what skyrocketed me.

Funnel Optimization

You may hear people mentioning you need to optimize your funnel. And as you grow, you absolutely must. At the beginning, don't worry about it. Focus on getting your first hundred customers. Those customers will help you understand what's working and what's not. Your job is to provide them with the best product and the highest quality of service possible. Your job is also to learn as much as possible from these customers.

Once you've learned as much as you can and amassed your first hundred customers, it's time to optimize your funnel. Here are five ways to optimize.

1. **Focus on your most valuable leads.** If you're going to optimize, begin with the leads you value the most. Know why you value them so much. Do they spend the most? Have they become true brand advocates? Decide the criteria that make them valuable to your company and focus your attention on these people first.

2. **How did they find you?** It's important to find out how these prized leads found you in the first place. So ask them. See if there's a common thread that runs throughout most of your leads because within that is your gold.

3. **Optimize your content.** As a growing business, it's vital to maximize the amount of time you spend on every aspect of your business, including your inbound marketing funnel. If your leads share a common theme, then optimize your content to find them and where they find you. Make sure to have a multi-channel approach that will help people know you're right beside them.

4. **Decide what makes a qualified lead.** We know when it's right, but we don't always know when to stop trying to close. Even if people come to us, they may not be in the position to do business with us. Instead of chasing everyone who comes knocking at your door, know what criteria matters most to help you qualify a lead (e.g., What's your budget for this product?).

5. **Measure, then, measure again.** No matter the size of your business, we recommend you measure everything. On average, you want to be closing at least twenty percent of your inbound marketing funnel. If you're not close to that number, then go back to step one and make sure that you thoroughly understood the identities of the valuable leads to optimize your marketing funnel.

GROWTH HACKING YOUR STARTUP

Whether you assign one person on your team or the entire team, *growth hacking* should be on your radar and part of your mix.

Growth hackers look for technological ways to disrupt normal channels and infiltrate markets via distribution. As you build your business, think of places to discover your target market. Begin to think of creative ways to break into new arenas in a way that no one else considered.

INBOUND MARKETING AND GREAT CONTENT Figure 13.12

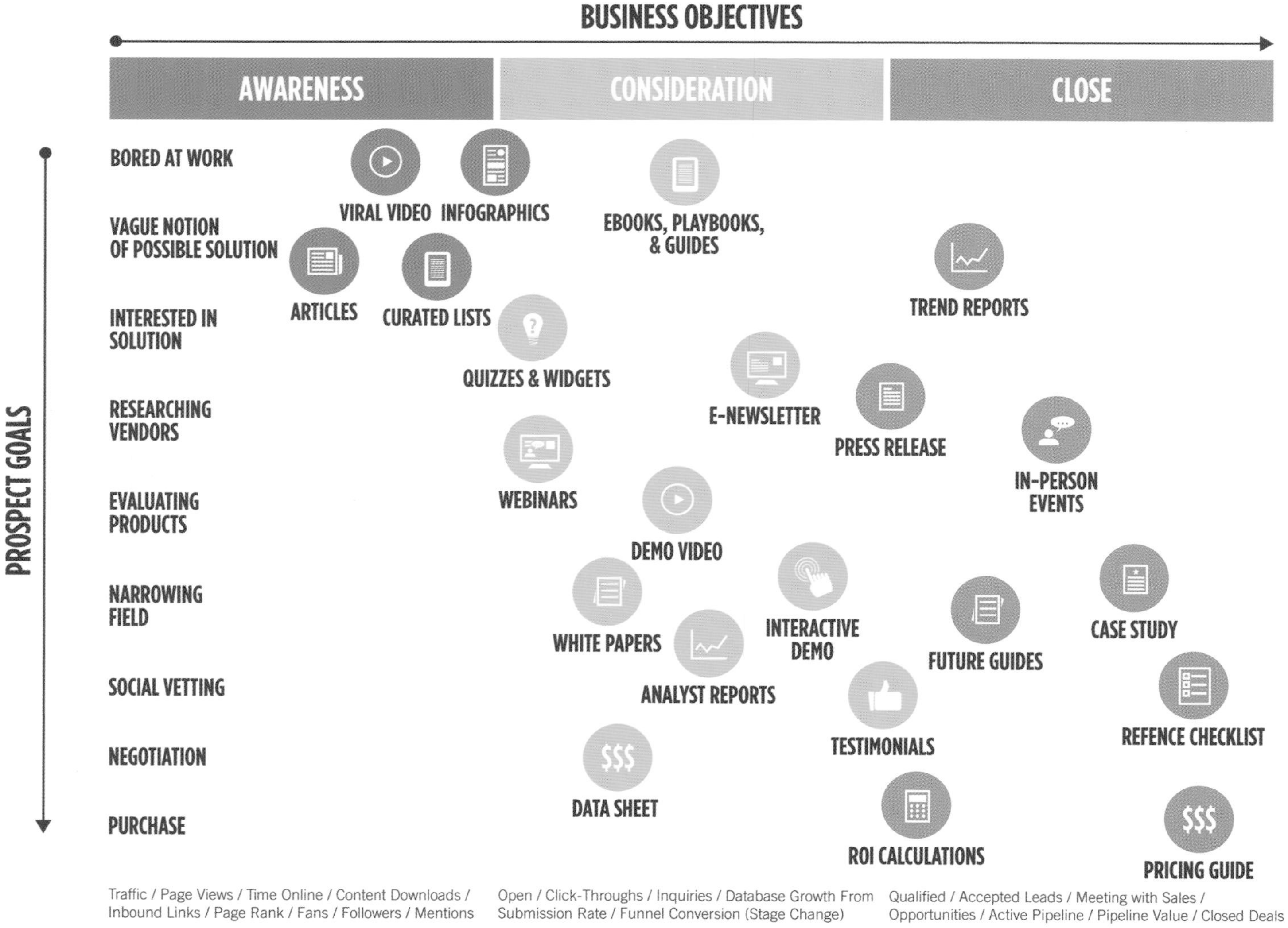

BUSINESS OBJECTIVES

AWARENESS	CONSIDERATION	CLOSE

PROSPECT GOALS

- BORED AT WORK
- VAGUE NOTION OF POSSIBLE SOLUTION
- INTERESTED IN SOLUTION
- RESEARCHING VENDORS
- EVALUATING PRODUCTS
- NARROWING FIELD
- SOCIAL VETTING
- NEGOTIATION
- PURCHASE

VIRAL VIDEO   INFOGRAPHICS

EBOOKS, PLAYBOOKS, & GUIDES

ARTICLES   CURATED LISTS

TREND REPORTS

QUIZZES & WIDGETS

E-NEWSLETTER

PRESS RELEASE

WEBINARS

IN-PERSON EVENTS

DEMO VIDEO

INTERACTIVE DEMO

WHITE PAPERS

FUTURE GUIDES

CASE STUDY

ANALYST REPORTS

TESTIMONIALS

REFENCE CHECKLIST

$$$
DATA SHEET

ROI CALCULATIONS

$$$
PRICING GUIDE

Traffic / Page Views / Time Online / Content Downloads / Inbound Links / Page Rank / Fans / Followers / Mentions

Open / Click-Throughs / Inquiries / Database Growth From Submission Rate / Funnel Conversion (Stage Change)

Qualified / Accepted Leads / Meeting with Sales / Opportunities / Active Pipeline / Pipeline Value / Closed Deals

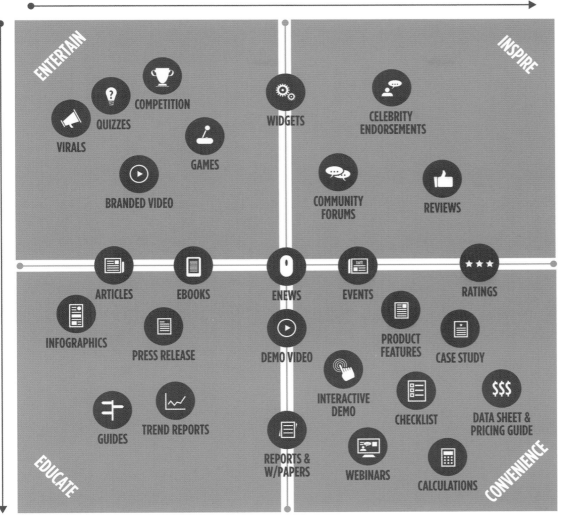

AWARENESS → PURCHASE

EMOTIONAL → RATIONAL

ENTERTAIN
- VIRALS
- QUIZZES
- COMPETITION
- GAMES
- BRANDED VIDEO
- WIDGETS

INSPIRE
- CELEBRITY ENDORSEMENTS
- COMMUNITY FORUMS
- REVIEWS

EDUCATE
- ARTICLES
- EBOOKS
- INFOGRAPHICS
- PRESS RELEASE
- GUIDES
- TREND REPORTS
- ENEWS
- DEMO VIDEO
- REPORTS & W/PAPERS
- EVENTS
- PRODUCT FEATURES
- INTERACTIVE DEMO
- WEBINARS
- CHECKLIST
- CALCULATIONS
- RATINGS
- CASE STUDY
- DATA SHEET & PRICING GUIDE

CONVENIENCE

Data Source: Eloqua, First 10, Smart Insights, and Jess3

As you begin to hack your business, it's important to have a lot of curiosity. It's also important to ask the questions and allow yourself to explore them.

Growth Hacking

No matter the stage of your business, **growth hacking (Grw)** is a vital part to building your business. Though *growth hacking* can be used in every area of your business, here are some ways to get started when using it for marketing.

- **Exclusivity:** If you're just starting out or launching a new product or service, then only offering it to a small group of beta testers is a great way to build mystery and demand, while receiving initial feedback. If you already have brand evangelists, then offer it to them first to build a partnership with your customers.

- **Automate:** Two of the biggest expenses that can eat up time and money are manpower and complicated processes. One way to have a handle on both is to use tools and services that can automate as many processes

CONTENT PUBLISHING BEST PRACTICES Figure 13.13

UNDERSTAND YOUR AUDIENCE

 KNOW YOUR AUDIENCE(S)
TIP: Get specific, get personal

 YOU'RE BUSY. SO ARE THEY
Don't waste your time or others'

 IT'S NOT ALL ABOUT YOU
Show interest in the needs of others, not just yours

 DO UNTO OTHERS...
Others like mentions and RTs as much as you

 LIMIT THE PLEAS FOR HELP
Ideally keep this below the 10% mark

 BE RESPONSIVE
Respond in 24 hrs but aim for a faster response

PLAN YOUR CONTENT

 HOW MUCH TIME DO YOU HAVE?
Be realistic and set a time limit

 MONTHLY: CONTENT STRATEGY
Identify what is coming up and set a schedule for it

 MONTHLY: KEY MESSAGES
Define key messages for campaigns and events

 USE AN EDITORIAL CALENDAR
Download a free one from TopNonprofits.com/edcal

 WEEKLY: BATCH CONTENT CREATION
Maximize time and maximize mental gear shifts

 SCHEDULING POSTS IN ADVANCE IS OK
TIP: Vary timing slightly to avoid :00 and :30

 CHECK FEEDS AT LEAST 2X PER DAY
If only 2x then mid morning and late afternoon

 HOW WILL YOU MEASURE SUCCESS
TIP: Set measurable goals and track progress

*Data Source: TopNonprofits.com

as possible. Look at every area of your marketing and see how you can simplify it and automate most of it.

Measuring What Is Important

Your KPIs are how you'll measure your marketing success. They will help you identify what content works and what does not. KPIs will also tell you whether a landing page performs well or if people are dropping off at a specific point. Use your KPIs as a guide so that you don't head too far down a rabbit hole. Your business deserves better than the casual treatment, and it's an avoidable mistake. Here's a list of marketing measurements you'll want to consider that will help to gauge the performance of your marketing mix through the funnel:

1. **Awareness**

    Main KPI: **Website Traffic**

    Secondary Metrics:

    - Inbound links
    - Referral visits
    - Inbound connections (subscribers, social followers)
    - New visitors
    - Returning visitors

2. **Leads**

    Main KPI: **Total Leads**

    Secondary Metrics:

    - Downloads
    - Lead source (advertising, direct, email, calls, social, offline)
    - Cost per lead (CPL)
    - Lead quality score
    - Prospects

3. **Conversion**

    Primary KPI: **Customers**

    Secondary Metrics:

    - Conversion rate
    - Cost of customer acquisition (COCA)
    - New customers
    - Revenue growth rate
    - Market growth rate

4. **Loyalty**

    Primary KPI: **Reoccurring Revenue**

    Supporting Metrics:

    - Customer retention rate
    - Customer lifetime value (CLV)
    - Net promoter score (NPS)
    - Customer satisfaction index
    - Customer engagement

There are many more KPIs and metrics that you can use to understand whether or not your marketing mix is working. Use this as a starting point to get you started.

GETTING READY . . .

It's no easy task to craft a marketing program that will work for you using the various elements. Finding the right mix sometimes takes time and can be appear daunting—at first. The best place to start is defining the big picture to gain perspective and the broader vision you need for your Startup Equation. Then, you need to understand and know your customers.

MARKETING METRICS THAT MATTER

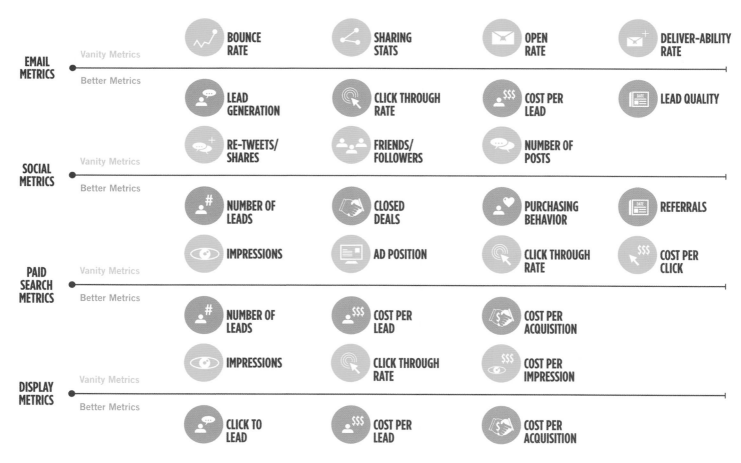

EMAIL METRICS

Vanity Metrics
- BOUNCE RATE
- SHARING STATS
- OPEN RATE
- DELIVER-ABILITY RATE

Better Metrics
- LEAD GENERATION
- CLICK THROUGH RATE
- COST PER LEAD
- LEAD QUALITY

SOCIAL METRICS

Vanity Metrics
- RE-TWEETS/ SHARES
- FRIENDS/ FOLLOWERS
- NUMBER OF POSTS

Better Metrics
- NUMBER OF LEADS
- CLOSED DEALS
- PURCHASING BEHAVIOR
- REFERRALS

PAID SEARCH METRICS

Vanity Metrics
- IMPRESSIONS
- AD POSITION
- CLICK THROUGH RATE
- COST PER CLICK

Better Metrics
- NUMBER OF LEADS
- COST PER LEAD
- COST PER ACQUISITION

DISPLAY METRICS

Vanity Metrics
- IMPRESSIONS
- CLICK THROUGH RATE
- COST PER IMPRESSION

Better Metrics
- CLICK TO LEAD
- COST PER LEAD
- COST PER ACQUISITION

*Data Source: Salesforce

MEASURE	REACH	ACT	CONVERT	ENGAGE
BRAND MEASURES	Unique Visitors New Visitors Brand/Direct Visits Audience Share (vs competitors)	Lead Volume % Product/Service interactions Pages per Visit	Sales Volume Lead Volume Follower or Fan Volumes	Email List Quality Repeat Transactions Repeat Visits Exit Survey - 4Q
CONTENT PERFORMANCE MEASURES	Share of Audience Key sites with your content visible in searches Follower/Fan Volumes Search of Search/Search Presence (Findability) Inbound Links Referring Domains	Page Engagement Rate (Bounce, page per visit) Shares by Users PostRank Score Comments and Site Interactions	Lead Sign-up and Conversion Rate by Engagement Tool Subscription to Email or RSS	Active Customer % (site and email active) Conversion to Fan or Follower % Social Interactions with content such as Fan page comments Repeat Conversion Rate Email open CTR
COMMERCIAL MEASURES	Cost per Click and Cost per Sale Brand Awareness	Goal Value per Visit Online Lead Contribution ($, % of total) Cost per Lead Customer Satisfaction	Conversion Rate to Sale Channel Conversion Rate Online-originated sales, revenue, and product Average Order Value or Cost per Sale	Retained Sales Growth and Volume Revenue per Visit Revenue per Channel and Category Lifetime Value of Customer/Loyalty

If you don't understand whom you're marketing to, you won't know how or what to focus on when you attract them to your startup.

In addition to the many charts and approaches in the chapter, make sure you complete the following exercises:

- Defining Clear Goals
- SWOT Marketing Analysis
- Building Your Marketing Strategy Mix
- Using the Positioning Statement Generator
- Building a Word of Mouth Campaign
- Crafting Your Growth Hacking Strategy

This is just the beginning of how to reach your potential customers. In the next chapter, we'll dive into the sales element of the equation so you can bring them "through the funnel" and convert them into paying, long-term customers.

Sa

Sales

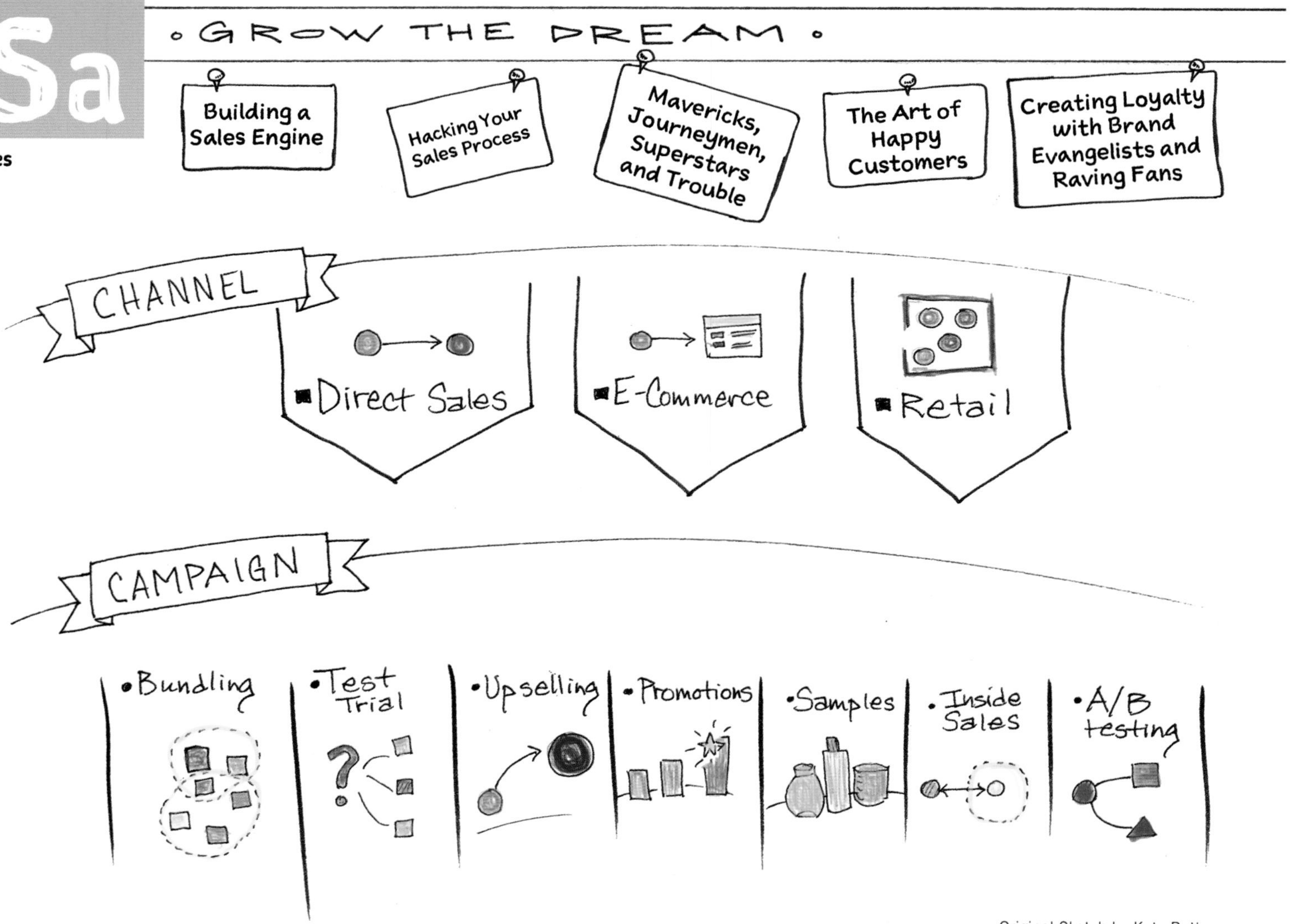

Building a Sales Engine

Hacking Your Sales Process

Mavericks, Journeymen, Superstars and Trouble

The Art of Happy Customers

Creating Loyalty with Brand Evangelists and Raving Fans

CHANNEL

■ Direct Sales

■ E-Commerce

■ Retail

CAMPAIGN

• Bundling

• Test Trial

• Upselling

• Promotions

• Samples

• Inside Sales

• A/B testing

Original Sketch by Kate Rutter

CHAPTER 14

We see our customers as invited guests to a party, and we are the hosts. It is our job every day to make every important aspect of the customer experience a little bit better. —*Jeff Bezos, CEO, Amazon.com*

ROI of Happy Customers

Back in 1995, Kevin Plank was captain of the University of Maryland football team. He realized a career in the NFL wasn't in his future, but he saw an opportunity. Compression shorts stayed dry during practice, so he decided to take that material and make other athletic gear that would wick away moisture. After a year in business, he was $40,000 in debt and broke. Then, he made his first sale to Georgia Tech and a few dozen NFL teams followed suit.

With that first customer, the rest began to fall like dominos because he would do whatever it took to get the product in places. He was the CEO and Under Armour's first salesperson. He was willing to do whatever it took to get the sale and get the product in the hands of people that could influence and grow the brand. According to Kevin, "the equipment manager called from Arizona State and asked, 'Do you guys make this for cold weather?'—they didn't but he knew he could, said 'Yes' and then drove to the designers house to figure out how to do it."

He's grown the company to a public entity (NYSE: UA) that did $2.3 billion in revenue last year. And it all started with a great idea, some seed capital, and a founder who was passionate about selling and creating fans, as well as customers, of his product.

In this chapter, we'll talk about sales in your startup and how to build a sales engine. We will also discuss the "Get-Keep-Grow" approach to customer development and various sales processes and strategies. This includes **Sales (Sa)** channel elements like **Direct Sales (Dsl)**, **E-Commerce (Ecm)**, and **Retail (Ret)**.

We will then dig into the essential elements for creating a Voice of the Customer program to listen and understand. You'll also learn how to create a positive relationship with everyone who crosses paths with your brand by turning them into brand evangelists and rabid fans. Using **Sales (Sa)** elements such as **Upselling (Usl)** and **Promotions (Pmt)** helps with retention and loyalty. Because in the end, no matter how you market

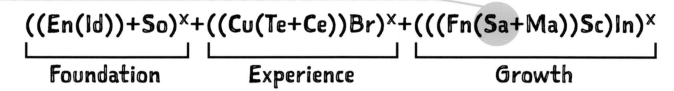

$$((En(Id))+So)^X+((Cu(Te+Ce))Br)^X+(((Fn(Sa+Ma))Sc)In)^X$$

| Foundation | Experience | Growth |

A startup is only a startup when it starts selling its product or service. Startups often struggle with lead generation or creating the right sales funnel that can scale with the company. The importance of sales when starting a startup cannot be denied.

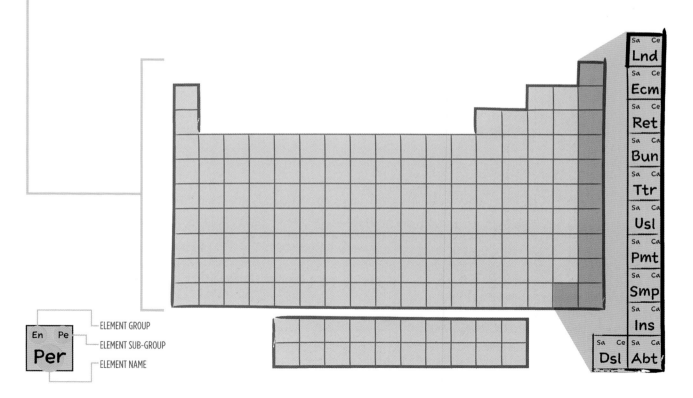

SALES (SA) CHANNEL ELEMENTS

A sales channel is a path in which a startup can sell to its consumers and through which a company or representative completes transactions with consumers.

Direct Sales (Dsl)
Direct selling is the selling of products or services directly to your consumers. This commonly occurs through home parties, one-on-one consultations, concierge or through a mobile location.

Landing Pages (Lnd)
A landing page is a single page on a website dedicated to a specific promotion or deal that the company is offering.

E-Commerce (Ecm)
E-commerce refers to commercial transactions conducted on the Internet. Commonly, transactions occur on a startup's personal website or through a third-party provider.

Retail (Ret)
Retail is the sale of products or services from businesses to consumers from a fixed location.

SALES (SA) CAMPAIGN ELEMENTS

Sales Campaign elements are activities that companies can use to sell more products or services. These programs can be stand alone or work in conjunction with other elements.

Bundling (Bun)
Bundling is the act of taking more than one product or service and creating a combined package for the consumer. Bundling can occur with a company's own products/services, other companies' products/services, or a combination of both.

Test Trial (Ttr)
A test trial allows for a prospective customer to try your company's product or service for a set duration of time.

Upselling (Usl)
Upselling occurs after the customer is within the sales funnel. As the customer is about to finalize their transaction, the seller induces either additional items, upgrades of current purchases or add-ons that would complement the original item being purchased.

Promotions (Pmt)
A sales promotion is a limited time offer to increase sales. A promotion can be direct to customer or through channels and partners.

Samples (Smp)
Samples are some offerings of your product/service to prospective consumers to give them enough exposure to your product/service to feel confident enough to purchase from you.

Inside Sales (Ins)
Inside sales is when the customer comes to you at a fixed location of business or the transaction is done remotely. Inside sales are sometimes a hybrid with account management.

A/B Testing (Abt)
A/B testing allows for a company to take two versions of a product, service, entity or promotion and test them. There is always an A version (the control) and a B version (the variation) and typically a startup will only test one item at a time in order to measure performance and conversion.

your company, you will have only one pinnacle KPI to measure against: the ROI of a happy customer.

BUILDING A SALES ENGINE

At the beginning of a startup, you'll experience your fair share of challenges. But as you deal with the challenges, build the team, and develop the product, you'll start to focus on selling your product and getting customers. In the beginning, odds are high you'll prove the best salesperson for your product and company.

As you think through this process, it's worth reviewing one of the most well-known customer development processes that comes from serial-entrepreneur Steven Blank. Mr. Blank argues that most startups fail from a lack of customer development, not product development.

Once a startup can prove product viability, they can start to execute and build their brand. But the key, as we've discussed previously, remains getting the minimum viable product right before you do anything else. After you've proven your product-market fit using tools like the Startup Equation Business Model Canvas outlined in Chapter 7, how do you connect it to the next step of selling to potential customers beyond the excited "true believers?"

The marketing tactics we outlined in Chapter 13 to get, keep, and grow your customers definitely come into play at this point. However, you can't forget that selling is a process and will always need your time and attention.

Know Thy Customer

In most cases, you're the best (and probably only) salesperson in the company as you start to build your sales engine. The first step is to

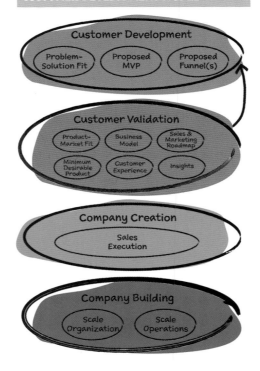

CUSTOMER DEVELOPMENT MODEL

Customer Development
Problem-Solution Fit · Proposed MVP · Proposed Funnel(s)

Customer Validation
Product-Market Fit · Business Model · Sales & Marketing Roadmap · Minimum Desirable Product · Customer Experience · Insights

Company Creation
Sales Execution

Company Building
Scale Organization · Scale Operations

re-validate who you believe is your ideal customer. You began this process back in Chapter 7 working on your business model canvas as well as in Chapter 10 with proto-personas. This helps you:

- Confirm your customer's biggest challenges
- Know where to focus your efforts
- Know where to look for highly qualified prospects
- Tailor your offerings and messaging to solve those exact challenges
- Convert potential customers more easily because they're a better fit
- Create an experience that speaks to them and their needs
- Provide more value

In order to confirm your ideal customer, take some of the target audience work from previous chapters and dig into the proto-personas exercise (Chapter 10). The more you can identify and relate to each persona, the more effectively you can guide them through the sales process while building a relationship.

EXERCISE: Build Your Own Ideal Customer Canvas

It's time to create your own Ideal Customer Canvas (see Figure 14.3). You can create a few ideal customer profiles, but it's best to focus on just one so you're not diluting the core, ideal customer profile. Ask yourself:

- What are the demographics of my ideal customer? What is their income, how many children do they have?
- What does their daily routine look like? How about at work?

- What kinds of objections might they have to using/buying your product/solution?
- What are the pain points of their problem that could be solved with your product?
- What would get them excited about your brand or product?

The Get-Keep-Grow Approach

Instead of thinking of your selling process as a sales funnel, view it as a get-keep-grow funnel.

"Get" Customers

"Get" customers falls on the left side of the funnel and references activities we discussed in Chapter 13 (e.g., earned or paid media) to attract, acquire, and activate new customers. Using your passion and product knowledge as a launch pad, you can craft a sales strategy that includes these key components:

- **Pipeline Building:** You must constantly fill the funnel with opportunities. You'll need to set up a system to track your leads, accounts, contacts, suspects and prospects, forecasts, activities, time management, products, and territories. There are many great, web-based tools out there to find your needs. Search on terms like sales software, CRM, and pipeline management to get you started.
- **Trust Selling:** At its core, a sale happens between two people. People buy from people they trust, not from people they like. Techniques like **word of mouth** (WOM) selling depend on trust selling. According to McKinsey, three-quarters of all industries are driven by WOM, and it should dominate your startup sales strategy, even when you're relying on the Internet. Other direct trust selling methods include public speaking at conferences, customer referrals, user conferences, training events, and demos.
- **Targeted Selling:** Every product has different ideal customers and requires a different strategy. Your strategy may require developing a personal human connection with the customer, marketing through email, or engaging with a social media campaign. You can assume

that doing a little bit of everything will work, and remember this stuff takes time.

- **Sales Targets:** You need to start building your success metrics from KPIs to track your efforts, including setting sales targets and goals associated with hitting key milestones. We'll dive into sales metrics later in the chapter.

"Keep" Customers

In this part of the funnel, we continue moving customers through the process and focus on what it takes to make them happy and stay with the brand, including how to keep customers and grow them for the long term.

- **Communications:** You must keep your customers in the loop and engage through all kinds of channels, including things like emails and blogs, for example.
- **Events:** Connecting with customers one-on-one can be incredible. Using events that have a focus and special appeal can help your brand awareness while attracting new customers to your brand.
- **Programs:** Different programs, like contests, have a limited window, but others engage in specific, long-term activities, like loyalty programs (discussed later in this chapter), that can help with retention and create fans of your brand.

"Grow" Customers

This is the really huge opportunity that doesn't get talked about much. Growing customers is about retention, but also about having them buy more or different things you offer. It also includes how to turn these fans into your free marketing and sales machine.

- **Up/Next/Cross Sell:** With a great group of customers, you have an opportunity to increase how much they buy from you, including other applicable products and services. It's also an opportunity to test new product ideas to see what appeals to various customers.
- **Referrals:** The best kind of new customer is one who is referred by an existing customer. The power of a referral creates trust and usually a better customer. Creating referral programs and incentives can build your customer base more cost effectively than many other types of sales programs.

Blank recommends starting with the testing of a series of hypotheses, particularly with the problem you are trying to solve for the customer and then the product or service concept. Within these tests, it is important to do some discovery once you have a small test group. Ask them:

• What are their top problems?
• What are they willing to pay to have those problems solved?
• Do they feel that your product/service solves those problems?
   • If so, how much would they pay for your product/service?

Once they have answered some of these initial questions, you can start to dig in a little deeper to see whether or not your product/service is truly scalable.

Opportunity Assessment:
• How big is the problem/need?
• How can you modify your product/service to truly meet the needs of your early adopters?
• How can you develop a repeatable sales process?

When in the feedback loop ask "Why" 5 times in order to get to the root cause. An example of this would be:

• Why did we change the software, so we do not make any money anymore?
• Why didn't operations get paged?
• Why didn't the cluster immune system reject the change?
• Why didn't automated tests go red and stop the line?
• Why wasn't the engineer trained not to make that mistake?

When you are able to take corrective action, Blank believes that you will be able to get to the root of why something isn't working within your product. Here is a flow of hypotheses and the process that Blank recommends that you follow:

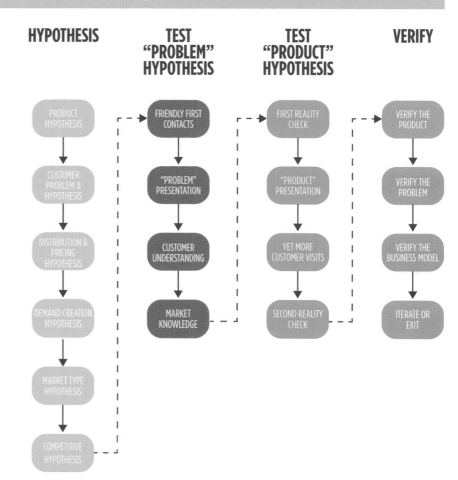

*Data Source: Steve Blank

IDEAL CUSTOMER CANVAS Figure 14.5

DEMOGRAPHICS

Are they married?
What is their annual household income?
Where do they live?
How old are they?
Do they have children?

DAILY LIFE

Exercise? If so, how?
Read? Tangible books or electronic?
Hobbies?
Personality type?
Prefer social gatherings over staying in?
Passions?
TV consumption?
What do they value?

WORK-RELATED

Where do they work? Home? Office?
What is their job title and description?
What goals would they have?
What level of seniority do they have?
Who else Would be involved in the
    decision-making process?

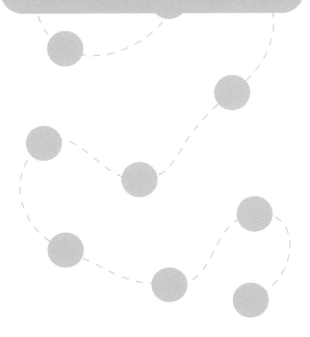

THE EXPERIENCE

What experience are they looking for when buying from your industry?
What should their sales experience be like for them?
How much time would they expect to spend within this experience?

OBJECTIONS

What objections would they have to buying
    from my brand?
What solutions can my brand provide for each
    of these objections?
What would make them switch to our brand
    from a competitor?

PAIN POINTS

What problems does their job description usually
    solve for a company?
What are some of the obstacles that get in the
    way of solving those problems?
Why would they get excited about my brand?

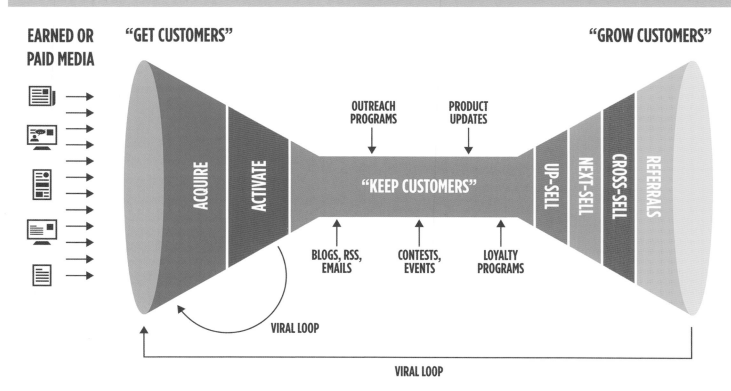

Data Source: Steve Blank from The Startup Owners Manual © 2012

HACKING YOUR SALES PROCESS

Most of the time, it can seem like all this planning is a waste and totally irrelevant before the ink dries on the whiteboard. A lack of planning can lead to sales efforts that can irreparably damage and even kill your startup.

Sales is usually the first time there's direct contact between a potential customer and your startup. It's critical that you attach significant weight to those first conversations. They're not just about building relationships, but also about establishing credibility, expertise and, most importantly, an understanding of the customer's perspective.

Depending on your business model, you may sell direct to consumers or to other businesses or maybe even both. The general sales process looks very similar for both as you move them through the funnel to convert and close them. In both instances, you may use online methods, a sales team, or a mix of both. Whatever your methods, it's critical that you define and refine your sales processes to work for your business.

Finding the Sales Process that is Right for You

Selling is the lifeline to your business. However, if there's one weakness that we consistently see across startups, it's the lack of a plan, process, and methodology. The other issue is hiring salespeople too early, but we'll get to that later in the chapter. So what exactly do we mean by a plan, a process and a methodology?

The Sales Plan
From the start of creating your sales plan, you'll need to pay attention to time. When you first start a company, you're in the street preacher phase of trying to persuade customers a product that you've worked on day and night for months will better meet their needs. While selling focuses on delivering revenue, there are usually more leads than there is time. Your sales plan can help you manage those leads effectively.

The Sales Process
When you achieve product/market fit, your company often ramps revenue very fast, and you need to build an organization to deal with the demand generation (e.g., marketing), sales discovery, implementation, and after-

sales support. But before you achieve product/market fit, you're often in "consultative sales" mode where your objective is to tease out customer needs. Your solution may not solve them entirely, so you'll often have to allow open access to your product or integrate it with other solutions.

Many confuse process with methodology, but for our purposes, a process is how a salesperson advances an opportunity from an unqualified lead to a close to a post-sale. Defining this process gives salespeople and management a clear understanding of how opportunities are progressing, what gaps exist, and where potential issues may arise.

A sales pipeline or funnel is the path in which a person goes from becoming aware of your business to becoming a customer. There are many potential sales funnels, and it's rarely one size fits all. However, by following a few simple steps, you can figure out your process.

1. **What do you want as the end result?** So many entrepreneurs focus on the beginning of the sales process they forget what they're really looking for: loyal customers who are happy to give repeat business. That said, you may have a different outcome in mind. Maybe you just want email addresses or a person to buy once from you. Either way, know what you want at the end and start working backwards to get to the beginning.

2. **How would they find you?** Now that you've identified your target and have a general sense of where they're most likely to be (online and offline), it's time to figure out how to engage in a conversation. When you're engaging at the top of the funnel, two things usually occur: (1) the customer knows that they have a problem and are looking for a solution or (2) the customer has absolutely no clue that they have a specific problem, let alone need your brand as their solution. Either way, the top of the funnel becomes an educational opportunity for you to connect with your potential clients.

3. **Where are you sending them?** It's one thing to engage with a potential customer, but if you don't have a place to send them for more information, then it's a moot point. Depending on the point of entry and the desired end result, you can pick the best sales channel.

4. **How can you simplify the funnel?** Many times, businesses will be caught in the marketing/sales loop. Diagram out all the possible sales channels. Have people walk through each process and solicit

feedback. What was the experience like? Where were the hang ups? Did you want to buy at all? If not, why? What questions did you still have? Collect data from your feedback loop and pick the most impactful changes to help you prioritize time and resources.

5. **How do you continue the experience?** The customer experience truly starts with awareness of your brand. They will decide immediately whether or not they wish to continue getting to know you. If a person decides to become a customer of yours, that's fantastic. But the experience doesn't end there. Remember to keep in mind what you want at the end of the funnel.

In Steve Blank's work with startups, he crafted a four-part method to create a teachable and reproducible sales process.

1. **Know Your BANT (Budget, Authority, Needs and Timeframe):** Understand your customer's procurement processes, budgeting cycles, decision-making authority, competing interests for time and resources, and key meetings that must take place to approve your sale. You need to know if you're speaking with the person who has the authority to approve your deal. You should also have knowledge of when people plan to buy.

2. **Handle Customer Objections:** If you're getting objections from the customer, it almost always means they're testing their understanding of the product and the deal. You can handle objections by clarifying their issue and empathizing with their concerns. It allows you to test or soft close with phrases like, "If we were able to resolve this issue, would you move forward with the product?" If the answer is no, then you have others issues you need to address.

3. **Get To the Top Quickly:** Without an insider helping you navigate and champion your offering, it can be nearly impossible to close a deal and can lead to wasting valuable resources on a deal that might not close this quarter—or ever. If you're selling online, it's easier because you're most likely leveraging inbound marketing techniques that we discussed in the previous chapter. If you do get someone higher up involved, their support will make it easier to move through the organization and get results.

4. **Prioritize Without Mercy:** It's your job to manage opportunities and know which deals are biggest and closest to closing. By prioritizing, you manage your pipeline efficiently, something that's hard to do when there's a live deal that's too small or a big, marquee deal that lacks a budget this cycle. We aren't suggesting you ignore smaller or less likely deals. What we do recommend is making the most of your available resources (e.g., self-service systems) to service those leads without hurting your more promising prospects.

Your job (and eventually the sales team's job) is to figure out whether the customer has a need, a budget, the resources, and an approval process to work with you. If the customer isn't ready for that final commitment, you can place your prospect in a "marketing funnel" managed by non-sales resources. They can stay in touch with potential customers through white papers or seminars while your sales people focus on the near-term deals and hitting your quarterly targets.

The Sales Methodology

In order to leverage the process you've created, there should be certain methods for meeting the stated objectives. Keeping this reality in mind, we'll focus on one method your startup could leverage: the PUCCKA methodology by Mark Suster. Mr. Suster is now an investment partner at Upfront Ventures and built out a standardized process to scale his own businesses. His goal was to create a common sales language that his teams could use with each other. So why is it called PUCCKA? It stands for Pain, Unique Selling Proposition, Compelling Event, Champion, Key Players, and Aligned Purchasing Process. Let's explore these areas in a bit more detail:[1]

- **Pain** is where you identify a business problem your prospect has and gain acceptance that there's a real need for a solution.

- **Unique Selling Proposition** or USP is the unique things that your product solves. USP answers the "Why buy me?" question in sales.

- **Compelling Event** is the thing that forces your prospect to realize they need to kick off a project immediately. It also answers "Why buy now?", the final question in sales, which is also the hardest question to answer. Often customers will think your product is useful, but they don't have the time, budget, or inclination to adopt your solution without a compelling event.

- **Champion** refers to the person who drives through the approval to give the go-ahead to your product or company. Orders don't fill out themselves. You need somebody who will take a risk on you and guide you through the process. A champion is somebody with both influence and authority.

- **Key Players** are the other people involved in the sales process, including enemies, technical experts, sponsors, etc. The most telling sign of an inexperienced salesperson is that they meet one person in an organization that's nice to them, and they spend all their time with this one individual.

- **Aligned Purchasing Process** is the act of your customer being ready to buy when you're ready to sell.

Someone who has a great deal of experience building sales organizations, discovering talent and creating many customer acquisition and retention programs is Carlos Diggs. Carlos is currently head of CDA Consulting, a sales and marketing consultancy, and has spent the last 20 years mastering the concept of why we buy and how companies should sell and keep their customers happy. We recently had the opportunity to sit down and talk about what startups need to build a sales engine.

SEQ: What do you think are the top three skills that an entrepreneur needs to start the customer acquisition process?

Diggs: It's probably the thing that they don't teach you in school. I believe that everyone needs to develop some fundamental selling skills. I think a sales course should be required in everyone's curriculum. I don't care if you're a scientist, an engineer, an astronaut, whatever. If you have an idea, one day you're going to pitch something and show that you have a solution to offer.

SEQ: When you're engaged with prospective clients who do you qualify them?

Diggs: You need to think about their profile, almost like a dating profile. What are the characteristics this company needs to have? If we're talking to business, you need to look at the type of company, and the vertical industry that they're in. Look at the revenues and a number of employees.

If it's a digital solution, you don't need to physically be there. Geography may not matter, but if you need to focus your marketing dollars, it's good to be try to become the big fish in the little pond.

Once you get that profile done, and you know who might be a good match for it, then it makes sense to have a qualifying set of questions you're going to ask. You go on that qualification call to get to yes or no. "Yes, I agree. That's a good assumption. Yes, you're right. We have that pay. Yes, we're willing to fix it and we need it done yesterday." Then, find out how much they're willing to pay.

Getting comfortable with talking money to see if you're in the ballpark is key. Figuring out when they're going to make the decision is key and who is going to make the ultimate decision.

Now, it's time to get out there. Talk to customers. Learn from your problem/solution pitches we discussed earlier. Always be listening to the customer and take the opportunity to experiment and test how you phrase things while learning to read reactions. Remember that sometimes the best learning experience may mean losing the deal. You don't have to win nine out of ten times. You can win one out of ten quickly and efficiently with a repeatable process.

EXERCISE: Draft Your Own S.I.M.P.L.E. Voice of the Customer (VoC) Program

1. **Create Your BANT:** List out the Budget, Authority, Needs and Timeframe of the sales campaigns you plan to run.

2. **Define Customer Objections:** Write out the objections that a customer might have and write out how you will handle them to turn them into a sale.

3. **Map Out Your Insiders and Champions:** Who are the insiders and champions that can help you get to the top quickly/close the deals you want?

4. **What is your Pitch?:** You need to focus and craft the 30 second sales pitch. Write out a few alternatives and read them aloud while someone is in the room to test it.

Using Sales Campaigns

Within the sales process in the previous section, we discussed the sales funnel and the need to test specific campaigns for effectiveness. Some of these elements include:

- **Bundling (Bun):** Bundling is when you offer more than one product or service within a package. It's a great way to add more value to an offering, as well as a great way to test what people are enticed to buy.

- **Test Trial (Ttr):** Sometimes people want to test a brand before purchasing. Much like taking a car for a spin before purchasing it, you can set up a test trial for potential customers to try your service for a set amount of time before purchasing. Many people do 30-day, risk-free trials.

- **Upselling (Usl):** Once you have someone in your sales funnel and they're ready to purchase, you can upsell. Upselling allows you to offer add-ons to the original intended purchase at an "additional cost."

- **Promotion (Pmt):** A promotion is a sale or series of integrated advertisements for a limited amount of time. Many sales promotions occur around a customer's buying cycle, such as the holiday season or the start of the school year.

- **Samples (Smp):** Much like the test trial, you can get people to try your product or service through a sample. Samples allow for people to see (and potentially taste or touch depending on the product) your product and get a sense of its quality.

- **Inside Sales (Ins):** Inside sales, also known as remote calling, involves selling remotely on the phone or web. These calls are usually with individuals who are somewhat familiar with your company. They may have downloaded a case study or asked for a quote through your website.

- **A/B Testing (Abt):** It's important within your business to test as many things as possible and see whether or not they're working for you. A/B testing is a simple way to test changes to a website, product, landing page, or copy to determine which ones produce positive results.

EXERCISE: Design Your Initial Sales Campaign

To prepare your sales team for a sales campaign, complete the following steps:

1. **Set a specific goal.** Know what you want the result of this campaign to be.

2. **Define a feeling.** Decide what you want a person to feel during your sales campaign. Work out what you would like them to feel as you keep your goal in mind. Then, remember to carry that feeling throughout the entire campaign.

3. **Decide on your initial campaigns.** Unless you've run a campaign before, we recommend testing one thing at a time to see what works for your business.

4. **Define a clear message.** No matter the campaign, make the messaging clear and remember to always lead with the benefit to the customer.

5. **Define a call to action.** Be very careful to avoid more than one call to action, otherwise the potential customer can be confused. You have one goal for this campaign, so align your CTAs with that goal.

Running a sales campaign is not an easy thing. It takes a lot of time and testing to get in the right groove. That's why starting with a small beta testing group is the best way to roll anything out. Again, let them be your guinea pigs and please remember to reward them for it!

MAVERICKS, JOURNEYMEN, SUPERSTARS AND TROUBLE

While it's true you're probably the best person to sell at your startup, you're going to be busy doing a million other things. You need people dedicated to the job, and not every salesperson is right for a startup.

Salespeople are divided into two general categories: the hunters and the farmers. The hunters are your pipeline fillers and deal closers. They get the new customers, close the deal, and move on to the next one. It's all

INBOUND MARKETING FUNNEL

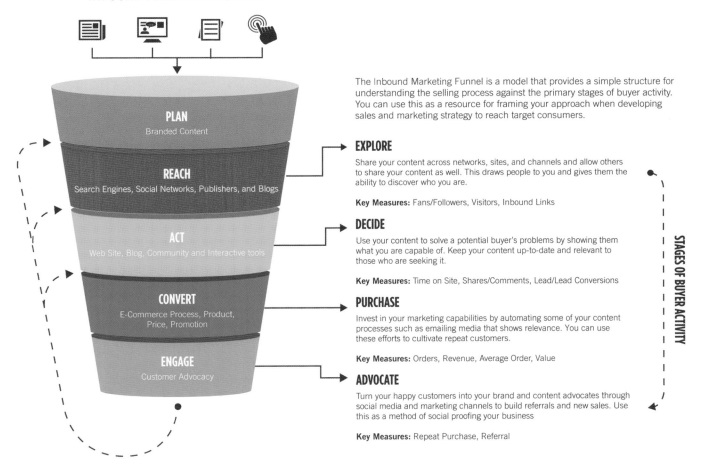

The Inbound Marketing Funnel is a model that provides a simple structure for understanding the selling process against the primary stages of buyer activity. You can use this as a resource for framing your approach when developing sales and marketing strategy to reach target consumers.

EXPLORE

Share your content across networks, sites, and channels and allow others to share your content as well. This draws people to you and gives them the ability to discover who you are.

Key Measures: Fans/Followers, Visitors, Inbound Links

DECIDE

Use your content to solve a potential buyer's problems by showing them what you are capable of. Keep your content up-to-date and relevant to those who are seeking it.

Key Measures: Time on Site, Shares/Comments, Lead/Lead Conversions

PURCHASE

Invest in your marketing capabilities by automating some of your content processes such as emailing media that shows relevance. You can use these efforts to cultivate repeat customers.

Key Measures: Orders, Revenue, Average Order, Value

ADVOCATE

Turn your happy customers into your brand and content advocates through social media and marketing channels to build referrals and new sales. Use this as a method of social proofing your business

Key Measures: Repeat Purchase, Referral

*Data Source: First 10, Smart Insights, and DemandResults

about the kill and close. These salespeople are key in the beginning, especially as you try to grow your customer base. But they're terrible when it comes to maintaining the customer. This is where the farmers come in.

Farmers harvest and grow the customer relationship. They develop the trusted relationship and grow the size of the account. They answer the calls at 2 a.m. because they know how to talk a customer off a ledge and keep them for life. You need these people, too, but when you're first starting out, you need the hunter first, and then the farmers about six months later when you've secured the relationship and can hand it off for the long term.

Here are 11 things a salesperson in a startup needs to have:[2]

1. Be willing to learn something new every day
2. Have the desire to make a real difference
3. Inspire everyone you speak with
4. Resist the urge to sell—be helpful instead
5. Connect with the right people
6. Embrace and be comfortable with change
7. Take a consultative approach
8. Differentiate from the pack
9. Have tough negotiation chops
10. Ditch the 9-to-5 work routine
11. Tell great stories

Mark Suster, a VC and author of the "Both Sides of Table Blog," breaks down another method for building a team, including the different types of salespeople in today's startups. He started with a tried and true four-quadrant matrix.

On the x-axis falls the scale of someone's innate talent for selling. Natural salespeople appear to be born with it, and it's a skill that can't always be taught. On the y-axis is the scale of process. Process can be taught, and only with experience and focus can someone be process driven. From that scale he defines four types: Journeyman, Maverick, Superstar, and Trouble.[3]

Wait for The Journeyman

The Journeyman learned the trade from another person. They're similar to the farmers Steve mentioned earlier. According to Mr. Suster:

> They are hugely process driven. These people take directions well from a sales manager on how to approach sales campaigns. . . . They're organized and methodical. They're great at orchestrating your company to deliver product demos. They know how to walk a deal from business owner, through IT, through procurement, and through legal to get a closed order. They are the LIFEBLOOD of sales organizations because they're plentiful and deliver great value relative to their costs.

They tend to fall short in two areas: (1) they don't tend to make great heads of sales departments, and (2) they aren't the people you want early in your company.

Don't Let Mavericks Crash Your Jet

In sales, the Mavericks are the complete opposite of Journeymen. Mr. Suster says, "Mavericks are by definition bad at following rules and bad at process." He goes on to add, "They can get access to senior executives and champion a sales campaign from the top. . . . They're chaotic by nature. But in the end they know how to put the big wins on the board. They can smell the person who holds the purse strings in a company and how to gain access to them." Mavericks do work well in early-stage companies and are probably your best bet for you first hire or two.

The Rarity of Superstars

A rare bird, Superstars have it all—an innate ability to sell, a desire for structure, and focused on process. Mr. Suster describes them as "[getting] all the benefits of a maverick but with more reliability and predictability. You also get somebody who can work well with leverage. They're able to manage and therefore harness the power of many journeymen to consistently deliver your sales numbers." These people are also the worst first hires to make in your startup.

Trouble is Well, Just Trouble

There is not much to say about this type. Trouble types can sell, but they aren't process driven and don't have the innate ability to sell ice to Eskimos. They're invariably a bad hire.

The bottom line if you're starting a company: Find a proven Maverick looking to make a big impact, then maybe hire another one. Soon, you'll need a Journeyman or two to manage the flow of business. After things take off, then you can bring in your Superstar.

The Art of Happy Customers

Every customer relationship comes with a value. It's often referred to as *relationship capital*. It can work for you or against you; depending on how much emphasis you put on building relationships. Here are a few examples:

- When you have unclear messaging, then you may be hurting your relationship capital and failing to attract the right target audience.
- When a customer has a crappy service experience with your brand, it dramatically hurts your relationship capital.
- When you violate a customer's trust by not delivering what you promised, then it really diminishes your relationship capital with that person.

It's safe to say that keeping customers happy is one of the hardest things you'll do in business, but where does customer service begin? Some argue that it's after the transaction. We strongly disagree with that approach. The art of creating happy customers begins with the first time a potential customer interacts with your brand.

Back in Chapter 10, we discussed customer experience and journey maps. Journey maps chart the interactions or "touch points" that a customer will have with your company. It doesn't matter if they find you online or meet you at a networking event. The first encounter is more important than any encounter that follows it.

But why does that first encounter matter so much? It's because you're fostering a relationship with a potential customer and the way you foster that relationship remains a crucial part of any successful business.

You should note the graphic "The Art of Happy Customers" and our ten point for creating happy customers. Because even after the first sale they need to stay happy for the long term for new opportunities (up/next/cross selling and referrals) that will help scale your business effectively.

It's also important to remember that at any moment, unhappy customers can share their opinions and negatively affect your business before you have a chance to react. Developing rapport and trust before someone becomes your customer will help you stay ahead of the game. But what will truly help is creating a customer-focused culture. One of the best ways is to create a voice of the customer program.

The S.I.M.P.L.E. Voice of the Customer Program

Voice of the Customer (VoC) is a term that describes your customer's feedback about their experiences with and expectations for your products or services. Perhaps you've been in business for a while, have a product/service that people will buy, and you're willing to scale. The voice of the customer is best heard as an ongoing conversation. The key to creating an effective VoC program is to gather and use information in a timely way that helps you to improve.

Characteristics of the Best VoC Programs

- Connect multiple types of feedback across data channels
- Provide automatic collaboration across functional departments
- Incorporate the voice of the employee
- Leverage dashboards and reports that integrate and display information from multiple customer voices regardless of source, survey or time
- Deliver clear ROI and business results
- Once you have a customer, you have someone who believes in you. Broaden that relationship by helping to solving important and meaningful problems. Listen to their issues and help educate them on how you can help them solve those problems. It will help to build up the trust that your customers have in you.

Happy customers are important at every step of the sales path. These simple pointers will help you be aware of the core skills necessary for making sales to your clients.

LISTEN

Listen to what you customers have to say and be attentive. Ask them return questions and summarize their responses to make sure you understand.

GOOD COMMUNICAITON SKILLS

Use strong communication skills to know when to speak, listen, and respond to your custom-ers. It will make the process simpler and improve the experience for you and them.

HONESTY IS THE BEST POLICY

Being honest and open builds trust and empathy with your client and shows them that you believe in ensuring their satisfaction.

BE THE EXPERT

Knowing your business and your market is import for your client as it builds their confidence in you. Be sure to know the products and services you are selling to clients and how they might be used in different situations.

HAVE CONFIDENCE

When you sound and act confident to your customers, you will have a greater ability to convince clients to purchase.

BE POSITIVE

Always use positive language in your conversations, even if the situation is not so. Positive language boosts confidence, can be motivating, and can be persuasive in your dealings with customers.

TIME MANAGEMENT

Maintaining good time management skills ensures you are providing your customers with enough time while also not wasting their time or falling behind on other callers.

KNOW THE ORGANIZATION

When you know the people around you and throughout the organization they can help you on more complex issues and tasks that need solving.

NEGOTIATE

Be adaptive and willing to find compromises with your customers that are mutually beneficial. The ability to negotiate will create more opportunities and win-win results that are essential for a business.

CLOSE THE DEAL

Knowing when and how to close a deal or arrive at a solution is essential to ensuring happy customers and will help not waste their time or yours.

*Data Source: Introhive Relationships Matter Study, Inc.com, MarketingSherpa, Forbes.com, Business.com

SIMPLE

S OLVE

I MPORTANT

M EANINGFUL

P ROBLEMS

BY

L ISTENING

E DUCATION

No Matter Where You Are, You Can Start Now

Will Carter of *CRN Magazine* states wherever you are in your VoC journey, if any of these issues sound familiar, here are three recommendations for how you can jump-start your program:

1. **Begin with the business decisions.** Why do you have a VoC program? What business decisions will the voice of your customer inform and influence? If you start with these decisions, you can focus on collecting the right data and performing the necessary analyses, thus limiting information overload. Starting with the business decisions also creates a compelling business case for your organization's stakeholders, to justify your resource requests and to elicit executive-level support.

2. **Align your VoC efforts to the customer journey.** Well-crafted VoC programs are designed around the most important aspects of the customer journey. Identify the leverage points that allow you to foster customer loyalty and create customer value. Understand the barriers in the customer journey where you lose loyalty and destroy value. Focus your VoC program in those areas.

3. **Integrate your VoC program across your organization.** VoC programs should not serve the needs of just one department or functional area. These efforts must be integrated across your marketing, sales and operations teams so that everyone knows how they can benefit from customer insights. While it won't be a quick process to get your entire organization to care about VoC, here are a few ideas to kick-start this process.

EXERCISE: Draft Your Own S.I.M.P.L.E. Voice of the Customer (VoC) Program

As you build out your sales engine you'll want to outline your own S.I.M.P.L.E. VoC program. Here are three things you need to complete in this exercise:

1. What are the top three meaningful problems you will solve?

2. What five insights do you want to measure and what tools will you use?

3. How will you let your customer know that you are listening and what activities will you and your VoC teams (e.g., sales, customer service)

CREATING LOYALTY WITH
BRAND EVANGELISTS AND RAVING FANS

So much in startup advice and theory is focused on the marketing side and getting the customer. It's true that these initial customers are your proving ground, your validation, and your key to the next level. However, that's just half of it. Once you get them bought into your vision and using your product, you need to keep them and keep them loyal. And we're talking beyond loyal, like true brand evangelists.

Building Brand Evangelists

Customers buy things. Brand evangelists preach the things that they have bought . . . for free. So, what do we mean when we say brand evangelist? They're very satisfied customers, who love to sing your praises. These people go beyond the customer role of just buying your product and make sure that everyone they know knows your product is the best.

The Temkin Group reports that brand evangelists are 5.2 times more likely to purchase from a company and are 5.8 times more likely to forgive a mistake made by the brand. In this era of customization and personalization, people truly rely on the brands that their friends and families trust and rely on. Wouldn't you rather be one of those brands than one they criticize? On the following page we outline a general approach to a stellar buying experience for a growing startup. It tracks concepts along two tracks: (1) customer engagement and (2) order fulfillment. Your customers need to feel supported and engaged every step of the way.

In order to build up evangelism, you need to give people reasons to evangelize for your startup:

- **Create a place for your community to connect.** People want to know that they are not the only one that likes your startup. Give customers a place where they can connect with one another and organically grow the community. One company who does this well is Spiceworks. They deliver a solid, reliable product, and provide a platform for people to ask each other questions, hold lively discussions and even have customer-initiated gatherings. Could you create a similar platform?

- **Acknowledge your brand evangelists:** Evangelists aren't doing it for the money. They're doing it because they love your company and believe in your products. So you reward them by acknowledging them. Highlight them and thank them. It validates their love for you and motivates them to promote you more.

- **Pay attention to criticisms.** Evangelists will tell you what you're screwing up, but then they'll help you fix it. While other customers might blog, "You suck," an evangelist will say, "Company X got it wrong, but here's what they should have done." Don't overlook their suggestions.

Making Everyone Raving Fans

When it comes down to it, you're in business because of people and the only way to get to know these people is to spend time with them and build relationships. Here are three components that can support your customer relationships.

1. **Personalize:** People want to feel like they're your only customer. Find multiple touch points within your relationship to personalize the experience for them. It will take a little more effort, but it will go a long way.

2. **Reciprocity:** Reciprocity is the practice of exchanging things with others for mutual benefit. It's been studied since the days of Aristotle. Our brains need to know that a transaction or an interaction has been done fairly or through a "fair exchange." Reciprocity has an amazing effect on customer service and customer relationships.

3. **Everyone's a VIP:** Everyone wants to know they matter. Sometimes just responding to their question can make a huge difference. People are willing to spend more with a business that they feel treats them with the respect they need and deserve. Plus, loyal customers will spend more with a company who sticks by them.

Creating a Loyalty Program that Rocks

You can create loyalty programs that allow for customers to rank against each other, redeem for rewards, or just have bragging rights and a way to tell others about how awesome your startup is to them. Here are things you can do:

- **Keep it elite.** If you keep participation limited to those customers who are the most loyal, send these invitations to a select few. It will

THE CHANGING DYNAMICS OF SALES

SOCIAL MEDIA
55%
of B2B Sales Professionals believe that social media has no impact on their sales efforts

SLOW RESPONSES
66%
of Sales Professionals believe that the buying process is changing faster than sales organizations

DEATH OF COLD CALLING
64%
of B2B Sales Professionals noted calling has not improved within the past three years

COST OF COLD CALLING
60%
Cold call efforts are 60% more expensive than generating inbound leads for sales

TRADITIONAL SELLING VS **MODERN SELLING**

The buying process begins with a call to or from a potential supplier.

Playing golf was traditionally the most effective way to nurture a prospect.

Treating a lead to dinner, paying their expenses and travel would typically increase the speed of making a sale happen.

93% of the buying process begins using internet searches.

Prospects want to buy from sellers that bring new value or offer new knowledge to the table.

Leveraging digital channels to engage and converse with leads has driven an increase in the ability to close a deal by 20%.

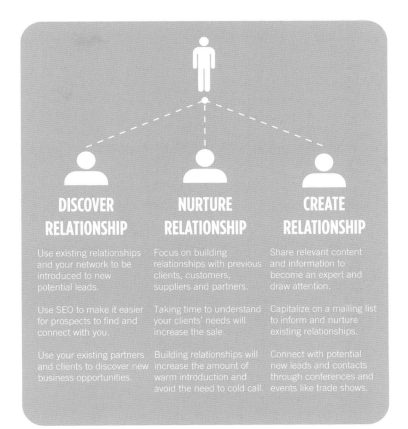

DISCOVER RELATIONSHIP

Use existing relationships and your network to be introduced to new potential leads.

Use SEO to make it easier for prospects to find and connect with you.

Use your existing partners and clients to discover new business opportunities.

NURTURE RELATIONSHIP

Focus on building relationships with previous clients, customers, suppliers and partners.

Taking time to understand your clients' needs will increase the sale.

Building relationships will increase the amount of warm introduction and avoid the need to cold call.

CREATE RELATIONSHIP

Share relevant content and information to become an expert and draw attention.

Capitalize on a mailing list to inform and nurture existing relationships.

Connect with potential new leads and contacts through conferences and events like trade shows.

*Data Source: Introhive Relationships Matter Study, Inc.com, MarketingSherpa, Forbes.com, Business.com create a more valuable membership while creating buzz and excitement around your brand.

- **Provide membership cards or numbers.** You probably have a ton of these connected to your keychain or as phone apps. Membership cards and numbers can be a major influence on customers' behavior. Create a real or virtual membership card that customers can use to track their purchases and work their way up to a discount. After all, if they know it will take just two more purchases at your business to earn their reward, why would they go to your competitor?
- **Regularly Communicate.** Set up channels like a private social media group or an email newsletter to communicate with loyalty program members so they feel like they're part of an elite group. These communications should be filled with useful content, descriptions of new products, and special offers.

EXERCISE: Outline Your Brand Evangelist Program

As you build your sales engine, you'll gain steam (pun intended) and acquire customers. It's important to identify those early influencers and invite them to become brand evangelists so you can empower and reward them. You can create an outline of your program using the following components:

- **Spaces:** Create a place or space to communicate with them (email, social group)
- **Ideas:** Generate 2–3 Loyalty Program Ideas to use initially with them and then roll out to everyone as you create new incentives for the brand evangelists to keep it fresh and special.
- **Recogntion:** Come up with 2-3 ways to recognize them and personalize the appreciation

---

Interview

Someone who knows what it is like to build a sales engine from the ground up is co-founder of Radian6, Chris Ramsay. We had a chance to chat with him about where to begin and scaling the machine. Here is what he had to say:

SEQ: Where did you first start as an entrepreneur?

Ramsey: I fall into the category of someone who didn't necessarily set out to be an entrepreneur. I went to work for a company in Ottawa called Fulcrum Technologies, came in writing code, ended up in product management. After they were acquired, I got a call out of the blue from a little company in Vancouver called NCompass Labs.

The product wasn't to market yet and the call was, "Hey, why don't you come out? We don't have anyone who has ever done this before in terms of getting product to market and we'd love for you to come out here." The stars aligned and I ended up out there. That was really my first entrepreneurial experience. Even though I wasn't the entrepreneur, but it was my first say startup experience.

We built that over three years, did great, sold it to Microsoft, ended up moving to Redmond and becoming a global product manager for our NCompass Labs Product at Microsoft which became Microsoft Content Management Server now prior to SharePoint. I spent a couple of years down there and at that time my wife and I were trying to figure out how to get back East and live in Fredericton. The path back ended up being a good friend of mine in Vancouver. He'd just become a COO of a small little start up there called Axonwave. There might have been 20 people at that time and again he was like, "Look, we need someone who knows how to get stuff very, very early stage to market. We know you know who we're going to sell this cool technology to and why. We need someone who can start there."

We did some great things with that one, but we missed a couple of elements of figuring out the go-to-market plan. We ended up shutting that one down, and I find myself for the first time in my life unemployed.

I start talking to a lot of people around Fredericton and one of the guys I bumped into is Chris Newton and another guy bumped into was this guy by the name of Gerry Pond who is the CEO of the Telco here for like 20 or 30 years and very entrepreneurial and an angel investor, and Newton and I just started going to Tim Horton's every day, I know it's cliché, but we started meeting at a coffee shop every day and 30 days later

Gerry Pond called us both into his office and said, "All right, I'm going to fund you guys, we're going to start this thing up." And that was May 2006 and that's the day we started Radian6.

SEQ: What was the first hire that really focused 100% on account growth?

Ramsey: Once we get the first handful of customers, we already had the name of Rich McInnis. It was a tricky profile. You're hiring someone not to carry a month-to-month quota, but someone who can think out of the box and has a good feel for what's happening in the market.

Rich fit that mold. He was a salesperson for another company when we hired him, but he was more than just your template salesperson. He would literally be on the phone dialing every day, doing his thing. And every day, he'd spend a half hour telling us about what he'd heard on his calls the day before. We would literally alter the product, the positioning, and the strategy based on what we heard from the first guy we hired. I think that's critical to have someone who thinks like an entrepreneur while doing the sales.

Customers are your company's reason for being, and the ability to communicate your value to them will help you build a sales engine that goes beyond those initial customers who tested and validated your product. You'll build out this sales engine by defining your ideal customers and using the Get-Keep-Grow method to create a valuable sales funnel that hopefully makes them customers for life.

To get ready to build your own custom Startup Equation Board, make sure you review and complete the following exercises in this chapter:

- Build Your Own Ideal Customer Canvas
- Design Your Initial Sales Campaign
- Draft Your Own S.I.M.P.L.E. Voice of the Customer (VoC) Program
- Outline Your Brand Evangelist Program

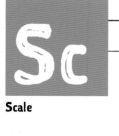

Sc

Scale

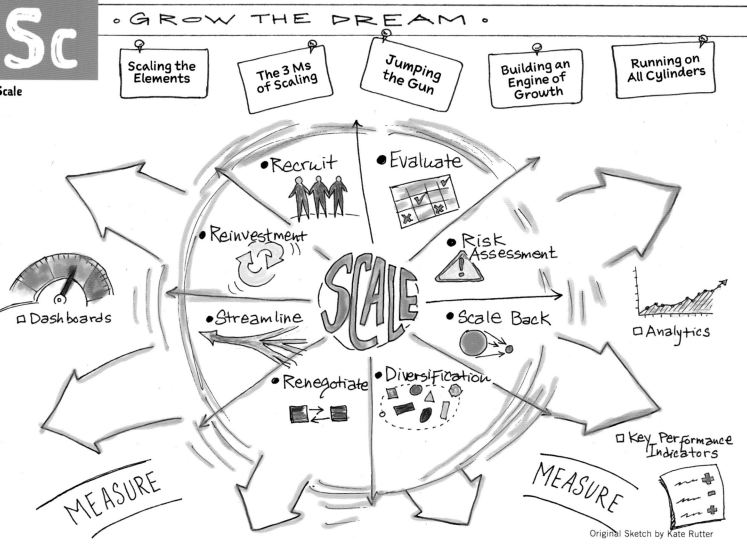

Scaling the Elements

The 3 Ms of Scaling

Jumping the Gun

Building an Engine of Growth

Running on All Cylinders

Recruit

Evaluate

Reinvestment

Risk Assessment

SCALE

Streamline

Scale Back

Renegotiate

Diversification

☐ Dashboards

☐ Analytics

MEASURE

MEASURE

☐ Key Performance Indicators

Original Sketch by Kate Rutter

Startups don't fail because they lack a product, they fail because they lack customers and a profitable business model.

—Steve Blank

Scaling to New Heights

When Steve was working on taking his startup Slipstream from a smaller product to a larger platform for a global marketplace he had to quickly learn about scaling a software company. It was a new term to him in the sense of startups. This company was his second startup, and the first one was services based and was "scaled" based on project backlog and billability. When you hear the term *scaling*, what comes to mind? Creating a billion dollar enterprise? Getting processes in place so the company can run itself? Having enough people you trust so that you can go on a vacation? These were all things running through his head and various answers from people he asked for advice. Even his father, a long-time entrepreneur, gave the answer "If you can't go on vacation without things coming to a halt, you really haven't built a company." The truth is that it's all of the above and depends on the kind of company you're building.

For startups, scaling in general is intended to happen after the following has occurred—gather a team, decide what you want to build, ship v1.0 of your product, raise money and demonstrate that people want your product.

Some define a startup as an organization formed to search for a repeatable and scalable business model. Many of the things we discuss in this chapter focus on scaling potential for high-growth organizations (i.e., firms that have a scalable business model) versus the more classic definition of a startup. The traditional startup implies we're talking about a business created less than five years ago. Many promising, buzz-worthy startups achieve these milestones but never scale.

We see scaling elements separated into two sub-groups—*Program* and *Measure*. On the following pages you will see how Program elements like **Reinvestment (Rei)**, **Diversification (Div)** and **Expansion (Epn)** set

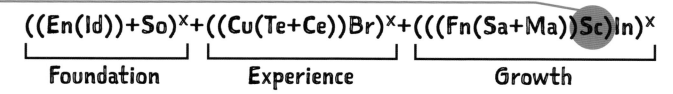

$$((En(Id))+So)^X+((Cu(Te+Ce))Br)^X+(((Fn(Sa+Ma))Sc)In)^X$$

Foundation   **Experience**   **Growth**

As your business grows, the desire to scale will become more important. Scaling is to not only grow the business but to create leverage and efficiencies that create economies of scale. There are different levels of scale depending on the kind of startup you want to build. However, there are common elements that all companies must leverage and they are separated into two groups: Program and Measure.

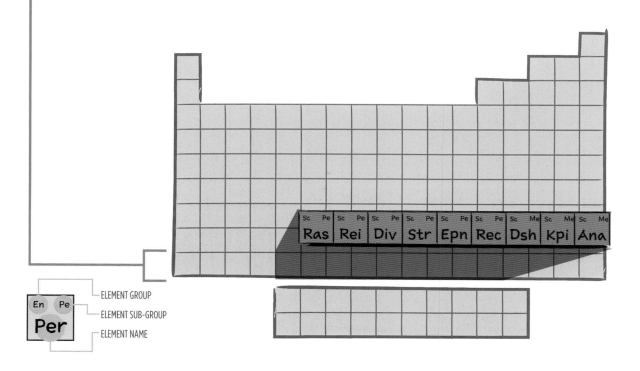

Sc Pe	Sc Pe	Sc Pe	Sc Pe	Sc Pe	Sc Pe	Sc Me	Sc Me	Sc Me
Ras	Rei	Div	Str	Epn	Rec	Dsh	Kpi	Ana

En	Pe	── ELEMENT GROUP
Per		── ELEMENT SUB-GROUP
		── ELEMENT NAME

SCALE (SC) PROGRAM ELEMENTS

To create economies of scale there must be specific programs put in place to create the leverage necessary to dominate your competitors.

Risk Assessment (Ras)
Evaluate your ability to scale from multiple dimensions (e.g., financial, customers) to see if they can support an expanded, scaled effort.

Reinvestment (Rei)
Review your resources and assess a reinvestment while looking for more investment from the outside to help you meet scaling goals.

Diversification (Div)
As you scale, you'll need a strategy to diversify your offering to appeal to a broader customer group, verticals, or geographies. Resource diversification extends your reach and may offer another potential scaling strategy.

Streamline (Str)
Even as you diversify your markets and reinvest resources, you'll need to be more lean and focused than ever. This means streamlining your processes and understanding the efficiencies and inefficiencies to maximize your growth engine.

Expansion (Epn)
With scale comes a desire to expand. Expansion is fueled by scale and vice versa. Expansion can be partnered with diversification since a company in a scaling model will expand to new markets, verticals, and geographies.

Recruit (Rec)
Scaling requires more resources and means putting in place a great recruiting engine to find talent, train people, and get them contributing to the scaling engine as quickly as possible.

SCALE (SC) MEASURE ELEMENTS

To measure the success of your scaling efforts, you must have systems in place to measure and report to all levels of the organization.

Dashboards (Dsh)
From defining KPIs to using analytic tools to collect and measure, most, if not all businessess will need to report and view this information. Dashboards provide the visualization of this information in ways that are easy to use and support taking action.

KPIs (Kpi)
Key Performance Indicators, or KPIs, help you measure your company's performance. They will come from a number of different places (i.e., financial, marketing, sales, technology) and be used in combination to measure various things.

Analytics (Ana)
Knowing your KPIs will allow you to use various systems to collect specific data and analyze it for relevancy, including potential relationships and connections, to inform new insights in your company's activities.

the groundwork for creating economies of scale. We will also explore the concept of measurement were key systems such as **Dashboards (Dsh)**, **Key Performance Indicators (Kpi)** and **Analytics (Ana)** must be in place to track the success of the programs and overall health of the company as it scales.

SCALING THE ELEMENTS

When planning to scale, the basic rule is to raise enough money to help the company hit a set of milestones that puts it in good shape to raise money at a higher valuation during subsequent rounds of financing and stages of growth. So, as you think about scaling your business, start with a ground-up analysis. How many people do you need to hire? How much do you need to pay them? How do you create a stellar customer experience? How many months will you need to get the product to market?

Another force at work is the unpredictability inherent to startup life. Everything costs more and takes longer than you think. The business you start with is often not what you end up launching. Even after the launch, many startups pivot to better meet the demands and needs of their customers. How do you deal with this? You plan and plan and plan again. Then, when you're confident about the amount of money you'll need to get to the next level, you add approximately 25%. Why? Companies historically always need about 25% more capital than they estimated initially.

At the most basic level, scaling involves:

- **Making sure your product can operate at scale.** You need to build the technical foundation for your product to operate at scale. This can involve setting up new servers to handle high traffic, establishing a smooth bug fix and product development pipeline, and building the backbone infrastructure (e.g., monitoring, testing, backups) of your website. Your infrastructure may require systems to support billing and invoicing, recovery of money owed by partners and customers, or industrialized frameworks for A/B testing your front-end.
- **Marketing your product at scale.** This involves figuring out how to market your product at scale, so plan to add users who are people in the real world, not just early adopters. It will also include building and

honing a repeatable customer process, understanding a sales process or conversion funnel, onboarding and supporting a customer, and ongoing CRM activities.

- **Designing your product for scale.** Optimize your product for (1) revenue and (2) the wide variety of use cases that you never imagined might exist when you shipped v1.0 of your product.
- **Building your team for scale.** You'll need to grow your number of employees significantly, but ensure you have competent management and established organizational routines to help drive your company forward.

You will always want to do a **Risk Assessment (Ras)** to understand your options and paths to scaling. You'll evaluate your ability to scale from multiple dimensions (e.g., financial, customers) so it can support your scaling efforts. A **Risk Assessment (Ras)** uses a scoring system with various criteria such as:

- **Business Risk Criteria:** Feasibility, Investment Costs, Payback and Profitability
- **Market Acceptance Criteria:** Compatibility, Need, Promotion, Distribution
- **Competitive Criteria:** Appearance, Price, Existing and New Competition
- **Demand Analysis Criteria:** Potential Market and Sales, Trend and Stability to Demand, Product Life Cycle and Potential
- **Experience and Strategy Criteria:** Tech Transfer, New Venture, Various Experience, Market Attractiveness

The idea is that once you've completed your risk assessment, the opportunities become a bit clearer. These options include **Reinvestment (Rei)**, **Diversification (Div)**, **Streamlining (Str)**, **Recruiting (Rec)**, and **Expansion (Epn)**.

As a startup, you don't have endless resources. With **Reinvestment (Rei)**, you can evaluate your existing resources and gain a better understanding of the additional investment you need to scale your business. As you scale, you'll need to create a diversification strategy to appeal to a broader customer group, verticals, or geographies. **Diversification**

(Div) of your resources helps extend your reach and support your scaling strategy.

Even as you diversify and reinvest, you'll need to be more lean and focused. You'll need to **Streamline (Str)** your processes and understand the efficiencies and inefficiencies in your business to maximize your growth engine. With the desire to scale comes the desire to expand. As a result, **Expansion (Epn)** fuels scale. Expansion can be partnered with diversification to support your company's scaling into new markets, verticals, and geographies. With expansion and diversification, your scaling efforts will require more resources. You'll need to **Recruit (Rec)** and build a system for finding talent, training people, and getting them involved in scaling the company as fast as possible.

Scaling ensures your company can survive and thrive to compete and beat the big competitors. It can require raising an appropriate amount of capital to support the almost inevitable cash-flow need that a scaling strategy requires. It's also the period that you take your company from cash-flow negative to cash-flow positive.

EXERCISE: Draft a Scaling Strategy

In order to prepare your startup to scale, here is an exercise that comes from the *Forbes* article – "Four Things to Consider When Scaling Your Startup."[1] Use our version to draft an initial scaling strategy.

1. **Grow your company without growing your staff exponentially.** Many companies require more people in order to scale their needs. The goal is to hire exactly what you need, no more, no less. It also means spending money on the best people like we discussed in Chapter 9 when we talked about hiring the A-Team. You need to **Recruit (Rec)** people who will keep a steady hand on the wheel during situations where other companies might collapse under the weight and speed of growth. The best people may feel expensive at first, but a team of great people can control the levers of growth so your company doesn't drive off a cliff.

2. **Automate what can be automated to serve 10x the customers.** If we were building a scalable company, we'd automate as much

as possible. This means using **Streamlining (Str)** tactics to use less people, but with the people you do have you can focus on the things that really need personal attention to grow the business. The automation approach can allow you to serve 200,000+ users with a staff of twelve, versus twenty clients with a staff of twelve. Before doing so, determine how this impacts your key resources (i.e., staff, leadership team, infrastructure) and what needs expansion (see #1). This should also include setting up great systems first.

3. **Estimate the shift from outbound to inbound marketing.** When working on marketing and sales, part of the strategy is to use inbound marketing to test and find the right fit. Not every company can afford to have a separate outbound sales team because of the large costs involved. In many cases, they may never need them. Instead, think about how to use **Reinvestment (Rei)** and **Diversification (Div)** tactics to bring customers to you rather than chasing after them. For example, having a small but dedicated content marketing team is turning out to be way more cost-effective than spending money on advertising.

4. **Evaluate all kinds of Expansion (Epn) strategies, including franchising.** Most of the discussion on scaling a startup revolves around growing the company's organization and operations. One option includes franchising to expand and scale the business. Let's say your startup is a successful retail shop or food truck in a big city. You get lots of great press and have loyal customers, but opening shops around town might be too difficult. However, if you focus on your idea/model/brand — and on packaging the best parts of what's working for you — and offer them to aspiring entrepreneurs, you will make a percentage of the sales without managing the staff it takes to run them. If you think about scaling from the outset, you'll be more likely to grow your company without huge hiccups.

THE 3 Ms OF SCALING

After many years of advising startups, we've seen the evolution of metrics, KPIs, and dashboards and how they've helped founders measure

THE 3M's OF SCALING Figure 15.3

MILESTONES

The term *milestones* gets tossed around quite a bit, usually when your business goes looking for an investment. However, as we mentioned earlier, there's no one metric or milestone that fits everyone. So what milestones offer a good starting point?

CUSTOMER
Clicks
Views
Conversion
Happiness
Loyalty
Referrals

PRODUCT
Activation
Engagement
Functionality
Channels
Platform

TEAM
Salaries
Culture
Turnover

BUSINESS MODEL
Channels
Markets

FINANCIALS
Revenue
Cashflow
Burn Rate
Receivables
Run Rate

Your startup will come with many available metrics to track, but you need to pick one core metric to optimize. We encourage you to research and test which metrics work for you. We could have written a whole book on startup metrics, so when you are ready to dive deeper, pick up a copy of *Lean Analytics* by Alistair Croll and Benjamin Yoskovitz and *Startup Metrics* by Brad Feld.

METRICS

In an early-stage company, you'll face the challenge of very little data. Look for data that avoids skewing your reporting. Key Performance Indicators or KPI (Kpi) help you quantify success in various areas. You can identify good KPIs if they:
• Validate or invalidate the assumptions you have
• Provide a Leverage Rate or Ratios (0.X or percent)
• Compare to whatever historical data you're gathering (e.g., A/B testing)
So how can you use these metrics?

TO EXPLORE
Investigating an assumption, validating feedback, looking for causality

TO REPORT
Measuring progress, measuring impact, measuring customer happiness

MEASUREMENT

The measurement aspect comes through (1) Analytics (Ana) and (2) Dashboards (Dsh). There are many tools you can use to measure, but Google Analytics is by far the easiest one to use at the beginning. Long term, it will depend on what you need to measure, and you may need to build your own tools eventually.

ANALYTICS

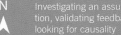

When we refer to analytics, we're talking about the tools used to collect the metrics.

DASHBOARDS

You'll present those metrics in a useful format with dashboards.

their success. Once they reach a milestone, then they receive the next round of funding. Investors, both big and small, have become more sophisticated, and they want to see results (e.g., hitting your numbers) so they can invest more wisely. We call this process the *3M's of Scaling: Milestones, Metrics, and Measurement.*

Dimensions of the 3Ms

First, your 3Ms may not look like anyone else's. Your business is completely different from every other business, and with some research, you can identify the best practices that fit your business. From the physical to the digital, there are metrics of all kinds that can be measured.

Milestones

The term gets tossed around a lot. Milestones are an action or event marking a significant change or stage in development. They usually are used in discussion when your business goes looking for an investment. As we mentioned earlier, there's no one metric or milestone that fits everyone. What milestones offer a good starting point?

- **Customer:** Clicks, Views, Conversion, Happiness, Loyalty, Referrals
- **Product:** Activation, Engagement, Functionality, Channels, Platforms
- **Team:** Salaries, Culture, Turnover
- **Financials:** Revenue, Cash Flow, Burn Rate, Receivables, Run Rate
- **Business Model:** Channels, Markets

Metrics

With so many metrics, how do you decide which ones are critical? You must distinguish which metrics are actually **Key Performance Indicators (Kpi)** or KPIs. KPIs are performance metrics explicitly linked to a strategic objective that help an organization translate strategy execution into quantifiable terms. Think of KPIs as the yardstick by which success and progress are measured; they are the measures most tightly linked to the organization's success or failure in executing strategy.

All KPIs are metrics, but not all metrics are KPIs.

Most organization have tons of metrics, but really haven't developed KPIs. While metrics can be a measure of just about anything, KPIs

are the measures that matter most. KPIs should also be actionable; if they are not actionable, how can they help you achieve your goals? In other words, don't measure something as a KPI that you can't change with specific actions.

So when is a metric a KPI? KPIs are metrics that are:

1. **Outcome-oriented:** tied to an objective
2. **Target-based:** have at least one defined time-sensitive target value
3. **Rated or graded:** have explicit thresholds that grade the difference (or gap) between the actual value and the target

The above three criteria, used in evaluating whether a metric meets KPI status, serve as a test to help ensure focus on the measures that truly matter to the success of your organization. So how can you use these metrics?

- **To Explore:** Investigating an assumption, validating feedback, looking for causality
- **To Report:** Measuring progress, measuring impact, measuring customer happiness

In an early-stage company, you'll face the challenge of very little data. Look for data that avoids skewing your reporting. You can identify good KPIs if they:

- Validate or invalidate the assumptions you have
- Provide a Leverage Rate or Ratios (0.X or percent)
- Compare to whatever historical data you're gathering (e.g., A/B testing)
- Can be explained, reported, and used to support milestones

Measurement

The measurement aspect comes through (1) **Analytics (Ana)** and (2) **Dashboards (Dsh)**. When we refer to analytics, we're talking about the tools used to collect the metrics. You'll present those metrics in a useful format with dashboards. There are many tools you can use to measure. Long term, it will depend on what you need to measure, and you may need to build your own tools eventually.

Your startup will come with many available metrics to track, but you need to pick one core metric to optimize. Otherwise, you'll become that

> *Your dashboard should shame you*
> *as much as motivate you.*
> *—Alistair Croll*

guy on TV spinning plates on poles, running back and forth to keep them all going (or at least trying).

EXERCISE: Create a 3M Dashboard

Incorporating the concepts of the 3M's (Milestones, Metrics and Measurement) you should come up with a list to track in each of the 3M's. For example:

1. Create a list of milestones for the next 18 months – this can include build dates, testing, launches, team members hired, funding received, etc.

2. Create a list of metrics you will want to track in relationship with the milestones. These should help you see if you are on track.

3. Create list of measurement thresholds since you need to see if the metrics are met, are exceeded (in a bad way) or totally blown out of the water (in a good way).

4. Take these lists and leverage some dashboard tools out on the web to build this out. You can even start with a spreadsheet and move to more analytical means of measurement.

JUMPING THE GUN

Over the last three decades, the power of technology has increased steadily. The current level of maturity triggered a domino effect throughout the global economy. As a result it's never been easier or cheaper to create a startup thanks to technologies like cloud hosting, software as a service (SaaS), open-source software, global payment systems, viral distribution channels, extremely focused advertising, real-time logistics, and collaboration.

Because of this rapid change, startups emerge faster and drive the new industrial revolution we discussed at the beginning of this book. While most entrepreneurs dream of growing their startups into a huge success like Zappos or Twitter, most never reach that level of global domination, receive Hollywood-like adoration, or become worth billions of dollars. In fact, when you look at the numbers, successful startups are a rare breed. One in ten startups fail eventually.

The Startup Genome Report identified "premature scaling" as a primary cause of failure. After surveying 3,200 companies, they discovered, *"Startups need 2–3 times longer to validate their market than most founders expect. This underestimation creates the pressure to scale prematurely."*[2]

You might think failure or success depends on age, location, experience, or education. Nope. None of these factors affect a company's chance to head down the path of failure. Sure, there are statistics about when many people start a business and the kind of experience and education required for some (e.g., professional services, law firms), but it's no predictor of future success.

The Startup Genome Report creates a framework for milestones and thresholds that clarifies the six stages of a startup lifecycle: (1) Discover, (2) Validation, (3) Efficiency, (4) Scale, (5) Sustain, and (6) Conservation. We won't dive into those stages here, but we recommend you read the full report (http://blog.startupcompass.co/) to get a sense of the structure. The other results from the survey were fascinating, too. Here are a few key findings:[3]

- Founders that learn are more successful; they raise 7x more money and have 3.5x better growth

- Startups that pivot once or twice raise 2.5x more money, have 3.6x better user growth, and are 52% less likely to scale prematurely than startups that pivot more than two times or not at all

- Solo founders take 3.6x longer to reach the scale stage

- Business-heavy founding teams are 6.2x more likely to successfully scale with sales-driven startups rather than product-driven startups

- Tech-heavy founding teams are 3.3x more likely to scale without network effects

THE LEAN STARTUP SCALING METHODS

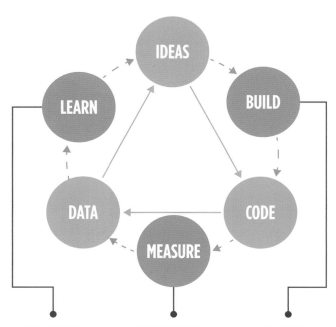

LEARN FASTER

Split Tests
Customer Interviews
Customer Development
Five Whys Root Cause Analysis
Customer Advisory Board
Falsifiable Hypotheses
Product Owner Accountability
Cross-functional Teams
Smoke Tests

MEASURE FASTER

Split Tests
Clear Product Owner
Continuous Development
Usability Tests
Real-time Monitoring
Custom Liaison
Funnel Analysis
Cohort Analysis
Net Promoter Score
Search Engine Marketing
Real-time Alerting
Predictive Monitoring

CODE FASTER

Unit Test
Usability Test
Continuous Integration
Incremental Deployment
Free & Open Source Components
Cloud Computing
Cluster Immune System
Just-in-time Scalability
Refactoring
Developer Sandbox

Data Source: KISS Metrics, Eric Ries

CRAFTING DASHBOARDS

There are many kinds of dashboards that can serve your startup. Below are two examples of these dashboards. There are many tools out there to create your own. Use a search engine and start with the term "startup dashboards" and you will find the most current offerings that might fit your business. They will enable quick creation out of the box and have the flexibility to report on the metrics you are looking to track.

EXAMPLE DASHBOARD: FINANCE

EXAMPLE DASHBOARD: CUSTOMERS

TOTAL MRR
$261K
Past 30 Days

MRR=Monthly Recurring Revenue

NEW MRR
1K
Past 30 Days

LOST MRR
50
Past 30 Days

NEW MRR
15
Today

NEW CUSTOMERS
30
Today

BASIC USERS
10.7K
Total

PRO USERS
1.5
Total

PLUS USERS
75
Total

There are so many different metrics you can create!

- Startups that haven't raised money overestimate their market size by 100x and often misinterpret their market as new (our personal favorite and so true).

So what are the most common reasons for startups to perform poorly or even fail because of premature scaling? The data points to scaling the team prematurely, paying people too much for early wins, failing to adapt the business model, lacking financial discipline, or overbuilding the product. We'll review each one in more detail.[4]

Dimension	Premature Scaling Examples
Customer	• Spending too much on customer acquisition before product/market fit and a repeatable scalable business model • Overcompensating and missing product/market fit with marketing and press
Product	• Building a product without problem/solution fit • Investing in product scalability before product/market fit • Adding "nice-to-have" features
Team	• Hiring too many people too early • Hiring specialists before they are critical (e.g., CFO's, Customer Service Reps, Database specialists, etc.) • Hiring managers (e.g., VPs, product managers, etc.) instead of doers • Having more than one level of hierarchy
Financials	• Raising too little money to get through the "Valley of Death" • Raising too much money • Note: Too much money isn't necessarily bad, but it usually makes entrepreneurs undisciplined and gives them the freedom to prematurely scale other dimensions (e.g., over-hiring and over-building). Raising too much is also more risky for investors than if they give startups how much they actually need and then wait to see how they progress.
Business Model	• Focusing too much on profit maximization too early • Over-planning and executing without a regular feedback loop • Not adapting the business model to a changing market • Failing to focus on the business model and discovering you can't get costs lower than revenue at scale

Someone who has seen many successful scaling examples but has seen their fair share of premature scaling failures is Rajesh Setty. As an investor he not only invests but is an active participant in their day-to-day growth. He writes about startups and life and it is filled with a ton of information that every entrepreneur can learn from. We had the opportunity to sit down with him about building great startups and where entrepreneurs should spend their energy when building and scaling their startup.

SEQ: What are the things that you look for in great startup teams?

Setty: I look for a cast of characters. When the cast is like an acronym C-A-S-T and *'C' is for competent people*. I want them to be good at whatever area they've picked because sometimes people pick areas that are hot and trendy because everybody else is making a lot of money. *'A' is for adaptable*, which I call the mindset of water. Whenever there are obstacles, they don't say, "Oh my God, there's a boulder there. Let me just not do anything." Water will keep flowing, so if they are adaptable, they will continue to be flowing irrespective of obstacles. The next one is *'S' for stickability*. My fundamental belief is if you're disciplined and when you stick to it for long enough, you'll hit a breakthrough sooner than later. The last one is *'T' for teachable*. It's basically, do they have the humility to learn some more, not just from me, but more than one person and be better compared to what they were yesterday. They have to be like an evergreen learning machine, absorbing things, growing and not assume that they have made it and then all they have to do is capitalize on what they have made it.

SEQ: When entrepreneurs are scaling their companies, their resources are usually pretty limited. Where should entrepreneurs focus their energy?

Setty: I always tell people that when resources are limited, the resourcefulness should become unlimited. You might have read or heard of Professor Saras Sarasvathy's paper *Effectuation*. It's the entrepreneurial mindset. Professor Sarasvathy studied hundreds of entrepreneurs and she found that there is a fundamental shift in the way entrepreneurs think about goals and where they are going and all those things. In her paper, she said, "In general, other people think about goals and then start worrying about what are the resources they need to reach those goals." It's like there's a path, a destination to reach and what are all the things they need? That's the standard way of thinking, but she says entrepreneurs think differently. They do an inventory of all the resources that

PREMATURE SCALING Figure 15.5

SCALING TOO SOON

A company's age is based on how it interacts with customers over time. When a startup prematurely scales it is typically due to a lack of synchronicity between its five core operational dimensions: customer, product, team, financials, and business model.

COMPANY A (PREMATURE SCALING)

COMPANY B (PROPER SCALING)

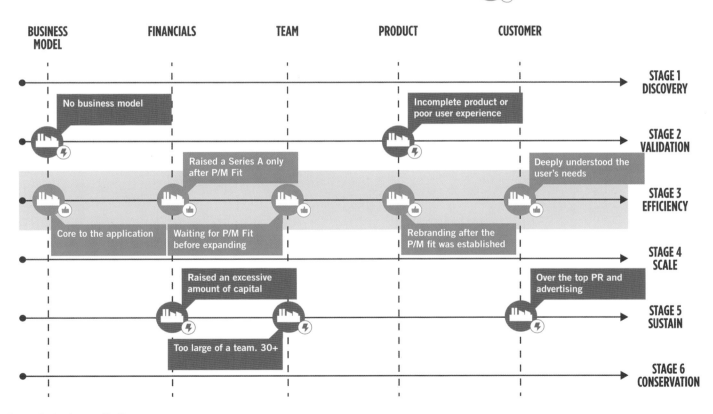

BUSINESS MODEL   FINANCIALS   TEAM   PRODUCT   CUSTOMER

STAGE 1 DISCOVERY

No business model

Incomplete product or poor user experience

STAGE 2 VALIDATION

Raised a Series A only after P/M Fit

Deeply understood the user's needs

STAGE 3 EFFICIENCY

Core to the application

Waiting for P/M Fit before expanding

Rebranding after the P/M fit was established

STAGE 4 SCALE

Raised an excessive amount of capital

Over the top PR and advertising

STAGE 5 SUSTAIN

Too large of a team. 30+

STAGE 6 CONSERVATION

*Data Source: Startup Genome, MadRaya

they have access to, like people, their skills and network and everything. Then they start thinking about what goals they can reach and looking for resources so they can do things with what they have. I like this model a lot because it changes the way people look at goals. I ask people to focus on three things. One is the innovation because innovation is state of mind, so you innovate with what you have rather than, "Oh my gosh, I don't have this, so let me first look for it." The next key skill is the choreographing skill, like how can somebody paint a picture with what they have and with the resources that they have access to. Lastly, building the ecosystem, so that they build their capacity for the future.

BUILDING AN ENGINE OF GROWTH

In the previous chapters on Sales and Marketing Mix, you were drinking through the fire hose of all the programs, channels, and technique elements to help form your startup equation for growth. There were many metrics for each area to gauge success. As you build an engine for growth, you must also remember to include metrics for your product (e.g., A/B testing, customer acquisition costs), metrics for financing (e.g., cash flow, revenues), and even metrics for the customer experience (e.g., satisfaction, user testing). Your KPIs will measure your success. KPIs will give you a target to aim at, like whether a landing page performs well or if people are dropping off via a specific page. Remember to use these as your guide to avoid getting too off track. Your business deserves better, and it's an avoidable mistake.

To scale as you grow, you have to put processes and structures in place that encourage everyone in your company to take more risks (not fewer), while keeping the right people informed of the risks, and protecting individuals from silly mistakes that would lead to unnecessary, embedded processes. This is where you'll continue to leverage growth hackers. Remember them from the marketing chapter? These are the people whose sole focus is growth, and they look through the lens of what produces scalable growth.

Fueling the Growth Engine

Hiring great people makes everything else easier. In Chapter 9 we discussed what it takes to build a great founding team and you will need to continue your recruiting efforts and hire great talent. Recruiting well is where you're most likely to struggle.

Say you need to hire thirty, high-quality inbound marketers and growth hackers in the next year, since you've figured out how to onboard, train, and measure salespeople. It's a massive endeavor! Recruiting quickly becomes a core competency, as well as training/retaining and all the other disciplines of team management. Your culture will change as you start managing through others, and some of your original team members may not scale or like this environment and that might be a challenge where they will either grow with you or find another place that is a better fit for themselves.

Recruiting Customers

Recruiting users manually sounds like the most unscalable thing founders have to do at the beginning. Nearly all startups have to. You can't wait for users to come to you. You have to go out and get them. According to Paul Graham, cofounder of the accelerator YCombinator, there are two reasons why founders resist recruiting customers.

> One is a combination of shyness and laziness. They'd rather sit at home writing code than go out and talk to a bunch of strangers and probably be rejected by most of them. But for a startup to succeed, at least one founder (usually the CEO) will have to spend a lot of time on sales and marketing. The other reason founders ignore this path is that the absolute numbers seem so small at first. This can't be how the big, famous startups got started, they think. The mistake they make is to underestimate the power of compound growth. We encourage every startup to measure their progress by weekly growth rate. If you have 100 users, you need to get 10 more next week to grow 10% a week. And while 110 may not seem much better than 100, if you keep growing at 10% a week you'll be surprised how big the numbers get. After a year you'll have 14,000 users, and after 2 years you'll have 2 million. You'll be doing different things when you're acquiring users a thousand at a time, and growth has to slow down eventually. But if the market exists you can usually start by recruiting users manually and then gradually switch to less manual methods.

Engine of Growth

A scaling "Engine of Growth" is working to grow from a number of different dimensions, including business model, customers (sales and marketing), product, team, and financials. As the company scales, they all start to come together and work in harmony. The chart below explores those dimensions and provides examples of goals you should consider as you scale out your "Engine of Growth."

Dimension	Engine of Growth Examples
Business Model	• Validating your revenue streams and profit model • Lowering costs while growing the customer base and revenues
Customer	• Understanding specific acquisition costs and conversion rates • Tracking successful activations and return visits • Tracking referrals who sign up and are also return customers
Product	• Successful A/B testing • Validating product/market fit through usability testing and surveys • Adding the right features based on user interviews and surveys
Team	• Staffing model is scaled and tied directly with increases in customers • Staffing costs are lower over time but produce exponential revenue growth
Financials	• Validating your revenue streams and profit model • Lowering costs while growing customer base and revenues • Having users generate minimum revenue • Having users generate break-even revenue

EXERCISE: Design Your Engine of Growth

While no two startups are the same, most look to grow in some way over the long run. This exercise is part strategy and part vision and it is about looking forward and putting yourself in the position of having to scale, so what does that look like?

- **Vision:** Draft a few paragraphs of what a fully scaled and operationally functional company looks like 3 years from now.

- **Parts of the Whole:** Use each of the dimensions in the "Engine of Growth" table and list at least one way your business would need to scale to realize that vision.
- **Fueling up the Machine:** Taking the ways your business can scale from the last bullet tie in metrics and ways you could measure it is success and detail how it could scale.

Two people who are really familiar with fueling an engine of growth are Marcel Lebrun, co-founder, and David Alston, former CMO, both of Radian6, a social measurement and monitoring platform which was purchased by Salesforce.com a few years ago. Marcel is now a Senior VP at Salesforce. Dave is now Chief Innovation Officer for IntroHive and a documentary film maker (*CodeKids*). We recently sat down with both of them to talk about their entrepreneurial adventures and how they lead Radian6 and helped scale it from a small startup to a global company.

SEQ: When you started Radian6, what were the things that were important to you and how did you go about creating an environment to grow and make the team effective?

Lebrun: When I met the guy who actually came up with the idea for Radian6, his name is Chris Newton, he's the CTO, and some of the others that were working around this, the biggest question in my mind was, "Would this be a great team? Can he be in a role that he loves and fits him like a glove and can I and can others?"

I started calling people that I knew were the kind of leaders we would need to grow the business to see if they were interested in the space, in the company. I knew that the team equation was probably even more important than the market and the idea. That is just so critical.

SEQ: What are the elements that need to be in place to really scale and grow a great product?

Alston: There's a bit of luck involved in terms of perfect timing. Usually what I find is when you think of an idea, oftentimes there's at least one other company trying to do the same thing. You generally don't go into the market by yourself, so you need a great product that people are willing to talk about.

Then, the team is going to make decisions. If you've got a great team, the odds are you're gonna make more correct decisions along the way. To me, that's how you get to be successful. I think it's important that you respect them and you appreciate them and you trust them and everyone's focus is on the customer and the company first. It's that dedication to do the right thing all the time and not second guessing yourself or second guessing everyone else.

SEQ: What are the things a startup needs to consider as they try to scale and grow?

Alston: I think you think global right from the beginning. You look, sound, act, and aim for being a global company. Don't be shy about that, and don't be timid. If you think global and you have ideas that are going to spread around the world and you find a way to help them spread, it doesn't matter where you're located. I've certainly seen that.

For example, in a B2B scenario you're selling to people. It's people to people, its person to person. The idea is that people generally buy from people they like. People like to have their relationship as well. Especially when they're in a B2B relationship. Being able to reach out and become friends or make connections with those customers and/or prospects and/or the community in general that is passionate about your space, I think it is an important thing to do.

SEQ: Did that help with raising venture in terms of scaling?

Lebrun: Absolutely. They invest as much in ideas as they do in people, so a lot of them are like, "You tell me where your next thing is." I had a great relationship with a number of those who had invested in companies in the past. When it came time, absolutely, it's like call this guy who's one of the executives at the largest agency in the world and ask him how central this problem set is to his business and how valuable it is to them and then they get on the phone and they say, "This is our future. The whole world is changing from traditional to on-line to social. We have to reinvent ourselves and these guys are helping us," they're like, "Whoa, they're onto something," and that was absolutely key to getting the venture financing.

SEQ: What kind of scaling techniques did you use to continue to really scale the company?

Lebrun: With Radian6, I wanted to build a starting team that I knew could scale to a large organization. That's the first thing that's important. Then as you grow, you're just making decisions all along. I hired a head engineer that I knew could run a hundred, two-hundred person R&D team, knew how to get product velocity out the door, was a grown-up, not a cowboy, but could also operate in the cowboy mode in the early days and that was key. Same in marketing, same in sales. Off we went.

RUNNING ON ALL CYLINDERS

Paint a picture in your mind of what effectively scaling a company looks like. When your startup enters a growth stage, you want to make sure you're not just thinking about the numbers. You need to have the right mindset for your current phase of development, and you need to make sure the people you're working with are on the same page.

Startups are especially vulnerable to mindset mistakes. They see that things are working well—something that's easier with ten people than 100—and they try to hold on to that feeling even as they recruit and acquire customers at breakneck speed.

"The hallmark of successful scaling is knowing when to hit the brakes so you can scale faster later," says Bob Sutton, organizational behavior expert at Stanford's School of Engineering. He goes on to explain, "And if anyone ever tells you they have solved all your scaling problems, they are lying to you, and you need to send them out the door immediately."[5]

Embracing Failure

Peter Drucker's quote highlights that just as many mistakes are committed by people being tentative as being aggressive. Moving fast often means making mistakes, though still not as many as you might think.

Flickr created a great award for a community member "who breaks flickr.com in the most spectacular way." Of course, it's a bit tongue-in-cheek, but the point about accepting mistakes is not. Spectacular failure means you were probably working on something big and had a spectacular learning experience.

"Rewarding" failure is not some crazy "everybody gets a trophy" kind of thing.

Catastrophic mistakes, on the other hand, aren't to be celebrated, but those mistakes are exceedingly rare, and you should have processes in place to deal with them. Most of the tension in companies around mistakes is about fairly mundane issues and is relatively unproductive (again, we point to Drucker's wisdom).

The good news about working at a startup is that you have the chance to spot all of these things as they pop up, and catch them before they become entrenched. In essence, as a founder, you should focus on removing roadblocks so that pockets of excellence can spread, unobstructed. When you envision it this way, you have a much better chance at getting your startup running on all cylinders and scaling smart.

GETTING READY . . .

As you prepare to build your own startup equation, you have worked on exercises to build your foundation and craft the experience with the last few chapters that get you thinking about growing the dream. To get ready to build your own startup equation make sure you review this chapter's exercises:

- Draft a Scaling Strategy
- Create a 3M Dashboard
- Design Your Engine of Growth

Over time you will come to find scaling as a big part of the success of your startup and with growth you have options—options for growth, options for an exit, options for taking a vacation.

Innovation

∘ GROW THE DREAM ∘

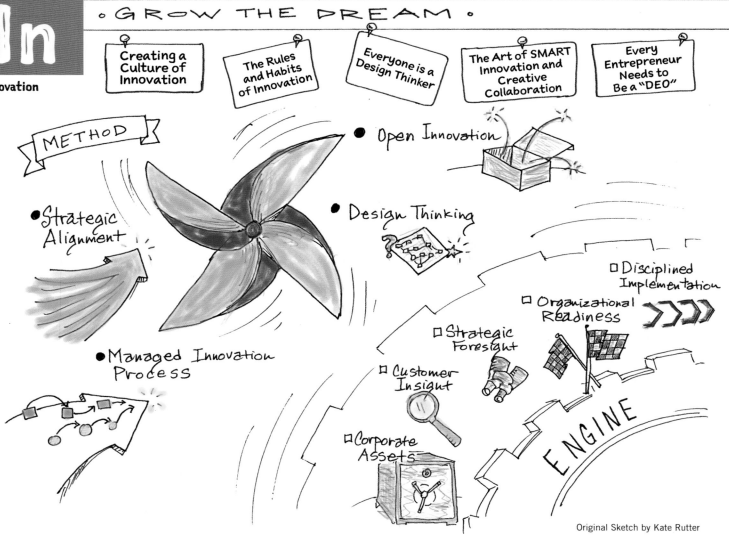

METHOD

- Strategic Alignment
- Managed Innovation Process

● Open Innovation

● Design Thinking

□ Disciplined Implementation

□ Organizational Readiness

□ Strategic Foresight

□ Customer Insight

□ Corporate Assets

ENGINE

Original Sketch by Kate Rutter

CHAPTER 16

If you always do what you always did,

you will always get what you always got.

—*Albert Einstein*

Always Be Innovating

Beyond a great idea and initial success, your startup will require the ability to continue innovating and pushing the envelope. When you think of innovative companies, the usual suspects come to mind—Nike, BMW, Coca-Cola, Starbucks and of course, Apple. Most of you probably know their stories, but we would like to share the story of one particular company, the fast food chain, Chipotle.

If you've ever been in a Chipotle, you wouldn't immediately think of it as a traditional, fast food restaurant. Their approach to dining has made them the face of a new restaurant trend called "fast casual."

Generally, the term fast food brings to mind places like McDonald's or KFC, places that emphasize "fast" and not necessarily the quality of the "food." Cultural changes over the last two decades led to consumers demanding healthier choices and expecting companies demon-

strate environmental awareness. Enter Chipotle and the fast casual experience.

Chipotle was started in 1993 by Steve Ells, a chef trained at the Culinary Institute of America, who only two years prior worked in San Francisco as a $12/hour line cook at the legendary restaurant Stars. But at his salary, he couldn't afford the food. So he usually ate the giant burritos found in the famous Mission District. One place in particular, Zona Rosa, made giant burritos. Mr. Ells watched how fast people went through the line, and it sparked the idea for Chipotle. Currently, the chain has 1,400 locations in the United States and is expanding internationally.

Mr. Ells and Chipotle demonstrate the importance of innovation to long-term business success. By looking for ways to innovate while staying true to their mission, they keep employees and customers happy. As

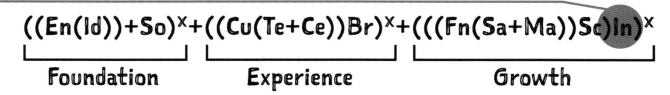

$$((En(Id))+So)^X+((Cu(Te+Ce))Br)^X+(((Fn(Sa+Ma))Sc)In)^X$$

| Foundation | Experience | Growth |

Every startup begins with that one great idea, but that is not the end of the innovation cycle—merely the beginning. In order to always be innovating and stay competitive and relevant, there are some key characteristics in what it takes to continuously innovate. In this diagram we separate Innovation (In) elements into two categories—Method and Engine.

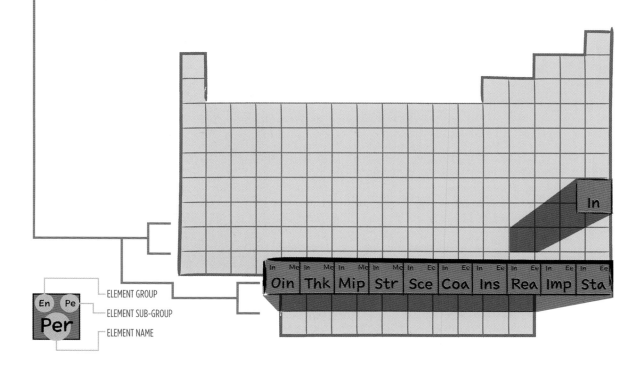

ELEMENT GROUP
ELEMENT SUB-GROUP
ELEMENT NAME

INNOVATION (IN) METHOD ELEMENTS

As your company looks to continuously innovate, there must be solid methods and programs in place so a culture of innovation is in the DNA of the company's everyday work.

Open Innovation (Oin)
The term "Open Innovation" was promoted as a way of thinking that "assumes firms can and should use external ideas as well as internal ideas, and internal and external paths to market"[i]. The central idea behind it is that in a world with so much distributed knowledge they should just stay in a silo and rely solely on their own research but innovate with partners by sharing risk and reward. This could mean buying or licensing processes or inventions (i.e., patents) from other companies. Additionally, inventions created by the company that are not being used by the company should be taken outside through licensing, joint ventures or spin-offs. This can also include idea competitions, customer immersion, collaborative design and innovation networks.

Design Thinking (Thk)
Design thinking is a broad concept that has come to be defined as "combining empathy for the context of a problem, creativity in the generation of insights and solutions, and rationality in analyzing and fitting various solutions to the problem context"[ii]. Design Thinking draws upon logic, imagination, intuition, and systemic reasoning to explore possibilities of what could be and to create desired outcomes that benefit the end user (the customer). A design mindset is not problem-focused, it's solution-focused, and action-oriented. When these principles are applied to strategy and in-novation the success rate for innovation dramatically improves. Design thinking is at the core of effective strategy development and organizational change. This can be applied to products, services, processes, physical locations… anything that needs to be optimized for human interaction.

Managed Innovation Process (Mip)
This is closely linked to Open Innovation and because this is a managed process, it is not a closed system. Quite the contrary: by providing a framework to manage the intake of ideas. This allows for a more rapid use of the open innovation concepts such as idea competitions, customer immersion, collaborative design and innovation networks. This also provides for the accelerated use of licensing and creation of joint ventures or spin-offs.

Strategic Foresight (Str)
Strategic foresight is the practice of creating a functional view of the future, or future events and possibilities, in such a way as to take full advantage of opportunities, as well as to prepare for any possible adversity. The idea of strategic foresight arose from the idea that while the future is not predictable, it is also not predetermined, and can be influenced in a positive way by actions we take in the present. Applied to innovation, this aligns future opportunities with those making business decisions to structure roadmaps based on future events.

INNOVATION (IN) ENGINE ELEMENTS

To 'Rev up' the engine of innovation, you and your company must leverage techniques and tools that finely tune your insight into what is coming and how your company can take advantage of the opportunity.

Scenarios (Sce)
Scenario planning is a strategic method used to make flexible long-term plans. Closely tied to strategic foresight, it details possible future events in order to prepare responses to what change can bring. This allows for decision makers to evaluate possible outcomes and help focus innovation efforts.

Corporate Assets (Coa)
When it comes to innovation in business, the goal is to create valuable intellectual property with financial returns. This can include physical or digital products that can be protected. Corporate assets can be created or improved through programs such as idea competitions, collaborative design and innovation networks. They can also be licensed or used for joint ventures or spin-offs.

Customer Insight (Ins)
Companies need to deliver new and innovative offerings to attract and retain customers whose expectations are changing. Customer Insight is where the interests of the consumer and features of your brand, product or service meet. Working with customers to understand why they care about you, and their mindset, motivation and desires that trigger their attitude toward your company.

Organizational Readiness (Rea)
There is no single thing that will trigger or ensure innovation in your startup. As you develop your innovation programs there will be points along the way where you need to check if the climate is receptive. By utilizing an organizational readiness assessment you will be able to gauge your company's readiness for innovation.

Disciplined Implementation (Imp)
We spoke of organizational readiness as being able to gauge readiness for continuous innovation in your startup. All of these innovation elements require a discipline in how they are implemented to ensure resources are being allocated properly.

Strategic Alignment (Sta)
As part of an organizational readiness assessment, strategic alignment means that each business unit, department, team and individual sees and understands their role and how it contributes to the overall innovation mandate of the organization.

a result, they've turned the concept of fast food on its head and put pressure on other fast food restaurants to do better.

Throughout this chapter, we discuss what's required to make innovation an active part of your business strategy, including the elements found in the **Innovation (In)** element group of the Startup Equation. The two element groups, *Method* and *Engine*, deal with elements that will help you create your own innovation method. These elements include **Open Innovation (Oin)**, **Design Thinking (Thk)**, **Managed Innovation (Mip)** and **Strategic Foresight (Str)**. Once you develop methods that work, you'll want to create an innovation engine that powers it through other elements like **Scenarios (Sce)** or **Customer Insights (Ins)** to name a few.

CREATING A CULTURE OF INNOVATION

As your startup grows, you'll need reinforce the role of innovation in your organization. It's hard to imagine that a company can be really good at innovation if its employees are not adequately motivated and engaged. When people are engaged in their work, they take a personal interest in the success of their company. Otherwise, they're likely to do what's expected, but lack the motivation to go much beyond the expected.

CultureAmp, a company that analyzes motivation and engagement in organizations, identified the top five drivers of employee engagement based on how employees perceive their company:[1]

- They feel confidence in the company's leadership.

- They see good opportunities for advancement in the organization and the possibility for transitioning to a different type of role.

- They understand how they're important to the success of the organization.

- They feel they can contribute to their field.

- They believe the company has a vision that motivates people.

In their analysis of these drivers, CultureAmp found two distinct themes:

- **Demonstrated Leadership:** Employers must demonstrate that people are important to the organization and show they're capable of making good decisions. This requires creating and communicating a motivating vision.

- **Strong Learning and Development:** Employees want to see a path forward in their organization. They want to know that opportunities exist to help them with personal development.

These two themes may surprise you because things like compensation or salary aren't in the top five. Now, the top five drivers of engagement aren't easy to deliver, but are worth the effort. If you're successful, you'll have a team of highly motivated, engaged employees invested in driving innovation.

Why Should Startups Innovate?

You might think that as a company moves past the startup phase and matures, it will handle innovation differently. However, if you've ever read Clayton Christensen's breakthrough book, *The Innovator's Dilemma*, you may remember that he found large companies are excellent at sustaining innovation, but struggle with, and usually fail, at "disruptive innovation."

It's tempting to say, "We're a startup. We're all innovative," but what happens next? Simply focusing on improving existing business models and products isn't enough anymore. To ensure their survival and produce satisfying growth, businesses need to invent a new products business model. Doing so requires an entirely new organizational culture and skill set. Companies will need an "innovation culture" to do two things at the same time:

1. Improving existing products, services, and business models

2. Inventing new and disruptive products, services and business models

Without motivation there is no innovation.
—*Phil McKinney*

This two-prong approach will allow your startup to build an "innovation portfolio" of ideas, concepts, and prototypes that will help your business maintain a competitive edge.

In Figure 16.3, you will notice a reference to "The Innovators Dilemma," which identifies motivating factors for innovation along three axes with six factors. We updated it for startups. Factors can range from regulations to business models that would motivate your startup to keep innovating. We also reference author Jean-Claude Biver, former CEO of Hublot Genève, who is a widely-renowned voice on innovation. Mr. Biver follows three major innovation tenets: (1) Be unique; (2) Be different; (3) Be first.

When innovation fails in startups, it's often traced back to a lack of discipline. Creativity may abound, but after the initial idea, the team can't "pivot" the company to implement the new idea. It's become clear that effective, disruptive and continuous innovation requires companies to have a structure that helps them to continue behaving just like a startup. It requires leveraging methods like **Open Innovation (Oin)** and **Design Thinking (Thk)**, which we cover later in this chapter, to ingrain a culture that everyone can innovate. It can also mean creating various programs or groups that continue this relentless pursuit while other parts of the business scale and grow what's already been created.

As you develop your innovation programs, there will be points along the way, particularly at the beginning, where you need to check if the climate is receptive. One way to improve the climate is to adopt **Organizational Readiness (Rea).** According to Derrick Palmer and Soren Kaplan of the consulting firm InnovationPoint, their work on a strategic innovation framework defines *Organizational Readiness* as covering three areas: cultural, process, and structural.[2]

Cultural readiness is about adopting values and a mission that supports an innovation culture. The practices that groups use to operate and collaborate effectively fall under process readiness. Structural readiness deals with organizational structures and technologies that support innovation. This last area also deals with an organization's ability to be flexible and assign talent to high-priority projects. As part of that assessment, you'll review your startup's **Strategic Alignment (Sta)** and measure how well each business unit, department, team, and individual sees and understands their role and how it contributes to the overall innovation mandate of the organization.

THE RULES AND HABITS OF INNOVATION

For decades, one company that was considered by many the model for modern startups is Hewlett Packard, or HP. A model innovator was Phil McKinney. For nine years, Phil was vice president and chief technology officer of the $40 billion (FY12) Personal Systems Group at HP where he also oversaw the global Innovation Office. He wrote a fantastic book called *Killer Innovations* and some of his approaches are detailed in this chapter. Currently president and CEO of CableLabs, which is the R&D and innovation industry group for cable operators around the world, Mr. McKinney also hosts a very popular podcast named after his book. We recently had an opportunity to talk to him about how startups can create their own killer innovations.

SEQ: Phil, you're recognized as an expert in the area of innovation. How should a startup approach innovation?

McKinney: The challenge in the innovation space falls into two categories, what I call the innovation gap and the innovation delay. The innovation gap is the lack of supply. There's lots of ideas I know are great. But how do you really discern the ones that are really, really great?

Once you've identified that, then the challenge becomes the innovation delay. The key is you've got to solve both the innovation gap and innovation delay. To solve the innovation gap, you need to have some form of an understanding of what are the key elements ideas need to have and how do you identify those ideas.

A lot of people think there's a complex ranking process that you've got to go through with the entire plan and the financial analysis. It's not. In fact, for a $120 billion corporation with 330 employees, the ranking process we put in place relies on five questions, right? First question is, will this idea follow through the customer's experience or expectation? Second question is, will this change the competitive positioning of the company? The third question is, will this change the economics?

If you can answer yes to one of those three questions, you need to be able to answer yes to the next two. That is, why you? Do you have some unique expertise or perspective? What is it about you that makes you the best to go execute this idea? The final question is will there be sufficient margin? Is that market big enough? Not a full economic model, but you understand who your target customer is.

There are different feelings on this topic. Some people feel that startups have to be innovative or they will die. While it is true that most startups chase the disruptive idea that Dr. Christensen talked about in the last section, in many cases they don't break through that first product into a continuous cycle in innovation that evolves their first product but also expands their offerings, revenue streams and long-term growth potential. One of the great examples of this shift is Google. Everyone knows about Google. But for the first 10 years of their existence they were primarily about search engines and their paid ad engine. Many thought of them as a one-trick company, a rich one trick pony, but nevertheless, a one-trick pony. Then in the last few years when Larry Page had matured to take the reigns as CEO, they had expanded into new technologies (e.g., mobile, driverless cars, wearable computing) and compelling acquisitions (e.g., Motorola, Nest) that made people take notice. All of a sudden, people were seeing them as a company that was not only going to index everything on the Internet but really connect everything and change the world.

But you don't have to be Google to recognize that when you build something successful you will eventually have competitors, the market will change and a whole bunch of other things can occur, putting your long term success at risk. There are six dimensions that identify motivating factors of why startups should innovate. They are— Jurisdiction, Personnel, Technology, Shareholders, Customers, and Competition. Which factors do you identify being a risk and an innovation motivator?

MOTIVATING FACTORS TO INNOVATE

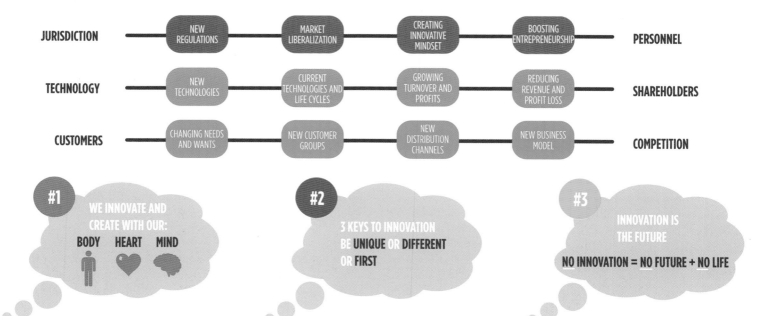

*Data Source: The Innovator's Delimma, Jean-Claude Biuer

McKinney: The law that tends to apply most to startup organizations is the law of patience, right? We didn't have everything right away. I said before there's this constant pressure to accelerate. At the same time, you've got to make sure what you're going to put out there is going to be something that the marketplace will respond to, right? You have to have some level of patience.

In the case of startups, patience falls into, "We've got to hurry up and get those products out because we promised the investors or we promised the board." There's this constant push between speed of getting it out there and getting the right thing out there.

The other one startups deal with a lot is resources. There's never enough resources. Now, I hear all the time some people saying, "Well, I've got this really great idea, but I've got to go raise $10 million to go do this." My general perception is someone uses money as the first excuse as to why their idea came to fruition, and so they don't believe enough in the product or believe enough in the idea.

Don't let resources, don't let the money side of resources be the restraining factor for you taking your idea and getting into the marketplace. I'm a big believer in early, what I call, market validation. If you've got an idea, then mark something up. Make it out of wood. Then, use that information to refine your thinking, refine your idea while at the same time you're building up information that could then actually lead you to getting the resources.

The Five Rules for Startup Innovation

Phil has created his "Seven Laws of Innovation" (Leadership, Culture, Resources, Patience, Process, BHAG, and Execution).[3] But it would be best to relate these laws more specifically to startups. We created the Five Rules for Startup Innovation.

1. **The Leadership Rule:** Be a leader, not a follower. As a startup, you're part of the executive team, but you must show the team why you believe innovation will drive the company's success.

2. **The Culture Rule:** Be an owner, not a player. As we discussed earlier, culture is critical to your success. You can make innovation a part of that culture DNA by rewarding good behavior (e.g., teamwork, collaboration, honesty) and getting rid of bad behavior (e.g., not-invented-here, passive/aggressive, turf battles).

3. **The Resources Rule:** Be a resource, not a drain. Innovation requires a committed level of resources (e.g., people, money, time, equipment) over an extended period of time. It helps validate the importance of innovation to an organization.

4. **The Vision Rule:** Be a visionary, not a pragmatist. You have to set the vision in order for leadership to outline an innovation agenda. This vision must present a clear and compelling target to act as the catalyst for the team.

5. **The Pioneer Rule:** Be a pioneer, not a pirate. No one likes a copycat and no one buys from one. If you're focused on attacking your competitors, you can't get out of your own way and be the original thinkers people will come to expect.

The Five Habits of Great Startup Innovators

Innovation requires a consistent commitment with an eye on the long game. You can start by encouraging your team to adopt what we call the Five Great Habits of Startup Innovation:

1. **The Patience Habit:** Innovation takes time. All too often, startups focus on short-term milestones to satisfy investors and keep the company growing. Keeping a steady focus on the long-term vision will help create a more valuable company.

2. **The Focus Habit:** Don't make your product a Swiss army knife. It impacts all of your resources (see The Resources Rule) and your product could lose its purpose (see The Vision Rule). Make it a habit to check in with the vision to ensure you've stayed focused on the end goal.

3. **The Process Habit:** To succeed at innovation, organizations need an innovation process that fits and works within their organization and culture. Create processes to cover the full innovation chain from idea capture through execution. Then, make it a habit to track a set of metrics and areas for improvement.

4. **The "Get Shit Done" Habit:** This is about the ability to execute on both the innovation agenda and the quarterly objectives of the operating business. Focusing on only one area of execution leaves the other to flounder. Successful organizations need leaders who can do both.

5. **The Humbleness Habit:** Sure, you have a great idea, but you must stay humble and resist the urge to rely on previous successes. You started your company by taking a risk. Don't be afraid to keep taking them but with a fierce passion and a humble heart.

> **EXERCISE: Your Startup Innovation and Rule Statements**
>
> After reading this section, you should do a brainstorming session with your startup team and come up with your own rules and habits for your startup. Take each of the rules and habits and write out a statement that aligns with your culture and what you will adhere to as the company grows. Things like:
>
> - **Our Culture Rule:** "We all have innovation weaved into our DNA. We will reward the innovative and work to eliminate bad behavior in every part of our company."
> - **Our Resources Habit:** "We will all be a resource to one another. We will commit the resources necessary for the organization to innovate".

EVERYONE IS A DESIGN THINKER

At its core, *The Startup Equation* is about innovation. One way for startups to embody that innovation depends on individuals seeing themselves as design thinkers and incorporating it into their startup culture.

So what's design thinking? Ask a bunch of people who are confident in design thinking to define what it is, and you'll get a variety of answers. There is no "unified field theory" for design thinking, but Wikipedia offers a reasonable definition:

> Design thinking is a formal method for practical, creative resolution of problems or issues, with the intent of an improved future result. In

this regard it is a form of solution-based, or solution-focused thinking, which starts with a goal (a better future situation) instead of solving one specific problem. By considering the present and future conditions, the parameters of the problem, and possible solutions, may be explored simultaneously.[4]

There are five modes within the design thinking process:

1. **Empathy:** To truly get to know the end user and understand what their true needs are in order to design something they will use.

2. **Define:** Allows you to sift through information and data in order to come up with a problem statement to solve for.

3. **Ideate:** This is the idea generation mode where you and your team allow yourselves to creatively "run free."

4. **Prototype:** Based on your point of view and problem statement that was identified in the Define mode, you and your team will pick an idea to build out as a prototype.

5. **Test:** The prototype that you build will need to go through some tests to see if it solves the problem that you have identified. Depending on the findings of your test, you may tweak your prototype in order to run further tests.

Design thinking starts without preconceived problem definitions and solutions with the goal of discovering hidden parameters and alternate paths to reach your goals. Because design thinking is also iterative, any solutions are also potential starting points for future phases.

Thinking Like a Designer

It's important to reinforce that design thinking is not exclusive to the realm of designers. But you do need to think like a designer. A designer brings two essential perspectives to every problem: *empathy* and *creativity*. They invent futures that don't exist and must understand how people currently do something in order to reimagine it.

In the ground breaking article, "Design Thinking," Tim Brown of IDEO lays out the five key characteristics you should adopt to think like a designer:[5]

1. **Empathy:** Empathetic thinkers can imagine the world from multiple perspectives. By taking a "people first" approach, design thinkers can imagine solutions that are inherently desirable and meet explicit or latent needs.

2. **Integrative Thinking:** The integrative thinker relies on analytical processes and exhibits the ability to see all of the important (even if they are conflicting) aspects of a problem and creates novel solutions that improve on existing alternatives.

3. **Optimism:** The optimistic thinker assumes that no matter how challenging the constraints of a given problem, at least one potential solution is better than the existing alternatives.

4. **Experimentalism:** The experimental thinker believes significant innovations don't come from incremental tweaks. Design thinkers pose questions and explore constraints in creative ways that proceed in entirely new directions.

5. **Collaboration:** The increasing complexity of products, services, and experiences has replaced the myth of the lone creative genius with the reality of an enthusiastic interdisciplinary collaborator.

Over the years of managing creative teams and getting others throughout the organization to think like designers, Steve created a flashcard with the following tips:

1. **You are a designer.** The key to thinking like a designer is to think of yourself as a designer. It's empowering, and you're in the position to design the solution.

2. **Create the ideal solution.** The existing situation that you want to change can be transformed into the preferred situation by your ideas.

3. **Reject the normal and boring.** Designers constantly reject the typical route and think of how it should be done, regardless of how radical the notion.

4. **Have ideas, lots and lots of ideas.** Crank out lots of ideas and don't pick one too quickly. The tendency exists to find a solution quickly by adapting what exists. Don't do it. Indulge in every idea to find the right solution.

5. **Build something.** Take the ideas and mock up the idea. People react to things they can touch and feel.

Design Thinking as a Strategy for Innovation

Innovation requires the ability to create value in a world powered by the constant flow of disruptive technology. When design principles are applied to strategy and innovation, the innovation success rate improves dramatically. As a result, design thinking can be applied to products, services, processes, physical locations, and really anything that needs to be optimized for human interaction.

To dovetail the focus on innovation, there are two elements that help power design thinking by exploring future uncertainties: **Strategic Foresight (Str)** and **Scenario Planning (Sce)**. **Strategic Foresight (Str)** is the practice of creating a functional view of future events and possibilities to take full advantage of opportunities and prepare for possible adversity. The idea of **Strategic Foresight (Str)** arose from the idea that while the future isn't predictable, it's also undetermined. However, it can be influenced in a positive way by actions we take in the present. Applied to innovation, this aligns future opportunities with those making business decisions to structure roadmaps based on future events.

Scenario Planning (Sce), also called scenario thinking or scenario analysis, is a strategic planning method that some organizations use to make flexible, long-term plans. Closely connected to **strategic foresight**, it details possible future events in order to prepare responses to the combinations and permutations that change can bring. In business, this allows for decision makers to evaluate possible outcomes and to help focus innovation efforts.

Develop Design Thinking Capabilities in Your Startup

While learning to be a good designer takes years, non-designers can learn to think like a designer and apply these skills to leadership and innovation in weeks and months. Here are six ways to develop design-thinking capabilities in your startup:

1. Explore the tool sets and skill sets used by designers, including empathy for your customers, idea generation, critical thinking, and

aesthetic ways of knowing, problem solving, rapid-prototyping, and collaboration.

2. Examine ways to connect with customers to uncover innovation opportunities.

3. Launch hands-on innovation challenges to work through the design thinking process from start to finish.

4. Transform insights and data into actionable ideas with measurable benchmarks.

5. Develop an active innovation portfolio with the SMART Innovation™ Method we cover in the next section to include a wide variety of concepts for products, services, experiences, messages, channels, business models, or strategies.

6. Create and implement new solutions that create value for your customers, faster and more effectively.

THE ART OF SMART INNOVATION

Sir Ken Robinson, an internationally recognized leader in the areas of creativity, innovation, and human resources, asserts that culture drives innovation and needs to involve everyone in the organization. "If you want a culture of innovation, there are certain conditions for it," Robinson says. "The culture of an organization is about habits and habitats—creating a habitat where people feel their ideas are welcomed, empowered and rewarded, and creating a physical environment that develops new ideas."

The core environment for new ideas is creative collaboration. As mentioned in the previous section, creative collaboration is about getting a diverse team together to create new ideas, technologies, or content. It helps foster the innovation process and impacts the culture of a startup by creating a shared mind. People learn by working with others in a variety of capacities, and co-creating new things together.

Five Insights on Creative Collaboration

In the McKinsey Global Survey on Innovation, they surveyed 3,000 executives and found "innovation faces ongoing challenges, such as increasing global competition, short-term priorities, and the need to integrate it into key organizational objectives. As a result it remains elusive, and leading organizations are looking to uncover every possible way to boost ability to innovate."[6]

The global workplace design company Steelcase studied a variety of innovation models, from internal models to external partnerships. Steelcase's research identified five overarching insights about how creative collaboration impacts innovation.[7]

1. **Innovation is a direct result of creative collaboration.**

   Creative collaboration is about forging something new—an innovation. It requires a team with a wide range of professions, diverse backgrounds, and experiences whose economic function is to create new ideas, new technologies, or creative content. People learn by working with others in a variety of capacities, and co-creating new things together is the highest form of learning and the highest form of collaboration.

2. **Creative collaboration requires a connection between sociology and technology.**

   Technology is a powerful configuring force in the ways we innovate because we use it to drive information and knowledge. When it becomes unobtrusive and intuitive for users, technology allows people to share information equally and democratically, improve transparency, and help users gain a shared understanding.

3. **Innovation is a team sport that, paradoxically, requires focused individual work to fuel collective creativity.**

   With so much focus on the social aspects of innovation, organizations sometimes forget about the power of individual, concentrated work. In order to be a strong contributor to a team, individuals need the time and place to think and let ideas germinate.

4. **Creative collaboration today is both physical and virtual.**

   To take advantage of the diverse backgrounds and experiences of a distributed team, interactions should happen in real time. It's not only about passing work back and forth between time zones to speed up development. Creative collaboration requires trust, which is built by teammates working together in real time.

5. **Creative collaboration happens in small groups.**

    The best collaboration often takes place in one-on-one or three-person subsets of the larger team. Even the larger team size should be managed. The trick is to get the right set of skills on the team without weighing it down.

Amplifying Creative Collaboration with Open Innovation

Open Innovation (Oin) remains one of the most powerful solutions. It relies on distributed knowledge, including things like buying or licensing processes or inventions from other companies. A recent example of this is the electric car company, Tesla. Elon Musk released Tesla patents to the public so people could innovate with the technology. The patent release creates the opportunity for Tesla technology to become the standard for electric cars, a benefit for the company long term. "Understanding Open Innovation Map" outlines four great ways to leverage creative collaboration.

Understanding the SMART Innovation Method

To help you develop your startup's innovation programs and portfolio, we recommend you leverage our SMART Innovation™ method. We came up with this method after hundreds of innovation projects. It is important to preface that no single organization has it all figured out, and no single thing will trigger or ensure innovation in your startup. But by taking an honest audit of your innovation programs, you can identify the areas that work and those that don't.

- **(S)tart with Opportunities:** It all begins with identifying opportunities that take advantage of with your company resources.

- **(M)ake Observations:** Meet with customers who could potentially benefit from the opportunities you've identified. Observed behavior can help validate or uncover ideas.

- **(A)ccelerate Ideas:** You can partner with larger companies and use open innovation techniques like innovation networks to discover new ideas. Internally, you can form brainstorming sessions or idea competitions like hackathons to pull together all the identified opportunities.

- **(R)efine Concepts:** Once the concept/idea/innovation is identified, use the exercises and tools we've covered previously to refine the idea [e.g., the Solution Element Equation (SEED) Board, proto-personas, customer journey maps]. It will make innovation less abstract for your organization and team.

- **(T)est and Validate:** Once you can get a refined concept in front of people, test it, and validate if this is an innovation deserving your company's full commitment. These results are measurable, helping you make the business case to other stakeholders and decision makers in the organization.

Leveraging the SMART Innovation Method to Enable Creative Collaboration

We'd love to do some of our best thinking at work. If you're like most people, however, work rarely provides the time or creative space to think. Most work environments aren't designed to empower creative thought. It's a paradox, right? Organizations turn to employees for new ideas or products, but most employees feel their work environment stifles creativity. Recognizing this reality, we came up with three ways to leverage the SMART Innovation Method to support creativity at work.

1. **Set clearly defined goals.** Many managers want to support creativity, but they're afraid of the perceived risk and the time required to come up with ideas. Counter the fear with clear goals based on specific objectives. A clear goal engages us and helps others understand what you want to achieve.

2. **Create intersections.** Great ideas often come from the intersections created when people with different backgrounds and different mindsets collide. Frans Johannsen described this phenomenon in his book *The Medici Effect*. Companies naturally have a few intersections built into them. As Johannsen notes, the key is to find them, encourage them, and use them to your advantage. Some intersections will already exist.

3. **Reward failure—strategically.** To encourage creative risk, reward failure strategically by encouraging the execution of ideas, only rewarding a failure the first time, and requiring that a person learn from the failure. Everyone fails from time to time, but you can use

OPEN INNOVATION MAP Figure 16.5

Open Innovation (Oin) offers several benefits to companies operating on a program of global collaboration:
• Reduced cost of conducting research and development
• Potential for improvement in development productivity
• Incorporation of customers early in the development process
• Increase in accuracy for market research and customer targeting
• Potential for synergism between internal and external innovations
• Potential for viral marketing

COLLABORATIVE OPEN INNOVATION

There are four ways to leverage creative collaboration in an Open Innovation environment:

IDEA COMPETITIONS

This model entails implementing a system that encourages competitiveness among contributors by rewarding successful submissions. Developer competitions such as hackathon events fall under this category of open innovation. This method provides organizations with inexpensive access to a large quantity of innovative ideas, while also providing a deeper insight into the needs of their customers and contributors.

CUSTOMER IMMERSION

While mostly orientated towards the end of the product development cycle, this technique involves extensive customer interaction through employees of the host organization. Companies are thus able to accurately incorporate customer input, while also allowing them to be more closely involved in the design process and product management cycle.

COLLABORATIVE PRODUCT DESIGN AND DEVELOPMENT

Here an organization incorporates their contributors into the development of the product. In addition to the provision of the framework on which contributors develop, the hosting organization still controls and maintains the eventual products developed in collaboration with their contributors. This method gives organizations more control by ensuring that the correct product is developed as fast as possible, while reducing the overall cost of development.

INNOVATION NETWORKS

Similar to idea competitions, an organization leverages a network of contributors in the design process by offering a reward in the form of an incentive. The difference relates to the fact that the network of contributors is used to develop solutions to identified problems within the development process, as opposed to new products.

Data Source: Stefan Lindegaard, The Open Innovation Essentials, Roadblocks to Leadership Skills. Wiley, 2010.

10 COMPONENTS OF AN OPEN INNOVATION CULTURE

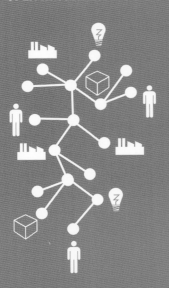

1. DYNAMIC PEOPLE

An open innovation culture requires open, dynamic people who can manage both customer and partner relationships while being able to accept and welcome new ideas from outside of the company.

2. OUTSIDE IDEAS

Not all great ideas or people come form within your organization. To be successful with open innovation you must be willing to actively seek out others from the outside to improve and grow the inside.

3. VALUE FAILURE

Failure is a great and humbling asset to learn from and leverage. Within an open innovation organization, failure is a key necessity for any company looking for growth and the ability to build new innovations.

4. SHARED KNOWLEDGE

To nurture a culture of innovation it requires a willingness to share knowledge and help educate team members, leaders, and partners about technology and how ideas and opportunities can turn into new business models.

5. WINNING COLLABORATIONS

Open innovation cultures do not require keeping a tight seal on concepts or intellectual property. Instead, they capitalize on winning collaborations with partners to innovate within the market.

6. BALANCING R&D

Successful open innovation cultures must find a balance between internal and external R&D operations for creating new value streams. External R&D can bring new, creative ideas while internal R&D helps to capitalize on them.

7. RISK TAKING

All cultures that look toward open innovation models must be risk takers rather than risk avoiders. The acceptance of failure, openness to learning, and rewarding of success is where the fruits of innovation lie.

8. INTELLECTUAL MURKINESS

A key reward and risk of innovation cultures is that at some point the ownership of intellectual property between partners can become murky; however, this can also work to the advantage of all the parties involved.

9. BUILDING TRUST

Open innovation requires trust and strong communication between those involved. By willing to be forthright and work around confidentiality or property ownership issues, you can actively form the bases of trust with your partners.

10. BEING BETTER NOT FIRST

Success for open innovation does not always require being the first to a new market, but rather, it requires refinement and building a better business model than those who initially entered into the space.

SIX CHARACTERISTICS OF A DEO Figure 16.8

In their bestselling book, *Rise of the DEO*, Maria Giudice and Christopher Ireland identify six key characteristics of a great DEO and they hold true for great founders and entrepreneurs from all walks of life.

INTUITIVE

DEOs are highly intuitive, either by nature or through experience. They have the ability to feel what's right, by using their intense perceptual and observational skills or through deep expertise. This doesn't mean they have a fear of numbers. They know that intuitively enhanced decision making doesn't preclude rational or logical analysis. They use both—and consider each valid and powerful.

CHANGE AGENTS

DEOs aren't troubled by change; in fact, they openly promote and encourage it. They understand traditional approaches, but are not dominated by them. As a result, they are comfortable disrupting the status quo if it stands in the way of their dream. They try to think and act differently than others. They recognize this ability as a competitive advantage.

THE DESIGN EXECUTIVE OFFICER

RISK TAKERS

DEOs embrace risk as an inherent part of life and a key ingredient of creativity. Rather than avoiding or mitigating it, they seek greater ease and command of it as one of the levers they can control. They recast it as experimentation and invite collaborators. A failed risk still produces learning.

SOCIALLY INTELLIGENT

DEOs have high social intelligence. They instinctively connect with others and integrate them into well-defined and heavily accessed networks. They prefer spending time with employees, customers, and strangers rather than equipment, plants, or spreadsheets. "Everyday people" are a source of strength, renewal, and new ideas.

SYSTEMS THINKERS

Despite their desire to disrupt and take risks, DEOs are systems thinkers who understand the interconnectedness of their world. They know that each part of their organization overlaps and influences others. They know unseen connections surround what's visible. This helps to give their disruptions intended, rather than chaotic, impact and makes their risk taking more conscious.

GSD

Finally, DEOs can be defined by a new set of initials: GSD—short for "gets shit done." They feel an urgency to get personally involved, to understand details through their own interaction, and to lead by example. DEOs make things happen.

Data Source: RISEOFTHEDEO.com

those moments to explore and reward creativity whenever possible, including creating an open innovation loop.

EVERY ENTREPRENEUR NEEDS TO BE A DEO

Authors Maria Giudice and Christopher Ireland discuss in their bestselling book, *Rise of the DEO*, the changing role of the leader in an organization. They define what they call a DEO, or Design Executive Officer.

> Part strategic business executive and part creative problem solver, the DEO views an organization as a design project that requires both skill sets. They see themselves as catalysts for transformation; as agents of cultural change. With this perspective and these abilities, the DEO looks at business problems as design problems, solvable through the right mix of imagination and metrics.

Giudice and Ireland write that "startup founders, and a growing number of progressive corporate leaders who emulate them, have learned to lead using these abilities." They go on to explain that entrepreneurs "realize their success rests on attracting and coalescing stakeholders who share their vision, goals and values." This is in line with why most entrepreneurs don't gel with the traditional "command and control" directives, nor adopt strategies focused primarily on bottom-line profitability.

As a result, great entrepreneurs with the "DEO gene" create resilient organizations that value expertise, but make room for failure. These organizations can evolve, and in Venn diagram style, they find interesting shared traits that are definitely in the camp of our "X-Factor" elements (we'll talk about those elements soon).

EXERCISE: DEO Quiz—Are You a Natural Born DEO?

Do you have the traits of a DEO? If you can honestly answer "yes" to most of the questions below, you possess the key characteristics of a next-generation leader:

1. **Are you comfortable taking risks on a regular basis?** DEOs embrace risk as an inherent part of life and a key ingredient of

creativity. They recast risk as experimentation and invite collaborators.

2. **Are you able to problem solve in a systematic manner?** Despite their desire to take risks and make change, DEOs are systems thinkers who understand the interconnectedness of their world.

3. **Can you integrate intuitive and analytic decision making?** DEOs know that the best decisions are informed by both intuitive and rational analysis.

4. **Can you easily empathize and connect with others?** DEOs have a highly refined creative intelligence and instinctively connect with others and integrate them into well-defined and heavily accessed networks.

5. **Are you driven to take action?** DEOs feel an urgency to get personally involved, to understand details through their own interaction, and to lead by example. They become adept at prioritizing and focusing on key tasks, and they often end discussions with "What's our deadline?"

GETTING READY . . .

Forging a path to continuous innovation within your startup is an ongoing process that builds over the weeks and months to support a sustainable process. With the awareness of your culture and approach (rules and habits), you'll need to empower everyone to be a design thinker and adopt the methods of SMART Innovation and creative collaboration.

To craft your own custom Startup Equation don't forget to review and complete/prepare for the exercises in this chapter:

- Map Out Your Startup's Innovation Dimensions
- Write Out Your Startup Innovation and Rule Statements
- Develop Design Thinking Capabilities in Your Startup
- Leverage the SMART Innovation Method to Enable Creative Collaboration
- Take the DEO Quiz—Are You a Natural Born DEO?

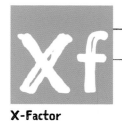

X-Factor

GROW THE DREAM

| Driven to Succeed | Bouncing Up, Not Bouncing Back | Curiosity Killed the Bad Idea | A Startup State of Mind | Serendipity Not Included |

CONSTANT

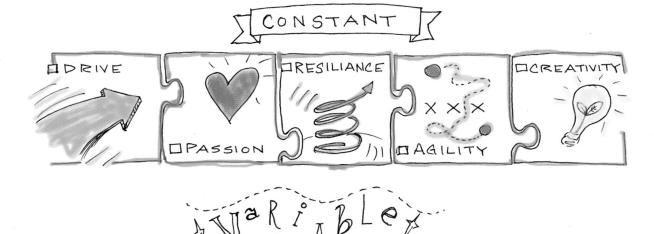

☐ DRIVE ☐ PASSION ☐ RESILIANCE ☐ AGILITY ☐ CREATIVITY

VARIABLE

 • CURIOSITY

• PLACE

 • TIMING

 • STATE of MIND

Original Sketch by Kate Rutter

CHAPTER 17

In reality, serendipity accounts for 1% of the blessings we receive in life, work, and love. The other 99% is due to our efforts.

—*Peter McWilliams*

The Exponential Power of the X-Factor

It was nearly sunrise in the city of Aguascalientes, Peru. We were waiting for buses that would take us and about 500 other people to the top of a mountain, a mystical place considered sacred by the Incas. To the rest of us, we know it as Machu Picchu. The Incas were an amazing civilization that only lasted 150 years and in that time built roads, mastered terrace agriculture on mountainsides, and engineered cities like Machu Picchu.

Once we reached the mountaintop, we climbed large, uneven stairs, taking time as we climbed to look out at the splendor of the valley. We were at an altitude of about 8,500 feet and there was no easy way down. As the morning broke and first light entered the valley you could feel the power of the place that was part royal living space, part observatory, and part place of worship.

We timed the trip to coincide with Steve's forty-third birthday, and we finished our climb around lunchtime on his birthday. We sat on the top of the plateau meditating, reflecting on life, and thinking about what had come before and what may lie ahead. It was an incredible moment that will stay with us forever, and it wouldn't have happened if Steve hadn't set the goal.

We all have goals of some sort. And some of us even have bucket lists. These are things we want to do on this earth before we go somewhere else. Machu Picchu was on Steve's list. And now there's a checkmark in that box. But what motivates people to reach for their goals while others remain complacent, even content with mediocrity?

It's the same thing that differentiates the successful entrepreneurs from the not-so-successful ones. You may have a great idea, a great product,

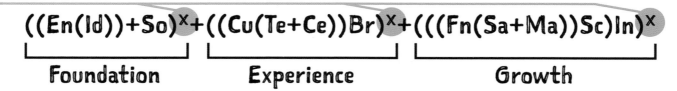

$$((En(Id))+So)^X+((Cu(Te+Ce))Br)^X+(((Fn(Sa+Ma))Sc)In)^X$$

| Foundation | Experience | Growth |

There are many elements that make up a startup, almost all of them are quantifiable or related to the path of building and launching a startup. However, there are intangible yet powerful elements that run throughout the life of a startup. They power your ability to surpass others and they are the X-Factors or the eXponential Factors that give your start up the advantage over everyone else. There are two groups of X-Factor elements: Constant and Variable.

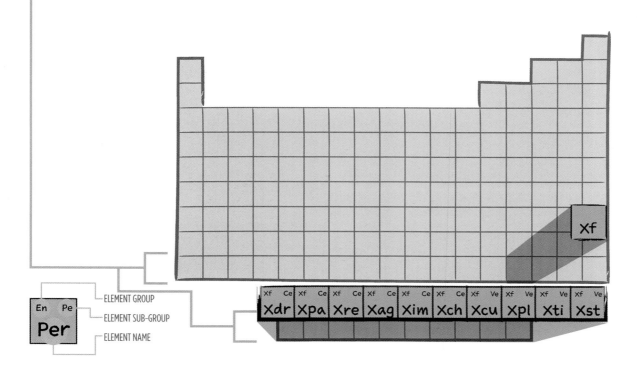

ELEMENT GROUP
ELEMENT SUB-GROUP
ELEMENT NAME

En   Pe
Per

Xf	Ce	Xf	Ce	Xf	Ce	Xf	Ce	Xf	Ce	Xf	Ve	Xf	Ve	Xf	Ve	Xf	Ve
Xdr	Xpa	Xre	Xag	Xim	Xch	Xcu	Xpl	Xti	Xst

Xf

X-FACTOR (XF) CONSTANT ELEMENTS

When you think of a startup that is successful, what is it that makes them stand out from the others? There are constants that are there throughout the life of the company. They embody the culture, come from the vision and even inhabit the personalities of people.

Drive (Xdr)
Drive is the constant urge to attain a goal or to overcome an obstacle. Drive will keep you up at night while your brain turns and turns. Drive will keep you going when everything else fails.

Passion (Xpa)
Passion is the emotion you feel when talking or thinking about your business and the problems you're helping your client solve. It's this emotional connection to your business that will help keep you fulfilled as a business owner.

Resilience (Xre)
Resilience is what we use to overcome adversity. Why do some people fail when they come up against obstacles while others thrive in the face of them? It's the latter's resilience that allows them to overcome the fear and quickly look for ways to problem solve. As an entrepreneur, resilience will be your best friend. Though everyone has their own level of resilience, it's absolutely something that can and should be built up over time.

Agility (Xag)
As entrepreneurs, you will pivot your company many times over the next few years. It may happen because of changes in the market or even when you're able to focus in on the customer needs. Being able to do so in a quick and nimble way will allow you to stay ahead of the game. Agility means staying lean so that you can move in a moment's notice.

Imagination (Xim)
Though many people do not consider themselves imaginative or creative, being able to have original ideas will fuel your business, its products, and how it interacts with its customer base. No one wants to see the same thing over and over again. As an entrepreneur, your job is to create something new, something different that helps customers solve their problems and come to you as a trusted source. That takes some creative thinking on your part.

Charisma (Xch)
Having a special appeal that causes people to feel connected and loyal to your leadership. It is a strong assuredness and confidence in your vision and being approachable. This also includes what is called "100% focused attention" on the person or persons you are speaking with.

X-FACTOR (XF) VARIABLE ELEMENTS

Building on the constants that are there in a startup's life are certain variables that become incredibly important at the right times. These variable elements super-charge the startup with curiosity and state of mind; and put you at the right place and time to take advantage of the right opportunity.

Curiosity (Xcu)
Curiosity is having the desire to know something by digging in and exploring. No one can teach you to be curious, but they can encourage it, like we encourage you to explore it. If you do not know an area of your business, poke around and get to know the basics. Want to be a better leader? Become curious about how others have done it. Find what piques your interest and begin your adventure.

Place (Xpl)
You can't ensure you'll be in the right place at the right time. However, there are things that you can do to improve your odds: Hanging in the same circles as the people you want to meet, going to the right events, and building a network can help you get to the places you need to be. It's an element that will take a lot of work, but it can also yield many rewards.

Timing (Xti)
There are things that come about and seem to hit at just the right time. A lot of what helps timing is preparation. If the time is right and you're not ready to move, then you miss your chance. However, if you've done your homework, then timing will be your ally as you build this company.

State of Mind (Xst)
Success is a mindset. Entrepreneurialism is a mindset. If you're going to do anything, it starts first with your thoughts, even before they translate into action. In order to grow your business, you have to have the right state of mind to do so.

a great team, funding, and many other operational elements, but it's not enough. You also need what we call the X-Factor.

What do we mean by X-Factors? These are the elements of entrepreneurship that people do not stress enough, but they have, in some instances, more power than the rest of our element table. X-Factors fall into two categories: *constant* and *variable*. You can see on the elements table page there are *constants* like **Drive (Xdr)** and **Passion (Xpa)** and *variables* like **Curiosity (Xdr)** and **Timing (XTi)**. Of course, there are many more, and they may seem obvious requirements for a successful startup, but it's amazing how often they're overlooked.

DRIVEN TO SUCCEED

There's an ongoing debate around whether **Drive (Xdr)** can be taught. **Drive (Xdr)** is the constant urge to attain a goal or to overcome an obstacle. It will keep you up at night. It will keep you going when everything else fails. A person's level of passion could determine the level of drive. We see something similar in athletes. Dr. Jim Taylor, a psychologist who works and studies professional athletes, says, "Professional athletes just work as hard as they possibly can. And that drive is usually propelled by an intense passion for their sport."

Running a business isn't much different. Writing at the *Huffington Post*, Dr. Taylor also discusses how perspective impacts your drive and ultimately your success. Here are a few questions to measure your drive to succeed:

• What are your reasons for selecting this industry?

• Do you have a sense of ownership over the final product your company puts out?

• How do you define your successes and your failures?

Every business will have its ups and downs. By asking the right questions, you can assess whether or not you have enough drive and passion to weather the storms that come your way.

Sylvia Woods, the "Queen of Soul Food," knows all about drive. She needed the drive to build Sylvia's over the last fifty years. She started as a waitress in Harlem at Johnson's Luncheonette in the '50s. He first day on the job was also her first day in a restaurant. With the help of her mother mortgaging the family farm, Sylvia bought Johnson's Luncheonette in 1962.

From its start as a soul food restaurant, Sylvia's has grown to include multiple cookbooks, as well as a food product line. Although her food has a lot to do with the success of the business, it was also her passion for community that helped the business thrive. "If you come alone, you're never going to dine alone," she said.

Taking a page from Sylvia's book, you need to ask the question, "What really drives me?" Think about what makes you passionate and include those elements in your startup. If your motivation is waning, think about what roadblocks might be standing in your way.

Fear, The Past and Perfection

Many times, people don't start businesses because they are afraid of what might happen. It helps to remember everyone is afraid of something. People will say "No" to you, but that's O.K. For every person who says "No," someone else will say "Yes!"

It's easy to say, "Let go of the past," but it's not always easy to forget the mistakes and ignore the expectations. The key is to know what you want and go after it. It may not turn out exactly as expected, but if you're flexible, then you may end up with better results.

Some of you will strive to have everything perfect, even before they start. Know this about businesses: They are never perfect. Allow yourself to make mistakes. People don't care if you make them. They just care that you own them and accept responsibility.

Having **Drive (Xdr)** helps you move forward, but you'll find it takes things like **Charisma (Xch)** to be that entrepreneurial leader that attracts people to your cause. One entrepreneur we know with both these elements is Peter Corbett. Peter started iStrategyLabs in his apartment after he got laid off from an agency. If you tried the SpongeBob arcade "skill crane" on the Nickelodeon site (the average SpongeBob fan age is 34) or shot apples out of a cannon from Redd Apple Ale, that was iStrategyLabs. We had the opportunity to talk to Peter about culture, failure, charisma, and humility.

SEQ: Failure is a great teacher. Any advice you'd share that really shaped you?

Corbett: I know there's this whole sort of tech-scene thing around, like celebrating failure and all the rest. Fail fast, etc., I think that's right, but I'm not a big, "Hey, let's fail fast." I'm more like, "Hey, let's succeed."

The kind of failing fast that we've done, and this is really the kind that I would suggest most people engage in, is non-fatal fast failure, which is things that didn't work, it doesn't matter that they didn't work. Failing at things that really matter, I'm deathly afraid of that and not interested in it.

SEQ: What traits or skills separate great entrepreneurs?

Corbett: One, I think, is charisma. It's maybe the most important and undervalued and under-appreciated. Charisma can correct a lot of things. Charisma can overcome your inability to sell. I think that humility is also an under-appreciated characteristic, especially in our hard-driven tech start-up culture where we're supposed to beat our chests all day. I think that perseverance is crucial. I don't think you can be an entrepreneur without extreme perseverance.

BOUNCING UP, NOT BOUNCING BACK

Every startup will experience failure. It's the risk of becoming an entrepreneur. But what happens when you hit rock bottom? What does it really take to bounce up?

At the core of the "Power of Bounce" is **Resilience (Xre)** and **Agility (Xag)**. **Resilience (Xre)** is what we use to overcome adversity. As an entrepreneur, **Resilience** will be your best friend. You'll also discover a need for **Agility (Xag)** as an entrepreneur. You'll pivot your company many times over the next few years. It may happen because of changes in the market or even when you're able to focus on what the customer needs. **Agility (Xag)** means staying lean so that you can move at a moment's notice, even though it may mean admitting things aren't working.

But failure can be rough. Though we may learn a ton from a failure, there's a bruise to the ego that occurs, and it's hard to get past it. Resilient people, however, are characterized by an ability to experience both negative and positive emotions, even in difficult or painful situations, according to Barbara Fredrickson, PhD, the author of *Positivity* (Crown Archetype, 2009).

They mourn losses and endure frustrations, but they also find redeeming potential or value in most challenges. When we come back from a failure, we're building our resilience. Resilience allows us to look at setbacks as minor bumps in the road. It allows us to acknowledge that something was tried, and even if the outcome isn't successful, resilience helps us to realize that it may not be our goal that's the problem, but how we're approaching it.

EXERCISE: The Resilience Builder

How do we build up resilience? Here are three ways to get started:[1]

- **Create Small Benchmarks:** Reexamine your goal. Then, make smaller, achievable goals. You'll set yourself up for success, while building momentum and resilience.

- **Create a Support Team:** It's sounds clichéd, but you need to surround yourself with people who have your back. When things go wrong, you'll want someone you trust. It needs to be someone with the experience to help guide you. Find those people and keep them close.

- **Sharpen Your Creative Problem Solving Skills:** There are always a plethora of solutions to a problem. Your job is not to find one, but to find the best one. When challenges arise, allow yourself to develop different strategies to test. This will help you focus on solving problems and better prepare you for the big ones that come your way.

CURIOSITY KILLED THE BAD IDEA

Albert Einstein famously said, "I have no special talents. I am only passionately curious." When you think of curiosity everyone thinks of cats or kids going places they probably shouldn't. We like to think of **Curiosity (Xcu)** as having the desire to know something by digging in and exploring.

In the *Harvard Business Review*, Tomas Chamorro-Premuzic had an article titled, "Curiosity Is as Important as Intelligence."[2] He poses the question:

Why are some people more able to manage complexity? Chamorro-Premuzic believes that although complexity is context-dependent, it's also determined by a person's disposition. He proposes three different psychological qualities that enhance our ability to manage complexity and the last one is the one that really caught our interest.

Complexity Measurement #1 (IQ): "IQ stands for intellectual quotient and refers to mental ability. The main reason is that higher levels of IQ enable people to learn and solve novel problems faster. In fact, IQ is a much stronger predictor of performance on complex tasks than on simple ones."

Complexity Measurement #2 (EQ): "EQ stands for emotional quotient and concerns our ability to perceive, control, and express emotions. EQ relates to complexity management in three main ways. First, individuals with higher EQ are less susceptible to stress and anxiety. Second, EQ is a key ingredient of interpersonal skills, which means that people with higher EQ are better equipped to navigate complex organizational politics and advance in their careers. Third, people with higher EQ tend to be more entrepreneurial, so they are more proactive at exploiting opportunities, taking risks, and turning creative ideas into actual innovations."

While IQ is great for intelligence, and EQ is great for leadership and entrepreneurship, number three trumps them all.

Complexity Measurement #3 (CQ): Curiosity quotient is a term originally put forth by author and journalist Thomas L. Friedman as part of an illustrative formula to explain how individuals can be powerfully motivated to learn about a personally interesting subject, whether or not they possess a particularly high intelligence quotient (IQ). The non-mathematical and fictitious formula is [[CQ + PQ > IQ]]; where CQ is "Curiosity quotient" and PQ is "Passion quotient," and according to Chamorro-Premuzic, "CQ concerns having a hungry mind."[3]

He theorizes that "people with higher CQ are more inquisitive and open to new experiences. They find novelty exciting and are quickly bored with routine. They tend to generate many original ideas and are counter-conformist. It has not been as deeply studied as EQ and IQ, but there's some evidence to suggest it is just as important when it comes to managing complexity in two major ways. First, individuals with higher CQ are generally more tolerant of ambiguity. This nuanced, sophisticated, subtle thinking style defines the very essence of complexity. Second, CQ leads to higher levels of intellectual investment and knowledge acquisition over time, especially in formal domains of education, such as science and art (note: this is of course different from IQ's measurement of raw intellectual horsepower). Knowledge and expertise, much like experience, translate complex situations into familiar ones, so CQ is the ultimate tool to produce simple solutions for complex problems."[4]

EXERCISE: Finding Your Curiosity Quotient

While no one can teach you to be curious, they can encourage it, like we encourage you to explore it. Find what captures your interest and begin your adventure. Start by measuring your "Curiosity quotient:"

1. **Explore Routes to New Opportunities.** A curious mind attracts new opportunities that are often overlooked by an incurious mind. Take a situation and come up with five different ways to you could reinvent a specific idea or process.

2. **Ask For More.** Understand that you don't know everything. Statistics say that forty-two percent of college graduates never read another book after college. As we grow up we tend to assume that we know everything and there is nothing more to learn. To stay mentally agile, make it a point to make learning a lifelong goal.[5]

3. **Observe and Explore.** Use all your senses to understand the people and the world around you. We can be as receptive as the sponge soaking in more and more information from our surroundings. One way to strengthen our receptiveness is by asking questions.[6]

4. **Experiment on New Things.** Dabble in different things. Having eclectic tastes and interests makes life more exciting. We all experience some level of resistance while trying something new. The only difference is that curious people break through this barrier more easily by entering the unfamiliar territory often. Persistent practice helps.[7]

A STARTUP STATE OF MIND

Both of us have spent our lives as entrepreneurs and helping other entrepreneurs. Along the way, we've discovered an invisible divide between certain entrepreneurs. Some have an entrepreneurial mindset, while others view their business as a job. Instead of taking a job and working for someone else, they created a job for themselves and are equally miserable.

Before you even begin your business, we strongly recommend asking, "Why am I doing this?" As an entrepreneur, your mission has to be about something bigger than yourself. It has to be a driving force in your life, otherwise it won't work, and you'll be left with just a job.

EXERCISE: Getting a Startup State of Mind

You need to find the perspective around being an entrepreneur that works for you. But how does one actually gain that perspective? Start with these simple steps:

- **Create a Mission:** You want to run your startup, but you've really been doing it for the money. Maybe it's for freedom. They're all good reasons, but they won't last. So, create a mission for yourself. Find something that you want to change. Then, when you feel bogged down with the minutiae, you can revisit this mission to refocus.

- **Empathize:** Many times as companies grow their startups, they lose sight of the customer. Look for ways to connect with your customers and empathize with them. Talk to them. Visit them, and let them be the fuel for your future progress.

- **Focus:** As an entrepreneur, it's very easy to get caught up in chasing shiny objects that may or may not help you grow your business. Instead, focus on what you want to grow. Check smaller benchmarks within that ultimate goal. And remember to focus on one business at a time. If you try to do too much, you'll dilute your brand and your focus.

An entrepreneur who knows about keeping a startup state of mind is Jeff Pulver. A co-founder of Vonage, the VON conferences, and the 140Conf. He's invested in many, including early investments in companies like Twitter. Jeff still remains an active angel investor. We had a chance to chat about his adventures and how startups are like rock bands.

SEQ: What role has Resilience (Xre) played in your entrepreneurship?

Pulver: In my case, you're talking to the Forrest Gump of communication. I'll never be critical if someone doesn't have the background to be successful in a certain area because I never did, and I believe that ignorance is a beautiful thing, no excuse but it's a beautiful thing because when you don't know you can't do something, anything in the world becomes possible. There are no boundaries, there's no "no," it's only "can." You just have to figure out how.

I kind of embrace that stuff. So, frankly, for me it's about drive and it's about fun, and it's about enjoying the ride. You may never actually solve the problem but you'll discover something else along the way and there's inherently a serendipity and synchronicity associated with almost everything I do.

SEQ: It's funny you mentioned serendipity, that was actually my next question. What are your thoughts on the concept of serendipity?

Pulver: I think that serendipity is something that you can enhance. I think that when opportunity knocks you should open the damn door and maybe be there, not to walk away from it, to walk into it. When you become aware of your own flow you need to be inside of it in order to benefit from it but if you stay away from where the action it, the action may never find you. I think that when you become more aware of who you are and more aware of who's around you, you can much better appreciate the chance to leverage life moments. If you're noticing lots of coincidences happening in your life, I'll just postulate that maybe it's not a coincidence at all.

SERENDIPITY NOT INCLUDED

Let's say you run into a friend you haven't seen in a while. Both of you became entrepreneurs around the same time and have shared war stories in the past. She shares with you that she recently sold her company and is starting something else. She explains how it came about and how she was at the right place at the right time. As you both wave goodbye, you wonder, "How did this happen? Why hasn't something like this happened to me?" What did she do differently that led to her cashing out while you're still trying to build something and exit? How did she get so lucky? The truth is, she didn't.

EXERCISE: Enabling Serendipity

Luck and serendipity are not things that you either have or you don't. They're the result of being prepared for the right moment. Those moments won't exist unless you do the following:

- **Know What You Want:** Have you noticed that when you know what you want or need, it's easier to find it? Many times we flounder and do not get what we need because we're not clear enough with ourselves when it comes to outcomes. Take a minute, and breathe. Now, figure out what it is that you really want to make happen.
- **Get Out:** As an entrepreneur, it's very easy to get into the trenches with your work and keep your head down. The problem with that approach? You'll never be able to network and make the connections you need in order to achieve what you want. On the flip side, you may be headed out to events, but they may be the wrong events for you. Take the time to know people and build relationships. Help them and see if they can connect you with networking connectors. This group specializes in creating serendipity for people.
- **Know That You Can:** There are people that think that they're lucky, but they're in the minority. Know this: You create your own luck and serendipity. Let go of your past. Get into that entrepreneurial state of mind and know that you can AND deserve to have it.

Serendipity comes to those who are open and ready for it. It comes to those who make it happen and are prepared to accept it. But you need to be true to yourself. Jonathan Fields, one of our good friends, has explored what it takes to be true to yourself and live a good life. He happens to be an entrepreneur who knows and understand the X-Factor elements from firsthand experience. Currently, he hosts a fantastic series called the "Good Life Project" where he interviews people from all walks of life and explores a simple question: What makes a good life? We sat down to discuss things like uncertainty, passion, and serendipity.

SEQ: As an entrepreneur, you face uncertainty almost on a daily basis. What have you seen people do to deal with that uncertainty?

Fields: There are a couple things. Number one, what most people do, and this includes entrepreneurs, is nothing. They just suffer. The reason they do that is because they make a wrong assumption, and that assumption is that you're either wired with the ability to go to that place and be okay, or you're not. If you're not, you just have to deal with and you have to live in pain all the time.

I got curious about whether that's trainable, or whether it's genetic. If it was trainable, how? It is indeed trainable. I started to drill into a lot of the practices and the strategies and things that people were doing to train it. There are a whole bunch of different things.

For me, under the umbrella, one of the most powerful things has been developing a mindfulness practice. Mindfulness is a very fundamental form of meditation that literally rewires your brain, rewires your cognitive function, amps your creativity. At the same time, it allows you to find a much more sustained sense of equanimity and clarity in the face of high levels of sustained uncertainty and stress. It's a really powerful tool for entrepreneurs.

One of the biggest challenges that we have as entrepreneurs is mind chatter. Especially a huge amount of negative self talk in the face of uncertainty and risk. Two big things that you spin in your head are, "I'm not good enough," and, "It's not good enough." You just keep rotating those over and over and over. Those become your default mode, and they become your truth eventually, when in fact very often they have no basis in reality or fact.

SEQ: How much do you think serendipity plays into it? Place, timing, all of that?

Fields: I think it's actually a lot more than most people give credit for. I'm not somebody that says luck is all about planning. I wish it was. That means you also have to take the negative with the positive, and all the horrible things, and take ownership. I think you do have to take ownership of a huge amount of your success. I also think serendipity can touch down in ways that are completely unforeseen and foreseeable. Your job is to simply be open to the notion that can happen.

GETTING READY . . .

The X-Factors are incredibly powerful yet intangible elements in the Startup Equation. While not every person has all the elements required to lead, we're certain you possess at least some of them. You wouldn't be an entrepreneur without them.

To ensure you have reviewed your X-Factor capabilities, make sure you complete the exercises we went through in this chapter:

- The Resilience Builder
- Finding Your Curiosity Quotient
- Getting a Startup State of Mind
- Enabling Serendipity

As we wrap up these equation elements, we are left with a big question: What is a great startup? It is yours, of course. In the next section, we bring everything together and help you finalize your unique startup equation.

You ready to build your own Startup Equation? Let's go . . .

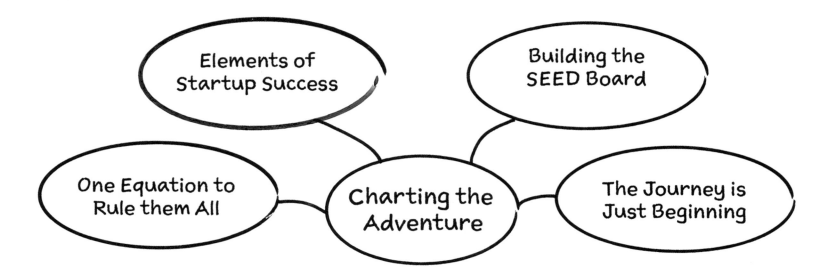

We've reached an exciting point in your startup journey. For seventeen chapters, we've been building to this moment. You've gotten a healthy dose of practical advice, plenty of stories from successful entrepreneurs, and knowledge about the nuts and bolts of starting a business. It's time to begin mapping your startup's course into the unknown. We think of it as "Choose Your Adventure—The Entrepreneur Edition."

Our journey started with the future of entrepreneurship, followed by an introduction to startup cities and the six forces igniting the new Industrial Revolution. From there, we explored the phases of building, crafting, and growing your business that culminated with the Startup Equation. It captures the essential functions and elements essential to building a successful startup.

In the chapter ahead you will review the Startup Equation and all of the elements. We will introduce the heart of this book, the Startup Equation Elements Design, or SEED, Board. This includes an overview that takes you through completing the SEED Board step-by-step. As part of this, you need to complete the exercises in each of the equation chapters. Once we are done walking you through the use of the SEED Board we will mention some examples of startups where the SEED Board can be applied. We also provide you with a blank version you can copy and draft many versions of as you go forward. As a result of completing the SEED Board you'll end up with a personalized Startup Equation that fits your chosen startup adventure.

Remember that going on an adventure should be a discovery, and like most adventures, you often don't know you're living one until you're right in the middle of it.

So let's go!!

SECTION

CHARTING
THE ADVENTURE

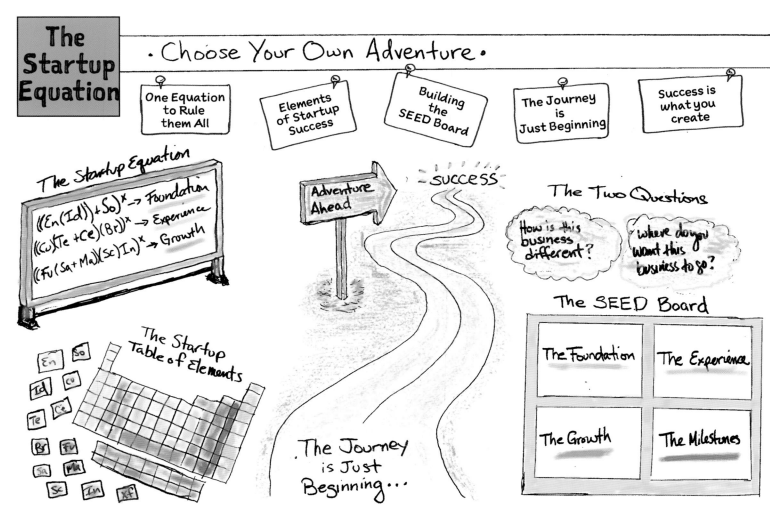

CHAPTER 18

Do not follow where the path may lead.

Go instead where there is no path and leave a trail.

—*Jonathan Swift*

Choose Your Own Adventure

rowing up, Steve consumed books at a steady clip with weekly visits to the library. For a stretch of time, his favorite books were the young adult "Choose Your Own Adventure" novels. Usually a mystery or suspense story, these books pulled readers in and let them guide the story's direction with choices. Based on your choice (e.g., "go out the door and run" or "turn and fight"), the reader would then turn to the directed page to continue the story.

It wasn't unusual for a choice to lead to a spectacular death by misadventure. However, if you chose the right path, the story continued towards a "happy" ending. In many cases you would reach a certain ending and start reading all of the pages to figure out the ending. If only life was like that. But overall, readers were active participants. And it's from these books that we drew our inspiration for this book.

The core message of this book is that your startup is your adventure. There are many choices to make. Some will lead you to mistakes and failures that you will learn from while others will take you down the path of success. And while ultimately the choices you make are up to you, we hope that by leveraging the Startup Equation you will have more knowledge and better understanding, so that when you are presented with different choices this book will help you create the startup and ultimately the business you have always dreamed of having.

Are you ready to embark on this final chapter and begin your journey? Awesome. Let's get started . . .

ONE EQUATION TO RULE THEM ALL

Yes, you've got an idea for a business. Some of us have lots of them. But it's not easy to separate the good from the bad or see the best path forward to turn the good into a real business. Regardless of their success, every entrepreneur we talked to wished they could execute better and feel more confident about the path their startup should take. They also expressed frustration about how hard it is to pull together everything they needed to learn to build their startup.

These insights made us look hard at the traditional flow and structure of how startups are built, operated, and grown into healthy operating companies. We started to see repeatable patterns:

- The kinds of startups
- How products and experiences were built
- How teams were assembled
- Sales and marketing tactics
- The scaling and innovation required to sustain growth

These patterns formed the structure for the Startup Equation.

Building the Foundation

The foundational elements in this portion of the equation are the bedrock of any startup ((Entrepreneur x Idea) + Solution). Too often, we heard stories about entrepreneurs with great ideas who stumbled early on because they didn't address these elements at the start.

To make the most of your idea, you need to understand who you are, what skills you bring to the table, and why you want to start a business (**Entrepreneur (En)**). Then, you multiply that with the concept or vision you have for the business (**Idea (Id)**). Together they're combined and applied to how you will actually build your startup (**Solution (So)**).

Crafting the Experience

A business is only as good as the experience. This rule applies to both employees and customers. In this part of the equation (((Culture + Team) x Customer Experience) x Brand), we look for answers that will help you craft the experience that you want people to have when they choose your business. First, look inward to who should be a part of a startup's core and extended **Team (Te)**. It's then time to build the company **Culture (Cu)**

The Startup Equation

$$((En(Id))+So)^x+((Cu(Te+Ce))Br)^x+(((Fn(Sa+Ma))Sc)In)^x$$

Foundation   Experience   Growth

through various core and additive elements followed by an exploration of what makes a great **Customer Experience (Ce)** through various programs and testing elements. All of this is multiplied, or rather amplified, by building a stellar **Brand (Br)** experience that leverages the identity and senses elements that communicate the experience customers and employees should expect from your startup.

Growing the Dream

A successful business only has value if you've built something that can survive without you for stretches of time. The part of the equation $(((Funding \times (Marketing + Sales)) \times Scaling) \times Continuous\ Innovation)) \times The\ X\text{-}Factors)$ focuses on finding answers that will help you grow and scale your startup. It starts with the core and model **Funding (Fn)** elements available to startups based on goals and size.

We then look to more operational functions with **Marketing (Ma)** programs and channels to attract customers and, by connection, **Sales (Sa)** channels and campaigns to close and retain them. Those elements are then multiplied by core and measurement **Scaling (Sc)** elements. In turn all are multiplied by the method and engine elements that underpin continuous **Innovation (In)**. Finally, the entire equation for all of the functions is amplified by our "eXponent" or **X-Factors (Xf)** through the core and additive elements that drive a startup to success.

We recognize that the equation is not a silver bullet for every startup issue. But many of the entrepreneurs we interviewed and studied made it clear there should be a better way to learn startup best practices and how to apply the knowledge gained from failing. They would say, "There are all these business concepts, but it's hard to know how to apply them." Based on this feedback and observation, we consider the equation key to a much larger framework that entrepreneurs of all kinds could leverage.

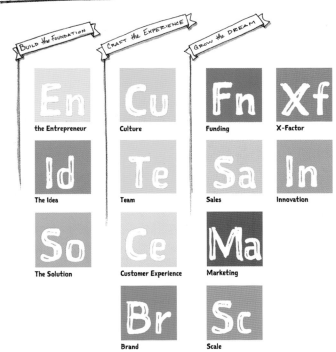

- THE ELEMENTS

BUILD the FOUNDATION   CRAFT the EXPERIENCE   GROW the DREAM

En the Entrepreneur
Cu Culture
Fn Funding
Xf X-Factor

Id The Idea
Te Team
Sa Sales
In Innovation

So The Solution
Ce Customer Experience
Ma Marketing

Br Brand
Sc Scale

THE ELEMENTS OF STARTUP SUCCESS

When we reviewed all the elements needed for the Startup Equation, it was clear that we needed a structure that would let you see all the elements in one place and their relationship to each other. The result: our Periodic Table of Startup Elements. We've grouped elements using distinct colors and their respective relationship to the major functions in the equation (e.g., En, Te, Cu). The use of a Table of Elements in modern science is used as part of a structure of basic laboratory techniques, theory, terminology, and the experimental method. As we dive into applying the elements we will also incorporate concepts such as activating agents and special mixes to frame and focus your use of *The Startup Equation* and the Startup Periodic Table of Elements.

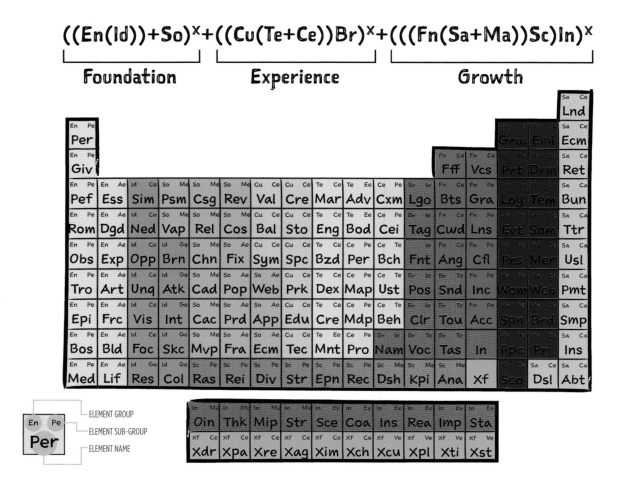

$$((En(Id))+So)^X+((Cu(Te+Ce))Br)^X+(((Fn(Sa+Ma))Sc)In)^X$$

Foundation   Experience   Growth

FOUNDATION ELEMENTS

En ENTREPRENEUR (EN)

ENTREPRENEUR PERSONALITY TYPE ELEMENTS
The Perfectionist (Per)
The Giver (Giv)
The Performer (Pef)
The Romantic (Rom)
The Observer (Obs)
The Trooper (Tro)
The Epicure (Epi)
The Boss (Bos)
The Mediator (Med)

ENTREPRENEUR APPROACH ELEMENTS
The Essentialist (Ess)
The Do Gooder (Dgd)
The Expert (Exp)
The Artist (Art)
The Franchisee (Frc)
The Builder (Bld)
The Lifestyle (Lif)

Id IDEA (ID)

IDEA CORE ELEMENTS
Simplicity (Sim)
Need (Ned)
Opportunity (Opp)
Uniqueness (Unq)
Vision (Vis)
Focus (Foc)

IDEA GENERATION ELEMENTS
Research (Res)
Brainstorming (Brn)
Attack Solution (Atk)
Intersections (Int)
Sketching (Skc)
Collaboration (Col)

So SOLUTION (SO)

SOLUTION MODEL ELEMENTS
Key Problem, Solution and
  Metrics (Psm)
Value Proposition (Vap)
Customer Segmentation (Csg)
Customer Relationships (Rel)
Solution Channels (Chn)
Competitive Advantage (Cad)
Customer Acquisition Cost (Cac)
Minimum Viable Product (Mvp)
Revenue/Profit Model (Rev)

SOLUTION APPROACH ELEMENTS
Fixed Space (Fix)
Pop-Up/Mobile Space (Pop)
Physical Product (Prd)
Franchises (Fra)
Online Presence (Web)
Mobile App (App)
E-Commerce (Ecm)

EXPERIENCE ELEMENTS

Cu CULTURE (CU)

CORE CULTURE ELEMENTS
Values (Val)
Balance (Bal)
Symbols (Sym)
Creativity (Cre)
Stories (Sto)

ADDITIVE CULTURE ELEMENTS
Spaces (Spc)
Perks (Prk)
Education (Edu)
Technology (Tec)

Te TEAM (TE)

CORE TEAM ELEMENTS
The Marketer (Mar)
The Technical
  Engineer/Hacker (Eng)
The Biz Developer or Hustler (Bzd)
The Domain Expert (Dex)
The Creative or Designer (Cre)

EXTENDED TEAM ELEMENTS
The Mentors (Mnt)
The Advisory Board (Adv)
The Board of Directors (Bod)

Ce CUSTOMER EXPERIENCE (CE)

CUSTOMER EXPERIENCE PROGRAM ELEMENTS
Customer Experience Personas (Per)
Customer Journey Map (Map)
Customer Experience Design and
  Prototyping (Pro)
Customer Experience
  Management (Cem)
Customer Experience Insights (Cei)

CUSTOMER EXPERIENCE TESTING ELEMENTS
Benchmarking (Bch)
Usability Testing (Ust)
Behavioral Targeting (Beh)

Br BRANDING (BR)

BRAND IDENTITY ELEMENTS
Name (Nam)
Logo (Lgo)
Tagline (Tag)
Font (Fnt)
Positioning (Pos)
Colors (Clr)

BRAND SENSES TESTING ELEMENTS
Voice (Voc)
Sounds (Snd)
Touch (Tou)
Taste/Smell (Tas)

GROWTH ELEMENTS

Fn FUNDING (FN)

FUNDING CLUSTER ELEMENTS
Friends/Family (Fff)
Crowdfunding (Cwd)
Angels (Ang)
Venture Capital (Vcs)

FUNDING PROGRAM ELEMENTS
Grants (Gra)
Loans/Microloans (Lns)
Cash Flow (Cfl)
Accelerators (Acc)
Incubators (Inc)

Sa SALES MIX (SA)

SALES CHANNEL ELEMENTS
Direct Sales (Dsl)
Landing Pages (Lnd)
E-Commerce (Ecm)
Retail (Ret)

SALES CAMPAIGN ELEMENTS
Bundling (Bun)
Test Trial (Ttr)
Upselling (Usl)
Promotions (Pmt)
Samples (Smp)
Inside Sales (Ins)
A/B Testing (Abt)

Ma MARKETING MIX (MA)

MARKETING PROGRAM ELEMENTS
Growth Hacking (Grw)
Partners (Ptr)
Loyalty Programs (Loy)
Events (Evt)
PR (Prs)
Word of Mouth (Wom)
Sponsorship (Spn)
PPC (Ppc)

MARKETING CHANNEL ELEMENTS
SEO (Seo)
Email (Eml)
Direct Mail (Drm)
Telemarketing (Tem)
Social Media (Som)
Merchandising (Mer)
Website (Web)
TV/Radio Broadcast (Brd)
Print (Pri)

Sc SCALE (SC)

SCALE PROGRAM ELEMENTS
Risk Assessment (Ras)
Reinvestment (Rei)
Diversification (Div)
Streamline (Str)
Expansion (Epn)
Recruit (Rec)

SCALE MEASURE ELEMENTS
Dashboards (Dsh)
KPIs (Kpi)
Analytics (Ana)

Xf X-FACTORS (XF)

X-FACTOR CONSTANT ELEMENTS
Drive (Xdr)
Passion (Xpa)
Resilience (Xre)
Agility (Xag)
Imagination (Xim)
Charisma (Xch)

X-FACTOR VARIABLE ELEMENTS
Curiosity (Xcu)
Place (Xpl)
Timing (Xti)
State of Mind (Xst)

In CONTINUOUS INNOVATION (IN)

INNOVATION METHOD ELEMENTS
Open Innovation (Oin)
Design Thinking (Thk)
Managed Innovation Process (Mip)
Strategic Foresight (Str)

INNOVATION ENGINE ELEMENTS
Scenario Planning (Sce)
Corporate Assets (Coa)
Customer Insight (Ins)
Organizational Readiness (Rea)
Disciplined Implementation (Imp)
Strategic Alignment (Sta)

• THE ELEMENTS

BUILD the FOUNDATION · CRAFT the EXPERIENCE · GROW the DREAM

En the Entrepreneur	Cu Culture	Fn Funding
Id The Idea	Te Team	Sa Sales
So The Solution	Ce Customer Experience	Ma Marketing
Br Brand		Sc Scale
		Xf X-Factor
		In Innovation

TWO QUESTIONS YOU MUST ASK

When building your startup, there are two vital questions that you must ask yourself:

- How is this startup different?
- How do I want this business to grow?

If you're just like everyone else, it's all but impossible for you to build a business. However, by focusing on finding opportunities untapped by others, you'll discover your path to startup success. These opportunities can manifest themselves in a few ways, including:

- The way you do business
- The creation of a new market segment
- The creation of a market ecosystem

By allowing yourself to explore ways to be different, you can discover where the true opportunity lies.

The answer to the second question doesn't always come as easily because people and startups change. However, as the founder, you set the direction of the ship. Even if you can only forecast the next three years, it will provide you with the ability to look at your business from a macro level and assess potential ways to scale it.

As you consider how to grow, here are some additional issues you'll want to address:

- As we scale, what is the one thing that cannot change about the business?
- How can we get our team involved in the process?
- What milestones do we want to hit 1–3 years from now?

Scaling remains an exercise in flexibility for a startup. Many variables can change your scaling strategy. However, if you know where you want to go and keep your company focused, it becomes much easier to find the right way to scale.

1 QUESTION 1: HOW IS THIS STARTUP DIFFERENT?

You have this amazing idea for your startup, but really why is it different? Differentiation is key to really evaluating your business's potential to create barriers of entry for competitors. Most likely you have competitors in some shape or form, so you will need to address how you are different from them and why your business stands out.

2 QUESTION 2: WHERE DO I WANT THIS BUSINESS TO GO?

So what type of business do you want to build? There are many valid approaches for different people. The other big question you need to ask is where you want the business to go. This will impact what kind of team you build, if you need funding, how/if you scale, etc.

THE SEED BOARD—WHERE THE RUBBER HITS THE ROAD

We've spent this entire book taking you through a journey of new ideas, new concepts, and an equation to frame your startup with the necessary elements to power it. To help you get a true sense of the scope of what you have learned and can apply to your startup, on the following page we introduce what we call the SEED Board. The SEED Board stands for "Startup Equation Elements Design" or SEED for short. This board is where the Startup Equation comes together to help you map out your startup. You SHOULD use this AFTER you have finished the exercises in the respective chapters but you can try and do it without that preparation. It just might require more time. Let's explore the high-level parts of the SEED Board and what you will be reviewing on the next few pages.

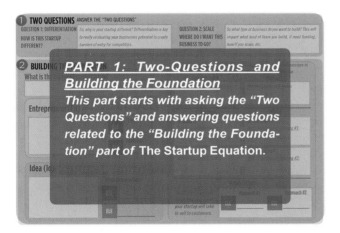

PART 1: Two-Questions and Building the Foundation
This part starts with asking the "Two Questions" and answering questions related to the "Building the Foundation" part of The Startup Equation.

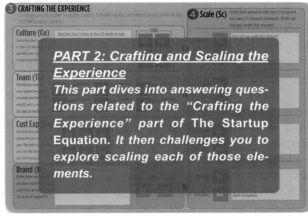

PART 2: Crafting and Scaling the Experience
This part dives into answering questions related to the "Crafting the Experience" part of The Startup Equation. It then challenges you to explore scaling each of those elements.

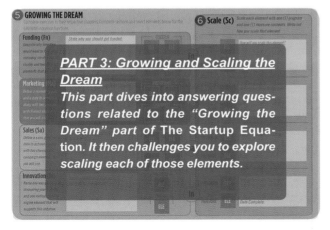

PART 3: Growing and Scaling the Dream
This part dives into answering questions related to the "Growing the Dream" part of The Startup Equation. It then challenges you to explore scaling each of those elements.

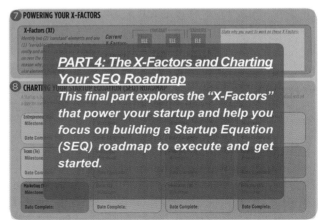

PART 4: The X-Factors and Charting Your SEQ Roadmap
This final part explores the "X-Factors" that power your startup and help you focus on building a Startup Equation (SEQ) roadmap to execute and get started.

STEP 1: Answering The Two Questions

Since we just covered the topic of "The Two Questions," they should be fresh in your mind. Before you dive into using the elements, test your choices based on the answers you've discovered about what makes your startup different and how you want to build it.

TWO QUESTIONS ANSWER THE "TWO QUESTIONS"

QUESTION 1: DIFFERENTIATION
HOW IS THIS STARTUP DIFFERENT?

Why is your startup different? Differentiation is key to really evaluating your business's potential to create barriers of entry for competitors.

QUESTION 2: SCALE
WHERE DO I WANT THIS BUSINESS TO GO?

What type of business do you want to build? This will impact what kind of team you build, if you need funding, how/if you scale, etc.

STEP 2: Building the Foundation

Whats the Name of your Startup?

There is so much in a name. And it may change but you should have a name for your startup. So write that in the space provided.

What Makes You Unique as an Entrepreneur (En)?

Becoming an entrepreneur starts with knowing yourself and what you really want out of building a business. As we get to our first element you are asked to write out how you are unique and contribute to your success as an entrepreneur. You also must select an **Entrepreneur (En)** element from the Type and Approach sub-groups. To help you with this, complete the exercises in Chapter 5 like "Discover Your Personal Entrepreneurship Approach and Type."

So What's Your Big Idea (Id)?

Ideas are fleeting unless we decide to make them a reality. In the **Idea (Id)** element section you will write out your business idea and identify two idea "Generations" you used or will use to work through and refine your idea. To help you with this, complete the exercises in Chapter 6 like "Fine Tuning Your Idea" and "Unique Snowflake."

What is the name of your startup?

e.g., INSERT AWESOME NAME HERE

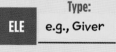

Entrepreneur (En) Write out what makes you unique as an entrepreneur then select the 'Type' and 'Approach' element you are and write them below.

This is about how you are unique that contibutes to your success as an entrepreneur with this startup

Type:
ELE e.g., Giver

Approach:
ELE e.g., Expert

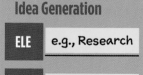

Idea (Id) Write out your business idea and identify two idea 'Generation' elements you will use below.

Idea Generation

Insert Awesome Idea Here.

ELE e.g., Research

ELE e.g., Sketching

STEP 2: Building the Foundation (Cont.)

Define and Refine Your Solution (So)

At this point in your startup journey, you probably have a good idea of what you want your business to be and how it might be different and valuable. Completing the following exercises in Chapter 7 will help with answering the questions in this part of the SEED Board.

- Forming Your Mission
- Craft Your Own BASE Board
- Identifying Your Business Approach and Structure
- Create Your First Financial Model
- Creating Your MVP

Understand the Opportunity and Market

In order to focus on the right solution, you must understand the opportunity. In this section you will fill in the spaces with a short description of the opportunity you are looking to address. This is the reason you are doing this startup and is a driving factor. You will also fill in the markets or customer segments you will serve.

Offerings and MVPs

In this section you will write out one or two products and/or services that your startup will offer customers. In order to get something launched you will need to create an MVP and you should write a short description of that MVP in order to get customer traction.

Approaches

In order to sell your product to customers you will need to decide on the approaches you will use. This includes approaches like **Fixed Retail (Fix)**, **Pop-up/Mobile Retail (Pop)**, **Physical Product (Prd)**, **Online Presence (Web)**, **Mobile App (App)**, **E-commerce (Ecm)**, and **Franchise (Fra)**.

Once you are done with this part of the SEED Board, you will have completed the "Building the Foundation" component. Now let's move onto the next step, "Crafting the Experience".

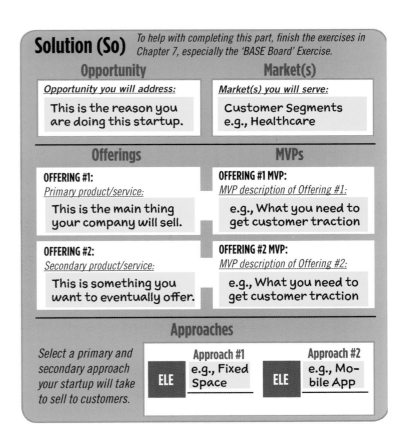

STEP 3: Crafting the Experience

Now that you have begun to build the foundation, you need to think about how to craft an amazing experience. You will note that in this group there are four primary functions—**Customer Experience (Ce)**, **Team (Te)**, **Culture (Cu)** and **Brand (Br)**. These elements explore how it is not just important to build a product and put it out there but to craft an experience within the company and the way customers perceive and experience the company too.

Building a Culture (Cu) of WOW

Building a Culture of WOW doesn't happen by accident. It takes commitment to build something greater. Here you will need to describe your culture in four (4) words or less. This is the mantra that defines your culture. You will also select two core and two additive culture elements that support your culture priorities. To help you with this, complete the exercises in Chapter 8 like "Setting Your Core Values" and "Crafting Your Startup Culture."

Rewards of Great Teams (Te)

Great teams can transform your company. However, from the founding team to scaling up, it's critical to find the right mix. Here you will identify your minimum viable team now and who is needed in six months. To help you with this, complete the exercises in Chapter 8 like "Which Member of the Startup Team Are You?" and "Design Your Minimum Viable Team or MVT."

Creating Great Customer Experiences (Ce)

Going beyond an MVP you need to craft a stellar customer experience. You must identify the program elements to work on and the benchmarks you will measure (analytics, SUS scores). To help you with this, complete the exercises in Chapter 10 like "Prototype Your Minimum Delightful Product" among many others.

The New Brand (Br) Order

Brand is about identity and differentation. Here you will write out your brand position statement and select elements in the Senses sub-group to focus on over the next six months. To help you with this, complete the exercises in Chapter 11 like "Draft Basic Brand Positioning" among others.

CRAFTING THE EXPERIENCE

Complete exercises in their respective chapters. Complete sections and select elements below for the CRAFTING equation functions.

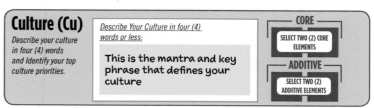

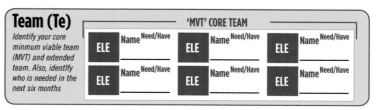

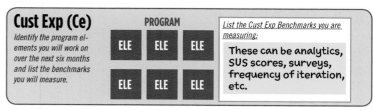

STEP 5: Growing the Dream

In this phase, Growing the Dream, we focus on finding answers that will help you grow and scale your startup. We begin with **Funding (Fn)** and then discuss more operational functions with **Marketing (Ma)** and **Sales (Sa)**. We then discuss **Innovation (In)** within your startup.

No Funding (Fn), No Excuses

You will need funding to build your business and you should state your differentiation and why you should get funded. You also need to select two elements from the cluster and program element sub-groups to support your funding efforts. To help you with this, complete the exercises in Chapter 12 like "Select Funding Strategies that Fit Your Startup".

Startup Marketing (Ma) Alchemy

To focus your efforts on crafting a marketing program that will bring customers into the funnel use the SEED to define one marketing goal and a date to achieve it. Also select two program and two channel elements to utilize. Also, complete the exercises in Chapter 13 like "Building Your Marketing Strategy Mix" in addition to many others.

The ROI of Happy Customers

To focus your efforts on building a sales engine that goes beyond initial customers, use the SEED board to define one sales goal and a date to achieve it. Also select two challenge and two program elements you will utilize. Also complete exercises in Chapter 14 like "Design Your Initial Sales Campaign" in addition to many others.

Always Be Innovating (In)

Making continuous innovation integral to your startup is an ongoing process. Use the SEED board to name one way you plan on innovating and a method and engine element you will use to execute on. Also complete the exercises in Chapter 16 like "Leverage the SMART Innovation Method" among the many others.

GROWING THE DREAM

Complete exercises in their respective chapters. Complete sections and select elements below for the GROWING equation functions.

Funding (Fn)
Describe why investors would want to fund your company. identify two (2) cluster and two (2) program elements that you will use.

State why you should get funded:

This is about real differentiation and why investors want to invest in you and your company.

CLUSTER — SELECT TWO (2) CLUSTER ELEMENTS

PROGRAM — SELECT TWO (2) CLUSTER ELEMENTS

Marketing (Ma)
Define a marketing goal and a date to achieve it along with two program and channel elements that you will use.

Define one marketing goal and a date to achieve it by:

Focus on a goal that brings customers into the funnel and ready to buy.

PROGRAMS — SELECT TWO (2) PROGRAM ELEMENTS

CHANNELS — SELECT TWO (2) CHANNEL ELEMENTS

Sales (Sa)
Define a sales goal and a date to achieve it along with two channel and campaign elements that you will use.

Define one sales goal and a date to achieve it by:

Consider how you will sell and convert the prospect into a customer.

CHANNEL — SELECT TWO (2) CHANNEL ELEMENTS

CAMPAIGNS — SELECT TWO (2) CAMPAIGN ELEMENTS

Innovation (In)
Name one way you plan on innovating your industry and one method and one engine element that will support this initiative.

Name one way you plan on innovating your industry:

This goes back to differentiation but continuing to stay ahead of the game.

METHOD — SELECT AN ENGINE ELEMENT

ENGINE — SELECT AN ENGINE ELEMENT

STEPS 4 & 6: Scaling (Sc) the Business

In the full SEED Board you will see Step 3 (Crafting the Experience) and Step 5 (Growing the Dream) have right side columns that are presented below. These are Steps 4 and 6, respectively, and extend the indvidual Startup Equation functions into the strategy of how you will scale each one.

On the SEED Board you will complete instructions for the the respective function (e.g., Culture) first and then you will write in the box how you will scale that startup function along with a date to complete it. You will also select a **Scale (Sc)** Program and Measure element. We highly recommend you review Chapter 15 and complete all of the exercises.

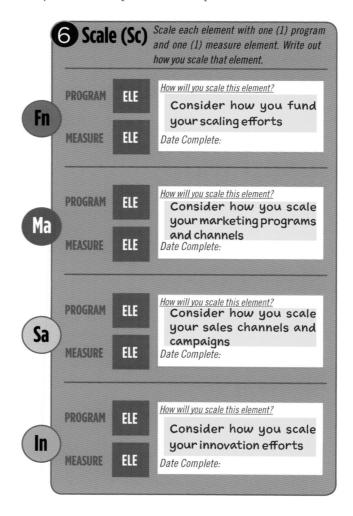

4 Scale (Sc) *Scale each element with one (1) program and one (1) measure element. Write out how you scale that element.*

Cu
- PROGRAM ELE
- MEASURE ELE

How will you scale this element?
Consider how you scale your startup culture
Date Complete:

Te
- PROGRAM ELE
- MEASURE ELE

How will you scale this element?
Consider how you scale a team
Date Complete:

Ce
- PROGRAM ELE
- MEASURE ELE

How will you scale this element?
Consider how you scale customer experience
Date Complete:

Br
- PROGRAM ELE
- MEASURE ELE

How will you scale this element?
Consider how you scale a brand
Date Complete:

6 Scale (Sc) *Scale each element with one (1) program and one (1) measure element. Write out how you scale that element.*

Fn
- PROGRAM ELE
- MEASURE ELE

How will you scale this element?
Consider how you fund your scaling efforts
Date Complete:

Ma
- PROGRAM ELE
- MEASURE ELE

How will you scale this element?
Consider how you scale your marketing programs and channels
Date Complete:

Sa
- PROGRAM ELE
- MEASURE ELE

How will you scale this element?
Consider how you scale your sales channels and campaigns
Date Complete:

In
- PROGRAM ELE
- MEASURE ELE

How will you scale this element?
Consider how you scale your innovation efforts
Date Complete:

STEP 7: Powering the X-factor (Xf)

The X-Factors are an incredibly powerful, yet intangible, function of the Startup Equation. These are those things that successful entpreneurs possess but you can't really quantify. While no person has all the elements, we're certain you possess at least some of them. We firmly believe you have it within you to also develop more of them, but it takes focus.

In the section below you will identify two constant and one variable X-Factor elements that you currently have and two constant and one variable you will work on. You will also state why you will work on those specifically. Also, we recommend completing the exercises in Chapter 17 such as "Getting a Startup State of Mind," "Finding Your Curiosity Quotient" among others.

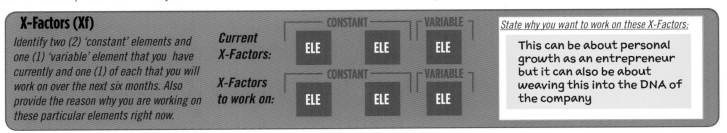

STEP 8: Charting your Startup Equation (SEQ) Roadmap

At this point in the SEED Board you have reached Step 8, which is about commitment and execution. The intent here is to lay out a roadmap. Review each of the steps of the SEED board that you filled out with various descriptions and goals. For each function of the equation you will identify a milestone that is achievable within the next six months. The point here is focus and execution. There might be many milestones but the one that is top of the list or most important you should list here along with a date to complete the milestone. This also makes the SEED Board a living strategy map that you can do often and update to track your progress but also to set new goals and milestones as your startup grows into a full-fledged business.

Now that you have had a chance to see the SEED Board broken down in its components and explained, you might be wondering how this might be applied in various scenarios. To get your brain moving we have come up with eight foundation "plays" that leverage the SEED Board. Please visit TheStartupEquation.com to see how the SEED Board is used in these.

EXCHANGE (BROKERAGE/MARKETPLACE)

This type of play is a startup that utilizes a digital commerce platform as its primary strategy. The products sold can be almost anything and it utilizes existing distribution channels and technologies to focus on their market and differentiators. An example could be a startup that links small, product retailers to a global marketspace with a focus on home and office consumer goods that have a personalized touch. The startup leverages emerging talent across the web and offers a market space for their work.

DISTRBUTOR GOODS & SVCS

This type of play is a startup with a brick-and-mortar storefront that sells direct to consumers. The differentiator to this startup play is the collaborative work with product and manufacturing firms to develop and market a range of goods each quarter. An example of a startup using this model could be offering a mix of seasonal styles from chic to modern that is still affordable at a variety of price ranges. This is through establishing ties with a variety of different manufacturers and established storefronts.

THE FRANCHISEE

This type of play is an entrepreneur who is skilled at running businesses but doesn't want to create their own from scratch. Purchasing a franchise license to operate a business out of the box and get going quickly is appealing for its quick ramp up time but also the long-term low maintenance that fits the entprreneur lifestyle. It also allows them to expand the territory should they decide to scale further.

COLLABORATIVE CONSUMPTION

This type of startup play leverages the "Collaborative Consumption"or "Sharing Economy" trend. It could be any number of business categories where consumers are interested in leveraging temporary items and not willing to purchase things outright because they don't need access to it all the time. An example of this could be a rideshare service. These are popular because more consumers are not interested in auto ownership but still need a method of getting around that is not a taxi or public transit. This startup is designed to connect those who need a temporary vehicle for a limited time to those who own and are willing to rent through its mobile app platform.

COLLABORATIVE CREATION

This play is a startup that leverages its community and crowd to utilize the "Collaborative Creation" process. In a specific example, it could be a gaming company that has created a cross-platform gaming experience. It uses an open innovation approach to allow for its gaming engine to be experimented and tested upon for new applications and used by other companies as a means for exploration. This type of innovation model when used as core to a startup is a powerful approach and differentiaor.

RAZORS + BLADES

This startup play is an old business model with a new twist. Anyone who has bought a good razor knows that the razor is the giveaway. The money is in the blades that you need to buy every few months. This startup is not literally selling razors and blades but it operates by providing the core of their technology at a one-time purchase fee and sells the replaceablle items at a significant discount to consumers. By leveraging digital channels or subscription services the scalability of this business model is huge.

PHYSICAL PRODUCT

A startup play of this type is about leveraging the New Industrial Revolution technologies to build something that doesn't exist and will make a strong impact on the marketplace. Startups like this are about the physical design and range from consumer wearables to medical devices among many other topics.The biggest thing about this type of startup is it is very capital intensive but can leverage rapid prototyping technologies and digital storefronts to have global reach with a continuous innovation path.

PROFESSIONAL SERVICES

This type of startup play is a company that is usually built based on a entrepreneur's background and extensive experience. In many cases they are launched out of necessity and scaled for opportunity. For example, it could be a firm that focuses on providing strategic business and design consulting for several Fortune 500 companies that want to enter new markets. They could have a differentiator of a collaborative network of freelancers and consultants for assembling dynamic teams to address any situation. This could be someone looking to create a lifestyle company or a large firm.

BUILD YOUR OWN SEED BOARD

Preparing for the Adventure

We have just spent the time in this chapter walking through the use of the SEED Board and reviewing the results of the element exercises (complete any you skipped), the Startup Equation Elements Design, and the SEED Board. To prepare you for your startup adventure, we've provided on the following pages a blank SEED Board for you to design your own Startup Equation.

Take it a section at a time and fill in the board in the order that it appears. As a quick recap from the previous SEED Board overview, to help you better understand the different phases of the startup life: you must answer the two questions before you can fill out anything else on the board. Why? Those two questions set the stage for the business you are building. Then, afterwards, move onto Part #2, Building the Foundation. This will give you insights into your strengths (**Entrepreneur (En)**), then help you capture the vision for your startup (**Idea (Id)**). Taking these elements into account leads to a better idea of how you'll actually build your startup (**Solution (So)**).

Next you will move to Part #3 to address how you want people to view and experience your company (Craft the Experience). It requires a hard look at your startup's **Team (Te)** and what company **Culture (Cu)** you want to promote. With these elements as a baseline, we explored what makes a great **Customer Experience (Ce)**, which creates the foundation for building a stellar **Brand (Br)** experience.

You will then look at Part #4 on how to scale your startup for success (Grow the Dream) and maintain that momentum. It means dealing with operational functions like **Marketing (Ma)** and **Sales (Sa)** by applying various **Scaling (Sc)** techniques along with how to support continuous **Innovation (In)**. Finally, we looked at the intangible (eXponent) or **X-Factors (Xf)** which underlie and amplify everything required to chart the best course for your startup journey.

If you find yourself in need of guidance within a section, then refer back to that section and its exercises. They are there to help you figure out the answers to these questions and the elements you need for your startup equation.

It is important to note that just like your business, your SEED Board will organically change over time. That's great. Feel free to revisit this board as frequently as you need to. It is here for you (just as the book is) when you need it.

Now You Are Ready to Begin the Adventure

We've reached an exciting point in your startup journey. It's time to choose your own adventure and build your very own Startup Equation. Now you are ready to walk through the use of the SEED Board. As a result you'll end up with a personalized Startup Equation that fits your chosen adventure.

Now it is time for you to build your own SEED Board.

Remember that going on an adventure should be a discovery, and like most adventures, you often don't know you're living one until you're right in the middle of it.

NOW IT'S YOUR TURN, SO GET STARTED!

BUILD YOUR SEED BOARD: PART 1 – TWO QUESTIONS & BUILDING THE FOUNDATION

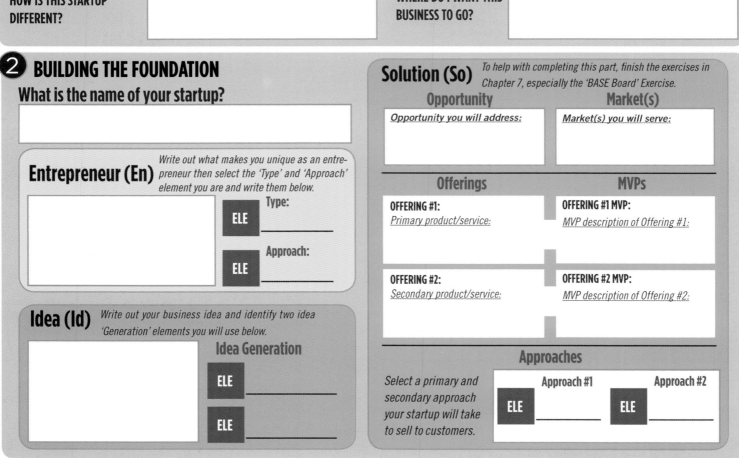

① TWO QUESTIONS ANSWER THE "TWO QUESTIONS"

QUESTION 1: DIFFERENTIATION

HOW IS THIS STARTUP DIFFERENT?

QUESTION 2: SCALE

WHERE DO I WANT THIS BUSINESS TO GO?

② BUILDING THE FOUNDATION

What is the name of your startup?

Entrepreneur (En) Write out what makes you unique as an entrepreneur then select the 'Type' and 'Approach' element you are and write them below.

ELE Type:

ELE Approach:

Idea (Id) Write out your business idea and identify two idea 'Generation' elements you will use below.

Idea Generation

ELE

ELE

Solution (So) To help with completing this part, finish the exercises in Chapter 7, especially the 'BASE Board' Exercise.

Opportunity

Opportunity you will address:

Market(s)

Market(s) you will serve:

Offerings

OFFERING #1:
Primary product/service:

OFFERING #2:
Secondary product/service:

MVPs

OFFERING #1 MVP:
MVP description of Offering #1:

OFFERING #2 MVP:
MVP description of Offering #2:

Approaches

Select a primary and secondary approach your startup will take to sell to customers.

ELE Approach #1

ELE Approach #2

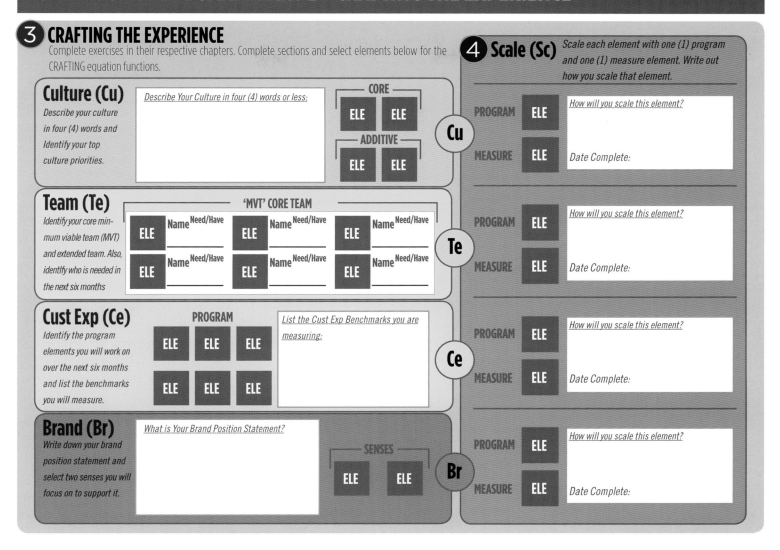

3 CRAFTING THE EXPERIENCE

Complete exercises in their respective chapters. Complete sections and select elements below for the CRAFTING equation functions.

Culture (Cu)

Describe your culture in four (4) words and Identify your top culture priorities.

Describe Your Culture in four (4) words or less:

CORE
ELE ELE

ADDITIVE
ELE ELE

Cu

Team (Te)

Identify your core minimum viable team (MVT) and extended team. Also, identify who is needed in the next six months

'MVT' CORE TEAM

ELE Name ___ Need/Have
ELE Name ___ Need/Have
ELE Name ___ Need/Have
ELE Name ___ Need/Have
ELE Name ___ Need/Have
ELE Name ___ Need/Have

Te

Cust Exp (Ce)

Identify the program elements you will work on over the next six months and list the benchmarks you will measure.

PROGRAM
ELE ELE ELE
ELE ELE ELE

List the Cust Exp Benchmarks you are measuring:

Ce

Brand (Br)

Write down your brand position statement and select two senses you will focus on to support it.

What is Your Brand Position Statement?

SENSES
ELE ELE

Br

4 Scale (Sc)

Scale each element with one (1) program and one (1) measure element. Write out how you scale that element.

PROGRAM ELE   *How will you scale this element?*
MEASURE ELE   *Date Complete:*

PROGRAM ELE   *How will you scale this element?*
MEASURE ELE   *Date Complete:*

PROGRAM ELE   *How will you scale this element?*
MEASURE ELE   *Date Complete:*

PROGRAM ELE   *How will you scale this element?*
MEASURE ELE   *Date Complete:*

BUILD YOUR SEED BOARD: PART 3 – GROWING THE DREAM

❺ GROWING THE DREAM

Complete exercises in their respective chapters. Complete sections and select elements below for the GROWING equation functions.

Funding (Fn)

Describe why investors would want to fund your company. identify two (2) cluster and two (2) program elements that you will use.

State why you should get funded:

CLUSTER
ELE | ELE

PROGRAM
ELE | ELE

Fn

Marketing (Ma)

Define a marketing goal and a date to achieve it along with two program and channel elements that you will use.

Define one marketing goal and a date to achieve it by:

PROGRAMS
ELE | ELE

CHANNELS
ELE | ELE

Ma

Sales (Sa)

Define a sales goal and a date to achieve it along with two channel and campaign elements that you will use.

Define one sales goal and a date to achieve it by:

CHANNEL
ELE | ELE

CAMPAIGNS
ELE | ELE

Sa

Innovation (In)

Name one way you plan on innovating your industry and one method and one engine element that will supports this initative.

Name one way you plan on innovating your industry:

METHOD
ELE

ENGINE
ELE

In

❻ Scale (Sc)

Scale each element with one (1) program and one (1) measure element. Write out how you scale that element.

PROGRAM — ELE — *How will you scale this element?*
MEASURE — ELE — *Date Complete:*

PROGRAM — ELE — *How will you scale this element?*
MEASURE — ELE — *Date Complete:*

PROGRAM — ELE — *How will you scale this element?*
MEASURE — ELE — *Date Complete:*

PROGRAM — ELE — *How will you scale this element?*
MEASURE — ELE — *Date Complete:*

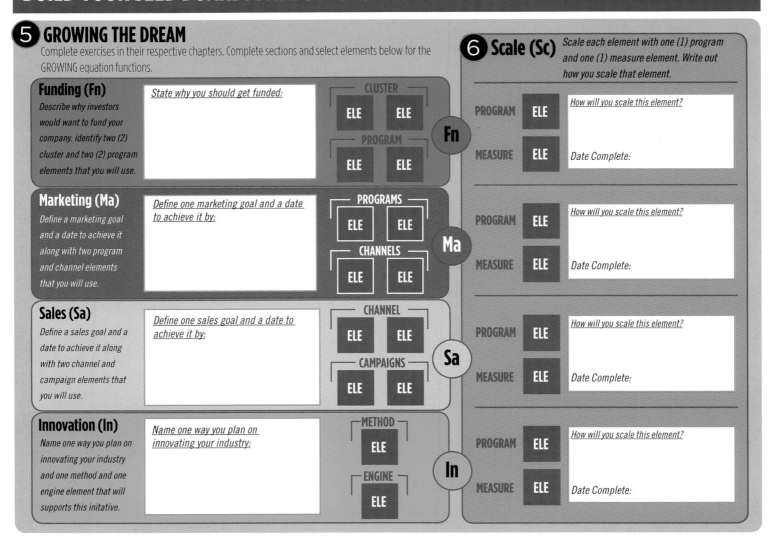

BUILD YOUR SEED BOARD: PART 4 – X-FACTORS & YOUR SEQ ROADMAP

⑦ POWERING YOUR X-FACTORS

X-Factors (Xf)

Identify two (2) 'constant' elements and one (1) 'variable' element that you have currently and one (1) of each that you will work on over the next six months. Also provide the reason why you are working on these particular elements right now.

Current X-Factors:

CONSTANT		VARIABLE
ELE	ELE	ELE

X-Factors to work on:

CONSTANT	VARIABLE
ELE	ELE

State why you want to work on these X-Factors:

⑧ CHARTING YOUR STARTUP EQUATION (SEQ) ROADMAP

A Startup is built one step at a time. Prioritize your roadmap based on urgency and importance. Select the first milestone from each element group (e.g., Marketing, Innovation) and set a date for completion. With the exception of Scale (Sc), where you have already set a milestone for that respective element group

Entrepreneur (En)
Milestone:

Date Complete:

Idea (Id)
Milestone:

Date Complete:

Solution (So)
Milestone:

Date Complete:

Customer Experience (Ce)
Milestone:

Date Complete:

Team (Te)
Milestone:

Date Complete:

Culture (Cu)
Milestone:

Date Complete:

Brand (Br)
Milestone:

Date Complete:

Funding (Fn)
Milestone:

Date Complete:

Marketing (Ma)
Milestone:

Date Complete:

Sales (Sa)
Milestone:

Date Complete:

Innovation (In)
Milestone:

Date Complete:

X-Factors (Xf)
Milestone:

Date Complete:

YOUR JOURNEY IS JUST BEGINNING

Your time is now.

Congratulations! Right now, in this very moment, you are embarking on a journey that you can barely believe to be something other than a dream. Luckily, with this book, you are not alone and you have already taken your first step toward creating something inspiring for the world to see. And it always begins with that first step.

One Billion Entrepreneurs and a New Industrial Revolution
You are one of the billion entrepreneurs in this golden age of entrepreneurship set to start a business in the next few years. In a nutshell, you are part of a new Industrial Revolution and it is entrepreneurs like you who will change and build a world that we can only imagine.

The Six Forces that Change the Game
As part of this new Industrial Revolution, there are six forces powering the opportunities that lay ahead. This includes the Liquid Workforce, the New Work Order, the Maker Movement, the Sharing Economy, the Connected Customer, and the evolved Creative Economy. More than any other time in history do you have the opportunity to create new industries, new business models and transform the world around you.

An Equation, a Table of Elements and a SEED Board
To help you along this journey we have provided you with the tools you need to begin and grow along the way. This includes, of course, the Startup Equation, which is the structural formula to build a foundation, create and experience and grow the dream that you have for your startup. Within the equation there are functions that have many elements you will leverage and we have provided the structure using the first "Periodic Table of Startup Elements". But we didn't stop there. You need to choose your own adventure. And in order to chart your own unique startup course we created two tools—the BASE (Business Approach & Structure Elements) Board which dives deep into questions you need to answer about your startup and set a good path. We also created the SEED

(Startup Equation Elements Design) Board which is the living map that will guide you along the way, and get you to where you need to go on your journey. Even if you decide to change directions, think of the BASE Board as your startup compass and the SEED Board as your startup map.

Remember, this is about the Journey and not just the Destination
Your journey will have its ups and downs but this is about the journey and not just the destination. You will have moments of doubt and moments of triumph. It is for moments like this that you are creating something great. It is moments like this that make you feel alive, feel strong, feel free. It is for these moments that you designed your own Startup Equation and for them that you are on a journey that is yours.

Success is what you create. So enjoy the journey.

Notes

Chapter 1

1. http://www.challengergray.com/press/PressRelease.aspx?PressUid=282
2. http://www.kauffman.org/research-and-policy/kauffman-index-of-entrepreneurial-activity.aspx
3. http://goldwaterinstitute.org/sites/default/files/PR254%20Increasing%20Entrepreneurship.pdf
4. Vaclav Smill, et all.
5. http://en.wikipedia.org/wiki/Post-industrial_society
6. Dunham-Jones, Ellen, "New Urbanism as a Counter-Project to Post-Industrialism," Places, vol 13.2 (2000) pgs 26-31.
7. Targ, Harry R. "Global Dominance and Dependence, Post-Industrialism and International Relations Theory." International Studies Quarterly (1976), pp 461-482.
8. Rifkin, Jeremy, *The Third Industrial Revolution, How Lateral Power is Transforming Energy, the Economy and the World*, St. Martin's Griffin, 2012.
9. Rifkin, Jeremy, *The Third Industrial Revolution, World Financial Review*, pg 10.

Chapter 2

1. ReferenceUSA, US Businesses Visual Data Summary http://0-www.reference-usa.com.library.scad.edu/UsBusiness/VisualDataSummary/Visualisation/fcd49413ab2c486da94832a63754f3fc
2. Feld, Brad, *Startup Communities*, page 25

Chapter 3

1. "The Rise of Talent Networks," Perkin, Neil, Oct 4, 2010, http://neilperkin.typepad.com/only_dead_fish/2010/10/the-rise-of-talent-networks.html
2. Global Coworking Census, Deskmag, March 3, 2013
3. Doug Palmer, Steve Lunceford and Aaron J. Patton, "The Engagement Economy: How Gamification Is Reshaping Business," Deliotte Review
4. Andrerson, Chris, "In the Next Industrial Revolution, Atoms are the New Bits," WIRED Magazine, Feb 2010.
5. http://www.kk.org/thetechnium/archives/2009/01/better_than_own.php
6. http://eur-lex.europa.eu/LexUriServ/LexUriServ.do?uri=CELEX:52012DC0537:EN:NOT
http://www.comitecolbert.com/assets/files/paragraphes/fichiers/20/Thevalueoftheculturalandcreative.PDF
7. http://www.uis.unesco.org/culture/Documents/FCS-handbook-1-economic-contribution-culture-en-web.pdf
8. http://www.mtc.gov.on.ca/en/creative_cluster/cluster_report_growth.shtml

Chapter 5

1. http://500hats.typepad.com/500blogs/2009/01/great-entrepreneurs-are-passionate-about-their-customers-products-not-about-being-great-entrepreneur.html
2. Wadhwa, Vivek, The Anatomy of an Entrepreneur, http://www.kauffman.org/what-we-do/research/2010/05/the-anatomy-of-an-entrepreneur
3. Owyang, Jeremiah, Web Strategist Blog, Four Traits of Effective Leaders, January 21, 2014, http://www.web-strategist.com/blog/2014/01/21/four-traits-of-effective-leaders/
4. http://www.amazon.com/Enneagram-Love-Work-Understanding-Relationships/dp/0062507214
5. http://www.kauffman.org/uploadedFiles/eship-ed-comes-of-age_report.pdf
6. http://www.linkedin.com/today/post/article/20121211162106-32702694-big-idea-2013-learning-fast-from-failure
7. http://www.forbes.com/sites/jmaureenhenderson/2012/12/10/meet-the-entrepreneur-who-eats-rejection-for-breakfast/

Chapter 6

1. Source: http://www.businesspundit.com/10-accidental-discoveries-that-generated-great-wealth/

Chapter 7

1. http://hbrblogs.files.wordpress.com/2013/05/canvas1.gif
2. Blagojevic, Vladimir, Ultimate Guide to Minimum Viable Products, August 2009, http://scalemybusiness.com/the-ultimate-guide-to-minimum-viable-products/
3. http://www.startuplessonslearned.com/2009/06/pivot-dont-jump-to-new-vision.html

Chapter 8

1. http://foundation.bz/25/
2. http://techcrunch.com/2012/12/19/foundation-tony-hsieh/
3. http://www.psychologytoday.com/blog/positively-media/201101/the-psychological-power-storytelling
4. http://www.adobe.com/aboutadobe/pressroom/pressreleases/201204/042312AdobeGlobalCreativityStudy.html

Chapter 9

1. Wasserman, Noam, *The Founders Dilemmas*, Figure 3.1, Pg 73
2. Frank Nouyrigat and Marc Nager, *Co-Founder Development*, October 2012, page 13
3. Frank Nouyrigat and Marc Nager, *Co-Founder Development*, October 2012, page 15
4. Frank Nouyrigat and Marc Nager, *Co-Founder Development*, October 2012, page 1
5. Frank Nouyrigat and Marc Nager, *Co-Founder Development*, October 2012, page 6
6. Cohen, David, The Mentor Manifesto, August 28, 2011, http://www.davidgcohen.com/2011/08/28/the-mentor-manifesto/
7. http://www.businessweek.com/stories/2007-10-18/directors-who-dont-deliverbusinessweek-business-news-stock-market-and-financial-advice

Chapter 10

1. http://en.wikipedia.org/wiki/Customer_experience
2. Bodine, Kerry, *Fast Company*, The 6 disciplines behind consistently great customer experiences, August 28, 2012 http://www.fastcompany.com/3000798/6-disciplines-behind-consistently-great-customer-experiences
3. https://uxmag.com/articles/using-proto-personas-for-executive-alignment
4. Stone, Dorian, McKinsey CMSO Forum, Dec 11, 2013
5. Wikipedia, Prototype
6. Wikipedia: Basic Prototype Categories
7. Sauro, Jeff, 10 Benchmarks for User Experience Metrics, Oct 16, 2012, https://www.measuringusability.com/blog/ux-benchmarks.php

Chapter 11

1. Source: http://farm4.static.flickr.com/3337/3306605711_1b9e4a807d_z.jpg and http://www.branddriveninnovation.com/2009/02/24/new-brand-relationship-model/

Chapter 12

1. Guy Kawasaki, The 10-20-30 Rule of Powerpoint, http://blog.guykawasaki.com/2005/12/the_102030_rule.html

Chapter 13

1. http://www.inc.com/guides/2010/08/get-more-sales-from-existing-customers.html
2. http://www.biakelsey.com/Company/Press-Releases/140402-Small-Business-Owners-Shift-Investment-from-Customer-Acquisition-to-Customer-Engagement.asp
3. http://www.nielsen.com/us/en/insights/reports/2012/global-trust-in-advertising-and-brand-messages.html
4. http://www.radicati.com/wp/wp-content/uploads/2013/04/Email-Statistics-Report-2013-2017-Executive-Summary.pdf

Chapter 14

1. http://www.bothsidesofthetable.com/2013/06/13/why-your-startup-needs-a-sales-methodology/
2. Pici. Michael, The 11 skills every sales startup sales job depends on to survive, Hubspot, June 19, 2014 - http://www.getsidekick.com/blog/11-skills-startup-sales
3. http://www.bothsidesofthetable.com/2010/04/08/journeymen-mavericks-superstars-understanding-salespeople-at-startups/

Chapter 15

1. http://www.forbes.com/sites/theyec/2013/06/03/four-things-to-consider-if-you-want-to-scale-your-startup/
2. Marmer, Max, et.al., *Startup Genome Report on Premature Scaling*, Pg 9, 2012
3. Marmer, Max, et.al., *Startup Genome Report on Premature Scaling*, Pg 8, 2012
4. Marmer, Max, et.al., *Startup Genome Report on Premature Scaling*, Pg 11, 2012
5. http://firstround.com/article/The-Dos-and-Donts-of-Rapid-Scaling-for-Startups

Chapter 16

1. http://blog.cultureamp.com/drivers-of-engagement
2. Palmer and Kaplan, *A Framework for Strategic Innovation*, Innovation Point, 2012
3. McKinney, Phil, http://philmckinney.com/archives/2011/08/the-7-immutable-laws-of-innovation-follow-them-or-risk-the-consequences.html , August 22, 2011
4. http://en.wikipedia.org/wiki/Design_thinking
5. Brown, Time, Design Thinking, Harvard Business Review, June 2008, page 87
6. Capozzi, Marla M., McKinsey Global Survey, September 2012, http://www.mckinsey.com/insights/innovation/making_innovation_structures_work_mckinsey_global_survey_results
7. Various Authors, *Amplify Your Innovation Quotient*, Steelcase 360 Magazine, Issue 66

Chapter 17

1. http://experiencelife.com/article/the-5-best-ways-to-build-resiliency/
2. http://blogs.hbr.org/2014/08/curiosity-is-as-important-as-intelligence/
3. http://en.wikipedia.org/wiki/Curiosity_quotient
4. http://en.wikipedia.org/wiki/Curiosity_quotient
5. http://www.pickthebrain.com/blog/what-is-your-curiosity-quotient
6. http://www.pickthebrain.com/blog/what-is-your-curiosity-quotient
7. http://www.pickthebrain.com/blog/what-is-your-curiosity-quotient

About the Authors

JA-NAÉ DUANE

For over 20 years, Ja-Naé Duane focused on one mission: make life better for as many people as possible. With that goal in mind she founded or co-founded five different organizations, including Wild Women Entrepreneurs, The Leaders, the National Artistic Effort, and the Massachusetts Artist Leaders Coalition.

She currently leads the Revolution Institute and works as a social science researcher while also teaching at Emerson College and Northeastern University. At Clark University, she holds the position of Entrepreneur-in-Residence.

The author of *How to Start Your Business with $100*, Ja-Naé excels at advising startups because she understands from personal experience what it means to be an entrepreneur. Over the years, her work has caught the attention of the Associated Press, NPR, *Classical Singer* magazine, the *Boston Globe*, and *BusinessWeek*. In 2007, she was nominated as one of New England's Most Innovative Leaders of 2007.

The Startup Equation marks her first official book collaboration with husband and best friend Steven Fisher.

STEVEN FISHER

Steven Fisher loves the future. So much so, he's spent the last 20 years as an award-winning designer and strategist helping companies, governments, and his own startups leverage the best innovations to compete and win. Steve delivers a valuable mix of venture creation, experience design, and innovation strategy. His slogan, "Unleash Your Innovation Rebel," serves as the foundation for his work around the world. In addition to his entrepreneurial experience, Steve serves as the Global Head of User and Product Experience for a technology company in Boston.

He is also an advisor and angel investor in a number of startups. For fun, Steve is a hot yoga instructor, beer maker and a filmmaker who is best known for co-creating and producing *Browncoats: Redemption*, a Joss Whedon Firefly/Serenity tribute. He is also a fast eater and a slow runner.

The Startup Equation is the first of many books that Steve hopes to write with his wife and best friend, Ja-Naé Duane.